# RECENT ADVANCES IN MODELING AND SIMULATION TOOLS FOR COMMUNICATION NETWORKS AND SERVICES

# RECENT ADVANCES IN MODELING AND SIMULATION TOOLS FOR COMMUNICATION NETWORKS AND SERVICES

*Edited by*

**A. Nejat Ince**
*Istanbul Technical University*

**Arnold Bragg**
*RTI International, Inc.*

 Springer

A. Nejat Ince
Istanbul Technical University

Arnold Bragg
RTI International Inc.

Recent Advances in Modeling and Simulation Tools for Communication
Networks and Services
Edited by A. Nejat Ince and Arnold Bragg

ISBN-13: 978-1-4419-4482-5          e-ISBN-13: 978-0-387-73908-3

9  8 7 6 5 4 3 2  1

springer.com

# ACKNOWLEDGEMENTS

As Chairman of COST Action 285 and co-editor of this book I wish to express my sincere thanks to all the members of the Management Committee for their full and active participation in the studies embraced by the Action including the decision to sponsor this symposium in which they presented the results of their individual research in different aspects of modeling and simulation of communication networks and services. I would particularly like to mention here Prof Dr Zhili Sun, a member of the Management Committee, made a unique contribution to the organization and success of the Symposium.

The symposium was very much enriched and gained much breadth and depth by the participation of many experts in the field from outside the Action Group, from the United States of America, and Europe who willingly accepted our invitation to attend and contribute to our deliberations. It would be invidious to single out names but I would like to mention Dr Arnold Bragg, of the Center for Advanced Research, RTI International NC/USA, who played a very important role inside the Committee as well as in the preparation and conduct of the symposium and in the editing of this book. I owe them all many thanks and much gratitude.

Last but by no means least I would like to express my appreciation to the COST Office Scientific Secretariat for the administrative and financial support given to the Action and Prof Dr Zhili Sun for making the facilities and staff of his Centre for Communication System Research, Surrey University UK, available for the symposium. Finally, it gives me pleasure to acknowledge the support I received from Prof Dr Ercan Topuz, Technical Secretary of the Action and Mr Zerhan Ener as well as from the staff of Springer Publishers in the preparation of this book.

Nejat Ince

# PREFACE

The papers which appear in this book were presented by their authors at a Symposium hosted by the Centre for Communication System Research, University of Surrey, Guildford, United Kingdom, on 28-29 March 2007. The Symposium was organized under the aegis of COST Action 285:

**Modeling and Simulation Tools for Research in Emerging
Multi-Service Telecommunications**

The Symposium focused specifically on recent advances in modeling and simulation methods, techniques, and tools for communications networks and services.

*COST* – the acronym for European **CO**operation in the field of Scientific and Technical research – is the oldest and most broadly focused European inter-governmental vehicle for cooperative research. COST was established by the Ministerial Conference in November 1971, and is presently used by the scientific communities of 35 European nations to cooperate in common research projects supported by national funds.

Hence, COST is a framework for scientific and technical cooperation, supporting the coordination of national research at the European level. COST's goal is to ensure that Europe holds a strong position in all fields of scientific and technical research by increasing cooperation and interaction among participating nations.

*COST Actions* are cooperative networks that focus on specific basic and pre-competitive research issues, as well as on activities of public interest. Actions are apportioned among fourteen key scientific domains such as social sciences, natural sciences, information technologies, and engineering. COST Action 285 is one of 22 Actions in the Information and Communication Technologies domain.

The main characteristics of COST Actions are a 'bottom up approach', in that the initiative of launching an Action comes from the scientists themselves; 'a la carte participation', in that only countries interested in the Action participate; 'equality of access', in that participation is also open to the scientific communities of countries not belonging to the European Union; and 'a flexible structure', characterized by the ease of implementation and minimal management oversight of the Actions. Funds provided by COST – less than 1% of the total value of the projects – support Actions involving more than 30,000 European scientists, and projects with research expenditures well in excess of 2 billion Euros per year.

As a precursor of advanced multi-disciplinary research, COST plays a very important role in: the realization of the European Research Area (ERA); in anticipating and complementing the activities of the Framework Programs; in constituting a 'bridge' between the scientific communities of Europe and the emerging nations; in increasing the mobility of researchers throughout Europe; and in fostering the establishment of Networks of Excellence in many key scientific domains and areas of societal importance.

*COST Action 285* comprises scientists from 15 nations. Its objectives are to enhance existing modeling and simulation tools, and to develop new ones for research in emerging multiservice telecommunications networks. Its primary focus areas are:

- Model Performance Improvements
- Multilayer Traffic Modeling
- Evaluation and Validation of New Modeling Tools.

The studies related to these areas are performed by members of the Action, with input from invited experts/scientists from academia and industry (when necessary), and are coordinated at Management Committee Meetings held 2-3 times per year. Members participate in other related projects and activities, both nationally and internationally (e.g., IST, ITU, ETSI, ESF). The Action provides opportunities for formal and informal contacts and dissemination of results. The Action hosts a Website*, and contributions/papers/presentations to the Action by members and specialists are available to the public.

---

* www.cost 285.itu.edu.tr

The Management Committee for COST Action 285 consists of:

- Chairman                Prof. Dr. Nejat INCE (Turkey)
- Deputy Chairman         Prof. Dr. Axel Lehmann (Germany)
- Technical Secretary     Prof. Dr. Ercan Topuz (Turkey)
- Other Members           Up to two representatives each from the 15 member nations: Bulgaria, Denmark, France, Germany, Hungary, Ireland, Italy, Macedonia, Malta, Norway, Slovenia, Spain, Turkey, Switzerland, and the United Kingdom.

*The March 2007 Symposium* – the Management Committee decided early in 2006 to convene a Symposium and to invite Members; external experts/scientists specializing in the areas of interest to COST Action 285; members from other COST Actions; and scientists/engineers from software houses, telecommunications companies, carriers and service providers, universities, and government research institutions of not only the COST countries but also of other continents. A letter of invitation was sent to known experts and institutions to participate in the Symposium, with the major aim of harnessing ideas and proposals for improved and new languages and tools to enable network designers, developers, and operators to model and simulate networks and services of emerging and future telecommunications systems.

Twenty-three papers presented at the Symposium were selected for inclusion in this book. The presentations covered six areas:

- Multilayer Modeling
- Wireless and Sensor Networks
- Verification and Validation
- High Throughput Systems
- Traffic
- Applications of Simulation.

Contributors and their coordinates are given in the list herewith attached.

The Symposium addressed a wide spectrum of subjects dealing with nearly all of the important aspects of simulation modeling, and with techniques and tools for the design and performance evaluation of emerging communications systems.

*Third in a Series* – the COST Action 285 Management Committee and Editors hope and expect that this book, which is the Proceedings of the 2007 Symposium, will be a useful reference work for academic researchers and practitioners. This book is the third in a series of works focusing on modeling and simulation methods, techniques, and tools in telecommunications. The previous works in this series are:

- *Modeling and Simulation Tools for Emerging Telecommunication Networks: Needs, Trends, Challenges and Solutions*, by A. Nejat Ince and Ercan Topuz (Editors), Springer, 2006, 510 pages, ISBN: 978-0387329215.

- *Modeling and Simulation Environment for Satellite and Terrestrial Communications Networks* (The Springer International Series in Engineering and Computer Science), by A. Nejat Ince (Editor), Springer/Kluwer, 2002, 424 pages, ISBN: 978-0792375470.

A. Nejat Ince
Arnold Bragg                                                    June 2007

# TABLE OF CONTENTS

# ALPHABETICAL LIST OF CONTRIBUTORS

**Eitan Altman**
INRIA Sophia Antipolis, France
altman@sohia.inria.fr

**Prof Leandro de Haro Ariet**
Universidad Politécnica de
Madrid. ETSI de
Telecomunicación. Ciudad
Universitaria s/n. 28040 Madrid
Spain

**Konstantin Avrachenkov**
INRIA Sophia Antipolis, France
avrachenkov@sophia.inria.fr

**Dr Irfan Awan**
Department of Computing
University of Bradford, UK
i.u.awan@bradford.ac.uk

**Prof. Osman Balci**
Department of Computer Science
660 McBryde Hall, MC 0106
Virginia Tech Blacksburg,
Virginia 24061, USA
balci@vt.edu

**Dr Chadi Barakat**
INRIA Sophia Antipolis, France
chadi.barakat@sophia.inria.fr

**Prof M. J. Bayarri**
Department of Statistics and
Operational Research, University
of Valencia, Spain and Adjunct
Professor of Statistics in ISDS,
Duke University, USA
susie.bayarri@uv.es

**Prof Monique Becker**
CNRS UMR 5157 SAMOVAR
Institut National des
Telecommunications
9, rue Charles Fourier
91011 Evry cedex,
France
monique.becker@int-evry.fr

**Dr. Markus Becker**
Communication Networks, TZI
ikom, University of Bremen,
28334 Bremen, Germany
mab@comnets.uni-bremen.de

**Dr. Arnold Bragg**
Center for Advanced Network
Research, RTI International, Inc.
Box 12194 Research Triangle
Park, NC 27709 USA
abragg@rti.org

**J. O. Berger**
University of
Valencia/SAMSI/Duke
University

**Janez Bešter**
Faculty of Electrical
Engineering, Ljubljana
Slovenia

**Gergő Buchholcz**
Telecommunications
Department, Budapest University
of Technology and Economics
Budapest, Hungary
buchholcz@hit.bme.hu

**Kartikeya Chandrayana**
Cisco Systems, San Jose, USA
kartikc@gmail.com

**Dr Haitham Cruickshank**
Centre for Communication
Systems Research
University of Surrey Guildford,
Surrey, UK, GU2 7XH
h.cruickshank@surrey.ac.uk

**Dr Tomaso de Cola**
CNIT - Italian National
Consortium for
TelecommunicationsGenoa
Research Unit, University of
Genoa, Via Opera Pia 13, 16145,
Genoa, Italy
tomaso.decola@cnit.it

**Ram Chakka**
Rajeev Gandhi Memorial
College of Engineering &
Technology
(RGMCET), Nandyal, India
ramchakka@yahoo.com

**Dr Tien Van Do**
Telecommunications
Department, Budapest University
of Technology and Economics
Budapest, Hungary
do@hit.bme.hu

**Francesco Furfari**
ISTI-CNR, Pisa, Italy

**Prof. Richard Fujimoto**
College of Computing, Georgia
Institute of Technology Atlanta,
Georgia 30332-0280, USA.
fujimoto@cc.gatech.edu

**Dr. Ivan Ganchev**
MIEEE Deputy Director,
Telecom Research Centre ECE
Department, University of
Limerick, Limerick, Ireland
ivan.ganchev@ul.ie

**Dr Christian Gaumier**
Ecole Polytechnique Fédérale de
Lausanne (EPFL), Switzerland.
christiangaumier@epfl.ch

**Dr Vincent Gauthier**
CNRS UMR 5157 SAMOVAR
Institut National des
Telecommunications
9, rue Charles Fourier
91011 Evry cedex, France
vincentgauthier@int-evry.fr

**F. Javier García**
Universidad Politécnica de
Madrid. ETSI Telecomunicación.
C. Universitaria s/n. 28040
Madrid, Spain

**Prof. Carmelita Görg**
Communication Networks, TZI
ikom, University of Bremen,
28334 Bremen, Germany
cg@comnets.uni-bremen.de

**Jen-Chih Huang**
College of Computing
Georgia Institute of Technology
Atlanta, Georgia 30332-0280
USA

**Xiaolong Jin**
Department of Computing,
School of Informatics,
University of Bradford,
Bradford, BD7 1DP, UK
x.jin@bradford.ac.uk

**Nauman Israr**
Department of Computing,
University of Bradford, UK
n.israr@bradford.ac.uk

**Dr. Gerta Köster**
Siemens AG-Corporate
Technology, Otto-Hahn-Ring 6
D-81730 München, Germany
gerta.koester@siemens.com

**Prof. Axel Lehmann**
Institut für Technische
Informatik, Universitaet der
Bundeswehr München, Germany
lehmann@informatik.unibw-
muenchen.de

**Xi Li**
Communication Networks, TZI
ikom, University of Bremen
28334 Bremen, Germany
xili@comnets.uni-bremen.de

**Zongyang Luo**
Centre for Communication
Systems Research
University of Surrey UK
z.luo@surrey.ac.uk

**Alfred Park**
College of Computing,
Georgia Institute of Technology
Atlanta, Georgia 30332-0280,
USA

**Mario Marchese**
DIST - Department of
Communication, Computer and
System Science, University of
Genoa Via Opera Pia 13, 16145,
Genoa, Italy

**Michel Marot**
CNRS UMR 5157 SAMOVAR
Institut National des
Telecommunications
9, rue Charles Fourier
91011 Evry cedex, France
michel.marot@int-evryfr

**Dr Geyong Min**
Department of Computing,
School of Informatics,
University of Bradford,
Bradford, BD7 1DP, UK
g.min@bradford.ac.uk

**A. Moloisane**
Telecommunications Research
Centre,
University of Limerick,
Limerick, Ireland

**G. Molina**
University of
Valencia/SAMSI/Duke
University

**Prof. A. Nejat Ince**
FIEEE, Member of the
International Academy of
Astronautics, Paris, Member of
the Russian Academy of
Technological Sciences, Member
of the New York Academy of
Sciences, Istanbul Technical
University Istanbul, Turkey
nejatince@ttnet.net.tr

**Luis Cuéllar Navarrete**
Universidad Politécnica de
Madrid, ETSI de
Telecomunicación. Ciudad
Universitaria s/n. 28040 Madrid
– Spain

**Dr M. O'Droma**
FIEE, SMIEEE
Director,Telecommunications
Research Centre, University of
Limerick,
Limerick, Ireland
martin.odroma@ul.ie

**Ramón Martínez
Rodríguez-Osorio**
Universidad Politécnica de
Madrid. ETSI de
Telecomunicación. Ciudad
Universitaria s/n. 28040 Madrid
- Spain

**Miguel Á. Fernández Otero**
Universidad Politécnica de
Madrid, ETSI de
Telecomunicación. Ciudad
Universitaria s/n. 28040 Madrid
– Spain

**William F. Ormsby**
Naval Surface Warfare Center
Dahlgren Division, Code W12
17320 Dahlgren Road Dahlgren,
Virginia 22448, USA
william.f.ormsby@navy.mil

**Dénes Papp**
Department of
Telecommunications
Budapest University of
Technology and Economics
Hungary

**Prof Chris Phillips**
Department of Electronic
Engineering, Queen Mary,
University of London, UK
chris.phillips@elec.gmul.ac.uk

**Giancarlo Portomauro**
CNIT - Italian National
Consortium for
TelecommunicationsGenoa
Research Unit University of
Genoa, Via Opera Pia 13, 16145,
Genoa, Italy
portomauro@cnit.it

**Dr. Francesco Potortì**
ISTI-CNR, Pisa, Italy
potorti@isti.cnr.it

**Dr. Stoyan A. Poryazov**
Institute of Mathematics and
Informatics, Bulgarian Academy
of Sciences Sofia, Bulgaria
stoyan@cc.bas.bg

**Dr Matevz Pustišek**
Faculty of Electrical Engineering
Ljubljana, Slovenia
matevz.pustisek@fe.uni-lj.si

**Prof Miguel Calvo Ramón**
Universidad Politécnica de
Madrid, ETSI de
Telecomunicación. Ciudad
Universitaria s/n. 28040 Madrid
– Spain
ramon@gr.ssr.upm.es

**Dr Sébastien Rumley**
Ecole Polytechnique Fédérale de
Lausanne (EPFL), Switzerland
sebastien.rumley@epfl.ch

**Ass. Prof Emiliya Saranova**
IMI - Bulgarian Academy of
Sciences, Sofia, Bulgaria
High College of
Telecommunication and Posts,
Sofia, Bulgaria
saranova@hctp.acad.bg

**Dragan Savić**
Faculty of Electrical Enginnering
University of Ljubljana Slovenia
dragan.savic@fe.uni-lj.si

**Prof Zhili Sun**
Centre for Communication
System Research, School of
Electronics and physical
Sciences, University of Surrey
Guildford, Surrey, GU2 7XH
United Kingdom
Z.Sun@surrey.ac.uk

**Xuan Mai Thi Truong**
Department of
Telecommunications
Budapest University of
Technology and Economics
Hungary

**Sašo Tomažič**
Faculty of Electrical
Engineering, Ljubljana, Slovenia

**Zhongshi Wang**
Institut für Technik Intelligenter
Systeme (ITIS e.V.), Universitat
der Bundeswehr, München,
Germany

**Lan Wang**
Department of Computing,
School of Informatics,
University of Bradford,
Bradford, BD7 1DP, UK

**Thushara Lanka**
**Weerawardane**
Communication Networks, TZI
ikom, University of Bremen
28334 Bremen, Germany
tlw@comnets.uni-bremen.de

# CHAPTER 1

# European Concerted Research Action COST 285
# Action Objectives and the Symposium

A. Nejat Ince

Istanbul Technical University

**Abstract.** *This paper covers the keynote address delivered by the Chairman of the COST Action 285 at the Symposium. It outlines the studies undertaken by the members of the Action with the objective of enhancing existing modeling and simulation tools and to develop new ones for research in emerging multiservice telecommunication networks. The paper shows how the scope of COST Action 285 has been enriched by the contributions made at the Symposium.*

## 1. INTRODUCTION

With reference to the information provided in the preface of this book regarding the COST framework and its actions, particularly our Action 285 entitled:

"Modeling and Simulation Tools for Research in Emerging Multiservice Telecommunications"

which is a sequel to COST Action 256 [1] entitled:

"Modeling and Simulation Environment for Telecommunication Networks",

we give here a short outline of Action 285 and of the contributions made by the attendants, particularly by the invited experts to the Symposium.

## 2.    BACKGROUND

Simulation for research and design accounts for a substantial fraction of engineering computation. With valid and credible models, simulation is often dramatically more cost-effective than are real experiments, which can be expensive, dangerous, or, in fact, impossible because a new system may not yet be available.

Modeling and simulation of today's wholly distributed and autonomously managed high speed/broadband networks present major challenges for the telecommunications society – some of which were addressed during the activities of the COST Action 256 [1] which was completed in June 2001. COST 256 had the objective of determining the need and making suggestions for the enhancement of existing tools, and for developing new ones supporting the modeling and simulation of emerging terrestrial and satellite communication networks. The Action had met its desired objectives within the known resource and time constraints. In the Final Report of the Action it was stated that there was a definite and urgent need for intensifying European R&D activities on simulation and modeling tools for research in emerging multi-service telecommunications systems, in order that Europe may become a key market player in this vital area.

In light of the above, and in order to make efficient use of the synergy obtained and the momentum gained during the four years of COST 256 activities, the members unanimously expressed their support for the creation of a new COST Action with the objective of further investigating the use of the powerful modeling and simulation techniques for research, and focusing on the specific area of multi-service telecommunications systems.

The contributions from COST 256 to the present Action 285 are in the following main areas:

- Requirements for new/improved tools: One of the accomplishments of COST 256 was to examine and analyze most of the commercially available simulation software packages and to assess their individual merits as well as their shortcomings and deficiencies.
- Modeling and simulation problems in mobile and fixed communication systems: Second generation TDMA/CDMA wireless

- networks, architecture and QoS in LEO/MEO satellite networks, DWDM optical networks, propagation in urban areas and in indoor environments.
- Advanced traffic source modeling. Traffic being the driving force behind all telecommunications activity, probability models for traffic streams are needed to the extent that they allow prediction of system performance measures to an acceptable degree of accuracy. During COST 256 activities traffic source modeling had been investigated in relation to the dimensioning of a cellular communication system including second and third generation systems and on fractal and self-similar traffic models which are used for the simulation of such networks as LAN, WAN, ATM and Internet.

## 3.   OBJECTIVES AND BENEFITS

The main objective of COST 285 is to enhance existing and develop new modeling and simulation tools for research in emerging multi-service telecommunications networks. To achieve the aims of the objective, several tasks are undertaken under the following three task headings:

Task 1    Model Performance Improvement

- Research in the area of new modeling tools based on analytic and hybrid cores for quick solutions of network design performance evaluation problems.
- Research in multimedia traffic.
- Research on how to improve the quality of the statistical analysis tools imbedded in commercial simulation products.

Task 2    Multilayer Traffic Models

- Research in the area of multilayer traffic modeling.

Task 3    Model Verification, Validation and Credibility (VVC).

- To address the important issue of how to evaluate and validate the new modeling tools above.

The work can be regarded as a natural extension and continuation of the work performed in COST Action 256.

Some of the expected outcomes of the COST 285 Action are:

- Provision of a European forum for specialists from University, Industry and R&D institutions engaged in current and anticipated modeling and simulation problems in Multiservice Telecommunication Systems.

- Evaluation of the suitability of existing models and tools, and determination of the need and making suggestions for their enhancement and/or for development of new tools including their verification, validation and credibility:

  - For obtaining quick solutions to network design and performance analysis problems utilizing tools based on analytic and hybrid cores.

  - For studying the convolutional and confounding effects of multi-layer traffic.

## 4.    SCIENTIFIC PROGRAMME

The details of the studies carried out under the three headings listed in the section above are described below:

### 4.1    Model Performance Improvement

### 4.1.1    Analytic and Hybrid Cores for Reducing Simulation Time

There are two basic techniques for simulating networks which treat the problem from different angles. The analytical technique examines the network in the steady-state and uses mathematical formulas employing assumptions about the network, such as the average arrival rate of packets at a node. The discrete-event simulation technique, in contrast, examines the dynamic behavior of the network and incorporates every event in the network. Discrete-event simulation tools can provide detailed and accurate results but may be prohibitively time-consuming for simulation of large networks, such as the Internet, which are becoming a pressing need. One of the research objectives of this Action is to investigate the strengths and limitations of modeling tools which are based on analytic cores (e.g., Analytical Engines Inc. NetRule) and use steady-state queuing theory formulas and mathematical modeling techniques to produce quick solutions. These tools, which do not capture nuances of protocol behaviors can, however, provide good first-order approximations and may be the only reasonable approach for very large networks.

Another approach to cut down on simulation time is the hybrid simulation in which one may focus the simulation on a portion of the network of special interest and model the remainder of the network using the analytic method. It is interesting to investigate the strengths and limitations of hybrid engines in terms of gain in speed and loss in accuracy.

### 4.1.2   Statistical Analysis Tools

Experience with available commercial simulation products have shown that the quality and depth of statistical analysis tools imbedded in them are rather disappointing and often require the simulation output captured to be analyzed in a statistical package like SAS. A more elegant solution, which would be to have the simulation tool itself "package" the output, is therefore to be investigated.

### 4.1.3   Multimedia Traffic

Multimedia traffic studies carried out in COST Action 256 and elsewhere give evidence that different protocols behave very differently at different time scales. A study is therefore undertaken of the network behavior in different time scales, e.g., 1, 10, 100 second intervals, including the method of validation of simulation results.

## 4.2   Multilayer Traffic Modeling

Some recently proposed models for TCP and their potential in addressing multilayer traffic modeling are to be investigated. Some of these models focus on window sizing and network issues separately but not independently, and when they can be coupled with a source level-model the outcome might be a valuable step toward multilayer modeling. It would be interesting to try combining good source and lower-layer models into two-layer or three-layer traffic models and to begin studying the convolutional and confounding effects.

## 4.3    Model Verification, Validation and Credibility (VVC)

### 4.3.1    Model Verification

Scientists and engineers deal with the complexity of the real world in terms of simplified models. There are, however, techniques that may be used for deciding on an appropriate level of model detail, for validating a simulation model, and for developing a credible model. Model relations between model objects abstract useful or interesting properties of corresponding real-world relations as objects. Well-defined relations between model objects are by definition mathematical relations, numerical or not. Model objects and their properties in different states are normally specified by numerical variables related to real measurements. Experiments can then check measured states predicted from model relations, and the model may be amended as needed. This is the basis of the scientific method and of the rational engineering design.

One of the basic questions is "Can network design tools help one to find the combination (complicated mix of applications, protocols, device and link technologies, traffic flows, and routing algorithms) that is right for the problem at hand?" It is argued that one of the most challenging decisions is to determine how accuracy can be sacrificed for speed, and that the trade-offs to be made in this respect depend on the user's role in the design process; network designers and engineers tend to wish to have accuracy and low cost for their benefit. Sales and marketing staff always appear to expect the results immediately and they want it to reflect the least cost result, whereas network managers ask for detail and realism when they review the design result. It appears that there are answers to most, if not all, of the questions that arise in respect to the above considerations.

The fundamental building blocks of a simulation are the real-world problem entity being simulated, a conceptual model representation of that entity and the computer model implementation of the conceptual model.

Conceptual model validity, software verification, and operational validity along with data validity are the technical processes that must be addressed to show that a model is credible. The technical experts of the Action, as well as experts from other institutions may be consulted to review the conceptual model to judge if it is valid. This activity, called face validity analysis, is performed to support the technical process of conceptual model validity.

Verification is the process of determining that a model operates as intended. The verification process is also referred to as "debugging." The aim is to try to find and remove unintentional errors in the model's logic and in its implementation. Verification will involve performing test runs in which a comprehensive set of tests will be devised to generate ideally all errors, and that all errors generated during these test runs are recognized.

Test cases that explore non-typical operating conditions are most likely to expose modeling errors (increase arrival rate and/or reduce service rate; increase the rate of infrequent events, etc.). Verification of the model should start at the module level. It is paramount that the programming language used presents facilities such as an interactive debugger and the capability of performing a localized "trace" of the flow of events within and between modules.

### 4.3.2 Model Validation

Validation is the process of assessing an acceptable level of confidence that the inferences drawn from the model correctly represent the real-world system modeled. The aim is to determine whether or not the simplifications and omissions of detail knowingly made in the model introduce unacceptably large errors in the results.

Validation focuses on three questions:

1. Conceptual Validity: Does the model adequately represent the real-world system?

2. Operational Validity: Are the model-generated behavioral data characteristic of the actual system?

3. Credibility: Does the user have confidence in the model's results?

Three variations of the real-world system have to be distinguished:

- The system exists and its outputs can be compared with the simulated results.
- The system exists but is not available for direct experimentation.

- The system is yet to be designed; validation here is in the sense of convincing others and ourselves that observed model behavior represents the proposed referent system if it is implemented.

The methods used for model validation are testing for reasonableness, for model structure and data and model behavior. A model's validation will be based on comparison of the results obtained from different analytical and simulation models and, where they exist, measurements in real telecommunication systems.

## 4.4    Network Emulation and Network Tomography

It was decided halfway through the action programme to include in the scientific programme an additional work item dealing with network emulation and network tomography.

# 5.    COST 285 INTERIM STUDY RESULTS

Study of the problems and issues outlined above is performed by the members of the Action Group. They are expected to complete their programme of work in the time frame assigned to the Action (2003-2007) by utilizing their own potential which may be augmented, where necessary, by external contributions from Symposia organized by the Group as well as from other sources. In this regard it should be mentioned that a formal association has been established with the Center for Advanced Network Research of RTI International Inc., USA, for cooperative research in the areas of mutual interest.

We give below a summary of the studies so far achieved with appropriate pointers in the present book.

## 5.1    Model Performance Improvement

### 5.1.1    Analytic and Hybrid Cores for Reducing Simulation Time

From a preliminary review and evaluation made of Task 1.1 it is clear that the network design tools available on the market are either general-purpose or special purpose tools. The first and most important decision to make for the user is to select the right tool to use, which implies challenging decisions to determine how much accuracy to sacrifice for speed which, depending on the application, can span four orders of magnitude, from tens of seconds to days.

A checklist of features to consider for different user groups was developed and introduced in [2] and [3]. This list has now been refined and extended [4] to address the needs of four categories of users (in terms of user features such as user interface, modeling paradigms, network topology, network types, supported traffic models, solution methods, simulation output, analysis tools, level of customization, etc.):

As part of Task 1.1 hybrid techniques are being investigated for modeling two types of telecommunications systems that are far too complex for commercial analytical or discrete event simulation tools. These studies are very relevant to the Action because they use a combination of methods to reduce simulation time (DES, analytical models, closed-form expressions, emulation, etc.) and because they appear to be a feasible way of modeling the very large and/or very complex infrastructures deployed in emerging multi-service telecommunication networks:

– The first is ultra high capacity optical networks, which are widely deployed in the core of emerging multi-service telecommunication networks. These networks have aggregate traffic volumes 4-5 orders of magnitude larger than what today's discrete event and hybrid simulators are able to handle. Modeling them in (near) real time requires a combination of techniques: emulators to mimic the network's control plane; an inference engine to deduce data plane behavior and performance from traffic observed in the control plane; analytics to model core network behaviors; a fast hybrid simulator to inject traffic and network impairments; and a supervisory kernel to interconnect and manage the components [5].

– The second is computing Grids, which is believed to be the next major computing paradigm. Grids are a major backbone technology in multi-service research test-beds, have been widely deployed throughout Europe (e.g., CERN), and are focus areas in at least three COST Actions (282, 283, 291). Grids are enormously complex dynamic systems. They require new modeling and simulation methods and tools to understand the behavior of components at various protocol layers and time scales, and to decipher the complex functional, spatial, and temporal interactions among the components. A "grid-in-lab" tool is under development, which is scalable, modular, configurable, and plug-and-play, for modeling grids and analyzing the performance of applications and middleware services offered on Grids [6].

A project has been undertaken to achieve "Faster-than-Real Time Distributed simulation Using Multi-Core FPGA Arrays" [7].

It is noted that discrete-event simulation tools may be prohibitively time-consuming for simulation of very large networks; distributed simulation, on the other hand, requires clusters of computers and is hence costly and could not be implemented without additional efforts.

Ref. 7 then describes a new approach which relies on using a 'system on a chip' rather than cluster of computers. The state of developments in this area which are currently being investigated includes a testbed system which uses Field Programmable Gate Arrays (FPGA). This system involves 25 processors per FPGA, 5 per board, and 8 boards per system, and comprises a total of about 1000 processors, each to simulate or emulate a wireless or satellite node. The goal of this project work is to achieve faster than real time performance.

On the analytic solution front, Markov chains has been used successfully to model burst errors on channels and on systems at access level for UMTS/DVB-T systems. New channel measurements on indoor environments are being conducted to improve Markov chain models, and to validate them.

This activity is being extended to models on Power Line Communication (PLC) systems which are expected to be used for communicating over power lines [8].

Verification of simulation using a computer and simulation/emulation using DSPs/FPGAs has been studied. Comparison between Matlab/C simulation programs and real time implementations on DSPs/FPGAs has been performed. The implemented systems are UMTS modems and smart antennas for UMTS. Moreover the antenna pattern produced by the smart antenna (which includes a UMTS modem and RF transmitters/receivers on it) has been measured, and the mutual coupling effect between RF chains and antennas has been corrected to obtain results close to simulation.

A paper entitled "Network Reference Scenarios for Pan European Architectures" is presented in [9]. The aim of this work is to model a realistic large scale pan-European optical network, including data links, ingress, egress or intermediate nodes and demands in terms of bandwidth. The requirements for the model are to: (i) Allow for several scenarios for simulation (variation among topologies, traffic estimation taking in account population and other parameters), (ii) Speed up the verification and validation, by comparing computed results on the basis of a common input scenario, (iii) Provide testing for different algorithms on a common base.

The network description/specification tool used in this project is based on the in-house developed software UND reported in [10], and the scenarios are derived from COST 266 topologies.

Detailed information on this work can be obtained via the web site, (http://itopwww.epfl.ch//TCOM/Recherchc/COST).

A paper, entitled "3P-AAA service simulation approaches on an ns2 Platform" has been completed [11]. The paper discusses the issues related to developing a Third Party Authentication, Authorization and Accounting framework, which would serve as a central authentication, authorization, and accounting system for Access Network Providers (ANP) and TeleService Providers (TSP) to handle all Service Level Agreements (SLAs) between ANPs/TSPs. This requires that a secure tunnel is set up between Mobile Consumer Users (MCU) and 3P-AAA-SP through which sensitive information can be passed. Data confidentiality is also a requirement between MCUs and ANP/TSP.

The paper describes an ns2 Model for the 3P-AAA Architecture and gives two possible approaches to simulating authentication in ns2: (i) Use sleep times to approximate encryptions/decryptions and possibly TLS signaling, and (ii) Adjust an existing TLS (or similar) implementation and layer it on top of ns2s SCTP model as an ns2 application. The second approach is preferable as it gives a more accurate view of how 3P-AAA authentication will work in the real world.

## 5.1.2  Statistical Analysis Tools

The MC has had some fruitful discussions on this Task and concluded that no "elegant solution" appears to have been implemented. The members agree that creating a standard format for exchanging simulation data between practitioners would be a worthwhile deliverable for the Action.

There are several solutions to the problem, ranging from XML, which is a general container for exchanging data, to specialized binary formats. Each solution has tradeoffs reflecting the problem's dimensions (performance, size, deployment, …); perhaps one should (1) identify the dimensions and the range of solutions in each, and (2) systematically lay out an approach for presenting the problem at large. It was concluded therefore that "Structured Formats for Simulation Results" outlined in [12] might be used to build upon for the deliverable for the Action. Sometimes an enumeration of alternatives and an indication of where each fits (or does not fit) is a more valuable contribution than a so-called 'point solution'. Helping practitioners understand the issues and build a strategy is perhaps all one can do, there is no 'one size fits all' [3].

Answers to a questionnaire from the MC members show that by far the most common format for data exchanging is the tabular form, where file names are used to store parameter values for different simulation runs. The questionnaire also highlights that typical simulations generate data quantities in the order of the gigabytes, and some of them generate several orders of magnitude more data. Since XML adds a large amount of overhead to data, specialized solutions for storing scientific data were analyzed, and HDF5 (Hierarchical Data Format version 5) was identified as the most appropriate format available today for storing big to huge quantities of scientific data. A software package, called *CostGlue*, was then jointly designed and implemented by some of our members. *CostGlue* can:

- **import** simulation or measurement results, in the form of trace files, into a common HDF5 data structure;
- **launch** post-processing (i.e., filtering and calculations) applications on the imported data, complement the raw data with the results of post-processing, feed stored data to other applications (e.g. for presentation);
- **export** data into various output formats (ASCII, XML, specialized formats).

*CostGlue* is implemented as

- a **core** (called CoreGlue), which is responsible for accessing the HDF5 archive and provides an API (application programming interface) for the modules;

- a collection of dynamically loaded **modules**, which are responsible for the user interface, for importing and exporting data into and out of the HDF5 archive, and for interfacing with external tools.

The status of the tool at the end of the Action [Chapter 23] is that of a usable prototype, released as free software: the core is implemented and modules exist that implement a command line interface, import/export of tabular data, and import/export of some measurement and simulation data. Work is in an advanced state for implementing modules to import and export data in ns-2 trace file format, tcpdump format and nam format. Work is in progress for implementing a module for a generic graphical user interface.

A study entitled "A new Paradigm for Traffic Engineering of Multi-Service Networks" [20] reviews the present state-of-art in traffic models including Erlang-B formula & Engset (& Pascal) formula, Erlang-C formula and Palm machine/repair model, Processor Sharing (Flow model) and Generalized Processor Sharing approaches, and points to their main shortcomings and limitations, viz., insensitivity to service and/or idle time distributions.

In connection with hybrid models it is pointed out that when combining two insensitive models, the issues to be considered would include the optimization of utilization, constructing reversible state transition diagrams, reversible scheduling, and allocation of resources between max-min scheduling and proportional scheduling. It is shown that the new paradigm yields a stable algorithm by normalizing probabilities after each new global state, finding individual performance for each traffic stream, and by truncating the state space final buffer for each traffic stream and/or all traffic streams. This new approach is applicable to network nodes (open and closed) and includes all classical loss/delay models.

Performance Modeling of MPLS Networks with Link Failures and Repairs has been studied [22]. The goal of this work is to propose a model which could calculate network performance parameters, taking into account LSP failures and repairs, and to offer an easy way to implement new repair strategies. The proposed analytical model is based on a generalized Markovian node model, called HetSigma, and is implemented on Mathematica (Wolfram), and Probabilistic Symbolic Model Checker, PRISM (University of Birmingham).

Preliminary results of numerical simulations are presented in [22]. The ongoing work in this area is concentrated on investigating a new repair strategy based on priority, and on refinement of determination of priority order.

### 5.1.3   Multimedia Traffic Modeling

The invariants in network traffic have been investigated [15]. It is concluded that different time scales need to be used at different protocol layers. Mathematical formulas are available to describe traffic at different protocol layers, and one has to be careful to understand and to identify the parameters or the characteristics of the traffic to be used for modeling and simulation purposes.

Several multiplicative SARIMA (s, p, d, q) models based on 30 fps MPEG-4 multimedia traces from TU-Berlin have been developed and their behavior at different time scales has been examined. Preliminary results suggest that the dominant factor at time scales up to 1 sec. is the seasonal effect induced by the MPEG-4 GOP structure. So-called "scene length" is the dominant factor at longer time scales.

IP network traffic measurement and modeling at packet level as well as network performance with self similar traffic has been carried out and discussed in [16, 17].

An analysis has been carried out of traffic traces from WWW traffic in terms of attributes common to all multimedia types – viz., heavy tailed distributions of object sizes, temporal locality, and conformance to Ziph's Law (i.e., quantity is inversely proportional to rank). This important commonality suggests that differentiating between multimedia types and implementations, and analytical modeling to improve performance may not be necessary [13].

An approach using analytical fluid models derived from a set of deterministic differential equations has been developed [18].The models account for randomness in TCP traffic, produce reliable performance predictions for networks that operate far from saturation, and are scalable with the number of long-lived connections, buffer size and link capacity. The models' accuracy and flexibility are based on considerations of static traffic patterns and dynamic conditions that require a transient analyses.

Auto Regressive Integrated Moving Average (ARIMA) models combined with Generalized Auto Regressive Conditional Heteroscedasticity (GARCH) models have been used to try to capture both short-and long-range dependence and fractal characteristics of the underlining data, especially for highly bursty data.

A parameter estimation procedure and an adaptive prediction scheme for the ARIMA/GARCH model has been developed which is capable of capturing the non-stationary characteristics of Internet data [13].

The GARCH component is used to account for dynamic variance, and is particularly well suited for traces that are variance non-stationary (which is commonplace in multimedia traffic).The ARIMA/GARCH model can also be used for near-term, one-step-ahead forecasts [14].

Characterization of Internet Traffic in Wireless Networks has been studied [21]. The objectives of this work are: To carry out systematic traffic measurements for wireless networks (IEEE 802.11 and IEEE 802.16); to investigate the impact of the distribution of different applications on traffic characterization in wireless networks; to provide valuable insights into the packet length and packet interarrival time distributions for both aggregated traffic and individual application traffic; and to determine the relationship between the packet length and packet interarrival time distributions. These provide the means to credibly predict traffic trends subject to a particular application for the design and development of wireless network equipment.

Reference [21] describes the aim and scope of a measurement campaign, and presents results of initial measurements which identify: IP packets analysis (packet components, their percentages and packet lengths), and packet inter-arrival time analysis (distribution analysis, probability density function, cumulative distribution function).

## 5.2  Multilayer Traffic Models

It has been shown that Task 2 on Multilayer Traffic Models which is probably the most intractable problem in the Action, Task 1.2 on Statistical Analysis Tools, and Task 3 on Model Verification/Validation and Credibility do not have elegant universal solutions and consequently one has to be content with "framework solutions" which, it was agreed, would be valuable contributions/deliverables for the Action.

These problems have a large number of dimensions (spanning an N-dimensional space) and the so-called solutions we see published represent cases in which someone has fixed each dimension and solved for only a single N-dimensional point. A particular research result may be important, but it usually does little more than firmly establish one point or a small set of points in N-space. Most neither provide insight about the N-dimensional performance response surface, nor attempt to explain how sensitive one parameter might be to other parameters. Another problem is that researchers make limiting assumptions so as to arrive at closed-form expressions. These assumptions ignore the potential convolutional, confounding, and interaction effects among the dimensions; hence, some of them are of little value because the assumptions are too limiting to be useful.

To demonstrate what can be achieved with multilayer traffic models, Padhye et al.'s [22] TCP Reno analytical model (layer 4), plus layer 2 and 3 extensions, have been used to investigate whether analytical multi-layer traffic models might provide credible results in (near) real time. Preliminary results suggest that such a model can provide a reasonable, steady-state, first-order approximation to TCP over a wireless infra-structure; TCP over an optical infrastructure; TCP over a source-routed IP network infrastructure; and TCP over a diffserv-like IP network infra-structure. The issue yet to be addressed is "steady state", as TCP techni-cally never reaches steady state in operational networks.

A heuristic has been developed for modeling encoding-specific and content-specific factors in multimedia traffic in order to build realistic multimedia traffic generators for discrete-event simulation [24].

## 5.3    Model Verification, Validation and Credibility (VVC)

Under this Task, the MC reviewed V&V problems in light of COST 285 and V&V goals which are defined as model quality improvement; increasing credibility of existing tools for telecommunication M&S; and introduction of new, credible M&S tools for telecommunication analysis (especially for multi-layer traffic). The Action's main contribution to this field would be in the area of introducing a framework/methodological approach for credibility assessment. Credibility depends on the perceived correctness, and on the perceived suitability of M&S. Analysis of correctness – known as verification – refers to consistency and com-pleteness testing. Analysis of suitability – mostly known as validation – refers to tests of capabilities, fidelity, and of accuracy. In this respect it has been noted that in order to ensure overall system integrity the accepted practice is to adopt "Independent Verification and Validation", which is accomplished organizationally as independent from the elements that acquire, design, develop or maintain the system [25].

"External PRNG's for OPNET", has been considered [26]. After a review of the characteristics of and performance metrics for Pseudo Random Number Generators (PRNG), the shortcomings of the built-in PRNG module of OPNET is described. It is stated that only one type of PRNG is implemented in OPNET, and this is an "uncertain type" of PRNG which fails several tests, indicating that its generated sequences are not independent. This shortcoming of OPNET could be removed by introducing tested PRNG's which are available in other libraries such as CNCL (Linux, GCC) and GSL (Linux, GCC) in this context. It is further noted that at least four different methods exist for integration of external PRNGs into OPNET: (i) Source Code Integration & Modification into OPNET process models, (ii) Use of a Compiler other than MSVC via the External Compiler Interface, (iii) a Linux version of OPNET, (iv) Modification of CNCL/GSL, and Compilation with MSVC and Linking of the library.

Simulation in the process of system design has been applied to traffic signal monitoring and control [27]. The scope of this work is the investigation of (i) the impact of simulation in the process of system design (as a methodology to go from specifications to implementation following a simulation approach), (ii) physical layer simulation, and (iii) simulation tasks in the process of developing a prototype. The aim is to make use of several commercial simulation tools. This approach requires answering the questions of "How do different tools interact and work together", and "How should validation and verification be addressed from simulation to measurement."

The tools used in the study included Matlab (for system design, cosimulation and verification), ISE 7.1 (for FPGA programming via the hardware description language VHDL), ModelSim (for hardware simulation and verification), and MultiSim (for design of printed circuit boards).

## 5.4    Network Emulation and Tomography

The MC considered that it would be appropriate to look beyond the tasks described in the Action program to see if there are other subjects in this area which would add value to the studies of the Action as originally conceived.

Two new subjects have been identified for inclusion in our program of work; Network Emulation and Network Tomography, for which there is adequate knowledge and expertise in some members of the MC who are willing to pursue these subjects in the timeframe foreseen for the Action [28].

Network emulation is a technique that is usually applied to testing experimental network protocols, especially in networks that use IP as the network layer. It is nearly impossible to thoroughly test an experimental protocol in an operational network because the test team cannot control the characteristics of the network, and cannot isolate the network from unforeseen disruptions or other effects caused by the experimental protocol. Emulators run actual unmodified protocol stacks on a small number of "instances" – commodity single-board PCs, or processes executing on multi-tasking hosts, or both – in near real time. The instances are physically interconnected over a simulated network core. The core realistically routes traffic, simulates network bandwidth and other resources, and models congestion, latency, loss, and error. Current implementations emulate about 100,000 packets per second per core node instance.

Network tomography is a discipline that borrows techniques from signal processing and medical imaging to solve network monitoring and inference problems in which some aspects of the network are not directly observable. For example, one can use tomographic techniques to estimate network performance (e.g., packet delay and loss) based on traffic measurements taken at a small set of nodes or links, or between a small set of sources and destinations. Other tomographic techniques can be used to infer a network's topology with a very small number of direct measurements, which is especially useful when operating over a com- mercial network whose topology and performance characteristics are not known.

An invited speaker to the MC presented a paper entitled "SatNEx meets COST 285" [29]. SatNEx is an European Satellite Network of Excellence, funded by the EC within the 6th FP. The first phase of this project is already concluded and the second phase initiated in April 2006 will conclude in March 2008. Key objectives of the project are: (i) Overcoming fragmentation in European SatCom research through closer networking of people and organizations, (ii) Advancing European research and knowledge in satellite communications, and (iii) Establishing durable integration of European research in satellite communications. The Consortium has 23 partners from 10 countries.

The Project involves simulation, emulation and trials on the field described as: (i) Simulation phase: the basic step to help researchers and scientists investigate and validate an analytical model; (ii) Emulation task: triggered by the inputs deriving from the simulation phase and dealing with implementation issues; (iii) Trials in the field: the final step of the research path in which novel solutions are tested on the real platform. The tools used in simulation and emulation studies include: Commercial tools (MATLAB, OPNET, SPW, STK, the Satellite Tool Kit), Open Source tools (ns-2, SaVi, TOSSIM TinyOS Simulator), and Proprietary tools (MuDiSP3, NePSing, Monet-s, etc.).

Emulation tools include: Commercial Tools (Galatea an UMTS emulator, by Wireless Future, Pontecchio by Marconi, BO), Open Source Tools (WTK 2.2 wireless tool kit, Iperf, Netperf, RudeCrude, NetPipe traffic generators), Proprietary tools (Multi-TCP, TCP-Peach Emulation System, Multicast Protocols Suite Testbed, S-WiNeTest, a remote access system to a Sensor Testbed, MaD-Wise, a sensor network testbed, ACE satellite Emulator, DTNPERF, and LATERE Platform, an interactive laboratory for remote testing of complex satellite scenarios).

The paper [29] concludes with a discussion on the activities under development in SatNEx.

## 6.    CONTRIBUTION TO COST 285 BY SYMPOSIUM PRESENTATIONS

### 6.1    Subject Areas

The major aim of the Symposium was to harness ideas and proposals for enhancing existing and developing new languages and tools to enable network planners, designers, developers, and operators to model and simulate networks and services of emerging and future communications systems.

Participation was invited from other COST Actions, software houses, telecommunications companies, Universities and government research institutions.

The Symposium was to concentrate on the following subject areas:

- Capabilities of existing simulation tools and languages and their shortcomings, considering present emerging and future telecommunications network problems.
- Uncertainties in traffic simulations.
- Calibration and validation of models (including input for simulation, and prediction accuracy).
- Tradeoff between simulation accuracy and speed.
- Methods (e.g., multilayer modeling) of maintaining simulation accuracy without sacrificing speed.
- Methods of resource allocation in dynamic environments.
- Characteristics of modeling and simulation tools (e.g., hybrid cores) to meet the needs of different user groups (e.g., researchers, network planners, operators).
- New requirements for modeling and simulation to cope with the problems of next-generation networks.
- Multimedia traffic at different time scales (e.g., modeling, measurement, forecasting, management, and control).
- Verification and validation.
- Other topics of interest for Next-Generation Networking (NGN).

A perusal of the chapters of the book would show that there is a good overlap between the subjects above and the papers presented at the Symposium.

Chapter 2 entitled "A Review of High Performance Simulation Tools and Modeling Concepts" covers nearly all Action Tasks and provides a summary of simulation techniques, focusing on enhanced forms of discrete event-driven simulation that are capable of modeling large and/or high-speed networks in a reasonable time-frame.

Other results obtained from the Symposium which are expected to enhance the various tasks undertaken in the Action are outlined below.

## 6.2    Model Performance Improvement

### 6.2.1    Analytic and Hybrid Cores for Reducing Simulation Time

Chapter 8 entitled "The Design of a FPGA-Based Traffic Light Control System: From Theory to Implementation" [27] deals with a M&S problem where real time results are required using something akin to a physical emulator to reduce simulation time. Simulation was also a major component of the system design process.

Chapter 13 "Towards Flexible High Throughput Parallel Discrete-Event Simulations" investigates flexible, high-throughput, parallel discrete event simulation; "Design and Performance Evaluation of a Packet Switching Satellite Emulator" Chapter 14 addresses the design and performance evaluation of a packet switching satellite emulator, and "Simulation Techniques for Peer-to-Peer Information Sharing Networks" Chapter 15 deals with simulation techniques for peer-to-peer information sharing networks. These are further examples of different approaches for reducing simulation time when modeling complex, high performance networks and systems.

### 6.2.2    Multimedia Traffic

Chapter 7 entitled "Modeling and Simulation of TCP performance with Link Layer Retransmission and Fragmentation for Satellite-UMTS Networks" indicates that TCP can be enhanced substantially by employing the relay function using On Board Processors (OBP) and appropriate configuration of radio link control parameters, thus showing the way toward designing next generation communication satellites with OBP.

In Chapter 9 "Distributed Multi-hop Clustering Approach for Sensor Networks", algorithmic and simulation results are presented demonstrating that uniform energy consumption of distributed wireless sensor networks are achieved by a distributed multi-hop cluster network.

The effects of bursty and correlated multimedia traffic on the performance of active queue management schemes are reported in Chapter 18 "Effects of Bursty and Correlated Traffic on the Performance of Active Management Schemes."

In Chapter 19 "Quality of Service Analysis of Priority Queuing Systems under Long-Range Dependent and Short-Range Dependent

Traffic" reports an efficient and comprehensive performance model for investigating the QoS of priority systems in the presence of heterogeneous long-range-dependent and short-range-dependent traffic. Closed form expressions of the queue length and loss probability distributions for individual traffic flows are derived and validated. The analytical model is used to evaluate the impact of LRD traffic on system performance under different working conditions.

A new repair strategy for MPLS multi-path routing is proposed in Chapter 16 entitled "Repair Strategies on the Operation of MPLS Routing" and the results obtained there are compared with several existing repair strategies in terms of performance measures. These comparisons show that this scheme outperforms most other repair strategies.

## 6.3    Multilayer Traffic Modeling

Chapter 3 "Visualization Techniques in Multilayer Traffic Modeling" describes traffic models that span several protocol layers, and traffic models of protocols that cross layers. Multilayer traffic modeling is challenging, as one must deal with disparate traffic sources, control loops, the effects of network elements such as IP routers; cross-layer protocols, asymmetries in bandwidth, session length, and application behaviors; and an enormous number of complex interactions among the various factors. In the present approach, visualization techniques are used to identify relationships, transformations, and scaling; to smooth simulation and measurement data; to examine boundary cases, subtle effects and interactions, and outlier; to fit models; and to compare models with others that have fewer parameters. Experience suggests that visualization techniques can provide practitioners with insight about complex multilayer traffic effects and interactions that are common in emerging next-generation networks.

Chapter 4 entitled "A Multilevel Approach for the Modeling of Large TCP/IP Networks" presents an analytical model for the calculation of network load and drop probabilities in a TCP/IP network with a general topology. The model does not require the predefinition of bottleneck links. It is based on analytical expressions for TCP throughput, which allows it to take into account diverse TCP features such as the receiver congestion window limitation. It can be used for TCP/IP networks with drop tail routers, as well as for TCP/IP networks with active queue management routers.

Chapter 5 entitled "Cross-Layer Interaction in Wireless Ad Hoc Networks: Practical Example" presents the design and the performance evaluation of a joined process between the physical layer and routing layer in multi-hop wireless ad hoc networks. This cross layer interaction between the physical and routing layers allows each node in an ad hoc network to evaluate the performance of each path in its routing table in terms of BER, and to classify each path accordingly. Routing information from poor quality links is not forwarded, leading to the selection of high quality links during the routing process.

Data exchange between various modules and tools causes interfacing difficulties in a multilayer environment. This aspect, which may be particularly critical in a distributed context, is investigated in Chapter 6 entitled "Multilayer Description of Large Scale Communication Networks." This paper proposes a multilayer descriptive framework for communication networks aimed at facilitating data exchange between different tools and models. The paper uses the extensible mark-up language (XML), which allows an increased flexibility and an improved visibility of relevant data.

## 6.4    Model Verification, Validation and Credibility

Chapter 11 entitled "Verification and Validation of Simulation Models and Applications – a Methodological Approach" presents a refined M&S verification and validation (V&V) process based on a multi-phase M&S development and application concept already developed and presented in COST Action 256 [1]. The Chapter shows how this method can be applied in various application scenarios, and how it can be tailored according to credibility criteria, or to cost, time and application requirements.

In Chapter 10 entitled "Scenario Simulation for Network-Centric Technology Assessment", network-centric system technologies are assessed for a number of quality characteristics including readiness, interoperability, and effectiveness. This assessment is carried out under a demonstration, trial, exercise or experimentation regime using a specially set up global multinational communications network and services infrastructure. This paper addresses the simulation of scenarios under which such technologies are assessed. Guidelines are given for scenario simulation model development and credibility assessment.

Chapter 12 entitled "Extending OPNET Modeler with External Pseudo Number Generators and Statistical Evaluation by the Limited Relative

Error Algorithm" focuses on the well known and widely used OPNET Modeler tool for communications networks and its Pseudo Random Number Generators (PRNG). The OPNET Modeler PRNG and its limitations are introduced, other available PRNG implementations and statistical evaluation libraries are reviewed, and an integration of those more refined PRNGs into the OPNET Modeler is described. An application of the PRNGs and statistical evaluation algorithm into an M/M/1 model is evaluated with regard to the simulation time needed to fulfill the requirements of a given certain maximum error.

Chapter 17 entitled "Incorporating Uncertainties into Traffic Simulators" investigates the effects of and the methodology for incorporating uncertainties into traffic simulators. The specific example described in the paper is a microsimulator for vehicular traffic, called CORSIM, which is studied with respect to its ability to successfully model and predict behavior of the traffic using data obtained from in situ measurements. Some of the data used in the simulation are accurate (video recordings), but some are quite inaccurate (observer counts of vehicles). The major conclusion of the studies reported in the paper is that it is possible to incorporate uncertainty in model inputs into analysis of traffic microsimulators like CORSIM using Bayesian techniques, and that incorporating this uncertainty can significantly change the variability of engineering simulations performed with CORSIM. The developments here should also be useful in dealing with general discrete network structures, including traffic in telecommunications networks.

The telecommunication market and, with it, telecommunication product design has undergone drastic changes in the past years. As a consequence, M&S tasks are confronted with new challenges. Chapter 22 entitled "Emerging Requirements for Telecommunication Product Design and System Modeling" outlines some requirement changes for simulation design. It is believed the focus must be on rapidity, robustness, simplicity and intuitiveness, and that for certain applications it should be acceptable to sacrifice exactness to some extent. The statement given in the paper is based on the assumption that M&S ultimately serves to facilitate decision making, and that most important decisions are made in the early design phase. It is herewith stressed that managers, who make decisions, prefer robust decisions to optimal decisions for singular cases. That is, they prefer decisions that are valid for a number of imaginable scenarios. Starting from the requirement of rapidity, robustness, simplicity and intuitiveness, the paper suggests a strategy to tackle a M&S :heterogeneous abstraction-level design approach (HALDA), where ideas from system test and system integration and test are developed and carried over to the early design phase.

The aim of Chapter 20 entitled "Redimensioning Network Resources Based on Users' Behavior" is to present a method for redimensioning network capacity (i.e., the number of internal switching lines) and some of their pre-designed parameters based on the detailed behavior of users of a telecommunications network and their demand for QoS. The approach described allows one to assess the sensitivity of various network parameters to the redimensioning task, and should be applicable directly to every (virtual) circuit switched network environment.

## 6.5    Network Emulation and Tomograpy

Chapter 21 deals with Internet performance measurement data extracted through Internet Tomography techniques and metrics, and how it may be used to enhance the capacity of network simulation and emulation modeling. The advantages of network simulation and emulation as a means to aid design and develop the component networks, which make up the Internet and are fundamental to its ongoing evolution, are highlighted.

## REFERENCES

[1]    Ince, A. Nejat, editor; "Modeling and Simulation Environment for Satellite and Terrestrial Communication Networks", Kluwer Academic Publishers, Boston, USA, 2002.

[2]    Bragg, A., "Features to Consider in a Network Design Tools", (TD/285/03/34)*.

[3]    Ince, A. Nejat and Topuz, Ercan Editors; "Modeling and Simulation Tools for Emerging Telecommunication Networks" Springer Science + Business media, Boston, USA, 2006.

[4]    Bragg, A., "Features to Consider When Evaluating Network Design Tool", (TD/285/05/07).*

[5]    Bragg, A., "Modeling and Analysis of Ultrahigh Capacity Optical Networks", (TD/285/05/09).*

[6]    Bragg, A., "An Architectural Framework and tool for Modeling Grids", (TD/285/05/10).*

---

*    The above references with their document numbers shown may be accessed at the Action's website www.cost285.itu.edu.tr

[7]    Bragg, A., "Faster-Than-Real-Time Distributed Simulation Using Multi-Core FPGA Arrays", (TD/285/06/13).

[8]    Henry, Paul, "Interference Characteristics of Broadband Power Line Communications Using Serial Medium Voltage Wires", IEEE Com. Magazine, April 2005.

[9]    Rumley, S. and Gaumier, C., "Network Reference Scenarios for Pan European Architectures" (TD/285/06/15).*

[10]   Rumley, S. and Gaumier, C., "Unified Description for Pan European Architectures" (TD/285/06/04).

[11]   McEvoy, E., Ganchev, I., O'Droma, M., "3P_AAA Service Simulation Approaches on an ns2 Platform" (TD/285/06/10).

[12]   Pustisek, M., "Structured Formats for Simulation Results" (TD/285/04/10).*

[13]   Khayari, R. E. A., Lehmann, A., "Multimedia Traffic Behavior, Analysis and Implications" (TD/285/05/17).

[14]   Zhou, B., He, D., Sun, Z., "Traffic Modeling and Prediction Using ARIMA/GARCH Mode" (TD/285/05/18).*

[15]   Sun, Z., "Invariants in Network Traffic", (TD/285/04/02).*

[16]   Liang, L. and Sun, Z., "IP Traffic Measurement and Modeling at Packet Level", (TD/285/03/23).*

[17]   Zhou, B. and Sun, Z., "Simulation Study of self-Similar Traffic and Network Performance", (TD/285/03/24).*

[18]   Marsan, M., "From Packet-Level Models to Fluid Models of IP-Networks: A Step Towards Scalability" (TD/285/05/19).

[19]   Bragg, A., "An Empirical Approach to Multimedia Modeling and Multilayer Modeling", (TD/285/05/16).*

[20]   Iversen, V. B., "A New Paradigm for Traffic Engineering of Multi-service Networks" (TD/285/06/11).*

[21]   Zhou, B., Sun, Z., "Characterization of Internet Traffic in Wireless Networks", (TD/285/06/14).*

[22]   Papp, D. et al., "Performance Modeling of MPLS Networks With Link Failures and Repairs" (TD/285/06/12).*

[23]   Padhye, J., et al., "Modeling TCP Reno Performance A Sample Model and Its Empirical Validation", Proc. IEEE/ACM Trans. Networking. Vol. 8, No.2, April 2000.

[24]   Bragg, A., "Encoding-Specific and Content-Heuristics for Building Multimedia Traffic Generators", (TD/285/06/05).*

[25]   Ince, A. N., "Independent Verification and Validation Implementation at NASA" (TD/285/06/09).*

[26]   Backer, M., "External PRNG's for OPNET" (TD/285/06/16).*

[27] Martinez, R., et al., "Simulation in the Process of System Design: Application to Traffic Lights Monitoring and Control" (TD/285/06/19).*

[28] Ganchev, I., "Network Tomography Measurement in Relation to Network Simulation and Emulation", (TD/285/03/32).*

[29] de Cola, T., "SatNEx meets COST 285", (TD/285/06/18).*

# CHAPTER 2

# A Review of High Performance Simulation Tools and Modeling Concepts

Chris Phillips

Department of Electronic Engineering, Queen Mary,
University of London

**Abstract.** *Simulation is used extensively to evaluate complex systems, including telecommunications networks. This paper provides a summary of simulation techniques, focussing on enhanced forms of discrete event-driven simulation that are capable of modeling large or high-speed networks in a reasonable time-frame. Various approaches are introduced though particular attention is paid to schemes that employ functional and/or spatial decomposition.*

## 1. INTRODUCTION: SIMULATION BASICS

A simulation is the execution of a model, represented by a computer program that gives information about the system being investigated. Simulation models are used to perform experiments that would be costly, dangerous or too time consuming with real systems. However, provided that models are adequate descriptions of reality (they are valid), experimenting with them can save money, suffering and even time.

Both continuous and discrete forms of simulation exist [1]. Discrete simulation is the modeling of a system as it evolves over time by a representation in which the state variables change only at a countable number of points in time. At these points an event occurs, where an event is taken to be an instantaneous occurrence that may change the state of a system.

Conventional simulation of packet-switched networks usually involves the use of discrete event simulators that model each individual packet through the network, typically called packet-level simulation. Each packet's arrival at, or departure from, a network element is represented by an event. Very large numbers of packets need to be simulated to obtain confidence in the results. This requires long simulation times, often amounting to many hours of real time just to simulate a few minutes of simulated time.

## 1.1    Discrete Event Simulation: Time Advancement

Discrete event simulation models are dynamic in nature, so there is a need for a mechanism to advance the simulation time from one event to the next. This requires a simulation clock that gives the current value of the elapsed simulated time. In addition, some means of storing all the current foreseeable events scheduled to occur within the system is necessary. This data structure normally takes the form of a single time ordered sequence of event records (with the next one to be executed being placed at the head) called an event-list. The simulation clock can be advanced according to either of two primary time-progression policies, namely fixed-increment time progression or next-event time progression.

The fixed-increment time progression method of time advance has been generally used in the simulation of systems where events are known to occur at fixed regular intervals. The simulation clock advances by constant amounts, called ticks. After each tick, a check is made to determine whether any events should have occurred during the previous time interval. If one or more events were scheduled, they are considered to occur at the end of the interval. The system state is then updated. The scheme can be inefficient if the tick magnitude is not carefully dimensioned. Choosing a smaller value reduces the probability of events occurring within a tick period and so increases the likelihood of simulator processing cycles that contain no useful event work. Selecting a larger tick interval, reduces the event time resolution.

With next-event time progression the times of occurrence of future events are generated. Then, the simulation clock is advanced to the time of the first of these events, which is subsequently processed. The system is updated to account for the effects resulting from this event and the simulation clock is then advanced to the next most imminent event and so on. This is the most common technique employed, primarily because periods of inactivity in the system are skipped since all state changes only occur at event times. This omission of inactive periods allows the simulation to proceed efficiently, especially when the time between successive events is large.

## 1.2    Generating Event Times

When it is necessary to select a suitable time for the completion of some future event, the simulator can adopt one of two main strategies. Firstly, it could use measured data from a real system that is fed into the simulator as a series of events. Although this method offers authenticity, it does have the disadvantage that for reasonable length simulations, a great deal of storage is required. A second and much more generally selected method is to use a Random Number Generator (RNG) along with models of the sources (e.g. probability distributions of inter-arrival times), from which particular event times can be calculated as required.

A truly random number sequence consists of a totally unpredictable stream of numbers that are in consequence unreproducible. This stream is normally obtained by observing some naturally random physical process such as the radioactive decay of a substance. In practice this can prove to be a difficult task in terms of correcting for experimental biases and maintaining a satisfactory generation rate. Storage of the ensuing data stream can also present a challenge. For these reasons, mechanisms for generating pseudo (false) random numbers have been introduced extensively. The principle of such pseudo RNG operation is that to an observer of the resulting number stream, it appears to be random in character.

Pseudo RNGs are used because the generation of any number is precisely defined according to some algorithm and so reproducibility of a given statistical experiment is possible. This is extremely useful in debugging software. Also, the storage and implementation requirements of the generator are very conservative and the simplicity of most of the coding algorithms facilitates very high-speed generation rates. These algorithms are completely non random and are usually periodic in nature, but the resulting stream of successive values is such as to appear random to an observer. However, provided the correlation between succeeding values is negligible, and the period of the RNG is large, then the resulting observed behaviour is usually considered to be independent of the generator.

## 1.3    Verification, Validation and Calibration

In order to satisfactorily prepare a simulation model verification, validation and calibration are necessary. Verification is the process of comparing the computer code with the model to ensure that the code is a correct implementation of the model, whereas, validation is the process of comparing the model's output with the behaviour of the phenomenon. In other words validation entails comparing the model to reality (physical or otherwise). A further consideration is calibration. This is the process of parameter estimation for a model. Calibration is a tweaking/tuning of existing parameters and usually does not involve the introduction of new ones, changing the model structure. In the context of optimization, calibration is an optimization procedure involved in system identification or during experimental design.

## 1.4    Challenges for Simulation

If the network simulation begins with an empty network each time the simulator is used, then an initial bias will always be present in the results. Obviously, if this is true of the system being studied, then this might be regarded as a desirable feature. Assuming the empty state is far removed from the typical operating conditions of the network, its effect could become very noticeable. The problem can be reduced, and even eliminated, by the adoption of one of three modifications:

1) Run the simulator for such a long time that this initial effect becomes a negligible influence upon the steady-state measures.
2) Only start recording observed data after a "warm up" period once a suitable steady-state has been attained.
3) When a suitable steady-state has been achieved, the status of the entire network is stored. In all subsequent simulation runs, the network is restarted from this frozen state.

A further challenge with simulation is determining the steady state. The term steady state is applied to systems that have reached a state of equilibrium. However, with most stochastic systems, there is no fixed steady state. One approach to determining an equilibrium condition might be to impose a tolerance on the output data such that when the parameter of interest remained within certain bounds of variability for a prescribed number of processed events, then the value would be considered to be in equilibrium. The concern with this method is deciding upon an acceptable tolerance. If it is too large the results may be inaccurate and selecting too small a tolerance might result in a terminating value never being attained.

Sometimes observation of the real system can help determine suitable bounds.

## 2.   FAST SIMULATION: MOTIVATION AND CLASSIFICATION

All modeling by simulation of stochastic systems requires a substantial quantity of information to be accumulated for results to be statistically viable. To enable such simulation studies to take place within a reasonable amount of real time, the designer could execute the program on a fast sequential computer or decompose the model into separate analytical and simulation components, a technique referred to as hybrid simulation. A further approach is to use parallel processing techniques employing a number of processors in some coherent manner to able certain tasks to be carried out concurrently. Both functional and spatial forms of decomposition are possible.

### 2.1   Races & Hazards

It is worth noting that in many systems comprising multiple connected, but autonomous, component processes there is a possibility of races and hazards occurring. A race is a competition between entities where the 'winner' is the one that completes some task, or arrives at some point, first. This is a natural feature of many systems, but the designer must ensure that this characteristic is dealt with correctly. A Hazard is an unintentional race whose outcome can distort the behaviour of the model and so lead to an inaccurate system characterisation. Although races are a concurrent phenomena, they can still be represented using conventional sequential simulation. The designer must be careful about the processing of events scheduled to take place at the same time.

### 2.2   Concurrency, Coupling and Consistency

Sequential event-driven simulations employ a global clock to indicate the current simulated time throughout the system. This clock is only advanced once all of the system's operations scheduled to take place at the current time instant have been accomplished; this allows each of these operations to physically be processed in series, although they may proceed concurrently in the network model. The limitation of this 'conventional' sequential method is that only a single instruction sequence is supported which processes a single data stream. This sequential processing of instructions is known as the Von Neumann principle. To improve performance, the CPU power must be enhanced. This leads to a potential bottleneck as the use of a single memory interface through which all data and control information must pass.

Actions are said to be concurrent when they overlap to some degree in time. This potential concurrency exists at various levels within an application. For example, concurrency may be exploited from the simulator architecture, by allowing unrelated simulator activities to proceed in parallel. Potential concurrency may also exist within the network model itself. By concurrent simulation, it is meant that some means is available to support the dedicated processing of two or more programming tasks in overlapping time. Assuming an unlimited quantity of processors to execute N jobs, each requiring t units of processor time, ideally all the tasks should be completed in t/N units of time. Relationships between individual jobs may require that certain tasks be accomplished before others can commence, resulting in reduced performance. This association between activities is referred to as coupling.

Some tasks may proceed independently, but others are related. This coupling results in order dependencies preventing certain jobs from being processed until others have been completed. Not only does this ordering lower the attainable performance, but also coupling by its very nature implies that some information is communicated between processes to determine when descendant jobs can be processed. These dependencies can be expressed as a directed graph enabling analysis to be used to evaluate an asymptotic upper bound on the attainable concurrency of a system. Order dependencies between entities may also dictate the processing sequence of events scheduled to occur at the same time. To model systems of this type, additional knowledge is required to enforce this ordering.

In distributed simulation, some method is always required to ensure consistency of the model. This implies that the processing of events within the model remains analogous to the behaviour of the real system, and that event causality relationships are never violated. The synchronous approach for maintaining consistency exerts a strict time-synchronous hand-shaking protocol between the concurrent event processing activities. The simulation time then advances from event to event such that, at any given instant, the simulated time across the model is the same, and is equal to the global earliest event-time. The asynchronous strategy relaxes this restriction somewhat, whilst remaining consistent, so that processing regions remain within bounded limits of some global earliest time. The range of simulated time that is supported by the simulation model, without violating consistency, is determined by the lookahead parameter.

## 2.3   Distributed Experiments

The distributed experiments multi-processor scheme recognises that many simulation studies take the form of a repeated series of trials, differing only in random number generator seed values, to enable batches of observed values of a parameter to be collected. Individual runs are simply assigned to separate processors and executed in parallel, and the individual results are collected and processed by one of the processors upon completion of the composite run. The appeal of this approach is that it is both simple to implement, with no communication required between the processors until the fruition of the experiment, and results in approximately N-fold performance gains. An alternative means of harnessing a multi-processor resource to improve performance is decomposition.

## 2.4   Decomposition

Different forms of decomposition exist for parallelizing an application. These can be broadly classified into functional and spatial decomposition. With functional decomposition, simulation programs consist of a number of functions that operate on data and data structures. Separating these into a number of component processes is called functional decomposition. This approach is sometimes called Algorithmic Parallelism. Conversely, with spatial decomposition the system model is decomposed into loosely coupled network components, or separate domains containing a few components, which are assigned to separate processes. These processes can then be mapped onto distinct processors for concurrent execution. This approach is sometimes called Geometric Parallelism.

Functional parallelism isolates loosely coupled functional units that are, at least to some extent, independent of each other and so can work concurrently. It allows the decomposition process to be tailored to the available resources. For example, mathematically demanding functions may be placed on processors supporting an integral Floating Point Unit [2]. The use of Task Farming is particularly relevant and can provide excellent speedups. It is also a strategy that is inherently load-balancing. Some researchers have chosen to isolate the event-list management functionality from that of the network model processing [3]. The attainable performance is highly related to the inherent parallelism in the algorithm.

With spatial parallelism [4] each spatial unit maintains its own local clock of how far it has progressed in elapsed simulated time and supports some data structure(s) of scheduled future events, which will occur at this location. The processing of an event is normally associated with some change of state in the physical process(es) it models; processing events may also induce changes of state within other spatial domains requiring information to be transferred between them. Some coordinated form of time-advancement is also required. With Synchronous techniques, akin to their time-driven counterparts, a global clock is implemented either in a centralized or distributed manner. Asynchronous event-driven schemes rely on time-stamped messages to convey timing information between the processes, each of which maintains a local clock record of elapsed time.

Generally in order to make the decomposition effective it is beneficial to arrange for the processing to arrange for the algorithm to be organised into coarse granularity structure where each processor can undertake a significant amount of useful work between intervals when it has to communicate with other system components. This is because communication is usually slow relative to the processing of data so avoiding undue communication, by keeping the processor busy performing local activities, improves the proportion of time spent fulfilling some useful operation. In addition, to reduce the time spent by processors waiting to initiate a communication, decoupling buffers can act as mediators, which temporarily retain the data until the receiver is ready. Finally, improved performance is achieved when the work assignment places more jobs, or jobs that are computationally more demanding, on processors with superior performance. When all processors offer the same processing capability, maximum performance is obtained when the workload is allocated equally, and time spent idle is minimum.

## 2.5  Lookahead

A significant parameter that increases the ability of processors to work concurrently is lookahead [5]. Lookahead defines the amount of time into the future a process can predict its behaviour unconditionally. It can at least be dimensioned to the smallest servicing time of any component within a network model. This is called the network-wide lookahead value. Events in spatially separate regions of a network model must be independent of each other provided the difference between their scheduled execution times differ by less than this network-wide lookahead value. They can thus be processed concurrently, even though these times are not identical, knowing that the processing of subsequent events cannot later invalidate resulting state changes in the network model. It is by this means that the inherent concurrency of the network model can be exploited. The term explicit lookahead is used when a lookahead value is invariant and is known prior to the start of the simulation.

## 2.6    Conservative and Optimistic Synchronization

Distributed simulation strategies must support some form of synchronization mechanism to ensure the model correctly simulates the behaviour of the system being modeled. This can be achieved by either employing conservative or optimistic synchronization policies. Optimistic schemes allow a component to process messages, even though there is uncertainty (i.e. some of its inputs are empty). This gives rise to a risk of inconsistent behaviour where the simulated elapsed time of the component may exceed that of the time-stamps of messages yet to arrive. Optimistic schemes allow a processor to simulate as far forward in time as it wants, without regard for the risk of having its simulation past affected, resulting in time warping [6] across the model. If its past is changed it must then be able to rollback [7] in time and correct any erroneous actions it has taken in its false future.

## 3.    DECOMPOSITION METHODS

Several forms of decomposition are now considered. The first approach based on [8], called centralized event-list, uses a combination of functional and spatial parallelism with a single event-list processor for events arising from all the spatial domains. Inter-processor communication typically introduces a significant performance penalty, aggravated when messages have to be relayed via intermediaries. It is illustrated in Fig. 1.

In this scheme functional parallelism allows the event-list management to proceed concurrently with the updating of the network model in the spatial domains. In addition, a lookahead windowing mechanism is employed with the event-list to enable multiple state-changes to take place in parallel. The operation of this Moving Time-Window mechanism [9] is shown in Fig. 2.

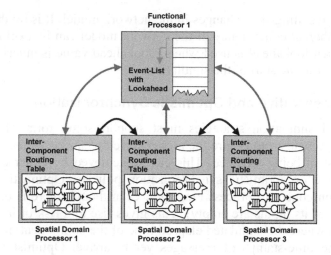

**Fig. 1  Centralized Event-List Decomposition**

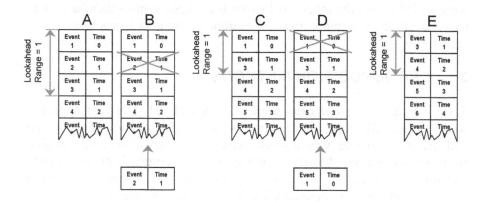

**Fig. 2  Moving Time Window Example**

To start with (A) as some events fall within the current lookahead window they are sent for processing. Upon return of the event-2-update the corresponding event record is deleted (B). However, as the event at time 0 is still outstanding, no further action is taken (C). The arrival of the event update at time 0, which relates to the leading outstanding event, causes the deletion of the corresponding event record (D). In addition, as there are no more events outstanding at this time, the window can be advanced, even though not all of the currently outstanding event updates have returned (E).

A significant disadvantage of this approach is that there is usually a significant performance overhead in transferring all events between the event-list processor and the spatial domain processors. To offset this, an alternative scheme, called the distributed event-list is to decompose the event-list into separate ones associated with each spatial domain [10] [11]. This reduces the communication burden but it requires coordination between these spatial domain processors to ensure the behaviour remains consistent.

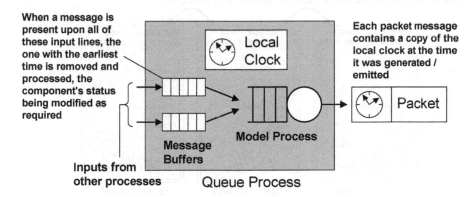

**Fig. 3  Distributed Event-List Decomposition**

As well as time-stamped packet messages, spatial domain processors exchange earliest event times in order for the Global Virtual Time to be established from which local lookahead bounds can be derived.

This scheme performs much better than the centralized event-list approach when the allocation of the network model regions to the different domain processes limits their interaction. Although a network-wide lookahead value can be used to determine which events can be processed without violating consistency constraints, further lookahead can be exploited between the spatial domains if the network model links between them can be arranged so that they are associated with queues that have an appreciable service time relative to the queues within each domain.

A more complete form of decomposition is that of distributed event buffering based on [12]. In this scheme the event-list is dispersed. Each queueing element is treated autonomously with its own event handling capability in the form of a message buffer associated with each input to the queueing element. The approach allows for fine-grain spatial parallelism.

Packets are tagged with timestamp information indicating the current local time at the upstream entity. When a packet message arrives it is placed at the end of the event buffer associated with that incoming line. Message buffers constitute an implicit event list should not be confused with any buffer associated with the component being modelled. When a message is present upon all of these input lines, the one with the earliest time is removed and processed, the component's status being modified as required. Each packet message contains a copy of the local clock at the time it was generated/emitted as shown in Figure 4.

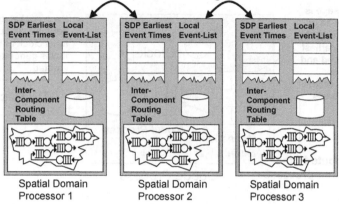

Spatial Domain      Spatial Domain      Spatial Domain
Processor 1        Processor 2        Processor 3

**Fig. 4  Queue Process with Message Buffers**

Deadlocks, or logical blocks, can occur where there is a cycle of blocked processes. A second form of deadlock or arrested simulation can arise in acyclic systems of processes when certain pathways, which culminate in a merge point, are not used. Neither of these Queues can proceed because they each have one input link with no messages waiting.

As shown in Figure 5, null-messages allow a process to inform others that no event messages will be sent along a particular link for a given time period [13]. Null messages are sent to all downstream adjacent processes whenever a process blocks. A block is deemed to have taken place when one of the input message buffers no longer contains any time-stamped messages. These Queues can now proceed because they have messages on all of their input links removing uncertainty.

To avoid deadlock within any cycle of communicating processes, the null-messages approach demands that there be a strict positive lower-bound on the lookahead of at least one process. The lookahead of each network component is set to its minimum service time. A process can then predict with absolute certainty that it will not transmit a cell to a remote process before a time given by its current clock value plus this lookahead. Null messages, time-stamped with this value, are sent to other processes so that they can identify occasions when it is legitimate to process event messages waiting on their other inputs. With implicit lookahead, via a future list mechanism, components use idle time to calculate the service times that messages will experience ahead of actual receipt of the messages. This information can then be sent as to other processes as null messages.

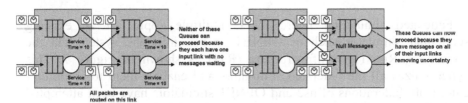

**Fig. 5  Arrested Simulation and the Use of Null Messages**

Within the distributed event buffering approach source processes are autonomous in nature and so can generate messages continually, up until some simulation stopping criterion without requiring input from other processes. This can be highly undesirable. Flow control is necessary to prevent message buffer saturation. To avoid an inordinate number of flow control messages, hysteresis is employed as illustrated in Figure 6.

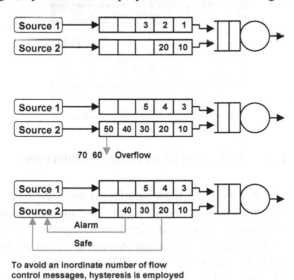

**Fig. 6 Flow Control to Regulate Autonomous Source Processes**

## 3.1  Federated Simulations

OPNET Modeler® is the leading commercial software for network simulation [14]. It includes an extensive well-document library of protocols and a powerful state-machine based representation of processes. Systems are represented hierarchically. ns2 is an open source network simulation that's popular with researchers [15]. It has good support for the TCP/IP protocol stack. ns2 provides very similar results compared to OPNET Modeler and is "freeware". However, the complete set of OPNET Modeler modules provides more features than ns2.

Federated simulation interconnects multiple copies of an existing sequential simulator such as OPNET or ns2 into one system via the underlying Run-Time Infrastructure (RTI) as shown in Figure 7. This synchronizes all the federated simulators and enables them to communicate. Both federations of ns2 and OPNET simulators have been attempted [16]. With OPNET, the existence of certain global data structures, zero lookahead interactions (i.e. Interface Control Information signals), and pointer data structures lead to dependencies between elements of the simulation that are hard to identify, making parallelization difficult and/or time consuming.

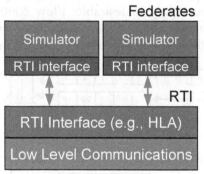

**Fig. 7  Federated Simulation Architecture**

The design of ns2 is such that simulation of very large networks is difficult, if not impossible, due to excessive memory and CPU time requirements. It uses a "federated simulation" approach where separate instantiations of ns modeling different sub-networks execute on different processors. Parallel/Distributed NS (PDNS) employs a conservative (blocking based) approach to synchronization. No federate in the parallel simulation will ever process an event that would later have to be undone due to receiving messages in the simulated past. This avoids the need to implement state saving in the existing ns2 code whilst still achieving good speedup figures [17] [18]. PDNS also includes emulation support for routing real application traffic via PDNS networks. This can be achieved using the Veil emulation framework, which captures the application data at the socket API layer.

## 3.2   Multi-Threaded Parallel Simulation

A thread can be defined as part of a program that can execute independently of other parts. Operating systems that support multi-threading enable programmers to design programs whose threaded parts can execute concurrently. The approach is well described in [19] where the authors consider modeling assembly line functions as a number of threads. The effect of decoupling "grain size" and the speedup versus the number of processors is shown and provides a good illustration of the typical characteristics observed with parallel simulation. For example, due to the inter-processor communication overhead, opting for a coarse thread granularity leads to improved performance. Indeed, in many cases this overhead is such that a performance benefit is never achieved, as the level of concurrency cannot compensate for this penalty. Even when it does, the speedup tends to plateau as the inherent parallelism of the underlying model is reached.

## 4.   OTHER FAST SIMULATION METHODS

In addition to decomposition various other methods of improving the performance of simulations. Some of these approaches are briefly considered in this section, starting with importance sampling.

## 4.1   Importance Sampling

Importance sampling is where the probabilities of the events are modified based on their relative importance to the required result [20]. Therefore in this method, a modified (or biased) probability distribution is introduced, in which the rare events of interest are forced to occur more frequently. This means the overall number of events to be simulated is reduced, requiring less computer resources. Further, the simulation outputs are weighted in order to correct for the use of the biased distribution.

## 4.2    Hybrid Simulation

This method focuses the simulation on a portion of the network of special interest and models the remainder of the network using analytic techniques [21]. It can be used to model network functions or characteristics with varying degrees of precision. For example traffic can be decomposed into foreground flows (modeled with simulation) and background flows (analytically) that simply influence the foreground traffic.

As an example of hybrid simulation it is possible to classify the network traffic into ForeGround (FG) traffic and BackGround (BG) traffic, and only the FG Traffic (which is of interest to us) is simulated. The BG Traffic is handled analytically; the service times of the FG Traffic is adjusted to compensate for the missing BG traffic. The magnitude of speed up depends on the ratio of FG: BG traffic. This gives a substantial reduction in the overall number of events to be simulated; however, validation tests typically show that there are some differences between the original and accelerated models. The analytical models do not capture nuances of protocol behaviours such as the feedback mechanism of TCP whereby the state of the network affects the source behaviour and, in turn, alters the network state. A further challenge remains how to interface data between the constituent tools such as network simulators and statistical analysis tools. There is no economical open-standard.

A further form of hybrid simulation is the use of aggregated models of sources to replace N multiplexed sources by a single equivalent source, such as an ON-OFF model [22]. This equivalent source generates traffic flows with the same characteristics as if they were derived from many individual sources. As the number of sources has a major impact on the run-time of a simulation, this aggregation can provide substantial performance benefits.

## 4.3    Emulation

Emulation is the ability of a program or device to imitate another program or device. Traditionally "emulator" implies hardware, and "simulator" is considered emulation via software. However, it is possible to employ electronic circuits to mimic the behaviour of routers and other telecommunications devices, though speedup is greatly affected by the complexity of the design [23]. A simple example would be to model simple queueing systems with hardware macrocells within an FPGA, originally expressed with VHDL/Verilog and then suitably synthesised.

(Re)configuration is possible by reprogramming the FPGA. Packet flows can be represented in a degenerate/simplified form only containing fields such as the destination address and the length of the packet. The approach appears to be relatively inflexible, except for modeling particular specific systems.

## 5.  CONCLUSIONS AND OBSERVATIONS

There is considerable motivation for developing faster simulations. Concerns about the stability of the Internet would appear to require large-scale models to capture the complex interactions between Autonomous Systems. Higher performance CPUs continue to be fabricated allowing legacy code to run faster but the computer architecture can remain a bottleneck. Hybrid simulation is appealing but often leads to compromises in the accuracy of the data that is generated due to simplifications needed to make the models tractable. Parallel simulation appears desirable as there is no loss of detail and scalable architectures are possible. Nevertheless overheads, typically in the form of communication delays, can outweigh the benefits. The trade-off/decisions regarding how to decompose a model into viable domains so that the workload is balanced is not trivial and usually requires appropriate selection of the fast simulation tool as well as specific calibration for each modeled environment.

Recent engineering developments are likely to reinvigorate interest in parallel simulation. Intel Corporation, for example, are considering multi-processor architectures for high performance computing that attempt to address speed, power and thermal considerations associated with high performance computing [24]. Their 80-tile architecture, shown in figure 8,

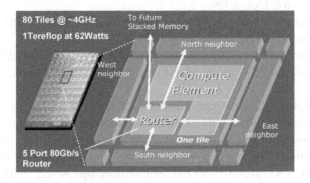

**Fig. 8  Intel's Teraflops Research Chip**

co-locates processing engines with local memory in order to reduce the communication burden and make this architecture appealing for decomposition schemes. When inter-processor communication is necessary a high-speed routing element on each tile provides four connections to adjacent tiles. This implies that information might have to be relayed via intermediary tiles to its destination depending on the decomposition placement. For parallel simulation the challenge will be to decompose the tool / model in order to make efficient use of the underlying processor architecture. Within previous parallel processing systems effective placement has typically relied on handcrafted configuration. However, compilers and parsers that are sensitive to the hardware architecture are likely to receive considerable attention as they meet analogous challenges addressed by the *place and route* algorithms for hardware synthesis.

## REFERENCES

[1]    P. Roth "Discrete, Continuous and Combined Simulation" in Proc. Winter Sim. Conf., pp. 56-60, 1988.

[2]    M. Barel "Performance Evaluation of the Discrete Event Simulation Computer DESC" in Proc. 18th Annual Simulation Symp., pp. 1-13, 1985.

[3]    D.W. Jones "Concurrent Simulation: An Alternative to Distributed Simulation" in Proc. 1986 Winter Simulation Conf., pp. 417-423.

[4]    P.F. Reynolds "A Spectrum of Options for Parallel Simulation" in Proc. Winter Sim. Conf., pp. 325-332, 1988.

[5]    Y.B. Lin, E.D. Lazowska "Exploiting Lookahead in Parallel Simulation" IEEE Trans. on Parallel and Distributed Systems, Vol.1 No.4, pp. 457-469, Oct. 1990.

[6]    D. Jefferson "Virtual Time" in ACM Trans. Prog. Lang. and Sys. Vol.7 No.3, pp. 404-425, July 1985.

[7]    A. Gafni "Rollback Mechanisms for Optimistic Distributed Simulation Systems" in Proc. SCS Multiconf. on Dist. Simulation, pp. 61-67, 1988.

[8]    D.W. Jones "Concurrent Simulation: An Alternative to Distributed Simulation" in Proc. 1986 Winter Simulation Conf., pp. 417-423.

[9]    L.M. Sokol, D.P. Briskoe, A.P. Wieland "MTW: A Strategy for Scheduling Discrete Simulation Events for Concurrent Execution" in Proc. SCS Multiconf. on Dist. Simulation, pp. 34-42, 1988.

[10] B.D. Lubachevsky "Bounded Lag Distributed Discrete-Event Simulation" in Proc. SCS Multiconf. on Dist. Simulation, pp. 183-191, 1988.

[11] D.M. Nicol, C.C. Michael, P. Inouye "Efficient Aggregation of Multiple LPs in Distributed Memory Parallel Simulations" in Proc. 1989 Winter Simulation Conf., pp. 680-685.

[12] K.M. Chandy, J. Misra "Asynchronous Distributed Simulation via a Sequence of Parallel Computations" in Comms. ACM, Vol. 24, No.11, pp. 198-206, 1981.

[13] K.M. Chandy, J. Misra, L. Haas "Distributed Deadlock Detection" in ACM Trans. on Computer Systems, Vol. 1, No.2, pp. 144-156, May 1983.

[14] OPNET, Available at: http://www.opnet.com/products/modeler/home.html.

[15] PDNS, Available at: http://www.cc.gatech.edu/computing/compass/pdns/

[16] H. Wu et al. "Experiences parallelizing a commercial network simulator", in Winter Simulation Conference, Dec. 2001.

[17] G.F. Riley et al. "A Federated Approach to Distributed Network Simulation", ACM Transactions on Modeling and Computer Simulation, vol. 14, pp. 116-148, 2004.

[18] Material from IMA Talks. ""Hot Topics" Workshop: Agent Based Modeling and Simulation", November, 2003, http://www.ima.umn.edu/talks/workshops/11-3-6.2003/ (accessed March 2006).

[19] C.C. Lim et al. "An Empirical Comparison of Runtime Systems for Conservative Parallel Simulations", 2nd Workshop on Runtime Systems for Parallel Programming, Florida, 1998, pp. 123-134.

[20] P.E. Heegaard "Comparison of speed-up techniques for simulation", 12th Nordic Teletraffic Seminar, Norway, pp. 407-420, August 1995.

[21] J.A. Schormans et al. "A hybrid technique for the accelerated simulation of ATM networks and network elements", ACM Transactions on Modeling and Computer Simulation, 11(2): 82-205, 2001.

[22] A. Ma "Accelerated Simulation of Power-Law Traffic in Packet Networks". PhD Dissertation, Department of Electronic Engineering, Queen Mary, University of London, 2002.

[23] Dong Xu, "Hardware-based Parallel Simulation of Flexible Manufacturing Systems". PhD Dissertation, Virginia Polytechnic Institute and State University, 2001.

[24] Intel Corporation, "Teraflops Research Chip", http://www.intel.com/research/platform/terascale/teraflops.htm (accessed March 2006).

# CHAPTER 3

# Using Visualization Techniques in Multilayer Traffic Modeling

Arnold Bragg

Center for Advanced Network Research
RTI International, Inc. Box 12194
Research Triangle Park, NC 27709 USA

**Abstract.** *We describe visualization techniques for multilayer traffic modeling – i.e., traffic models that span several protocol layers, and traffic models of protocols that cross layers. Multilayer traffic modeling is challenging, as one must deal with disparate traffic sources; control loops; the effects of network elements such as IP routers; cross-layer protocols; asymmetries in bandwidth, session lengths, and application behaviors; and an enormous number of complex interactions among the various factors. We illustrate by using visualization techniques to identify relationships, transformations, and scaling; to smooth simulation and measurement data; to examine boundary cases, subtle effects and interactions, and outliers; to fit models; and to compare models with others that have fewer parameters. Our experience suggests that visualization techniques can provide practitioners with extraordinary insight about complex multilayer traffic effects and interactions that are common in emerging next-generation networks.*

# 1.    INTRODUCTION

A multilayer traffic model comprises a traffic stream, and changes made in that stream as it transits various protocol layers. The reference model usually consists of an application that generates traffic, followed by transport (e.g., TCP, UDP), network, link, and physical layer protocols that alter the characteristics of the traffic stream in some way. The reference model may also include components from protocol sublayers that affect the stream in some way (e.g., the effects of MPLS tunnels, ATM segmentation and reassembly, load balancing, LLC fragmentation). Reference models are briefly discussed in the next Section.

Modeling and analyzing multilayer traffic is challenging, as one must deal with disparate traffic-source characteristics (greedy, bursty, periodic, non-stationary, autocorrelated, short- and long-range dependent, stochastic, streaming, elastic, multiplexed, etc.); various control loops and their inter-actions (within TCP, imposed by traffic shapers, etc.); various routing strategies and their interactions (e.g., $\lambda$ routing and IP routing in optical networks); network elements (buffering, blocking in switches, active queue management in routers, etc.); cross-layer protocols (common in mobile and wireless protocol stacks); broad differences in bandwidth, session lengths, and application behaviors; and various convolutional and confounding effects and other interactions among these factors [1]. Most practitioners lack insight about the various effects and interactions; hence, traffic modelers either make simplifying assumptions which may reduce model *fidelity*; or include every protocol layer and component in their models – including superfluous ones – which reduces run-time *efficiency*.

## 1.1    Relevance to the Networking Research Community

The choices made vis-à-vis traffic models have a significant impact on simulation accuracy and run-time efficiency. The visualization techniques described herein have several advantages:

- They provide practitioners with *insight* about complex traffic streams found in emerging next-generation networks.
- They can be used to improve the calibration and validation of new traffic models.
- They can help in maintaining simulation accuracy without sacrificing speed.
- They can be applied to traffic at various time scales.

- They can be applied to measurements from experimental and production networks, to simulation output, to output from analytical and hybrid models, and to output from network emulators.

The US National Science Foundation's Global Environment for Network Innovations (GENI) initiative – an effort to redesign the Internet – has proposed an end-to-end research process for taking ideas from conception, through validation, to deployment (Fig. 1). Modeling and simulation play an important role in this process, but also have limitations (Fig. 1):

*"It is well known within the networking research community that we lack effective methodologies and tools for rigorously evaluating, testing, and deploying new ideas. Today, most new ideas for how the Internet might be improved are initially evaluated using simulation, emulation, and theoretical analysis. These techniques are invaluable in helping researchers understand how an algorithm or protocol operates in a controlled environment, but they provide only a first step. The problem is that the simulations tend to be based on models that are backed by conjecture rather than empirical data; [and] models that are overly simple in virtually every attribute of practical significance."* [2]

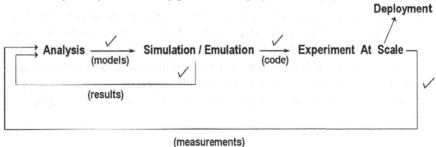

**Fig. 1 Process for networking research (US NSF GENI Initiative, [2]).**

Visualization techniques can be applied at several points in this process (denoted by checkmarks in Fig. 1) – following the Analysis step using test data, following the Simulation/Emulation step using simulation output, and following Experiments At Scale using measurement data from operational networks or experimental test beds. These techniques can significantly reduce the dependence on conjecture by identifying the key components and relationships for the analyst.

## 1.2    Multilayer Traffic Models

Visualization techniques can be applied to a number of multilayer traffic modeling scenarios. Fig. 2 depicts a set of multilayer traffic reference models in which a traffic stream transits, and is altered in some way, by various protocol layers. A particular reference model may represent an analytical, simulation, or hybrid implementation.

Fig. 2 (a) is a full model in which each protocol layer acts on the traffic stream serially. This approach is often used in discrete-event simulation, and can provide very high fidelity but may also incur prohibitively long run times.

Fig. 2 (b) and (c) combine two or three protocol layers into a multilayer model. This is often done when only one or two layers are the focus of study, but the effects of all layers must be represented at least superficially. When combining layers, one usually combines adjacent layers. In this example there are seven adjacency 2- and 3-sets – (1) application/transport, (2) transport/network, (3) network/link, (4) link/physical, (5) application/ transport/network, (6) transport/network/link, and (7) network/link/physical. Combining layers can reduce run times, but may sacrifice accuracy because the interactions between layers may not be captured.

Fig. 2 (d) is an example of a cross-layer network protocol, which is another type of multilayer traffic model. E.g., small unmanned aerial vehicles (UAVs) use modified transport and network protocols in which performance data from the link layer is passed directly to the transport and network layers where it is used to modify the operating characteristics of those layers [3]. Cross-layer protocols can be enormously complex to analyze [4].

Fig. 2 (e) is another variation of a multilayer traffic model based on a single-layer analytical model for which certain assumptions about higher and lower layers been made, and for which static data is provided via input parameters (e.g., round-trip delay, packet loss rate, timeout interval, congestion window size). A widely-used transport layer model uses mathematical formulas to estimate the TCP source sending rate and TCP end-to-end throughput at steady state [5,6,7,8]. This (and comparable) models provide reasonable first-order approximations for TCP throughput and 'goodput', but obviously cannot capture the dynamics of TCP, nor subtle nuances of its behavior. However, this is often the only practical approach for simulating TCP flows over large and complex networks [1].

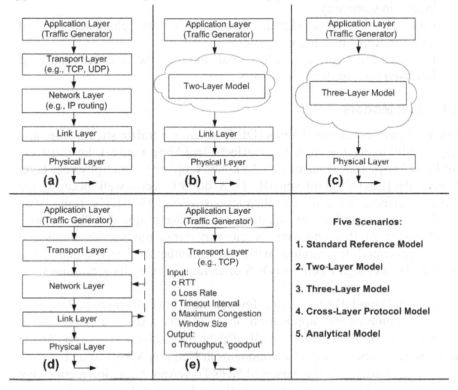

**Fig. 2  Full (a), and multilayer (b, c, d, e) protocol reference models.**

Zhang describes yet another multilayer protocol for enhancing TCP performance in secure wireless networks [9]. TCP's performance enhancement proxy conflicts with IP-security (IPsec). Zhang uses a multilayer protection protocol that gives wireless routers controllable access to TCP headers for performance enhancement purposes.

## 2.    CHALLENGES IN MULTILAYER MODELING

Consider a protocol stack consisting of:

1.    An application's traffic stream (App), with
2.    Transport layer effects (Trn) that modify the characteristics of App in some way,

3. Network layer effects (Net) that modify the characteristics of Trn[App] – the application's traffic stream modified by the transport layer – in some way,
4. Link layer effects (Lnk), that modify the characteristics of Net[Trn[App]] in some way, and
5. Physical layer effects (Phy) that modify the characteristics of Lnk[Net[Trn[App]]] in some way.

## 2.1  Full Models

Many discrete-event simulations (DES) generate a traffic stream App, and sequentially apply transport layer effects Trn[App], network layer effects Net[Trn[App]], link layer effects Lnk[Net[Trn[App]]], and physical layer effects Phy[Lnk[Net[Trn[App]]]]. DES do this very well because the protocol effects are realistic abstractions – e.g. OPNET's finite state machine representations of standard networking protocols. The obvious disadvantage of this approach is the very large number of simulation events generated for models with large numbers of traffic-generating sources. Hence, high fidelity in DES often requires very long run times.

In the 'full model' case as in reference model (a) of Figure 2, Trn[App] has $2^2$-1 components: application layer effects (App), transport layer effects (Trn), and the effects of all of their interactions Trn⊗App. At the network layer, there are $2^3$-1 components in Net[Trn[App]]: App, Trn, Net, Trn⊗App, Net⊗Trn, Net⊗App, and Net⊗Trn⊗App. Some interactions are superfluous, while others are realistic and cannot be ignored – e.g., Net⊗App might represent the effects of router priority queuing to support delay- and jitter-sensitive voice traffic at the expense of other traffic; and Trn⊗App might represent characteristic behaviors applied by a real-time transport protocol.

## 2.2  Two-Layer Models

A two-layer model might, for example, combine the effects of the transport and network layers into a single abstraction, NetTrn – which is not the same as Net⊗Trn – giving Phy[Lnk[NetTrn[App]]] as in reference model (b) in Fig. 2. In this case, NetTrn[App] has App, Net⊗Trn, and NetTrn⊗App components. The latter component is challenging to model, because it more or less embodies the Trn, Net, Trn⊗App, Net⊗App, and Net⊗Trn⊗App components from a comparable full model. A protocol modeling expert may have the skills to combine the Net and Trn components and to craft a realistic NetTrn⊗App ≅ {Trn, Net, Trn⊗App, Net⊗App, Net⊗Trn⊗App} representation, but only if most of the interactions are superfluous.

## 2.3 Three-Layer Models

A three-layer model might combine the effects of the transport, network, and link layers into one abstraction, LnkNetTrn, giving Phy[LnkNetTrn[App]] as in reference model (c) in Fig. 2. Note that LnkNetTrn[App] has App, LnkNetTrn, and LnkNetTrn⊗App components, and the latter two terms embody a large number of abstractions – Trn, Trn⊗App, Net, Net⊗Trn, Net⊗App, Net⊗Trn⊗App, Lnk, Lnk⊗App, Lnk⊗Trn, Lnk⊗Trn⊗App, Lnk⊗Net, Lnk⊗Net⊗App, Lnk⊗Net⊗Trn, and Lnk⊗Net⊗Trn⊗App. Note also that LnkNetTrn is not the same as Lnk⊗Net⊗Trn. A protocol modeling expert must be quite adept in separating the influential effects and interactions from the superfluous ones.

As noted, one cannot assume that most interactions are superfluous, as real protocol stacks may have important interactions between non-adjacent layers. Net⊗App might represent a router protocol that prioritizes traffic in its buffers based on the type of application – e.g., voice over IP. Lnk⊗Trn might represent the effects of a cross-layer protocol – reference model (d) in Figure 2 – that passes link-layer loss rates up the stack to the transport layer for use in window sizing.

If there is feedback then Trn[App] may be stochastic: e.g., Trn[App](t) = SomeFunctionOf(Trn[App](t-1), Trn[App](t-2), ..., Trn[App](t-N)) at times (t), (t-1), ..., (t-i). There may be situations in which routing decisions are made at two different layers, and those decisions may conflict (e.g., λ routing and IP routing in optical networks). These are very important components in multilayer and cross-layer protocols, and must be accounted for in realistic traffic models of them.

## 3.    APPROACH

Model builders usually begin with a basic traffic model and use empirical data and/or simulation output to refine the model over several iterations. Unfortunately, coarse-grained modeling approaches such as full-factorial designs may require hundreds of 'experiments' to determine which factors and interactions are most important, and to differentiate among competing models. This is even more difficult when modeling is based on traffic measurements from operational networks over which the model builder has little or no experimental control.

Practitioners require high fidelity and short run times (Fig. 3, point a). Currently this is achievable only with models based on emulators (and perhaps only massively parallel ones at that).

DES can provide high fidelity at long run times (Fig. 3, point b), although various specialized techniques have been proposed to reduce run times without significantly sacrificing fidelity.

An expert modeler may be able to remove superfluous components and achieve relatively high fidelity at reduced run times (Figure 3, point c). However, as models become more complex – moving from a two-layer to a three-layer model, or using nearly any cross-layer protocol model – the likelihood that a specialist can craft a high-fidelity model is diminished (Figure 3, points c to d to e as complexity increases).

Visualization techniques, which are widely used in exploratory data analysis, data mining, computational physics, etc., can be exploited to greatly accelerate a multilayer traffic model builder's understanding of underlying processes, to identify influential factors and interactions, and to provide insight early in the model building phase. Visualization helps one see behaviors related to the main effects and their various interactions – the behavior of a specific component (e.g., App) or components (e.g., Trn[App]). One can also use visualization to focus on complex interactions like $Net \otimes Trn \otimes App$ by visualizing components of the transport layer (e.g., window size) and the application layer (e.g., offered traffic load) at the same time, while varying loss rates (e.g., incurred by active queue management in routers). Visualization provides one with the *insight* required to develop better models, and lets one move point (e) in Fig. 3 toward the right by understanding main effects and interactions.

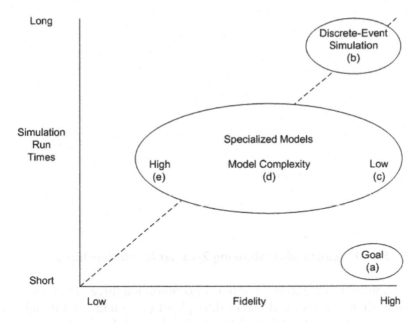

**Fig. 3 Model fidelity vs. performance; visualization techniques move from (e) toward (c).**

We conclude this Section with seven examples showing how we have used visualization techniques to develop and analyze multi-layer traffic models.

## Example 1 – Relationships, Transformations, and Scaling

The first step is to look for relationships (or lack of relationships) between variables, and to determine whether transformations to logarithmic or other scales might be useful. Fig. 4 (left) shows simple scatter plots for throughput ($Tp$), packet loss rate ($p$), and end-to-end round trip delay or round trip time ($RTT$). (In practice, many more variables would likely be assessed.) Fig. 4 (right) shows similar relationships between round trip time, maximum TCP window size ($Wm$), and throughput. The relationship between window size and throughput in the bottom right of the Figure is particularly interesting, as is confirmation that $Tp$ and $p$ have a more or less linear relationship (upper left of the Figure) in this particular model. (Both are check-marked in Fig. 4.)

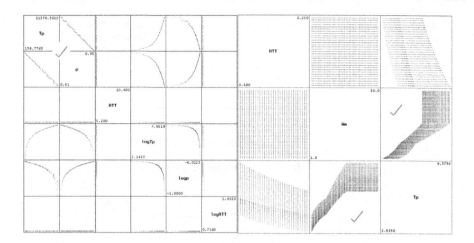

**Fig. 4  Scatter plots showing 2-variable relationships.**

Fig. 5 (top two rows) shows relationships involving three variables for a completely different protocol stack: throughput (*Thr*) and log throughput (*l Thr*), packet loss rate (*Ls*) and log packet loss (*l Ls*), and round trip time (*RTT*) and log round trip time (*l RTT*). Note that logarithmic transformations on some variables make the response surfaces more uniform, which can be useful in analyzing them.

Similar exploratory analyses can be performed for throughput (*Tp*), packet loss rate (*p*), and congestion window size (*Wm*) (Fig. 5, bottom two rows). In general, analysts avoid 'peaked' surfaces such as on the first and third rows of Fig. 5. In practice, many more variables would likely be assessed, and automated tools might also be used to suggest transformations that reduce variability in multivariate relationships. One might link descriptive statistics and correlations to graphics to numerically confirm visual relationships. One might also generate plots of principal components of highly dimensioned models in two or three dimensions (as in Figs. 4 and 5) to better understand the structure of multidimensional data.

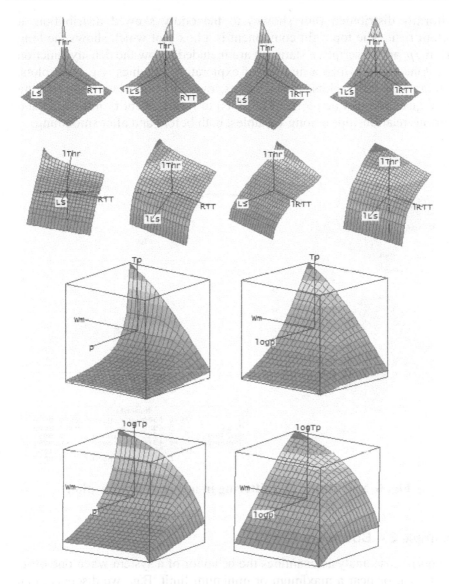

**Fig. 5  Scatter surfaces showing 3-variable relationships.**

## Example 2 – Smoothing

Another important step is to filter or otherwise remove, if possible, experimental 'noise' from measurements and simulation output. Fig. 6 shows a 3-dimensional plot of throughput (*Tp*), round trip delay (*RTT*), and congestion window size (*Wm*) as measured (top left), and smoothed (bottom left). Once smoothed, the density of *Tp* goes from more or less uniformly distributed (not shown) to the oddly skewed distribution at bottom right. The top right component is a box plot which shows the long tail in *Tp*, and descriptive statistics are included below the density function plot. One might utilize a number of exploratory graphics (e.g., box plots, histograms, scatter plots, mosaic plots, overlaid line plots, 3-D rotating plots, quantile-quantile plots, CDF plots) to further identify influential and spurious relationships among variables, both before and after smoothing.

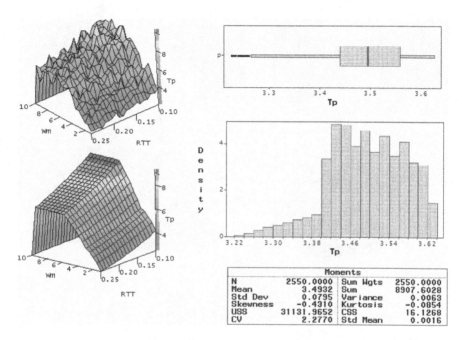

**Fig. 6  Smoothing and filtering in a three-variable plot.**

## Example 3 – Boundary Cases

Boundary case analysis examines the behavior of a system when one of its inputs is at or near a maximum or minimum limit. E.g., we discovered an odd phenomenon (described in [1]) when we varied TCP's maximum congestion window size *Wm* and timeout interval *T0* over practical operating ranges at three slightly different packet loss rates using a well-known analytical model [5,6]. Fig. 7 shows a plot of TCP throughput *Tp* at packet loss rates *p* of 0.010, 0.011, 0.012, 0.013, and 0.014 with a round trip delay *RTT* of 2.0 seconds. Note the ridge near *Wm* = 12 in the leftmost plot, and how it progresses across subsequent plots as loss rates are slightly increased. We believe this is an artifact of an imperfect TCP analytical model rather than an odd interrelationship between $Tp$, $p$, $Wm$, and $T0$. (The phenomenon more or less disappears when a revised model is used [8].)

In general, it is important that the analyst can render boundary cases in three dimensions. Equally important are capabilities to 'spin' a three-dimensional plot and to support dynamic and interactive user-initiated selection of subsets of data (e.g., loss rates in a very narrow range) that can be added or excluded, with analyses and graphs automatically recomputed in real time.

## Example 4 – Subtle Effects and Interactions

We also reported results from simulating TCP over a wireless network infrastructure with relatively high packet loss rates and relatively short round trip times in [1]. Fig. 8 (top left) shows a plot of TCP throughput $Tp$ at a packet loss rate $p$ of 0.05, round trip delays $RTT$ between 0.1 and 1.0 second, and a maximum TCP congestion window size $Wm$ between 1 and 10. We noted an unusual bulge in the leftmost Figure (arrow).

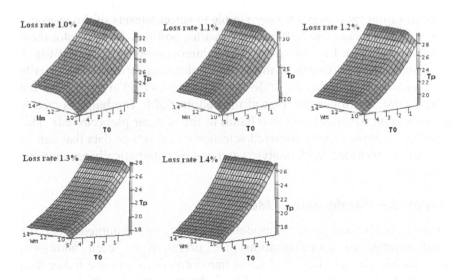

**Fig. 7  TCP throughput ($Tp$) vs. $Wm$ and $T0$ at five slightly different packet loss rates.**

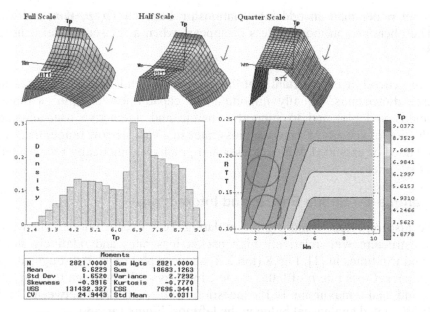

**Fig. 8  Wireless TCP throughput (*Tp*) vs. *RTT* and *Wm*.**

Visualization tools make it very simple to select subsets of the response surface – in this case one-half and one-quarter portions – and to plot them at higher resolution. I.e., the center and rightmost plots at the top of Fig. 8 are one-half and one-fourth of the leftmost plot, respectively. The density and moments of *Tp* in this expanded sample are provided at the bottom left of the Figure, and a contour plot at the bottom right. The bulge is clearly indicated as an irregularity in two bands of the contour plot (circled). This is another example of user-initiated selection of subsets of data that can be expanded or excluded, with analyses and graphs automatically recomputed in real time.

## Example 5 – Parsimonious Models

In general, traffic and protocol models with the fewest parameters and the fewest number of transformations are preferred as each additional parameter adds uncertainty, and some transformations confuse rather than clarify an analyst's understanding. Fig. 9 shows a case in which a simple model was the best choice. We analyzed a high speed wireless bulk data transfer scheme loosely based on Reliable Blast UDP (RBUDP) [10]. (The protocol transmits an entire file using UDP, then performs selective retransmissions to fill gaps caused by packet loss.)

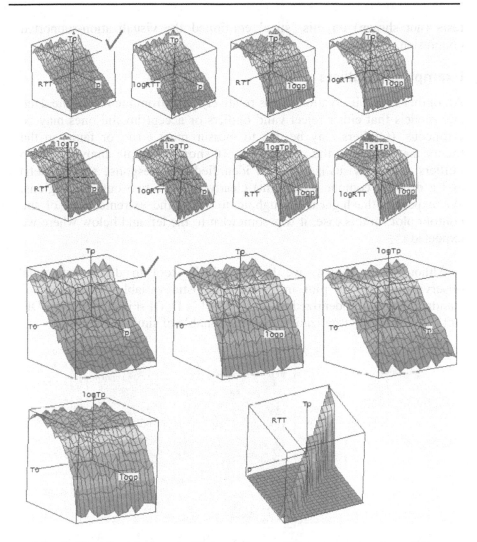

**Fig. 9  Simple wireless bulk transfer multilayer protocol model.**

Fig. 9 indicates that the best response in the throughput (*Tp*) vs. round trip delay (*RTT*) vs. packet loss (*p*) relationship was the leftmost one in the top row (checked) – with no transformations. Smoothing (not shown) confirmed that throughput was dominated by loss, and the relationship was more or less linear. A similar linearity was observed when processing time at the destination (*T0*) was evaluated (third row, leftmost plot, checked). Again, normalized throughput depended almost entirely on the packet loss rate. The plot in the lower right of Fig. 9 shows how the visualization tool was able to extract a cross-sectional view of one of the plots. Linearity tests (not shown) on this 'slice' confirmed the visualization-supported conclusion.

## Example 6 – Outliers

An outlier is an observation that is relatively 'far' from the rest of the data, and models that either reject valid outliers or accept invalid ones may be erroneous. (Outliers may be due to measurement error, or faults in the theory that generated the values.) Fig. 10 shows a simple analysis of two outliers that the visualization tool identified. The response surface (left) and a detailed contour plot (right) clearly indicate two outlying regions. We expected the highest throughput to be in the extreme right of the contour plot; in this case, it was somewhat to the left and below where we expected.

Although not shown, we have used the tool to detect influential observations, and to plot influence diagnostic variables (hat diagonal, standardized and studentized residuals, Cook's D, DF-Fits, CovRatios, DF-Betas, etc.). Most visualization tools are capable of similar analyses.

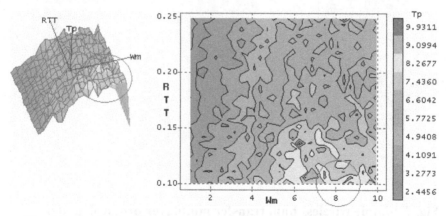

**Fig. 10  Analysis of two outliers, and confirmation via contour plot.**

## Example 7 – Model Fitting

Dynamically fitting models is another important component. Fig. 11 shows a three-dimensional plot of throughput ($Tp$), end-to-end delay ($RTT$) and congestion window size ($Wm$) (top left). The distribution of $Tp$ fits a Weibull distribution reasonably well (Fig. 11, top middle), so there is no need to utilize an artificial empirical distribution (Figure 11, top right). The cumulative distribution functions of the $Tp$ distribution and a three-parameter

Weibull distribution confirm the fit (Fig. 11, middle left, and middle right with confidence bands).

The Weibull distribution's parameters can be dynamically adjusted using sliders (Fig. 11, bottom). In this case, the three parameters – shape, scale, and location – are adjusted to achieve the 'best' fit. Once a model is fit, the analyst may be able to replace a great deal of simulation code with mathematical expressions.

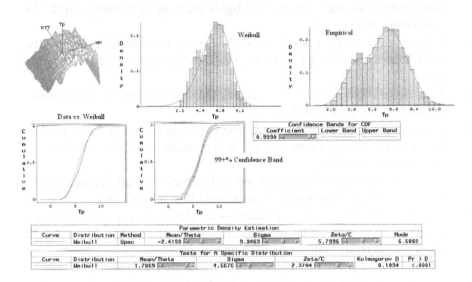

**Fig. 11 Fitting distributions and models.**

# 4. VISUALIZATION TOOLS FOR MULTILAYER MODELING

There are a number of commercial visualization tools for exploring and analyzing simulation and measurement data. We used SAS/INSIGHT software from SAS Institute Inc. in the examples herein, but other tools may be comparable in price and/or features (e.g., AVS DataDesk, IDL, JMP, MATLAB, PVWave, S-Plus, XGobi).

In general, a visualization tool used to analyze multilayer traffic and protocol models, simulation output, and measurements from networks should [11]:

- Be dynamic and interactive.
- Be capable of visualizing univariate distributions, multivariate data, and fitting models using linear regression, analysis of variance, logistic

regression, Poisson regression, other generalized linear models, and various non-linear models.

- Render in three dimensions, with the ability to spin a three-dimensional plot.
- Support user-initiated selection of subsets of data that can be added or excluded, with analyses and graphs automatically recomputed in real time.
- Support multiple windows, dynamically linked so that 'coloring' observations in one window highlights them in all windows with the same coloration.
- Support exploratory graphics (e.g., box plots, histograms, scatter plots, mosaic plots, overlaid line plots, 3-D rotating plots, quantile-quantile plots, CDF plots).
- Link descriptive statistics and correlations to graphics to numerically confirm visual relationships.
- Generate plots of principal components of highly dimensioned models in two or three dimensions to better understand the structure of multidimensional data.
- Fit and dynamically adjust polynomial curves with confidence bands, kernel estimates, smoothing splines, and other smoothers.
- Evaluate models with summary statistics, analysis of variance, parameter estimates, collinearity diagnostics, residual-by-predicted plots (to identify outliers), and partial leverage plots (to examine changes in the residuals with and without explanatory variables).
- Detect influential observations, and plot influence diagnostic variables (e.g., hat diagonal, standardized and studentized residuals, Cook's D, DF-Fits, CovRatio, and DF-Betas).
- Check the distribution of residuals (e.g., tests for Gaussian, lognormal, exponential, Weibull, and similar distributions).

## 5.  SUMMARY

We have described several visualization techniques for multilayer traffic modeling and analysis and have illustrated each technique with examples that identify relationships; perform transformations, smoothing, and scaling; examine boundary cases, subtle effects and interactions, and outliers; fit models; and compare models with others that have fewer parameters.

Our experience suggests that visualization techniques can provide practitioners with extraordinary insight about complex multilayer traffic effects and interactions that are common in emerging next-generation networks, and may be especially valuable for traffic models in which several protocol layers are combined.

## REFERENCES

[1]  Bragg A. "An Empirical Approach For Multilayer Traffic Modeling And Multimedia Traffic Modeling At Different Time Scales". Chapter 3 in Ince, A. Nejat (editor) *Modeling and Simulation of Telecomm. Networks*. Springer/Kluwer. London. 2006.

[2]  Anderson T. et al., *GENI: Global Environment for Network Innovations – Conceptual Design Project Execution Plan*, GDD-06-07, January 10, 2006, US National Science Foundation, http://www.geni.net

[3]  Baldine, I., A. Bragg, D. Stevenson, "Cross-layer protocols for small UAVs," unpublished, 2006.

[4]  Gurtov, A. et al., "Multilayer protocol tracing in a GPRS network," *Proc. IEEE 56th Vehicular Technology Conference*, 2002, 24–28 Sept. 2002 Page(s) 1612–1616.

[5]  Padhye J. et al., "Modeling TCP throughput: a simple model and its empirical validation", *Proc. ACM SIGCOMM '98*, August 1998.

[6]  Padhye, J. et al., "Modeling TCP Reno Performance: A Simple Model and Its Empirical Validation," *Proc. IEEE/ACM Trans. Networking*, Vol. 8 No. 2, April 2000.

[7]  Padhye J. and S. Floyd, "On inferring TCP behavior", *Proc. ACM SIGCOMM '01*, August 2001.

[8]  Chen Z. et al., "Comments on 'Modeling TCP Reno Performance: A Simple Model and Its Empirical Validation'," *IEEE/ACM Transactions on Networking*, Vol. 14, No. 2, April 2006, pp. 451–453.

[9]  Zhang Y. "A multilayer IP security protocol for TCP performance enhancement in wireless networks." *IEEE Journal on Selected Areas in Communications*, May 2004, Vol. 22 , Issue 4, page(s): 767–776.

[10] He E. et al., "Reliable Blast UDP: Predictable High Performance Bulk Data Transfer," *IEEE Cluster Computing 2002*, Chicago, Illinois, Sept, 2002.

[11] SAS/INSIGHT, www.sas.com.

# CHAPTER 4

# A Multilevel Approach for the Modelling of Large TCP/IP Networks

Eitan Altman[1], Konstantin Avrachenkov[1], Chadi Barakat[1],
Kartikeya Chandrayana[2]

[1]INRIA Sophia Antipolis, France
[2]Cisco Systems, San Jose

**Abstract.** *We present in this paper an analytical model for the calculation of network load and drop probabilities in a TCP/IP network with general topology. Our model does not require the predefinition of bottleneck links. The model is based on analytical expressions for TCP throughput, which allows it to take into account diverse TCP features as the receiver congestion window limitation. It can be used for TCP/IP networks with drop tail routers as well as for TCP/IP networks with active queue management routers. First, we formulate our model as a Non-Linear Complementarity problem (NCP). Then, we transform the model into two equivalent formulations: fixed point formulation and nonlinear programming formulation. Thereupon, using asymptotic analysis, we prove existence of a unique solution to the NCP by casting it into the well known utility optimization framework. In addition to uniqueness of rates and end-to-end drop probabilities, the NCP shows the ability to provide unique solutions in terms of link drop probabilities. We explain the relationship between the utility optimization, fixed-point approach and our complementarity approach. Specifically, we show how these models can be*

[2] This work was done while the last author was visiting INRIA. The work of the first two coauthors was supported by the EuroNGI network of excellence.

*derived from each other. Finally, we illustrate the utility of our proposed approach by solving some benchmark examples and showing how the distribution of load varies with network parameters. The distribution of load is sometimes counter-intuitive which cannot be detected by other models making prior assumptions on the locations of bottlenecks.*

**Index Terms.** TCP/IP modelling, general network topology, fixed point approach, complementarity problem, utility optimization.

## 1.    INTRODUCTION

Modeling and prediction of network behavior is an important task for good network design, upgrade and provisioning. Specifically, it is important to predict the location of bottleneck links, the steady state loss probabilities on those links, average throughput of users, etc, in order to dimension the network properly. For example, it might be required that the network be upgraded (or capacities of links be increased) so as to mitigate congestion. For such an upgrade, we will require a map of the network, specifically a map of the bottlenecks on the network. In absence of such information, a network upgrade might unintentionally create more bottlenecks in the network. We illustrate this point with the help of an example later in the paper, wherein by increasing the capacity of a link, the provider may create more bottlenecks. Similarly, a map of bottlenecks might be required before new links are added in the network. Thus, prediction of network behavior is an important task for dimensioning the network properly.

Most applications in the Internet use the TCP protocol which reacts in a well known way to the loss of packets in the network [17]. Given this behavior of the protocol, different models have been proposed to predict the average throughput of a TCP connection [1], [14], [21]. These models consider the network as an entity that drops packets with a certain probability and that delays them for some period equal to the round-trip time. Expressions for TCP throughput together with a certain model for the network (e.g., how packets are dropped in a router for a certain rate of TCP packets) can be used to give some insights on how the network and TCP connections will behave.

In [4], the authors use a fixed-point approximation to calculate some metrics in a network crossed by long-lived TCP connections and implementing Active Queue Management techniques in routers. Their model requires the *a priori* identification of bottleneck routers. An equation is written for each bottleneck router, which results in a system of non-linear equations to solve. The drop probability and the average queue length in every bottleneck router as well as the throughput of the different TCP connections are then calculated. In [12], the authors use the technique of stochastic differential equations to calculate the behavior of network traffic in the transitory regime. Again, their model requires the identification of bottleneck routers before the calculation of metrics. In [5], the authors used Markov chains as well as fixed-point approach to model one and two routers TCP/IP networks. It is not clear however if their approach can be easily extended to the case of general network topology.

Several recent papers (see [8], [9], [10], [13], [23] and references therein) have analyzed TCP-like congestion control based on the optimization of some aggregated utility function for general network topology. These models all have similarities with TCP, especially to versions based on ECN (Explicit Congestion Notification), but also differences. Discussions on the differences are given for instance in Section 4.1 in [9]. In particular, most of the above models assume that ACKs arrive continuously in time [8], [10] (or very frequently [9]). A common feature of all these models is that the utility optimization approach is related to explicit simplified dynamic evolution equations for the transmission rate of connections. Our approach, in contrast, requires as starting point only a relation between the average throughput of a connection and its average packet loss rate and round-trip time. The obtained results do not rely on the exact dynamics that leads to that relation, and could be applied to variants of congestion control mechanisms, which need not have a linear increase and an additive decrease behavior. Another difference between our model and [8] is that we do not need to use an ECN version of TCP; in particular, our model assumes that losses occur if and only if a link is saturated. This means that the rate of acknowledgment is not a continuous function of the global throughput in the congested router, as required in [8]. In spite of the differences between our model and those based on utility optimization approach [8], [9], [10], [13], [23], it is remarkable to note that our approach also leads to a global optimization problem.

In the present paper, we investigate the problem of network performance prediction without the bottleneck pre-identification requirement. First, we introduce a system of non-linear inequalities, which guarantees that the sum of TCP throughputs on each link does not exceed its capacity. The structure of the inequalities that we propose is simpler than those in [4], as we consider networks with large delay-bandwidth products (i.e., smooth traffic and small queues in routers compared to end-to-end delay). Then, we add *complementarity* type conditions that ensure the *automatic* localization of bottlenecks. We call this model as Non-Linear Complementarity Problem (NCP). To find a feasible point which satisfies both capacity constraint inequalities and complementarity type conditions, we use the fixed point formulation as well as the mathematical programming formulation. By using the fixed point formulation, we are able to prove the existence of a solution to our model. As a solution of our model, we obtain packet loss probabilities, the distribution of load in the network and the location of bottleneck routers. We would like to note that our model includes the possibility of having source rate limitation (e.g., the limitation imposed by TCP receiver window); this feature of TCP is not included in the above mentioned models. Other features as Timeouts can be included as well. This flexibility of our approach is the result of using analytical expressions for TCP throughput rather than subjective measures as in the utility-based framework [8], [10].

As mentioned earlier, a drawback of existing optimization models is that while they give us unique end-to-end loss probabilities for connections, they are unable to quantify the loss rates of the different bottlenecks in a systematic way. Bottleneck loss rates are uniquely identified in the sole case of a full row rank incidence (or routing) matrix. However, our Non-Linear Complementarity model presented in this paper is able to solve this problem. We prove this analytically on some network topologies and we conjecture that it is the case for general topologies. Nonetheless, in spite of these differences between our model and existing optimization approaches [8], [10], [9], we would like to point out that our approach also leads to similar global optimization problem. We show the relationship between the complementarity, fixed-point approach and the utility function based flow optimization models. Our results indicate that all these different approaches are maximizing a similar objective function. Finally, we test our general approach on several benchmark network examples, for which we are able to obtain some analytical results and good approximations. In particular, the analysis of the examples shows clearly that the problem of bottleneck identification is not an easy task and that it is very sensitive to network resources distribution. For example, by slightly changing the bandwidth on a link, the bottleneck can move from a link to another link and it happens that this move is not immediate so that the two links can be bottlenecks at the same time. Thus, the change in bottleneck position alters significantly the behavior of the network. We also observe that in some cases, the addition of bandwidth to some parts of the network might deteriorate the performance of other parts.

The rest of the paper is organized as follows. In Section 2, we present our TCP network model and provide methods for its solution. Thereupon, in Section 3, we first briefly review the utility optimization framework and show the relationship between the fixed-point approach, optimization framework and the Non-Linear Complementarity model. Specifically, we show how the utility function model can be derived from the complementarity model. We use this derivation in Section 4 to prove uniqueness of the solution under some conditions on the throughput expression and routing matrix (also called incidence matrix). In Section 5, we present some benchmark network examples to show how the bottleneck position and the load distribution are sensitive to network parameters. The results of the analysis are validated by ns-2 simulations [18]. The conclusions and future work are presented in Section 6.

## 2. TCP NETWORK MODEL

Consider a network $G$ formed of $V$ nodes (the routers in data network terminology). Let $I$ be a set of groups of persistent TCP connections. We denote the source node of group $i$ in $I$ by $S_i$ and its destination node by $D_i$, respectively. Connections of group $i$ in $I$ follow a fixed path $\pi_i = \{v^i_1 ,...,v^i_{n(i)}\}$, where $v^i_1$ corresponds to the first node that the connections cross after leaving the source node $S_i$, and $v^i_{n(i)}$ is the last node that the connections cross before reaching the destination node $D_i$. We also define $\pi_i(u) = \{v^i_1 ,..., u\}$, that is, $\pi_i(u)$ corresponds to the part of the path $\pi_i$ from the source node $S_i$ up to node $u$. Of course, we are aware of the fact that the routing in the Internet is dynamic and that packets from the same TCP connection may follow different routes if some links in the network go down. We suppose that these deficiencies are not frequent and that the routing tables in Internet routers do not change during short periods of time of the order of TCP transfer times so that our assumptions can hold. Indeed, this has been shown to be the case in the Internet [22], where more than 2/3 of routes persist for days or even weeks.

We also introduce the following objects:
- $C = \{c_1 ,..., c_{|V|}\}$ is the capacity vector, where $c_v$ is the capacity of node $v$. In reality, a capacity is associated to a link rather than a router. A router may have different output interfaces and hence different capacities. For such routers, we associate a node to each

outgoing link. So based on this terminology, nodes and links are the same. In our abstract network, one can see a node as being the part of the router where the multiple TCP connections routed via the same output interface are multiplexed together. We focus on routers where each output interface has its own buffer. The routing engine in a router decides (at a high rate) on how the different arriving packets are distributed on the different output interfaces. Packets are queued (and possibly dropped) in the buffer at the output interface before being transmitted on the link to the next router.

- $A = \{\gamma_{vi}, v$ in $V, i$ in $I\}$ is the incidence matrix (also called routing matrix), where $\gamma_{vi} = 1$ if connection $i$ goes through node $v$, and is equal to zero otherwise.

- $\mathbf{p} = \{p_1, ..., p_{|V|}\}$ is the vector of loss probabilities; $p_v$ corresponds to the probability that a packet is lost at node $v$, or in other words that it is lost in the buffer at the entry of the link between node $v$ and the adjacent router. We suppose here that packets from all connections are treated in the same manner in network nodes. This can be the result of some randomization in the drop policy in router buffers (e.g., RED [15]) or the result of some randomization in the multiplexing of flows in routers (in the case of drop tail routers). Thus, we suppose that all packets are dropped with the same probability in a node and this probability is independent from that in other nodes. It follows that the probability that a packet of a connection of type $i$ is lost in the network is equal to

$$\kappa_i = \sum_{v \in \pi_i} p_v \prod_{u \in \pi_i(v) \backslash v} (1 - p_u). \tag{1}$$

- $T = \{T_1, ..., T_{|I|}\}$ is the sending rate vector, where $T_i$ is the sending rate of a connection of type $i$. The sending rate can be expressed [1], [19], [14], [21] as a function of the probability with which packets of the connection are dropped within the network. It is also function of the round-trip time calculated in our case from the propagation delays of links crossed by the connection.

- $N_i$, $i$ in $I$, is the number of connections of type $i$. Denote $NT = \{N_1 T_1, ..., N_{|I|} T_{|I|}\}$ the vector whose $i$-th entry is the sending rate of all connections of type $i$.

We shall make the following assumptions:

**A1:** All links in the network have large delay-bandwidth product. This allows us to neglect queuing delays in routers, and hence, their impact on TCP throughput.

**A2:** The sending rate $T_i(\kappa_i)$ is a continuous function of the packet end-to-end loss probability $\kappa_i$.

We shall consider in particular some well known forms of relations between loss probability and sending rate. The following expression (so-called "square root formula" [21]) is well suited for a small number of timeout events, which is typical in large delay-bandwidth product networks

$$T_i(\kappa_i) = MSS_i \min\{\frac{1}{\theta_i}\sqrt{\frac{\beta_i}{\kappa_i}}, \frac{W^i_{max}}{\theta_i}\}, \quad i \in I, \tag{2}$$

where $MSS_i$ is the maximum segment size, $W^i_{max}$ is the receiver window size, $\theta_i$ is the average round-trip time of the connection and $\beta_i$ is a constant that depends on the version of the TCP implementation and on the characteristics of the process of inter-loss times [1]. For example, if we assume that inter-loss times are exponentially distributed and the delay ACK mechanism is disabled, then $\beta_i = 2$ [1].

The next expression [14] (which we shall refer to as "PFTK formula") is known to be more suitable when the timeout probabilities are not negligible:

$$T_i(\kappa_i) = \begin{cases} MSS_i \dfrac{\frac{1-\kappa_i}{\kappa_i}+W(\kappa_i)+Q(\kappa_i,W(\kappa_i))}{\theta_i(\frac{b_i}{2}W(\kappa_i)+1)+\frac{Q(\kappa_i,W(\kappa_i))F(\kappa_i)T_0^i}{1-\kappa_i}}, \\ \quad \text{if } W(\kappa_i) < W^i_{max}, \\ MSS_i \dfrac{\frac{1-\kappa_i}{\kappa_i}+W^i_{max}+Q(\kappa_i,W^i_{max})}{\theta_i(\frac{b_i}{8}W^i_{max}+\frac{1-\kappa_i}{\kappa_i W^i_{max}}+2)+\frac{Q(\kappa_i,W^i_{max})F(\kappa_i)T_0^i}{1-\kappa_i}}, \\ \quad \text{otherwise,} \end{cases} \tag{3}$$

where

$$
\begin{aligned}
W(q) &= 2/3 + 2\sqrt{(1-q)/(3q)} + 1/9, \\
Q(q,w) &= \min\{1, (1-(1-q)^3)(1+(1-q)^3 \times \\
&\quad \times (1-(1-q)^{w-3}))/(1-(1-q)^w)\}, \\
F(q) &= 1 + q + 2q^2 + 4q^3 + 8q^4 + 16q^5 + 32q^6,
\end{aligned}
$$

and where $\beta_l$ is the number of packets acknowledged by an ACK (typically 2), and $T^i_0$ is the basic timeout duration (typically $4\theta_i$).

It is clear that the capacity at each node cannot be exceeded by the rate of packets that cross it. This leads to the following system of inequalities,

$$
\sum_{i \in I} \gamma_{vi} \left( \prod_{u \in \pi_i(v)} (1 - p_u) \right) NT_i(\kappa_i) \leq c_v, \quad v \in V. \tag{4}
$$

where the left-hand term represents the sending rate of TCP connections crossing node $v$ reduced by the number of packets dropped before reaching the output interface of $v$.

Thus, we have obtained a system of $|V|$ inequalities for $|V|$ unknowns $p_1$ ,..., $p_{|V|}$ that we have to solve in order to model the performance of TCP connections and the distribution of load on network nodes. This is what we call a multilevel model for large TCP/IP networks. The first level is the network level where load is related to routing and link capacities. The second level is the TCP level where expressions for TCP sending rate are used. As for the third level, it would be the application level where the performance perceived by TCP can be used to model quality of service perceived by applications. Latency is a typical performance metric that can be computed. We refer to [2] for an illustration of this approach for the case of single bottleneck network.

## A. The Non Linear Complementarity Problem Formulation

First, let us show that the aforementioned system of inequalities is feasible.

*Proposition 1:* Under **A2**, the system of inequalities (4) is feasible. Moreover, there is a continuum of feasible solutions.

*Proof:* There is an obvious feasible solution: $p_v = 1$, for all $v$ in $V$, which results in a strict inequality in (4). Since this point is interior, and $\kappa_i$ are continuous in $p_v$, and consequently $T_i$ are continuous in the $\kappa_i$, there is a feasible region with nonzero measure.

Even though there is a continuum of feasible solutions to (4), most of them do not correspond to a real TCP network state. An example of such solutions is a one that gives high drop probabilities so that all nodes are poorly utilized. On contrary, TCP is designed to fully utilize the available resources of the network, if both sender and receiver windows allow. We observed from numerous simulations carried out with the help of the network simulator ns-2 [18] that a network link can be either bottleneck with a substantial amount of packet losses at its input, or it can be underutilized with negligible packet-loss probability. These two states of a link are quite mutually exclusive. The latter observation led us to propose the following *complementarity* type conditions

$$p_v \left( c_v - \sum_{i \in I} \gamma_{vi} \left( \prod_{u \in \pi_i(v)} (1 - p_u) \right) NT_i(\kappa_i) \right) = 0, \tag{5}$$

for $v$ in $V$. These conditions say that packets are only dropped in nodes which are fully utilized. These are the bottleneck nodes that limit the performance of TCP connections. Other nodes are well dimensioned so that they do not drop packets and thus they do not impact the performance of TCP.

We shall refer to the system of (4) and (5), plus the natural condition

$$0 \le p_v \le 1, \quad v \in V, \tag{6}$$

as the *Non-Linear Complementarity Problem Formulation* (NCP formulation). Next we show that the Non-Linear Complementarity Problem Formulation is equivalent to a *Fixed Point Formulation* (FP formulation).

## B. The Fixed Point Formulation

*Lemma 1:* The NCP formulation (4), (5) and (6) is equivalent to the following Fixed Point formulation

$$p_v = \Pr_{[0,1]} \left\{ p_v - \alpha \left( c_v - \sum_{i \in I} \gamma_{vi} \left( \prod_{u \in \pi_i(v)} (1 - p_u) \right) NT_i(\mathbf{p}) \right) \right\}, \tag{7}$$

where $\alpha > 0$ and $\mathrm{Pr}_{[0,1]}\{x\}$ is the projection on the interval $[0,1]$, that is,

$$\mathrm{Pr}_{[0,1]}\{x\} = \begin{cases} 0, & x < 0, \\ x, & 0 \le x \le 1, \\ 1, & 1 < x. \end{cases}$$

*Proof:* First, let us prove that any solution of NCP is a solution of FP. Take any $v$ in $V$. According to the complementarity condition (5), if the inequality (4) is strict, $p_v = 0$. Hence, we have

$$\mathrm{Pr}_{[0,1]}\{-\alpha(c_v - \sum_{i \in I} \gamma_{vi}(\prod_{u \in \pi_i(v)} (1 - p_u))NT_i(\mathbf{p}))\} = 0,$$

and consequently, $p_v$ satisfies (7). Now, if $p_v > 0$,

$$\Delta_v := c_v - \sum_{i \in I} \gamma_{vi}(\prod_{u \in \pi_i(v)} (1 - p_u))NT_i(\mathbf{p})) = 0$$

we have $p_v = \mathrm{Pr}_{[0,1]}\{p_v\}$, that is true, since $p_v$ in $[0,1]$. In case both $p_v = 0$ and $\Delta_v = 0$, the equality (7) holds trivially.

Now we show that any solution of FP is also a solution of NCP. The condition (6) follows immediately from the definition of the projection. Let us show that the inequality (4) holds. Suppose on contrary that $\Delta_v < 0$. Then, it follows from (7) that $p_v$ is necessarily equal to one. However, if $p_v = 1$, $\Delta_v = c_v > 0$. Thus, we came to the contradiction and hence (4) holds.

Finally, we need to show that the complementarity condition (5) holds, namely, we need to show that it is not possible to have $p_v > 0$ and $\Delta_v > 0$ simultaneously. Suppose on contrary that these two strict inequalities hold. The inequality $\Delta_v > 0$ implies that $p_v - \alpha \Delta_v < 1$. Hence, according to (7), $p_v = p_v - \alpha \Delta_v$. The latter implies that $\Delta_v = 0$, which is the contradiction. Thus, the complementarity condition (5) holds as well. This completes the proof.

Using the FP formulation, we are able to prove the existence of a solution to our model.

*Theorem 1:* The TCP network model (4), (5) and (6) has a solution.

*Proof:* From *Lemma 1*, we know that the TCP network model (4), (5) and (6) is equivalent to the Fixed Point formulation (7). Under Assumption **A2**, the mapping (7) is well-defined and continuous on the compact and convex set $X_{v \text{ in } V} [0,1]$. Furthermore, (7) maps the set $X_{v \text{ in } V} [0,1]$ into itself. Hence, all conditions of Brouwer Fixed Point Theorem [7], [20] are satisfied and we can conclude that the system of (4), (5) and (6) has a solution.

Note that the FP formulation provides not only the theoretical means to prove the existence of a solution to our model, but it also gives a practical algorithm for its calculation. Namely, we can calculate a solution by using the following fixed point iterations

$$p_v^{(k+1)} = \Pr_{[0,1]} \left\{ p_v^{(k)} - \right.$$

$$\left. \alpha \left( c_v - \sum_{i \in I} \gamma_{vi} \left( \prod_{u \in \pi_i(v)} (1 - p_u^{(k)}) \right) NT_i(\mathbf{p}^{(k)}) \right) \right\}, \tag{8}$$

where $\alpha$ is a parameter that can be chosen to control stability and the speed of convergence.

Next, we propose yet another formulation which also leads to an efficient computational algorithm for the solution of the system (4), (5) and (6). This third formulation is based on the application of the nonlinear mathematical programming to complementarity problems [6]. Therefore, we shall refer to it as *Nonlinear Programming formulation* (NP formulation).

## C. The Nonlinear Programming Formulation

Consider the following nonlinear mathematical program

$$\min \sum p_v z_v \qquad \text{subject to}$$

$$\sum_{i \in I} \gamma_{vi} \left( \prod_{u \in \pi_i(v)} (1 - p_u) \right) NT_i(\mathbf{p}) + z_v = c_v, \tag{9}$$

$$0 \le z_v, \quad 0 \le p_v \le 1, \quad v \in V.$$

Note that variables $z_v$ play the same role as the supplementary variables introduced in linear programming. They transform a system of inequalities into a system of equations. The intuition behind the mathematical program (9) can be explained as follows: we start from a feasible point inside the region defined by inequalities (4), and then, by minimizing $\sum p_v z_v$, we try to satisfy the complementarity conditions (5). Since in (9) we minimize a continuous function over a compact set, this program has a global minimum. Furthermore, the value of the objective function evaluated at this minimum is zero if and only if the original system (4), (5), (6) has a solution. Thus, due to *Theorem 1*, the mathematical program (9) provides a solution to the system (4), (5), (6).

We would like to emphasize that the main advantage of using either FP formulation or NP formulation is that one does not need to care as in [4] about locating bottleneck nodes in order to establish a system of equations that solves the problem. If there is no *a priori* information on the location of the bottlenecks, then one might need to check up to $2^{|V|}$ cases. As we shall see later in the section on the Benchmark examples, the localization of bottleneck nodes is not always so intuitive. A small change in network parameters may shift the bottleneck from one node to another.

## D. The Rough Approximation Model

For TCP/IP networks with large delay-bandwidth products, the packet loss probabilities $p_v$ are typically small (connections operate at large windows). Therefore, one can simplify our model even further. Equations (1) and (4) take now the form

$$\kappa_i = \sum_{v \in \pi_i} p_v,$$

$$\sum_{i \in I} \gamma_{vi} N T_i \leq c_i.$$

As an example, if we use the square root formula for TCP sending rate, which is known to perform well in case of small loss rates, we obtain the following system of equations and inequalities

$$\sum_{i \in I} \gamma_{vi} \frac{k_i}{\sqrt{\sum_{v \in \pi_i} p_v}} \le c_i, \quad v \in V, \qquad (10)$$

$$p_v \left( c_v - \sum_{i \in I} \gamma_{vi} \frac{k_i}{\sqrt{\sum_{v \in \pi_i} p_v}} \right) = 0, \quad v \in V, \qquad (11)$$

where we denote $N_i\sqrt{\beta_i}/\theta_i$ by $k_i$ to simplify notations. In the sequel, we shall refer to the above system as the *rough approximation model*. Note that the rough approximation model can be written in an elegant form by using the matrix notations introduced in the beginning of the present section. Namely, the inequalities and the equations for the rough approximation model can be written as follows:

$$A \cdot NT \le C, \quad \mathbf{p}^{\mathrm{T}} \cdot [C - A \cdot NT] = 0$$

## 3.   RELATION BETWEEN COMPLEMENTARITY FORMULATION AND UTILITY OPTIMIZATION

We start by briefly reviewing the utility optimization framework presented in [8], [9], [10], [13], [23]. Using this introduction to utility function formulation, we will illustrate the difference between the complementarity and utility function formulation. Specifically, we will argue that utility function formulation *cannot always* identify the bottlenecks in the network, at best it can uniquely identify the end-to-end loss probability for a connection. Then, we will show that the utility function formulation can be derived from complementarity framework. Thereupon, later in the section, we will argue that the complementarity framework presented in this paper can uniquely identify the loss rates of bottleneck links. These results together with the results from the previous section, which show the relationship between the fixed-point formulation and complementarity framework, the arguments presented in this section will tie up all the flow optimization frameworks together.

### A. Utility Function Based Flow Optimization Framework

In the utility function based optimization models, a user $s$ is described with the help of its rate, $x_s$, a utility function $U_s$ and the set of links which he uses, $L(s)$. The rates are taken to be bounded, i.e., $m_s \le x_s \le M_s$. It is further assumed that the utility functions are *increasing* with rates and *strictly concave*. The network is identified with links $l$ of capacity $c_l$, and the set of users using a link, $l$, is given by $S(l)$.

The optimization problem can then be defined as users trying to maximize their individual utility functions and the network trying to maximize the resource allocation subject to link capacity constraints. Thus, the primal problem can be defined as:

$$maximize \ \sum_{s \in S} U_s(x_s) \tag{12}$$

$$subject \ to \ \sum_{s \in S(l)} x_s \ \le \ c_l, \ \forall l \tag{13}$$

for all $x_s \ge 0$. The dual formulation, $D(\mathbf{p})$, for the above problem was defined in [10] as:

$$D(\mathbf{p}) = \underset{p \ge 0}{min} \sum_{s \in S} \underset{x_s}{max} (U_s(x_s) - \sum_l p_l x_s) + \sum_l p_l c_l \tag{14}$$

The authors in [10] show that using the Karush Kuhn Tucker (KKT) conditions and gradient projection algorithm, the dual yields the following update algorithm:

$$x_s(t) \ = \ U_s'^{-1} (\sum_l p_l) \tag{15}$$

$$p_l(t+1) \ = \ [p_l(t) + \gamma (\sum_{s \in S(l)} x_s - c_l)]^+ \tag{16}$$

Since the primal is strictly concave and the constraints are linear, there is no duality gap and hence dual optimal is also primal optimal. Further, the strict concavity entails a unique global optimum $(x^*_s, p^{s*})$, where $p^s = \sum_l p_l$. So even if the primal optimal $x^*_s$ is unique, we may not have a unique dual optimal $p^*_l$; all what we are sure about is having a unique optimum end-to-end loss probability for every source, $p^{s*}$. Thus, the utility optimization *cannot uniquely identify* the bottlenecks except in the case of a full row rank incidence matrix, which we will prove later in the paper. Next, we illustrate this point with the help of an example.

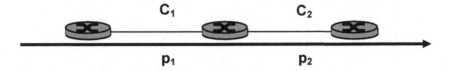

Fig. 1  Single Flow – 2 Bottleneck Links Example

**Example 1:** Consider a network where a single TCP flow traverses two bottlenecks as shown in Figure 1. Let the utility function of this flow be $U$ and its rate be $x$, where (15) shows the relationship between the two. Further, we assume that the flow is TCP Reno whose utility function is given as $U = -1/x$. Let us denote by $p_1$ and $p_2$ the loss probabilities on links 1 and 2 respectively. It follows that the capacity constraints for the two links can be written as

$$g_1(p) = C_1 - x(p_1 + p_2) \geq 0 \qquad (17)$$

$$g_2(p) = C_2 - x(p_1 + p_2) \geq 0 \qquad (18)$$

Given the above notations, the utility optimization problem for this specific model can be posed as

$$maximize \ \frac{-1}{x_s} \qquad (19)$$

$$subject \ to \quad g_i \ \geq \ 0, \quad \forall i \qquad (20)$$

The solution to this problem can be written as

$$p_1 + p_2 = \frac{1}{(min(C_1, C_2))^2}, \qquad (21)$$

which does not allow to uniquely determine the bottleneck, irrespective of the choice of link capacities. To understand this result, we write the incidence matrix in this case, $A = (\ 1 \quad 1\ )^T$. Clearly, this is not a full row rank matrix (or the rank of the matrix is not equal to the number of links). Thus, a simple observation can be made at this stage: If the routing matrix is not full row rank (where number of rows is equal to the number of links in the topology), bottleneck links cannot be always uniquely determined by the Utility function based approach. An intuitive justification for this claim is that in absence of full row-rank incidence matrix, all the link capacity constraints are not linearly independent, thus making it hard to identify the bottleneck links. A more formal proof will be presented in Section 4.

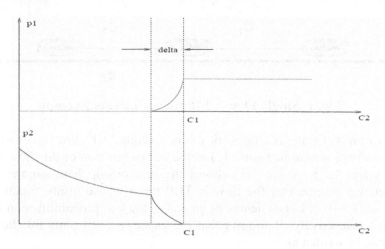

**Fig. 2  Link Loss Probabilities in a Single Flow – 2 Bottleneck Links Example**
**($C_1$ is held constant while $C_2$ is varied)**

Let's now look at the same scenario from the viewpoint of our approach. Figure 2 shows the actual loss probabilities obtained by solving the system of equations in (5). As the plot shows, when $C_1$ is slightly greater than $C_2$, both the links become bottlenecks and they cannot be identified using the Utility function model. $C_1 = C_2$ marks the end of the indecision boundary because for all the cases where $C_1 \leq C_2$, only the first link is the bottleneck, i.e. $p_2 = 0$. So for the case $C_1 \leq C_2$, the bottlenecks can be uniquely determined in the utility function model. However, when $C_1 > C_2$, the utility function model cannot uniquely identify the bottleneck. As Figure 2 shows, for some value of $\delta = C_1 - C_2$, $\delta > 0$, both the links are bottlenecks while for the rest, only link 2 is the bottleneck. So one can conclude that equation (21) is insufficient to deduce which link will be the bottleneck.

The example cited in this section is especially interesting when the capacity of the first link is slightly greater than that of the second, i.e., $C_1 = C_2 + \delta$. In such scenario, if a provider adds a small bandwidth to a link to "ease" congestion, inadvertently he might be worsening the congestion in the network by adding more bottlenecks!

## B. Relationship between Utility Function Framework and NCP Model

With the introduction to the Utility function formulation presented in the previous section, we are now ready to present arguments showing how it is related to the complementarity framework. Later in this section we will revisit the example presented in the previous section and show that the NCP framework can uniquely identify the bottleneck links. Suppose that all link capacities are sufficiently large. Then, one can expect the packet loss probabilities to be small. If it is indeed the case, in (1) one can approximate the path loss probability as $\kappa_i \approx \sum p_l$. Also, the expression $\prod(1-p_u^{(k)})$ in (4) and (5) can be approximated by one. Then, the Complementarity Formulation takes the following matrix form

$$\kappa = A^T \times \mathbf{p}, \tag{22}$$

$$A \times NT(\kappa) \leq C, \tag{23}$$

$$p^T \times (C - A \times NT(\kappa)) = 0, \tag{24}$$

which we refer to as the *Approximate Complementarity Formulation* (ACF). In the rest of this paper, we interchangeably refer to the ACF as the approximate model and sometimes use Exact Model to refer to the NCP. The following theorem states that the Approximate Complementarity Formulation (ACF) is equivalent to the Utility Optimization Approach [8], [9], [10].

*Theorem 2:* The Approximate Complementarity Formulation is the Karush-Kuhn-Tucker (KKT) optimality conditions of the following optimization problem .

$$\max_{\mathbf{x}} \sum_s U_s(x_s)$$

subject to

$$\sum_{s \in S(l)} x_s - c_l \leq 0, \forall l$$

where $x_s$ represents the rate of source $s$, $U_s$ its utility function and $l$ represents a link of capacity $c_l$.

*Proof:* Consider the ACF given by equations (22), (23) and (24). Let's assume that $T(\kappa)$ is an algebraic expression in $\kappa$, which relates the sending rate, $x_s$, of a source $s$ to $\kappa_s$. Further, let's make the natural assumption that $T(\kappa)$ is strictly decreasing in $\kappa$. Then, we may express $\kappa_s$ for a source $s$ as $\kappa_s = T^{-1}(x_s)$. Without loss of generality, by taking $N_i$ equal to 1 for all $i$, and using the above equations, we may write the ACF as

$$T^{-1}(x_s) = A^T \mathbf{p}, \tag{25}$$

$$A\mathbf{x} \leq C, \tag{26}$$

$$p^T(C - A\mathbf{x}) = 0. \tag{27}$$

The KKT conditions for the utility optimization problem can be written as

$$U_s{}'^{(-1)}(x_s) = A^T \mathbf{p}, \tag{28}$$

$$A\mathbf{x} \leq C, \tag{29}$$

$$p^T(C - A\mathbf{x}) = 0. \tag{30}$$

where $\mathbf{p}$ may be interpreted as the vector of Lagrangian multipliers. Then, the ACF corresponds to the KKT conditions of the utility optimization where the utility function is defined by the following relationship

$$T^{-1}(x_s) = U'_s(x_s). \tag{31}$$

Since $T$ is a decreasing function in $\kappa$, we have if the above relationship holds,

$$U''_s(x_s) < 0$$

or in other words ACF corresponds to the KKT conditions of a strictly concave utility optimization problem where the utility function for a source can be found using equation (31).

*Remark 1:* Since ACF corresponds to the KKT conditions of a strict concave maximization problem, a unique solution in the rate vector $\mathbf{x}$ exists. Further, this solution is also unique in end-to-end loss probabilities, $\kappa$. However, the solution to the ACF is unique in the link-loss probability vector $\mathbf{p}$ iff the incidence matrix is full row-rank. We prove this uniqueness in $\mathbf{p}$ for the ACF by an alternative method in Section 4.

**Example 1 Revisited:** In Section 3-A, we had presented an example scenario to show that utility function formulation cannot always identify the bottleneck links. We had also claimed that complementarity formulation can solve the problem by uniquely identifying the link loss probabilities of bottleneck links. We will now substantiate our claims by providing a solution to the example discussed in Section 3-A.

If we assume link capacities to be large, then the loss probabilities will be small and we can write

$$\prod_{s\in\pi_i(l)} (1-p_s) = (1 - \sum_{s\in\pi_i(l)} p_s) \tag{32}$$

Using this equation, the non-linear complementarity problem can be restated as

$$c_l - \sum_{i\in I}\gamma_{li}\left(\left(1 - \sum_{s\in\pi_i(l)} p_s\right) NT_i(\kappa_i)\right) \geq 0 \tag{33}$$

$$p_l\left(c_l - \sum_{i\in I}\gamma_{li}\left(\left(1 - \sum_{s\in\pi_i(l)} p_s\right) NT_i(\kappa_i)\right)\right) = 0 \tag{34}$$

$$0 \leq p_l \leq 1 \tag{35}$$

However, since we are only worried about the loss probabilities on the congested links, we are restricted to solving the following problem

$$c_l - \sum_{i\in I}\gamma_{li}\left(1 - \sum_{s\in\pi_i(l)} p_s\right) NT_i(\kappa_i) = 0 \tag{36}$$

$$0 \leq p_l \leq 1 \tag{37}$$

which can then we written as

$$\Lambda(NT)\,\mathbf{p} = \Omega(C\,,NT), \tag{38}$$

where $\Lambda(NT)$ is called the loss-probability matrix and $\Omega$ is a matrix which has the capacities $C$ and throughputs $NT$ as members. For the two links Example 1, the capacity constraints for both the links can be written as

$$(1 - p_1)T(\kappa) = C_1, \tag{39}$$

$$(1 - p_1 - p_2)T(\kappa) = C_2. \tag{40}$$

or

$$\begin{pmatrix} -T(\kappa) & 0 \\ -T(\kappa) & -T(\kappa) \end{pmatrix}\begin{pmatrix} p_1 \\ p_2 \end{pmatrix} = \begin{pmatrix} C_1 - T(\kappa) \\ C_2 - T(\kappa) \end{pmatrix} \tag{41}$$

which has an unique solution in $p_1$ and $p_2$ because the loss probability matrix is invertible. We conjecture that for any network topology, the NCP can uniquely identify the link loss probabilities of bottleneck links at the opposite of the utility optimization model. None of the numerical examples we considered within the framework of this study shows an irregularity in this regard.

## 4.    UNIQUENESS OF SOLUTION TO THE COMPLEMENTARITY FORMULATION: INCIDENCE MATRIX WITH FULL ROW RANK

In this section we will prove the existence of unique $\kappa$ and $p_l$ when the Incidence matrix is full row-rank, i.e. it has full rank in the number of bottleneck links. This constraint of full-row rank can also be thought of as the case when we can uniquely *identify* the bottleneck links. We summarize these arguments in this section in *Theorem 3*, but before that, we will state the following *Lemma 2* which we will require later.

*Lemma 2:* Let $F = (f_1 ,..., f_n)$ be a vector of real-valued functions defined on $R^n$. If the Jacobian matrix of $F(x)$ exists and is positive semi-definite for all $x$ in $R^n$, then there is at most one $x$ such that $F(x) = 0$ holds.

*Proof:* See *Lemma 5* in [13].

Let there be $n$ sources using a network with $J$ links. Out of these lets assume that $m$ links are bottleneck links, which can be *uniquely* identified. Then we can restate the original complementarity problem as:

$$A\mathbf{T} \leq C, \tag{42}$$

$$\mathbf{p}A = \kappa, \tag{43}$$

$$T_i = f_i(\kappa_i) \qquad \text{for all } i \text{ in } 1 \ldots n, \tag{44}$$

where the last equation expresses the throughput as a function of $\kappa$. Specifically $f_i$ represents the throughput formula for source $i$ and is decreasing in $\kappa_i$. Note, we do not place the requirement that the throughput formula has to be the same for every source, it just has to be a decreasing function of end-to-end loss probability.

*Theorem 3:* Given a network of $J$ links, $n$ users and the corresponding set of bottlenecks $m$ ($m$ in $J$), then the end-to-end loss probability vector, $\kappa$, that solves equations (42-44) is unique.

*Proof:* For links which are not bottlenecks, clearly $p_j = 0$. Henceforth, we will not consider the non-bottleneck links for our problem. Let us assume that there are $m$ bottleneck links. Then we can rewrite equation (42) as $A\mathbf{T} = C$, where $C$ is now the link capacity vector for the $m$ bottleneck links and $A$ is the incidence matrix on these bottleneck links. Then by renumbering the connections and the network nodes, we can rewrite A as

$$A = (\,E\,F\,),$$

where $E$ is a $m$x$m$ matrix and $F$ is a $m$x$(n-m)$ matrix.

Further, let us define by $U$ the null space of $A$, i.e. $U : AU = 0$. Clearly $U$ is a $n$x$(n-m)$ matrix. Let us further partition $U$ as two matrices, an $m$x$(n-m)$ matrix $U_E$ and an $(n-m)$x$(n-m)$ matrix $U_F$. Then we have

$$F = -E\,U_E\,U^{-1}_F \qquad (45)$$

Using this null space matrix we can rewrite our original problem as

$$A\mathbf{T} = C, \qquad (46)$$

$$\kappa^T U = 0, \qquad (47)$$

$$T_i = f_i(\kappa_i) \qquad \text{for all } i \text{ in } 1\ ...n. \qquad (48)$$

Let us also partition the $\kappa$ matrix as two 1x$m$ and 1x$(n-m)$ matrices $\kappa_E$ and $\kappa_F$ respectively. Similarly we partition the throughput and the function $f$ as 1x$m$ ($T_E$, $\mathbf{f}(\kappa_E)$) and 1x$(n-m)$ ($T_F$, $\mathbf{f}(\kappa_F)$) matrices. Then, from the definition of null-space matrix $U$ we have

$$\kappa^T_F = -\,\kappa^T_E U_E U_F^{-1} \qquad (49)$$

$$E\,T_E + F\,T_F = C \qquad (50)$$

$$E\,\mathbf{f}(\kappa_E) + F\,\mathbf{f}(\kappa_F) = C \qquad (51)$$

Using equations (46) and (48), we define a function $G(\kappa_E)$

$$G(\kappa_E) = E^{-1}\,(E\,\mathbf{f}(\kappa_E) + F\,\mathbf{f}(\kappa_F) - C) = 0 \qquad (52)$$

$$= \mathbf{f}(\kappa_E) + E^{-1}F\,\mathbf{f}(\kappa_F) - E^{-1}C \qquad (53)$$

as $\kappa_F$ can be expressed just in terms of $\kappa_E$ (from equation (49)). The derivative of this function with respect to $\kappa_E$ can then be written as follows. For, i,j = 1 ,.., m

$$\frac{\partial \mathbf{f}(\kappa_E)_i}{\partial \kappa_j} = \frac{\partial f(\kappa_E)_i}{\partial \kappa_j}\delta_{ij} \tag{54}$$

and for k = m+1, .., (n-m)

$$\frac{\partial \mathbf{f}(\kappa_F)_k}{\partial \kappa_j} = \frac{\partial f(\kappa_E)_k}{\partial \kappa_k}\frac{\partial \kappa_k}{\partial \kappa_j} \tag{55}$$

But, using equation (49) we may rewrite the above equation as

$$\frac{\partial \mathbf{f}(\kappa_F)_k}{\partial \kappa_j} = \frac{\partial f(\kappa_E)_k}{\partial \kappa_k}(-U_E U_F^{-1})^T \tag{56}$$

Using the equations (53,54,56,45) we get

$$\frac{\partial G(\kappa_E)}{\partial \kappa_i} = diag\left(\frac{\partial f_E(\kappa_E)_i}{\partial \kappa_i}\right) + \Gamma \tag{57}$$

$$\Gamma = (U_E U_F^{-1})\, diag\left(\frac{\partial f(\kappa_E)_k}{\partial \kappa_k}\right)(U_E U_F^{-1})^T$$

where $\delta_{ij} = 1$ if i=j and 0 otherwise. Since the function $\mathbf{f}$ is a decreasing function in corresponding $\kappa_i$, it is easy to see that the Jacobian of $G$ is negative definite. Therefore using *Lemma 1*, the equation $G=0$ has unique solution. Further, since $E$ is full rank, hence the mapping $\kappa_E : G(\kappa_E) \rightarrow EG(\kappa_E)$ is one to one and $G(\kappa_E) = 0$ has unique solution. Also, since $U_F$ is an invertible matrix, by equation (7) we can conclude that $\kappa$ is unique.

*Corollary 1:* If the incidence matrix is full row rank, then not only the set of end-to-end loss probabilities $\kappa$ are unique, but the set of link loss probabilities $\mathbf{p}$ are also unique.

*Proof:* It follows from equation (43).

## 5.    BENCHMARK EXAMPLES

In this section we present several benchmark examples. Even though we have succeeded to prove the existence of a solution to our model, the uniqueness of this solution in terms of packet loss probabilities and TCP sending rates is still an open problem. We are able to show the uniqueness for some benchmark examples. Using these examples, we compare the analytical results and approximations with the fixed-point iterations (8), the numerical solution of mathematical program (9) and with simulations obtained via ns-2. Actually, the numerical solutions obtained via (8) and (9) coincide within the computer precision. However, we would like to note that the method of fixed-point iterations reaches the solution much faster in comparison with (9). We also note that the solution has been shown to be unique for the Approximate Formulation and full rank incidence matrix.

We choose the parameters of the simulations so that to avoid timeouts. Thus, we can use the simple square root formula (2) for TCP throughput. We are interested in the case when TCP has no restrictions on its throughput other than the network capacity. Hence, we take $W_i^{max} = \infty$ for our analytical calculations and $W_i^{max} = \max\{c_v\}$ for our numerical calculations. In all our experiments, we use the New Reno TCP version and we set $MSS_i = 512$ Bytes. For routers, we choose RED as queue management policy with the following parameters: min_thresh=10 packets, max_thresh=30 packets, queue_limit=50, p_max=0.1, and averaging_weight=0.002.

## A. One Node Case

For completeness of the presentation, let us consider a single node example. Namely, let $m$ different type TCP connections cross a single node. In the case of the rough approximation model, we have the following equation for the packet loss probability

$$\sum_{i=1}^{m} \frac{N_i}{\theta_i} \sqrt{\frac{c_i}{p}} = c.$$

Clearly, the above equation always has a unique solution which is given by

$$p_* = \frac{1}{c^2} \left( \sum_{i=1}^{m} \frac{N_i \sqrt{c_i}}{\theta_i} \right)^2. \tag{58}$$

Note that if the delay-bandwidth products are large ($c\theta_i \gg 1$), the above formula gives a small packet loss probability. We may expect that the rough approximation model and the following more precise model have close solutions

$$\sum_{i=1}^{m} \frac{N_i}{\theta_i} \sqrt{\frac{c_i}{p}} (1-p) = c.$$

The above equation leads to the following equivalent quadratic equation

$$p^2 - (\frac{1}{p_*} + 2)p + 1 = 0,$$

with $p_*$ as in (58). It has two roots:

$$p_{1,2} = \frac{1}{2} \left( (\frac{1}{p_*} + 2) \pm \sqrt{\frac{1}{p_*}(\frac{1}{p_*} + 4)} \right).$$

The root corresponding to "+" in the above expression is greater than one. Therefore, we choose the root corresponding to "-". For small values of $p_*$, this root has the following asymptotic,

$$p = p_* - 2p_*^2 + o(p_*^2).$$

Thus, we can see that indeed for the case of large delay-bandwidth products, the rough approximation model gives results that are very close to the ones of the original model (4), (5) and (6). In particular, the two models have unique solutions.

## B. Simple Two Node Tandem Network

Let a group of $N$ TCP connections of the same type successively cross two nodes with capacities $c_1$ and $c_2$ as in Example 1 (see Figure 1). We denote the probability of packet loss at the first node by $p_1$ and the probability of packet loss at the second node by $p_2$. From (2), the sending rate of a TCP connection is given by

$$T(p_1, p_2) = \frac{1}{\theta} \sqrt{\frac{c}{p_1 + (1-p_1)p_2}}.$$

Then, according to (4), we have

$$T(p_1, p_2)(1-p_1) \le c_1, T(p_1, p_2)(1-p_1)(1-p_2) \le c_2, \tag{59}$$

where $k = N\sqrt{c}/\theta$. The complementarity conditions (5) take the form

$$p_1 (c_1 - T(p_1, p_2)(1 - p_1)) = 0,$$
$$p_2 (c_2 - T(p_1, p_2)(1 - p_1)(1 - p_2)) = 0. \tag{60}$$

First let us consider the rough approximation model:

$$\frac{k}{\sqrt{p_1 + p_2}} \le c_1, \quad \frac{k}{\sqrt{p_1 + p_2}} \le c_2, \tag{61}$$

$$p_1 \left( c_1 - \frac{k}{\sqrt{p_1 + p_2}} \right) = 0, \ p_2 \left( c_2 - \frac{k}{\sqrt{p_1 + p_2}} \right) = 0. \tag{62}$$

We note that for the rough approximation model, the analysis of the two cases: $c_1 < c_2$ and $c_1 > c_2$ is the same. Let us consider for example the case $c_1 < c_2$. Clearly,

$$\frac{k}{\sqrt{p_1 + p_2}} < c_2$$

and hence from complementarity conditions (62), we conclude that $p_2 = 0$. The first inequality in (61) becomes equality. The latter leads to the expression for the packet loss probability in the first node.

$$p_1 = \frac{k^2}{c_1^2} = \frac{N^2 c}{c_1^2 \theta^2}$$

Now let us consider the case $c_1 = c_2 = c$. Inequalities (61), which become equalities, and conditions (62) are now satisfied for all $p_1$ and $p_2$ such that $p_1 + p_2 = N^2 c/c^2 \theta^2$. That is, the rough approximation model has a non unique solution if $c_1 = c_2$.

Next, we analyze the more precise model (59),(60). In particular, we shall see that (59) and (60) always possess a unique solution. First, we consider the case $c_1 \le c_2$. According to conditions (60), there could be three possibilities: (a) only the second node is a bottleneck ($p_1 = 0$, $p_2 > 0$); (b) both nodes are bottlenecks ($p_1 > 0$, $p_2 > 0$); and (c) only the first node is a bottleneck ($p_1 > 0$, $p_2 = 0$). In case (a), (59) and (60) imply

$$\frac{k}{\sqrt{p_2}} \le c_1, \quad \frac{k}{\sqrt{p_2}}(1 - p_2) = c_2.$$

The above inequality and equation lead to

$$c_2 = \frac{k}{\sqrt{p_2}}(1 - p_2) \le c_1(1 - p_2) < c_1.$$

The latter means that $c_2 < c_1$, which is a contradiction, and hence possibility (a) cannot be realized. In case (b), according to complementarity conditions (60), inequalities (59) become equalities, which lead to

$$c_2 = c_1(1 - p_2) < c_1.$$

This is again the contradiction, and consequently, possibility (b) cannot be realized as well. Only possibility (c) is left. In this case, (59) and (60) imply

$$\frac{k}{\sqrt{p_1}}(1 - p_1) = c_1, \tag{63}$$

$$\frac{k}{\sqrt{p_1}}(1 - p_1) \le c_2. \tag{64}$$

If equation (63) has a solution, inequality (64) is satisfied as $c_1 \le c_2$. The existence and uniqueness of a solution to (63) has been shown in the previous subsection. Therefore, the system (59), (60) has a unique solution if $c_1 \le c_2$. In particular, we conclude that in this case the first node is a bottleneck.

The case $c_1 > c_2$ is more difficult to analyze. It turns out that if we set $c_1 = c_2 = c$ and we start to increase the value of $c_1$, then initially there will be an interval $(c, c^*)$ inside which there is a solution to the system of equations

$$T(p_1, p_2)(1 - p_1) = c_1, \ T(p_1, p_2)(1 - p_1)(1 - p_2) = c_2, \tag{65}$$

with both $p_1$ and $p_2$ positive, and then for the interval $[c^*, \infty)$, only the second node becomes a bottleneck ($p_1 = 0$). To analyze this phenomenon, one can directly solve the system of equations (65) for the interval $(c, c^*)$. However, it is simpler to use the "perturbation approach". Take $c_1 = c + \varepsilon$ and $c_2 = c$ and look for the solution of the system (65) in the following form $p_1(\varepsilon) = p^*_1 + q_1 \varepsilon + \ldots$ and $p_2(\varepsilon) = q_2 \varepsilon + \ldots$ $p^*_1$ is the solution of equation (63) and $q_1$ and $q_2$ are two coefficients to calculate. After the substitution of these series into equations (65), expanding nonlinear expressions as power series and collecting terms with the same power of $\varepsilon$, we obtain the next system for the first order approximation

$$q_1 + (1 - p_1^*)q_2 = 0,$$

$$(1 + p_1^*)q_1 + (1 - p_1^*)^2 q_2 = -\frac{2p_1^*\sqrt{p_1^*}}{k}.$$

The solution of the above equations gives

$$p_1(\varepsilon) = p_1^* - \frac{\sqrt{p_1^*}}{k}\varepsilon + ..., \tag{66}$$

$$p_2(\varepsilon) = \frac{\sqrt{p_1^*}}{(1-p_1^*)k}\varepsilon + ... = \frac{\varepsilon}{c} + ... \tag{67}$$

Using the approximate expression for $p_1(\varepsilon)$, we can estimate $c^*$. Namely, $c^* = c + \varepsilon^*$, where $\varepsilon^* = k\sqrt{p^*}_1$. By using either the fixed point iteration method (8) or the nonlinear programming (9), we can obtain the packet loss probabilities $p_1$ and $p_2$ (see Figure 3). At the same Figure 3, we also plot the packet loss probabilities obtained by ns-2. The following parameters were used: $N = 40$, $\theta = 204$ ms, $c = 10$ Mbits/s.

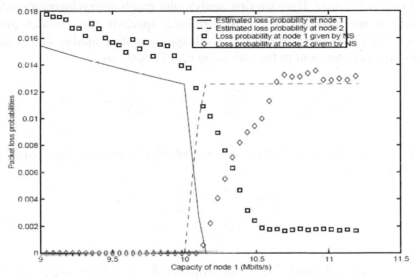

Fig. 3 Simple two-node tandem network

We would like to note that the analytical approximations (66) and (67) are so good that they cannot be distinguished from the plots obtained via (8) or (9).

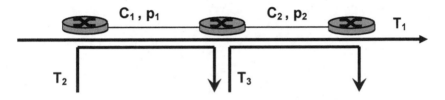

Fig. 4 Topology for Example 3

## C. Two-Node Network with Cross Traffic

Next, we consider a two-node tandem network with cross traffic (see Figure 4). Let us show that both nodes in this example are bottlenecks. Namely, we need to show that the following system of equations always has a solution

$$\frac{k_1}{\sqrt{p_1 + p_2}} + \frac{k_2}{\sqrt{p_1}} = c_1, \tag{68}$$

$$\frac{k_1}{\sqrt{p_1 + p_2}} + \frac{k_3}{\sqrt{p_2}} = c_2, \tag{69}$$

where $k_i = N_i \sqrt{c_i} / \theta_i$. Here we first analyze the rough approximation model. Later on we shall show that the refined approximation model gives practically the same results as the rough approximation model. The system (68), (69) is equivalent to the following set of equations

$$\frac{k_1}{\sqrt{p_1 + p_2}} = x, \quad \frac{k_2}{\sqrt{p_1}} = c_1 - x, \quad \frac{k_3}{\sqrt{p_2}} = c_2 - x.$$

In turn, the above set of equations gives the following single equation for unknown $x$.

$$\frac{k_1}{\sqrt{\dfrac{k_2^2}{(c_1 - x)^2} + \dfrac{k_3^2}{(c_2 - x)^2}}} = x \tag{70}$$

Denote the left hand side of this equation by $f(x)$. Next, we prove that the graph of $y = f(x)$ intersects the line $y = x$ only at one point (see Fig. 5).

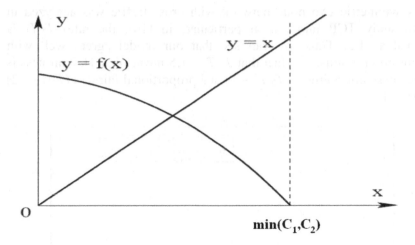

**Fig. 5 Uniqueness of the solution for Example 3**

Towards this end, we compute the derivative

$$f'(x) = -\frac{k_1\left(\dfrac{k_2^2}{(c_1-x)^3} + \dfrac{k_3^2}{(c_2-x)^3}\right)}{\left(\dfrac{k_2^2}{(c_1-x)^2} + \dfrac{k_3^2}{(c_2-x)^2}\right)^{3/2}}$$

and observe that it is negative for $x$ in $[0;\ \min\{c_1, c_2\})$. Hence, the function $f(x)$ is monotonous on the interval $[0;\ \min\{c_1, c_2\})$, and consequently, equation (70) always has a unique solution. The latter implies that the system (68), (69) has a unique solution as well. Note that the system (68), (69) can be solved via the direct application of Newton type methods for the solution of nonlinear systems.

Let us now consider a particular symmetric case where we are able to obtain exact analytical expressions. Let $c_1 = c_2 = c$, $\theta_1 = \theta_2 = \theta_3 =: \theta$ and $N_1 = N_2 = N_3 =: N$. Clearly, in this case $p_1 = p_2 = p$. After straightforward calculations, we get

$$p = \frac{(1+\sqrt{2})^2}{2}\frac{cN^2}{(\theta c)^2} = \frac{3+2\sqrt{2}}{2}\frac{cN^2}{(\theta c)^2}.$$

We also obtain

$$\frac{T_2}{T_1} = \frac{T_3}{T_1} = \sqrt{2}.$$

This symmetric two node network with cross traffic was analyzed in [16] to study TCP fairness. In particular, in [16], the ratio $T_2/T_1$ is estimated as 1.5. Thus, we can see that our model agrees well with previous observations. The fact that $T_2/T_1 \approx 1.5$ means that TCP fairness is between max-min fairness ($T_2/T_1 = 1$) and proportional fairness ($T_2/T_1 = 2$) [3], [8], [11].

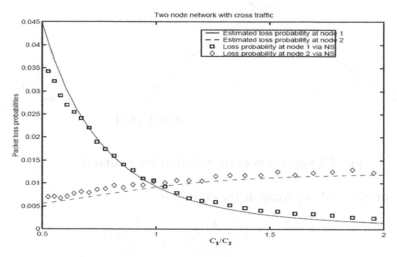

**Fig. 6 Two-node network with cross traffic: Packet loss**

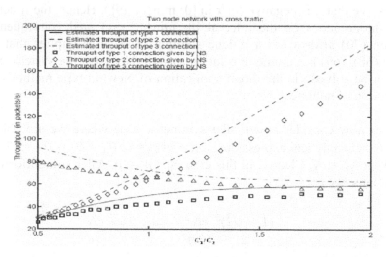

**Fig. 7 Two-node network with cross traffic: Throughput**

Next we study a non symmetric case. We fix $c_2 = c = 10$Mbits/s and we vary the value of $c_1$ (the other parameters are $N_1 = N_2 = N_3 = 20$, $\theta_1 = \theta_2 = \theta_3 = 204$ ms). We plot the packet loss probabilities $p_1$, $p_2$ and the values of throughputs $T_1$, $T_2$, $T_3$ with respect to the ratio $c_1/c_2$ in Figures 6 and 7, respectively. Note that if we increase $c_1$ from the value $c$ and keep $c_2$ unchanged, the throughput of connection 3 is deteriorated. At the first sight, this fact might appear to be surprising, as we are only increasing the total capacity of the network. However, we can propose the following explanation for this phenomenon: with the increase of the capacity of node 1, the throughput of type 1 connections increases as well; the latter creates an additional load on node 2, which leads to the deterioration in the performance of connections of type 3. Finally, we plot the same graphs for the more precise model (4), (5) and it turns out that for the set of the network parameters under consideration, the results from the rough approximation model and the results from the more precise model (4), (5) are practically indistinguishable. The figures also show graphs from ns-2 simulations which validate our modeling results.

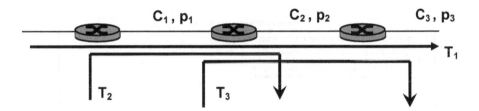

**Fig. 8  Topology for Example 4**

## D. Three Node Tandem Network

Finally let us consider a three node tandem network (see Figure 8). We set the following values of the parameters: $\theta_1 = 304$ ms, $\theta_2 = \theta_3 = 204$ ms, $N_1 = N_2 = N_3 = 20$, $c_1 = 12$ Mbits/s, $c_3 = 8$ Mbits/s and we vary capacity $c2$ over the range [10 Mbits/s; 22 Mbits/s]. In Figures 9 and 10, we plot the packet loss probabilities $p_1$, $p_2$, $p_3$, and the sending rates $T_1$, $T_2$, $T_3$, respectively. The probabilities are calculated with the help of the fixed-point iteration method (8).

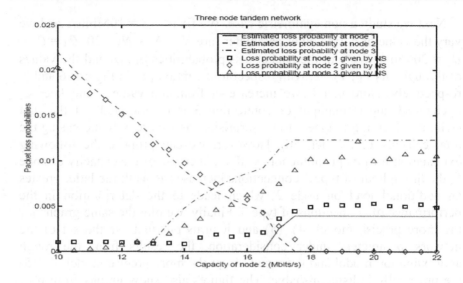

**Fig. 9  Three-node tandem network: Packet loss**

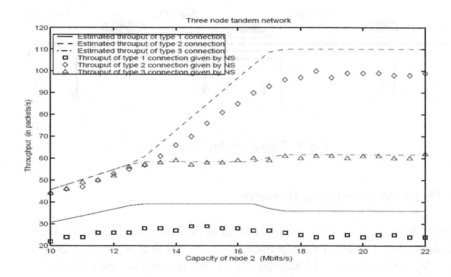

**Fig. 10 Three-node tandem network: Throughput**

The plots show that first only node 2 is a bottleneck (we call it, phase 1), then node 3 also becomes a bottleneck (phase 2), then with the further increase in the value of $c_2$, all three nodes become bottlenecks (phase 3), and finally for large values of $c_2$ only nodes 1 and 3 are left as bottlenecks (phase 4). Even though this sequence of changes in the network is quite intuitive, it is practically impossible to relay on intuition to predict the boundaries for these phases. This fact highlights utility of the formal approaches such as FP and NP formulations.

The non monotonous behavior of the sending rate $T_1$ is another interesting fact. We have already noticed such behaviour in the previous Example 3; the increase in the capacity in one part of the network can sometimes lead to the decrease in throughputs of some TCP connections. We also note that the previous examples of one node network and two-node tandem network with cross traffic, are the limiting cases of this more general topology and can be used to construct approximations when either $c_2 << c_1$, $c_3$ or $c_2 >> c_1$, $c_3$.

## 6.  CONCLUSIONS

Several approaches exist for modeling and analyzing TCP/IP networks. On one hand, there is the approach that focuses on a single TCP connection and calculates its throughput as a function of the characteristics of the packet loss process. On the other hand, there are approaches that consider the whole network and try to predict the throughput of all connections simultaneously, taking into account their mutual interaction. This paper belongs to the second research direction. We proposed a model for the network and we presented three equivalent formulations (NCP, FP and NP) of it. In particular, FP and NCP formulations lead to efficient computational procedures and FP formulation helps us to prove the existence of a solution. More importantly, the NCP problem is shown to uniquely identify bottlenecks and quantify the drop probabilities in routers for some network topology examples. We conjecture that this extends to general network configuration.

In summary, the model presented in this paper does not require the pre-identification of bottleneck links and includes the possibility of the source rate limitation as well as other features of TCP. We have demonstrated how various optimization frameworks such as utility optimization, FP and NCP models can be derived from each other. Finally, through some simple benchmark network examples we demonstrate that the localization of bottlenecks is not intuitive and TCP throughput is not always a monotonous function of the total capacity of the network.

# REFERENCES

[1]    E. Altman, K. Avrachenkov, and C. Barakat, "A stochastic model of TCP/IP with stationary random losses", *ACM SIGCOMM'2000*, Stockholm, pp. 231-242.

[2]    Urtzi Ayesta, Kostya Avranchenkov, Eitan Altman, Chadi Barakat, Parijat Dube, "Multilevel Approach for Modeling Short TCP Sessions", in proceedings of ITC-18, Berlin, September 2003.

[3]    T. Bonald and L. Massoulié, "Impact of fairness on Internet performance", *ACM SIGMETRICS 2001*, pp. 82-91.

[4]    T. Bu and D. Towsley, "Fixed point approximation for TCP behaviour in an AQM network", *ACM SIGMETRICS'01*, June 2001.

[5]    Claudio Casetti and Michela Meo, "A new approach to model the stationary behavior of TCP connections", *IEEE INFOCOM'2000*, March 2000.

[6]    R.W. Cottle, J.-S. Pang, and R.E. Stone, *The linear complementarity problem*, Academic Press, Boston, 1992.

[7]    V. Istratescu, *Fixed point theory*, Dordrecht, Holland: Reidel, 1981.

[8]    F.P. Kelly, A. Maulloo, and D. Tan, "Rate control for communication networks: shadow prices, proportional fairness and stability", J. Oper. Res. Soc., v.49, 1998, pp. 237-252.

[9]    S. Kunniyur and R. Srikant, "End-to-end congestion control schemes: Utility functions, Random losses, ECN marks", *IEEE INFOCOM 2000*.

[10]   S.H. Low and D.E. Lapsley, "Optimization flow control I: Basic Algorithm and Convergence", *IEEE/ACM Trans. on Networking*, v.7, no.6, Dec. 1999.

[11]   L. Massoulié and J. Roberts, "Bandwidth sharing and admission control for elastic traffic", *Telecommunication Systems*, v.15, pp. 185-201, 2000.

[12]   V. Misra, W.-B. Gong, and D. Towsley, "Fluid-based Analysis of a Network of AQM Routers Supporting TCP Flows with Application to RED", *ACM SIGCOMM*, Aug 2000.

[13]   J. Mo and J. Walrand, "Fair end-to-end window-based congestion control", *IEEE/ACM Trans. Networking*, v.8, no.5, Oct 2000.

[14]   J. Padhye, V. Firoiu, D. Towsley, and J. Kurose, "Modeling TCP Throughput: a Simple Model and its Empirical Validation", *ACM SIGCOMM*, Sep 1998.

[15]   S. Floyd and V. Jacobson, "Random Early Detection gateways for Congestion Avoidance", *IEEE/ACM Transactions on Networking*, Aug 1993.

[16] R. Gibbens and P. Key, "Distributed control and resource pricing", *ACM SIGCOMM'2000 Tutorial*.

[17] V. Jacobson, "Congestion avoidance and control", *ACM SIGCOMM*, Aug 1988.

[18] NS-2, Network Simulator (ver.2), LBL, http://wwwmash.cs.berkeley.edu/ns.

[19] M. Mathis, J. Semke, J. Mahdavi, T. Ott, "The Macroscopic Behaviour of the TCP Congestion Avoidance Algorithm", *ACM Computer Communication Review*, 27(3), July 1997.

[20] J.M. Ortega and W.C. Rheinboldt, *Iterative solution of nonlinear equations in several variables*, Academic Press, 1970.

[21] T. Ott, J. Kemperman, and M. Mathis, "The stationary behavior of the ideal TCP congestion avoidance", ftp://ftp.telcordia.com/pub/tjo/TCPwindow.ps

[22] V. Paxson, "End-to-End Routing Behavior in the Internet", *ACM SIGCOMM*, Aug 1996.

[23] M. Vojnovi'c, J.-Y. Le Boudec, and C. Boutremans, "Global fairness of additive-increase and multiplicative-decrease with heterogeneous roundtrip times", *IEEE INFOCOM 2000*.

[24] E. Altman, K. Avrachenkov, and C. Barakat, "TCP network calculus: The case of large delay-bandwidth product", *IEEE Infocom'2002*, New York.

# CHAPTER 5

## Cross-Layer Interaction in Wireless Ad Hoc Networks: A Practical Example

Vincent Gauthier, Michel Marot, Monique Becker

CNRS UMR 5157 SAMOVAR
Institut National des Telecommunications
9, rue Charles Fourier
91011 Evry cedex,
FRANCE

**Abstract.** *This paper presents the design and the performance evaluation of a joined process between the PHY (PHYsical) layer and routing layer in multi-hop wireless ad hoc networks. This cross-layer interaction between the PHY and routing layers allows each node in an ad hoc network to evaluate the performance of each path in its routing table in terms of Bit Error Rate (BER) and to classify each path accordingly. Routing information from poor quality links are not forwarded leading to the selection of high quality links during the routing process. An implementation of our cross-layer algorithm based on Ad-hoc On-demand Distance Vector (AODV) is presented along with simulation results showing significant improvements in terms of additional throughput and lower BER. Furthermore, inherent of our mechanism's design, the network overhead introduced by routing protocols is reduced..*

## 1. INTRODUCTION

In Mobile Ad hoc NETworks (MANET), each node is involved in the process of forwarding packets and maintaining a set of valid routes. As a MANET topology is mobile and the connectivity is unpredictable, it is rather challenging to establish and maintain routing tables. Additional challenges lay in the fact that wireless communications are impacted by stochastic and time-varying phenomena such as fading or interference. Hence, alike-wired networks, the behavior of ad hoc networks becomes very complex to predict and the Cross-layer interaction is a new way of managing interactions between layers introduced in previous works [1,2]. The reader can refer to [9] for a detailed survey of cross-layer design. In wireless networks there are a large number of phenomena that have an effect on the end-to-end performance. A layered architecture like the seven layers of the OSI model has divided each networking task into the services provided by one layer. This architecture enables each layer to communicate directly only with an adjacent layer. Alternatively cross-layer design allows direct communication between non-adjacent layers. This design clearly violates the OSI model in order to enable different types of interaction between layers. This new way of managing the network stack is mainly studied in the case of wireless networks, because some effects, such as time-varying link quality or mobile architecture, lead to develop a dynamic layer model and algorithm which take into account information from several layers at the same time.

In ad hoc networks cross-layer design could help to solve the key issues like scalability, collision, noisy link, lowered throughput, reduce the waste of bandwidth due to routing overhead, save energy. But on the other hand, with cross-layer design the performance could potentially be worsted, because different layers could try to improve the same metric at the same time but in a different direction. This phenomenon could be avoided by using a central entity which pilots the information flow between layers.

In [4], the authors show that the scalability of wireless ad hoc networks is bad when only the probability of packet loss at the reception, due to noise and interferences, is taken into account. The cross-layer mechanism described in this paper takes into account this phenomenon, based on the SNIR (Signal to Noise and Interference Ratio) of each link.

To design cross-layer interactions, various approaches have been proposed in the literature. In [1], Raisinghani *et al.* have proposed a new layer design for wireless networks that allows the possibility to exchange information between layers through a new stack component, the Devices Management Entity (DME), which stores information about each layer. In Kawadia *et al.* [2] the authors have developed the idea that using cross-layer interactions for wireless networks could improve the performance, and have given a few examples of ad hoc networks, which can use interlayer interactions to choose the path with the best throughput with the help of link information. In [5], Klemm *et al.* try to improve the performance of TCP in Ad Hoc networks by reducing the number of packet losses. To avoid errors, they measure the signal strength at the physical layer, and the MAC (Medium Access Control) layer estimates whether the failure is due to congestion or due to the neighbor moving out of range. There are two ways of reducing the number of dropped packets. First, the proactive approach: a node searches for a new route when a node detects a possible link failure to a neighbor and the second one is to increase the transmission power in case where a neighbor has just moved out of range. The simulation results show that in high mobility, the proactive approach can improve performance of a TCP session by 75% when the network is lightly loaded. In [6], Chiang describes a distributive power algorithm to improve the end-to-end performance of TCP Vegas in ad hoc networks. He uses the standard formulation of the network utility maximization and adapts it to the case when the sum of each individual source is constrained by a variable data rate on the logical link function of interferences and the power of transmission. The algorithm needs to have an inter-layer interaction between the transport and the physical layer to compute the optimal power of transmission of each frame. The author shows that the end-to-end throughput per watt of power transmitted is 82% higher with a power control and a co-design across the physical and transport layers. In [4], Mhatre *et al.* determined asymptotic bounds on the capacity of a random ad hoc network, with the assumption that the mapping from SINR (Signal to Interference and Noise Ratio) to packet success probability is continuous. Hence, over each hop, for every finite SINR, there is a non-zero probability of packet loss. Consequently, it is shown that the cumulative effect of packet loss per-hop results in a per-node throughput of only $\Theta(\frac{1}{n})$ (instead of $\Theta(\frac{1}{\sqrt{nlogn}})$) as shown previously in [7] for the threshold-based link model. However, some works are interested in analyzing the effect of physical phenomena on the network performance [8] [9].

Finally the authors in [10][11] propose new metrics, ETX and WCETT, based on measurements to select the path in function of criteria like the packet loss for ETX metric, and the Expected Transmission Time for WCEET metric. Authors in [12] [13] propose two MAC algorithms, the Receiver Based Auto Rate (RBAR) and the Opportunistic Auto Rate (OAR) algorithm to enhance the Auto Rate Fallback (ARF) protocol. Theses two mechanisms use active probe to have feedback about the quality of the channel. In the cross-layer design introduced here, we present a modified routing AODV routing algorithm that selects only paths with a enough high SNIR level to have no loss (cf. Section § 2). This mechanism has two consequences on the overall performance (cf. Section § 3). First, in the case of a network with high connectivity or low connectivity, only high throughput links will be used, and packet delivery ratio will be improved. Secondly the routing overhead will be decreased by two, because only a link with high quality will carry the routing packets. Some researchers already tried or suggested to integrate a kind of SNIR based criteria in the routing algorithms (cf. [16], [17] and [18]), but no maintenance process is proposed in [17] and [18] uses a quite different approach.

The paper is organized as follows. In Section 2 we recall briefly the Cross-layer interaction schemes for Ad Hoc networks. In section 3, We present the algorithm based on a cross-layer interaction between the physical layer and the routing layer, this cross-layer interaction uses a modified version of the AODV protocol to take into account information about the link layer, such as the average received power of a link and the BER of a link. In section 4, some numerical analyses are presented. Section 5 includes simulation results and a discussion. Finally sections 6 and 7 present our conclusion and some promising directions for future works.

## 2.   ALGORITHM AND DESIGN

The designed algorithm is divided in two parts: first, the feedback process, which enables the routing layer to give information about the QoS (Quality of Service) performance from the MAC/PHY layer. The second part is the process implemented in the routing layer to select the most accurate path as a function of the PHY/MAC layer information.

Let us describe now the process performed at the routing layer. We have used here an AODV based protocol, which takes into account feedback information about the stability and the physical performance of each neighboring link. Depending on this information the routing protocol decides to enable packets to be routed on one link according to the performances of this link. First, the AODV protocol uses two functions to look for a path: searching for a function in the routing table and/or broadcasting a route request through the network. This algorithm acts on these two processes, first for each neighboring link added to the routing table; we join a new parameter that represents the QoS of the link (during the hello broadcast process defined in the AODV protocol). Secondly when a node receives a route Request it replies or forwards this packet only if the link of the previous hop has an acceptable QoS level or discards it as a function of the information, which is stored in this routing table, or the information, which comes directly from the lower layer. This optimization has two effects: it reduces the routing load because each node drops routing packets which come from poor performance links and does not forward it. And secondly, only paths, which have been judged acceptable, will be carrying packets, because the other links that have no acceptable QoS level will not participate in the process of broadcasting the route discovery through the network.

Information, which is used at the network layer, comes from the PHY/MAC layer. This cross-layer interaction or joint process between the PHY/MAC and the network layer is done through a new design of layers. First of all, this metric exchange between layers to define the QoS of each link, is the $BER_l$ (bit error rate) and the $FER_l$ (frame error rate) of each packet through one particular link $l$. The $BER_l$ and the $FER_l$ are calculated as a function of the $SIR_l$ (signal to interference ratio) measured by the physical layer on link $l \in L(s)$ as follows:

$$SIR_l(P) = \frac{P_l G_{ll}}{N_l + \sum_{k \neq l}^{N} P_l G_{lk}}$$

$$BER_l = \hat{\alpha}_M \, Q\left(\sqrt{\hat{\beta}_M \, SIR_l(P)}\right) \qquad (1)$$

$$FER_l = 1 - (1 - BER_l)^n$$

where :
- $n$ : number of bits in a packet
- $G_{lk}$ : Path losses from the transmitter on the logical link $l$ to the receiver on the logical link $k$
- $P_l$ : Transmission Power from the transmitter on the logical link $l$
- $N_l$ : Background noise on the logical link $l$
- $FER_l$ : Frame error rate on the logical link $l$
- $BER_l$ : Bits error rate on the logical link $l$

- $Q()$: Q function, $Q(z)$, is defined as the probability that a Gaussian random variable x with mean 0 and variance 1 is bigger than z [15]
- $\alpha_M$: in $\hat{\alpha}_M = \alpha_M/(log_2 M)$ where $\alpha_M$ is the number of nearest neighbours to the constellation at the minimum distance [15]
- $\beta_M$: in $\hat{\beta}_M = (log_2 M)/\beta_M$ is a constant that relates minimum distance to average symbol energy, $\alpha_M$ and $\beta_M$ are constants depending on the modulation and the required bit error rate is given by BER [15].

This metric (the $BER_l$) comes from the PHY/MAC layer to network layer and we stored the $FER_l \in [0,1]$ in the routing table during the moving average calculation process, which smooths the noise variation of the $FER_l$ ($\gamma$ is the smoothing factor) and enables us to calculate and average $FER_l$.

$$\overline{FER_l} = \gamma\, FER_l + (1-\gamma)\, FER_l(t-1) \qquad (2)$$

The network layer has the opportunity to distinguish which link is acceptable or not as a function of the $FER$ and a determined threshold for each link to all its neighbors. The FER is used as a metric to determine if we could forward or reply to routing solicitation, but it doesn't change the normal routing process that selects the link which leads to lowering the number of hops.

With this cross-layer mechanism a node will forward or process an RREQ packet only if the $\overline{FER_l} < \zeta$ or $FER_l < \zeta$ and $\zeta$ is a predefined threshold and the $\overline{FER_l}$ is the average Frame Error rate for one link stores in the routing table and the $FER_l$ is the instantaneous Frame Error Rate measured by the PHY layer. This proposal is to avoid routes that have poor capacity in terms of the number of errors at the physical layer and throughput.

## 3.    ANALYSIS

With CSMA/CA, the impact of the interference is rather low. Instead, the transmission errors are mainly due to path losses and fading. That is why we are more interested in observing the effect of the algorithm as a function of the connectivity, that is as a function of the transmission range or, which is the same, the transmission power.

Let us assume that there is no fading to simplify the analysis, but that the only transmission errors are due to path loss. Between two hosts, because of the three hand-shakes, a data packet is received in one hop after an RTS/CTS exchange at MAC level between the intermediary source and the destination, plus the sending of the data packet and its acknowledgment. In this case, the probability that a data packet sent by a node $x_k$ to a node $x_{k+1}$ separated by a distance $d$ is never received, is (no packets, either RTS, CTS, data or acknowledgment is retransmitted after three times):

$$
\begin{aligned}
p_\varepsilon(d) \;=\;& 1 - \big[ (1 - p_{RTS/CTS}(d)) \\
& (1 - p_{er}(d))(1 - p_{ack}(d)) \\
& (1 - p_{RTS/CTS}(d))^2 \\
& [p_{er}(d) + (1 - p_{er}(d))p_{ack}(d)] \\
& + (1 - p_{RTS/CTS}(d))^2 \\
& [p_{er}(d) + (1 - p_{er}(d))p_{ack}(d)] \\
& (1 - p_{er}(d))(1 - p_{ack}(d)) \\
& + (1 - p_{RTS/CTS}(d))^3 \\
& [p_{er}(d) + (1 - p_{er}(d))p_{ack}(d)]^2 \\
& (1 - p_{er}(d))(1 - p_{ack}(d)) \big]
\end{aligned}
\tag{3}
$$

where

- $p_{ack}(d)$ is the probability that an acknowledgment is lost;
- $p_{er}(d)$ is the probability that a data packet is lost;
- $p_{RTS/CTS}(d)$ is obtained by

$$
\begin{aligned}
p_{RTS/CTS}(d) =\;& 1 - \big[ (1 - p_{RTS}(d))(1 - p_{CTS}(d)) \\
& + (p_{RTS}(d) + p_{CTS}(d))(1 - p_{RTS}(d))(1 - p_{CTS}(d)) \\
& + (p_{RTS}(d) + p_{CTS}(d))^2 (1 - p_{RTS}(d))(1 - p_{CTS}(d)) \big]
\end{aligned}
\tag{4}
$$

where $p_{RTS}(d)$ and $p_{CTS}(d)$ are the probabilities that an RTS and an CTS are lost respectively. $p_{RTS}(d)$, $p_{CTS}(d)$, $p_{ack}(d)$ and $p_{er}(d)$ can be computed with the formula:

$$p_X(d) \;=\; \left[1 - BER_X\big(SINR(d)\big)\right]^{v_X} \tag{5}$$

where,

- $v_X$ is the number of bits per packets of type X (RTS, CTS, ACK or data);
- $BER_X(y)$ is the bit error rate function giving the probability that a bit is received with an error for an SNR equal to y, for the packet of type X.

and

$$SNR(d) \;=\; P_0\left(\frac{\lambda}{4\pi d}\right)^2 \times \frac{Rxthres}{No} \tag{6}$$

where:

- $P_0$ is the transmission power;
- $\lambda$ is the wave length;
- $Rxthres$ is the reception threshold;
- $No$ is the ambient noise.

The loss rate on the path between A and B is then:

$$\tau_{AB} = 1 - \sum_{k}\Big[P(k)\times$$

$$\int_{d_{Ax_1}}\int_{d_{x_1x_2}}\int_{d_{x_{k-1}x_k}}\int_{d_{x_kB}}$$

$$p_\varepsilon(d_{Ax_1})\Pi_{i=1}^{k}p_\varepsilon(d_{x_ix_{i+1}})p_\varepsilon(d_{x_kB}) \tag{7}$$

$$f\left(d_{Ax_1},d_{x_1x_2},,d_{x_kB}\right)$$

$$\mathrm{mod}\,3ex \times dd_{Ax_1}\,dd_{x_1x_2}\,dd_{x_1x_2}\,dd_{x_kB}\Big]$$

where:

- $P(k)$ is the probability to have k nodes on the path;
- $d_{Ax_1}$, $d_{x_1x_2}$, $,d_{x_kB}$ are the distances between nodes $A$ and $x_1$, nodes $x_1$ and $x_2$, , nodes $x_k$ and $B$;

- $f\left(d_{Ax_1}, d_{x_1x_2}, , d_{x_kB}\right)$ is the probability function of these distances;

Discarding bad routes in terms of bit error rates produces a lower loss rate and result in suppressing from the integral above, all the infinitesimal elements corresponding to a big $BER(d)$, and so all the infinitesimal elements with a high distance. It leads to have shorter distances between nodes.

On the other hand, to allow only a shorter distance between nodes leads some routes to be broken. This appears in equation (7) through a decreasing of the $P(k)$ terms for small $k$, thus weighting the paths for which the loss rates are lower.

So, adding the cross-layer threshold leads to modifying the path, the number of hops and the distances in between, that is exactly $P(k)$ and $f\left(d_{Ax_1}, d_{x_1x_2}, , d_{x_kB}\right)$. Indexing respectively by $XL$ and $NXL$ the quantities corresponding to respectively the cross-layer and non cross-layer cases, the gain is then:

$$G = \sum_k [P_{XL}(k) \times$$

$$\int_{d_{Ax_1}} \int_{d_{x_1x_2}} \int_{x_{k_{XL}-1}} x_{k_{XL}} \int_{x_{k_{XL}}} B$$

$$p_\varepsilon(d_{Ax_1}) \Pi_{i=1}^{k_{XL}} p_\varepsilon(d_{x_i x_{i+1}}) p_\varepsilon(d_{x_{k_{XL}} B})$$

$$f_{XL}\left( d_{Ax_1}, d_{x_1 x_2}, , d_{x_{k_{XL}} B} \right)$$

$$\mod 3ex \times dd_{Ax_1} dd_{x_1 x_2} dd_{x_1 x_2} dd_{x_{k_{XL}} B} \Big]$$

$$- \sum_k [P_{NXL}(k) \times \tag{8}$$

$$\int_{d_{Ax_1}} \int_{d_{x_1x_2}} \int_{x_{k_{NXL}}-1} x_k \int_{x_{k_N}} XL B$$

$$p_\varepsilon(d_{Ax_1}) \Pi_{i=1}^{k_{NXL}} p_\varepsilon(d_{x_i x_{i+1}}) p_\varepsilon(d_{x_{k_{NXL}} B})$$

$$f_{NXL}\left( d_{Ax_1}, d_{x_1 x_2}, , d_{x_{k_{NXL}} B} \right)$$

$$\mod 3ex \times dd_{Ax_1} dd_{x_1 x_2} dd_{x_1 x_2} dd_{x_{k_{NXL}} B} \Big]$$

Unfortunately, it is not possible to compute analytically this gain, since it involves connectivity measures which are not known at the moment. This problem is closely related to the percolation theory, and to predicting the probability of having a path between two node.

## 4.    PERFORMANCE ANALYSIS

### 4.1    Simulations Parameters

We have used the event-based simulator Qualnet [19] with a simulated area of $1500 \times 1000$ m with 50 nodes. For the MAC layer we have picked the unmodified IEEE 802.11b model and a modified AODV [14] protocol, which uses cross-layer interaction. The traffic sources are CBR, and the source destination pairs are spread randomly over the network. In the case of mobility the mobility model is *The Random Trip Mobility Model* [20], which generalizes random waypoints and random walks to realistic scenarios. We have selected *The Random Trip Mobility Model* because this implementation performs perfect initialization, i.e. the mobility model has no transient phase. In our simulation, a packet is considered receivable if its reception power to take into account the noise and interference is above a certain threshold. After that we calculate the packet SIR and pick a random number to simulate the error probability that normally occurs during transmission.

### Table 1 Simulation Parameters

| Summary of Simulation Parameters | |
|---|---|
| Parameter | Value |
| Simulation Time | 2000s |
| Number of Nodes | 100 |
| Pathloss Model | Two Ray Ground |
| Physical Model | 802.11b |
| Mac layer Data Rate | 11 Mbps |
| Transmission Power | 5 to 13 dBm |
| Receiver Sensibility at 11Mbps | -83 Dbm |
| Typical Transmission Range | 271.979m at 11Mbps |
| *Traffic* | |
| Number of Traffic Sources | 50 |
| Packet Size | 1460 bytes |
| Average Flow duration | 200s |
| Number of Flow | 500 |
| *Movement* | |
| Mobility Model | Random Trip Mobility Model |
| Speed | 5 m/s |
| Pause time | 100s |

## 4.2   Performance Results

The performance evaluation in the case where all nodes move according to the *The Random Trip Mobility Model* mobility model defined by [20] with an average speed of 5m/s and a pause time of 100s. All simulations were made for the transmission power range of 5 dBm to 13dBm (cf. Table 1). This lets us show an evaluation of the performance as a function of the network connectivity, because the transmission range varies according to the transmission power. Figure 1 shows that in the cross-layer case the packet delivery fraction increases by a magnitude of 80% or 75% more in the best case according the threshold $\zeta$ which is the minimal FER (Frame Error Rate) authorized for a link. On the other hand, Figure 2 shows the ratio of RREQ not carried by the network in cross-layer case for different values of $\zeta$ versus the non cross-layer case. The result is that the cross-layer case carries around 54% less RREQ packets in the case of poor connectivity and 66% in the case of a fully connected network for $\zeta = 0.1$.

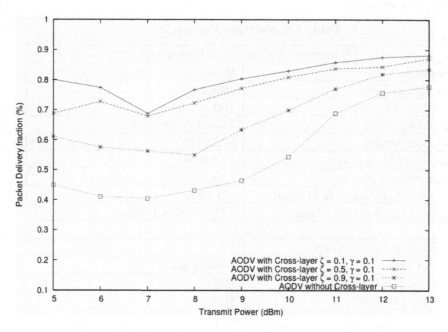

**Fig. 1 Packet delivery fraction as function of the transmission power**

The performance shows that the cross-layer mechanism reduces the routing load by carrying fewer RREQ packets, because with the cross-layer mechanism we carry only packets from links with a Frame Error Rate under the threshold $\zeta$. This is more obvious in the case of a fully connected networks (when transmission power equals 13 dBm). On the other hand the packet delivery fraction is greatly improved when the network coverage is low (when the transmission power is equal to 5dBm), because in this case the path through the network is close to the optimal, in terms of the number of hops and distance. It also appears from the simulations that a large proportion of the links is of very poor quality (cf. Fig. 1 for $\zeta = 0.9$). Over these links with a measured $FER > 0.9$ transmission will be very poor, and theses links are the main source of damage to the end-to-end performance. For all communication over the wireless link, this kind of link must be avoided.

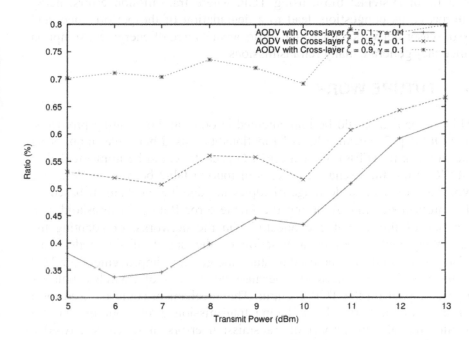

**Fig. 2  Ratio of RREQ not carry by the network in the cross-layer case for different value of $\zeta$ versus non cross-layer case**

## 5.    CONCLUSION

We presented a cross-layer framework based on an AODV protocol. It consists of allowing the routing algorithm to only select routes with sufficiently high quality according to information that comes from the Physical layer. The quality of the links is periodically measured by exchanges of HELLO messages between nodes. It leads to suppressing poor quality routes, and also to reducing the data load, which would be transmitted in poor conditions. When the connectivity is sufficient, this mechanism allows routes to be found with more hops but with a lower loss rate. Simulations show some significant improvement in terms of packet delivery fraction that improve by 10% to 80% depending on the transmission power and also in terms of routing load which is reduced by half.

This framework could be used for a large set of other protocols and mechanisms, which need a QoS information. It would be of great benefit to a lot of systems: those using TCP, where transmission errors, being interpreted as congestion, lead to a degradation of the performance, and also, sensor networks, for which errors are a source of energy consumption since they generate many retransmissions.

## 6.    FUTURE WORK

This mechanism could be implemented in other ad hoc routing protocols, like OLSR [17] because lots of functionalities used here, like monitoring the link quality (FER) of each HELLO packets, could be implemented in OLSR during the exchange process of routing table between nodes. This work also raises a wide range of topics in adaptive mechanism based on this mechanism, like Adapting the Frame error Rate ($\zeta$) threshold as a function of the available connectivity in the networks, or adapting the smoothing factor ($\gamma$) as a function of the speed of the node. This framework could even be used to study the goodput improvement for TCP connection in ad hoc networks, because the loss rate of a wireless link has a great impact on the TCP goodput. This mechanism could be used for a large set of networks. By reducing transmission errors, our mechanism would alleviate the impact of transmission errors in wireless networks. It would be of great benefit to a lot of systems: those using TCP (Transmission Control Protocol), where transmission errors, being inter-preted as congestion, lead to a degradation of the performance, and also sensor networks, for which errors are a source of energy consumption since they generate many retransmissions.

## ACKNOWLEDGEMENT

This study is led within the Programme Initiative "Réseaux Spontanés" of the Groupe des Ecoles des Télécommunications.

# REFERENCES

[1]    V. T. Raisinghani and S. Iyer, Cross-Layer Design Optimization in Wireless Protocol Stacks, in Computer Communication, vol. 27, num. 8, May, 2004, pp. 720–724.

[2]    V. Kawadia and P. R. Kumar, A Cautionary Perspective on Cross Layer Design, in IEEE Wireless Communication Magazine, vol. 12, num. 1, July, 2003, pp. 3–11.

[3]    V. Srivastava and M. Motani, Cross-layer Design: A Survey and the Road Ahead, in IEEE Wireless Communication Magazine, vol. 43, num. 12, December, 2005, pp. 112–119.

[4]    Vivek P Mhatre and Catherine P Rosenberg, The Capacity of Random Ad hoc Networks under a Realistic Link Layer Model, submitted to IEEE Transactions on Information Theory, April, 2005.

[5]    F. Klemm and Z. Ye and S. Krishnamurthy and S. Tripathi, Improving TCP Performance in Ad Hoc Networks Using Signal Strength Based Link Management, Ad Hoc Networks Journal, 2004.

[6]    M. Chiang, To Layer or not to Layer: Balancing Transport and Physical Layers in Wireless Multihop Networks, in Proc. of IEEE INFOCOM, March, 2004.

[7]    P. Gupta and P. R. Kumar, The capacity of wireless networks, IEEE Transactions on Information Theory, vol. IT-46, num. 2, March, 2000, pp. 388–404.

[8]    H. Lundgren and E. Nordstrom and C. Tschudin, The Gray Zone Problem in IEEE 802.11b based Ad hoc Networks, in Mobile Computing and Communication Review (MC2R), July, 2002.

[9]    J. Mullen and T. Matis and S. Rangan, The Receiver's Dilemma, in Proc. of International Conference in Mobile and Wireless Communication Networks, October, 2004.

[10]   Douglas S. J. De Couto and Daniel Aguayo and John Bicket and Robert Morris, A high-throughput path metric for multi-hop wireless routing, in Wirel. Netw., vol. 11, num. 4, 2005, pp. 419–434.

[11]   Richard Draves and Jitendra Padhye and Brian Zill, Routing in multi-radio, multi-hop wireless mesh networks, in MobiCom '04: Proceedings of the 10th annual international conference on Mobile computing and networking, 2004, pp. 114–128.

[12]   Gavin Holland and Nitin Vaidya and Paramvir Bahl, A rate-adaptive MAC protocol for multi-Hop wireless networks, in MobiCom '01: Proceedings of the 7th annual international conference on Mobile computing and networking, 2001, pp. 236–251.

[13]   B. Sadeghi and V. Kanodia and A. Sabharwal and E. Knightly, Opportunistic media access for multirate ad hoc networks, MobiCom '02: Proceedings of the 8th annual international conference on Mobile computing and networking, 2002, pp. 24–35.

[14]   Charles Perkins and Elizabeth Royer, Ad hoc on-demand distance vector routing, in Proceedings of the 2nd IEEE Workshop on Mobile Computing Systems and Applications, pp. 90–100, Febuary, 1999.

[15]   A. Goldsimth, Cambrige University Press, Wireless Communications, 2004.

[16]   A.-L. Beylot and R. Dhaou and V. Gauthier and M. Becker, Cross-Layer Simulation and Optimization for Mobile ad-hoc Networks, in Proc. of International Conference in Mobile and Wireless Communication Networks, October, 2004.

[17]   Wing Ho Yuen, Heung-no Lee, T.D. Andersen, A simple and effective cross layer networking system for mobile ad hoc networks, in Proc. of The 13th IEEE International Symposium on Personal, Indoor and Mobile Radio Communications, vol. 4, September, 2002, pp. 1952--1956,

[18]   S. Toumpis, A.J. Goldsmith, Performance optimization, and cross-layer design of media access protocols for wireless ad hoc networks, in Proc. of The IEEE International Conference on Communications. ICC '03., vol. 3, May 2003, pp. 2234–2240.

[19]   Qualnet, http://www.scalable-networks.com/.

[20]   J.-Y. Le Boudec and M. Vojnovic, Perfect Simulation and Stationarity of a Class of Mobility Models, in Proc. of IEEE INFOCOM, 2005.

[21]   T. Clausen and P. Jacquet and A. Laouiti and P. Muhlethaler and A. Qayyum and L. Viennot, Optimized Link State Routing Protocol, in Proc. of IEEE INMIC, Pakistan, 2001.

[22]   Biswas, Sanjit and Morris, Robert, Opportunistic routing in multi-hop wireless networks, in SIGCOMM Computer Communications Review, vol. 34, num 1, 2004, pp. 69–74.

[23]   Henrik Lundgren and Erik Nordstro and Christian Tschudin, Coping with communication gray zones in IEEE 802.11b based ad hoc networks, in WOWMOM '02: Proceedings of the 5th ACM international workshop on Wireless mobile multimedia, 2002, pp. 49–55.

# CHAPTER 6

# Multilayer Description of Large Scale Communication Networks

Sébastien Rumley, Christian Gaumier

Ecole Polytechnique Fédérale de Lausanne (EPFL)

**Abstract.** *Data exchanges between various modules and tools raise interfacing difficulties in a multilayer environment. This aspect may become particularly critical in a distributed context.*

*This paper proposes a multilayer descriptive framework for communication networks aimed at facilitating data exchange between different tools and modules. This description uses the extensible mark-up language (XML) which allows an increased flexibility and an improved visibility of relevant data.*

## 1. INTRODUCTION

Multilayer modelling of communication networks has emerged in recent years for many reasons. Certain technologies are by definition multilayer. Wavelength division multiplexing (WDM), for instance, spans over OSI layers 1 and 2, or even 3 (IP-over-WDM) and thus needs an integrated multilayer approach. On the other hand, well known specific algorithms provide effective solutions to particular problems, such as routing, wavelength assignment or protection and restoration. These algorithms concern generally a single layer, which implies the integration of the results provided by several of these algorithms within a multilayer context. Often, separate optimization of each layer does not necessarily imply a global optimum. Being suboptimal on one layer may lead to valuable improvements in upper layers. Multilayer sensitivity analysis may be very helpful in these situations [1]. Moreover, upper layer algorithms generally contain control loops and feedback mechanisms which may affect in turn lower layers [2]. Only multilayer models may take into account these special behaviours.

An integrated and monolithic model encompassing all layers at the same time is difficult to achieve. Therefore, a partition is envisaged and a modular approach becomes necessary. Existing tools, methods and algorithms associated with each layer or sub-layer can be successfully reused. They should however not been considered as stand-alone blocks anymore, but as interacting components [3].

In many cases, the results coming from one given block are supplied as input data for another component. With rare exception, output data furnished will need an intermediate processing stage (filtering) to be turned into valid input data for the next component. This processing stage could go from simple data reformatting to advance statistical analysis.

Fig. 1 depicts the block diagram of a multilayer simulation, where the global system plans some iteration among various components. To be able to easily iterate a large number of times, data flow between components must be fluid and automated since data exchange between components is one key issue of a multilayer approach.

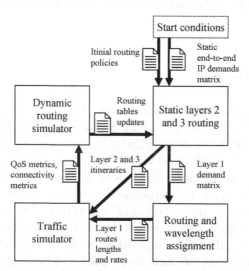

**Fig. 1   An example of multi-component planning environment for IP-over-WDM architectures.**

For a multilayer planning environment using $n$ distinct components called here tools, between $n$-1 and $n(n$-1) intermediate processing blocks (interfaces) are needed. Fig. 2 illustrates this situation. This multiplication of additional processing blocks may be particularly harmful: a change in one tool may necessitate a change in each preceding or following interface associated to that tool. Moreover, interfaces, unlike algorithms, are difficult to debug and particularly exposed to bugs. They are known in the software engineering field to occupy a large part of total code, and thus to be largely time and effort consuming [4], and crror-prone.

In case of a multilayer planning and performance analysis driven in an extended context like international scientific collaboration, the integration of the tools of distinct participants may be particularly difficult if several common guidelines are not decided. Furthermore, some groups may support a given file format while others not. Some groups may decide to include or discard certain data while other groups will neglect or regret them. A group may change its input or output dataset, which again forces all other collaborating entities to adapt their own interfaces. Finally, a group may have interest to mask private data and/or any information about the tool itself [5].

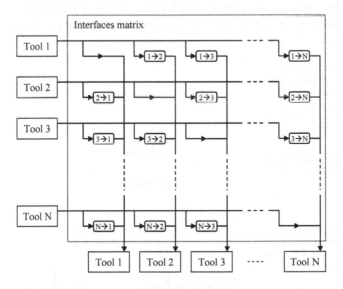

**Fig. 2  A collection of N tools may imply the use of $n(n$-1) interfaces.**

Data input and output (I/O) has therefore a key importance in a multilayer. In [5], the authors address this problem on the quantity side, putting emphasis on specific post-processing operations, large data amount handling and archiving. In this paper, on the other hand, a large emphasis is put on the generality, universality and flexibility. A Multilayer Network Description (MND) framework is proposed, aiming to assist the multilayer modelling by improving the data exchange between various components and tools in addition with offering a clear view on the overall studied case. In the next section, the advantages of MND are illustrated in a generic context. An example related to an IP-over-WDM architecture is shown in section 3. Conclusions and future work directions form the object of section 4.

## 2.    MULTILAYER NETWORK DESCRIPTION

A universal data description format would resolve all aforementioned impairments. As shown in Fig. 3, a common I/O format cancels the need for interfaces. It however fixes strict rules on the exchange configuration and requires appropriate adjustment for each tool. This is of course not realistic, as this would probably imply heavy code rewriting and testing. In addition, the common inter-tool data format called "Universal Format" in Fig. 3 is itself hypothetic, as specific tools may require or produce data that does not fit at all into it.

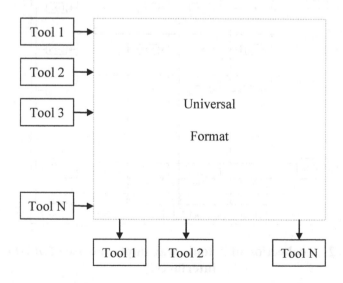

**Fig. 3  An hypothetic "Universal Format" suitable to all tools.**

As shown in Fig. 4, the MND framework approaches in some extent the Universal Format as it defines a common intermediate data format. It however keeps a pre-processing (MND to tool format translation) and post-processing (tool format to MND translation) modules for each tool. In comparison to Fig. 2, the maximal number of interfaces is reduced to $2n$. In addition, a new tool, if supplied with appropriate I/O interfaces adapted to MND, is automatically compatible with the existing planning environment. Moreover, a radical change in the data format of a given tool implies only some modifications in its I/O interfaces.

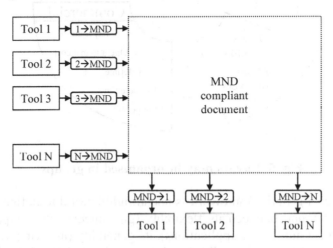

**Fig. 4 Using the Multilayer Network Description (MND), each tool has its dedicated pre and post processing unit, which limits the number of interface to $2n$.**

MND, unlike the Universal Format, is feasible as it does not define a fixed file or data format. It is a flexible framework able to integrate each specific data types. MND can be defined as a list of rules of variable length and is aimed to be a generic descriptive framework intended to structure input and output data.

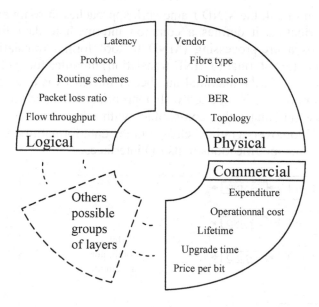

**Fig. 5  Layers may be organised in groups.**

The role of a generic framework is not straightforward to define. Trade-offs must be found between its flexibility (guaranteeing its compatibility with the largest number of applications), its generality (allowing synergies between tools and code reusability) and its complexity (allowing advanced data extraction operations). The exchange format shown in Fig. 2 has high complexity and flexibility, but no genericity. In Fig. 3, the Universal Format has high genericity and complexity, but poor flexibility. A simple text file with tab-separated values has high flexibility and genericity, but poor complexity.

MND tries to balance these three issues by adopting an approach suitable to both graph and list structures associated to communication networks.

The MND framework is based on the well-known extensible mark-up language (XML [6]). According to section 1, the multilayer description should be the meeting point of various tools (network planners, simulators, etc.) which may be related to various computer platforms, programming technologies or even to various human languages. XML is Unicode which avoids problems with specific characters (é, ç); XML is promoted by the World Wide Web consortium (W3C) which is a proof of multi-platform and multi programming language availability; XML is wide spread, easing its implementation by importing open source handling libraries; XML is intuitive and limits itself to its main purpose: formatting and organisation of data; finally, XML document can be consulted through an internet browser. For all these reasons, XML has been the natural candidate for the MND framework.

The MND is organised around three abstract objects: nodes, links and layers. These objects are each represented with an XML element, which are placed in a certain manner in the document. Element inheritance and attribute set are the two main mechanisms of XML. The first mechanism is used to include an element in another: a link is included in a layer; a layer is included in a network or a group of layers. The latter mechanism permits association of values to elements. This allows in particular cross-referencing between elements: each node defines an id attribute and each link defines two attributes to reference origin and destination nodes, using their ids. Using that principle, incidence matrices may be included in MND, as well as more complex data structures.

A full multilayer description contains several layers, which may be organized in groups. Fig. 5 illustrates three possible layer groups (physical, logical and commercial) together with some included layers.

Fig. 6 illustrates this organisation, showing the "topology" and "demands" layers of particular four-node network architecture. By a simple "click" in the browser, the user may inspect the content of one specific layer while keeping the contents of other layers hidden. This feature greatly improves the readability of the document.

```xml
<?xml version="1.0" encoding="UTF-8"?>
  <network>
    <main_description>
    <layer id="topology">
        <node id="0" pos_x="100" pos_y="340"/>
        <node id="1" pos_x="282" pos_y="362"/>
        <node id="2" pos_x="76"  pos_y="168"/>
        <node id="3" pos_x="230" pos_y="87"/>
        <link orig="0" dest="1"/>
        <link orig="2" dest="3"/>
        <link orig="0" dest="2"/>
    </layer>
    <layer id="demands" unit="mbps">
        <link orig="0" dest="3" rate="30"/>
        <link orig="0" dest="2" rate="55"/>
        <link orig="1" dest="0" rate="60"/>
```

```
            <link orig="1" dest="2" rate="50"/>
            <link orig="1" dest="3" rate="50"/>
            <link orig="3" dest="1" rate="80"/>
            <link orig="3" dest="0" rate="100"/>
            <link orig="3" dest="2" rate="50"/>
            <link orig="2" dest="3" rate="10"/>
            <link orig="2" dest="1" rate="40"/>
            <link orig="2" dest="0" rate="80"/>
        </layer>
    </main_description>
  </network>
```

**Fig. 6 "Topology" and "demands" layers of a four-node network.**

Any MND file must conform to the structure depicted in Fig. 7. It should also comply with the elements and attributes namespaces listed in Tables 1 and 2. For instance, a link element must always be the direct children of a layer element. To permit reconstruction of the incidence matrix, node element must absolutely define an "id" attribute.

Similarly, each link must defined an "orig" and "dest" attributes, which will act as pointer to start and end nodes. Note that a link can connect a node without being in the same layer. Note besides that "orig" and "dest" attributes must also be used in case of undirected graph. An additional attribute can be attached to the containing layer to specify the undirected property.

To completely segment the information among the different layers, a precise link or node may have multiple roles and thus be defined in multiple layers. This becomes possible, through the usage of unique id numbers.

The document structure is also wide open and flexible. Additional attributes can be added according to the needs. To associate a more complex data structure to a node or a link, sub-elements may be included into links or nodes elements. For special purpose, additional information may be stored in an independent element, below the "main_ description" element. These extension capabilities are also visible in Fig. 7, where additional attributes or elements are shown in dotted lines.

**Table 1: MND defines five element names. Each of these elements has its own place into the structure and imposes several rules for its containing attributes and sub-elements.**

|  | Father element | Purpose | Contains |
|---|---|---|---|
| network | none (root) | root of the document | • one and only one sub-element named "main_description", plus possibly additional ones<br>• no attributes |
| main_des cription | network | define the intrinsic properties of the network | • at least one sub-element named "layer", plus possibly others named differently<br>• no attributes |
| layer | main_descr iption | describe one part of the network | • "node" and "link" sub-elements, plus possibly different ones named differently<br>• an "id" attribute, plus possibly additional ones |
| node | layer | describe a node | • possibly some sub-elements<br>• one and only one "id" attribute, plus possibly other attributes, like position identifiers ("pos_x", pos_y") |
| link | layer | describe a link or a connection | • possibly some sub-elements<br>• one (and only one) "orig" attribute, one "dest" attribute, plus possibly additional ones |

**Table 2: Five attributes complete the list of element name. They permit to define unambiguously complex graph structure. Ids for links are optional since their origin, destination and containing layer are generally sufficient to define them.**

| Attribute name | Contained in | Purpose |
|---|---|---|
| id | node, link, layer | Key object identifier (optional for links) |
| pos_x | node | Horizontal position attribute |
| pos_y | node | Vertical position attribute |
| orig | link | Link's origin node |
| dest | link | Link's destination node |

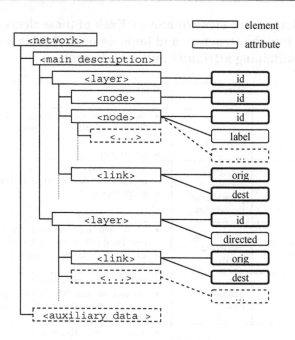

**Fig. 7  Organisation of an MND file. Mandatory attributes are highlighted.**

XML documents are in theory neither limited by size, structure nor content type. They may include all sorts of data, even binary data. However, it is recommended to restrict their content to textual information. Pure textual information allied with a clear document structure facilitate a visual consultation, and a by hand edition. In the extreme ease, very large data blocks or binary dataset can be stored in an external file, while the XML document contains a pointer to it.

## 3.    AN EXAMPLE

The use of the MND is illustrated by the IP-over-WDM network depicted in Fig. 8. The network description contains four layers called: geographical, physical topology, traffic demands and IP connectivity. Resulting MND file is listed in Fig. 9.

Geographical layer only contains nodes, considered as cities or population centres. Beside their ids, nodes include the two position attributes, and several other general data, for instance, city names and population.

Physical topology layer represents the wired connections between cities and points-of-presence. It contains thus a collection of links, plus some additional nodes representing backbone routers, which cannot be considered as population centres and therefore do not appear in geographical layer. A link element holds here for an undirected fibre span. Beside the two mandatory attributes origin and destination, additional data inherent to fibre are to be added (length, fibre type).

Traffic demands layer contains inter-cities logical connections. We assume an n-to-n demand set. Again, a collection of link elements are defined, with bandwidth requirements in terms of megabytes or light paths.

IP Connectivity layer should model the IP layer of the network. Each node of this layer has an IP address, and a routing table. We assume that this layer additionally defines a large set of connections under the form of a dump file. To limit the size of the original MND document, the file reference is given here, with the regular expression permitting the easy extraction of each line.

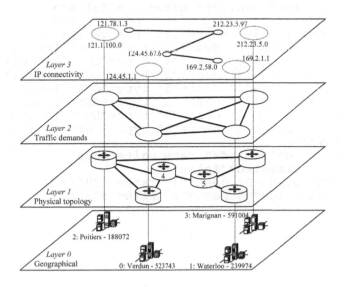

**Fig. 8  A four-layer problem instance.**

Remark that nodes 0 to 3 appear in the geographical and in the connection layer. They have to be defined in two distinct locations to comply with the layer separation rule: IP routing information does not have anything to do with geography.

Reversely, if in the Fig. 8 nodes 0 to 3 appear in all the four layers, no mention of their subject is made neither in physical layer nor network layer: no additional information is needed on these layers. They have however connecting links on theses layers, which is fully allowed.

```xml
<?xml version="1.0" encoding="UTF-8"?>
<network>
 <main_description>
   <layer id="geographical">
     <node id="0" pos_x="151" pos_y="237">
       <city label="Verdun" population="523743"/>
     </node>
     <node id="1" pos_x="342" pos_y="231"/>
       <city label="Waterloo" population="239974"/>
     </node>
     <node id="2" pos_x="151" pos_y="81"/>
       <city label="Poitiers" population="188072"/>
     </node>
     <node id="3" pos_x="344" pos_y="89"/>
       <city label="Marignan" population="591004"/>
     </node>
   </layer>
   <layer id="topology" directed="false">
     <node id="4" pos_x="199" pos_y="185"/>
     <node id="5" pos_x="281" pos_y="129"/>
     <link orig="0" dest="2" type="DCF" length="23"/>
     <link orig="0" dest="4" type="DCF" length="19"/>
     <link orig="4" dest="2" type="DCF" length="17"/>
     <link orig="4" dest="5" type="DCF" length="26"/>
     <link orig="5" dest="3" type="DSF" length="45"/>
     <link orig="1" dest="5" type="DCF" length="42"/>
     <link orig="1" dest="0" type="DSF" length="9"/>
   </layer>
   <layer id="demands" rate_unit="mbps"
          directed="false">
   <link orig="0" dest="1" rate="429"/>
   <link orig="0" dest="2" rate="523"/>
```

```
        <link orig="0" dest="3" rate="7008"/>
        <link orig="1" dest="0" rate="819"/>
        <link orig="1" dest="2" rate="416"/>
        <link orig="1" dest="3" rate="5840"/>
        <link orig="2" dest="0" rate="1245"/>
        <link orig="2" dest="1" rate="900"/>
        <link orig="2" dest="3" rate="6453"/>
        <link orig="3" dest="0" rate="3544"/>
        <link orig="3" dest="1" rate="4912"/>
        <link orig="3" dest="2" rate="815"/>
    </layer>
    <layer id="connection" directed="true">
        <node id="0" ip="124.45.1.1">
          <routing_table>
            <route dest="169/24" next="169.2.1.1"/>
            <route dest="121/24" next="169.1.100.0"/>
            <route dest="212.23/16" next="212.23.5.0"/>
          </routing_table>
        </node>
        <node id="1" ip="169.2.1.1">

  ...

        </node>
        <node id="2" ip="121.1.100.0">

  ...

        </node>
        <node id="3" ip="212.23.5.0">

  ...

        </node>

        <node id="6" ip="124.45.67.6" gway="124.45.1.1"/>
        <node id="7" ip="121.78.0.3" gway="121.1.100.0"/>
        <node id="8" ip="169.2.58.0" gway="169.2.1.1"/>
        <node id="9" ip="212.23.5.97" gway="212.23.5.0"/>
        <external_file filename="ip_dump.xml"
            content="connections with start time, dura-
tion,
            origin, destination and rate"
            regexp="[^,]*,[^,]*[^,]*[^,]*"/>
    </layer>
  </main_description>
</network>
```

**Fig. 9  A MND document related to an IP-over-WDM architecture.**

Once the first data set has been included, an application, RWA for instance, will read the structure using an XML parser, extract the needed information (from the physical and network layers) and feed it into the algorithm. When algorithm terminates, the results produced may be included into the initial MND document as illustrated in Fig. 10.

```
<layer id="demands" rate_unit="mbps"
         lightpath_rate= "2500" >
   <link orig="0" dest="1" rate="429" l_paths="1">
     <route path="0-4,4-5,5-1" wavelength="0"/>
   </link>
   <link orig="0" dest="2" rate="523" l_paths="1">
     <route path="0-2" wavelength="0"/>
   </link>
   <link orig="0" dest="3" rate="7008" l_paths="3">
     <route path="0-2,2-3" wavelength="1"/>
     <route path="0-2,2-3" wavelength="2"/>
     <route path="0-2,2-3" wavelength="3"/>
   </link>
   <link orig="1" dest="0" rate="819" l_paths="1">
     <route path="1-5,5-4,4-0" wavelength="2"/>
   </link>

     . . .

   <link orig="3" dest="2" rate="815" l_paths="1">
     <route path="2-3" wavelength="4"/>
   </link>
</layer>
```

**Fig. 10  The "demands" layer of the architecture described in Fig. 9, augmented with RWA results.**

## 4.    CONCLUSION

Integration of independent components is one of the most treated subjects in computer science, and has even connections with management theory [7].

An analysis of I/O data formats and characteristics of data exchange in a multilayer context shows that neither a unique nor a universal data format could be a suitable solution. The network description framework proposed in this paper aims at reaching a trade-off between these two extreme cases.

It facilitates the data exchange between various tools of a planning environment dealing with multilayer communication networks. In addition, it offers a good readability either for initial data or for intermediate and final results.

## ACKNOWLEDGEMENT

The authors wish to thank the Swiss Secretariat for Education and Research for supporting this work within the COST Actions 285 and 291.

## REFERENCES

[1]    A. N. Ince, *"European Concerted Research Action COST 285 Modelling and Simulation Tools for Research in Emerging Multiservice Telecommunications"*, Modelling and Simulation Tools for Emerging Telecommunications Networks, Springer, ISBN 0-387-32921-8, 2006.

[2]    A. Bragg, *"An Empirical Approach For Multilayer Traffic Modelling And Multimedia Traffic Modelling At Different Time Scales"*, Modelling and Simulation Tools for Emerging Telecommunications Networks, Springer, ISBN 0-387-32921-8, 2006.

[3]    M. Lackovic, C. Bungarzeanu, *"A Component Approach to Optical Transmission Network Design"*, Modelling and Simulation Tools for Emerging Telecommunications Networks, Springer, ISBN 0-387-32921-8, 2006.

[4]    M. Shaw, J. Bentley, *"Programming Pearl's"*, Communications of the ACM p. 898, Vol. 28, September 1985.

[5]    M. Pustisek, D. Savic, F. Potorti, *"Packaging Simulation Results With CostGlue"*, Modelling and Simulation Tools for Emerging Telecommunications Networks, Springer, ISBN 0-387-32921-8, 2006.

[6]    N. Walsh, *"A Techninal Introduction to XML"*, xml.com, O'Reilly Media, Inc. October 1998.

[7]    D. Garlan, R. Allen, J. Ockerbloom, *"Architectural mismatch or why it's hard to build systems out of existing parts"*, Proceedings of the 17th internation conference on Software engineering, p. 179-185, 1995.

# CHAPTER 7

# Modelling and Simulation Study of TCP Performance with Link Layer Retransmission and Fragmentation for Satellite-UMTS Networks

Zongyang Luo, Zhili Sun, Haitham Cruickshank

Centre for Communication Systems Research
University of Surrey
Guildford, Surrey, United Kingdom, GU2 7XH

**Abstract.** *Satellite-based Universal Mobile Telecommunications System (S-UMTS) is used to provide all kinds of Transmission Control Protocol/ Internet Protocol (TCP/IP) based Internet services for global end users. However, due to the high propagation delay and high bit error rates over satellite links, the TCP performance degrades considerably and affects many qualities of TCP based services. In this work, we focus on studying the TCP performance in S-UMTS using radio link control (RLC) with fragmentation and retransmission mechanisms. Analytical and simulation studies have been carried out to study this cross-layer problem. Two scenarios have been studied, i.e., the satellite operates in either transparent mode or with onboard processor (OBP) mode. The results indicate that the TCP performance can be enhanced substantially by employing the relay function using OBP and appropriate configurations of RLC parameters, thus providing useful information to the design the next generation communication satellite with onboard processing.*

## 1. INTRODUCTION

In the next generation mobile networks, users can use all kinds of TCP/IP based Internet services. However, when using wireless links, terrestrial or satellite links, we need to consider that the characteristics of these links are quite different compared to wired links. Wireless links usually have high bit error rates (BER), often combined with channel fading. At the same time, the uplink and downlink are usually asymmetric in nature and have very high propagation delay, particularly for geostationary (GEO) satellites. All the above link characteristics or even a subset of them can degrade the performance of the traditional TCP considerably. Initially, TCP was designed for wired networks; its congestion avoidance mechanism assumes that packet losses are caused by traffic congestion somewhere in the network, and attempts to alleviate congestion by reducing the packet sending rate. In wireless networks, packet losses mainly occur due to bad channel conditions; unfortunately, TCP regards these losses as consequences of network congestion, thus the sender reduces the packet sending rate accordingly, resulting in severe degradation of TCP throughput. In order to enhance TCP performance in wireless networks, researchers have proposed a number of solutions, which can be classified into three categories. The first one is lower layer solutions [1], such as Automatic Repeat reQuest (ARQ) and Forward Error Correction (FEC) at the link layer. The second one entails splitting connections [2]. This solution splits the connection between the wired networks and wireless networks. Normal TCP is used in wired segments and modified TCP or another protocol is used in the wireless networks segment. This approach destroys the end-to-end connection and requires the modification of the protocol stack on the nodes connecting wired networks and wireless network. The last solution is to adapt a new transport protocol to replace TCP [3, 4].

Many proposed solutions to enhance TCP performance over satellite, and the analysis on the interaction between TCP and link layer protocols [5, 6], have only considered satellites as a bent pipe transponder so far. Herein, we propose a novel RLC relay mechanism. We compare these two scenarios, i.e., satellite working in a bent-pipe mode and a satellite equipped with an onboard processor and Radio Link Control (RLC) protocol stack. For the rest of the text, we refer the first scenario as transparent mode and the second scenario as relay mode. In relay mode, the satellite segment can be considered as a two-hop network. The uplink and downlink can be considered as two separate RLC links unlike the transparent mode where the uplink and downlink constitute one RLC link.

## 2.    S-UMTS ARCHITECTURE

S-UMTS is a very important enhancement to the UMTS terrestrial networks, and aims to provide true global seamless mobile multimedia services [7]. The reference architecture of S-UMTS is depicted in Figure 1. It can be considered as two parts, the UMTS Satellite Radio Access Network (USRAN) and the UMTS IP Core Network (CN). USRAN has User Equipment (UE), satellite, and ground station. The ground station acts as the Base Station and Radio Network Controller (RNC). Here, the satellite is considered as a geostationary satellite. CN consists of the Serving GPRS Support Node (SGSN) and Gateway GPRS Support Node (GGSN). In our studies, the Node B and the Radio Network Controller (RNC) are assumed to be collocated in the S-UMTS gateway, which means that intra Node B handover is managed by the gateway. The NCC provides the fault, anomaly, configuration, performance, and security functions for management of the network and also co-ordinates the use of satellite resources among all gateways.

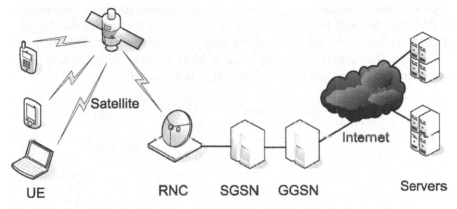

**Fig. 1  S-UMTS Architecture**

According to [9], the S-UMTS standard is originally derived from 3GPP UMTS with the inclusion of satellite channel characteristics. In the specifications, S-UMTS has user and control planes. Figure 2 depicts the protocol architecture of user plane. The RLC protocol runs in both the UE and RNC [8, 9]. It implements the regular link layer functionality over the WCDMA interface and provides segmentation and retransmission services for both user and controlling. Every RLC entity operates in one of the following three modes: Transparent Mode (TM), Unacknowledged Mode (UM) or Acknowledged Mode (AM). AM implements the ARQ function and it can provide reliable link layer data transmission. Here what we only care about is user plane and Acknowledged Mode. When an RLC entity is working in AM, ARQ is enabled and it usually works with FEC to provide more reliable data transfer. There are several ARQ methods, such as Stop and Wait (SW), Go Back N (GBN), Selective-Repeat (SR) and Negative ACKnowledgement mode (NACK).

## 3.    LAYER 2 DATA FLOWS

To help building the mathematic modelling, we illustrate some examples of how data flows are processed across the layer 2 to upper or lower layers. Data flows through layer 2 are characterized by the applied RLC transfer modes, acknowledged, unacknowledged or transparent mode, as mentioned above, in combination with the data transfer type on MAC (whether or not a MAC header is required). Since our interest is TCP performance with link layer fragmentation and retransmission, we use Dedicated Channel (DCH) as example to illustrate the data flow through layer 2.

Fig. 2 depicts the data flow when either Dedicated Traffic Channel (DTCH) or Dedicated Control Channel (DCCH) is mapped onto DCH. In the case when an acknowledged RLC retransmission mode is employed, the RLC header will be 2 to 4 bytes depending on the use of the length indicator (LI). When MAC multiplexing is assumed (i.e. DTCH and DCCH logical channels are multiplexed in MAC), then a MAC header of 4 bits; otherwise a transparent MAC operation is assumed.

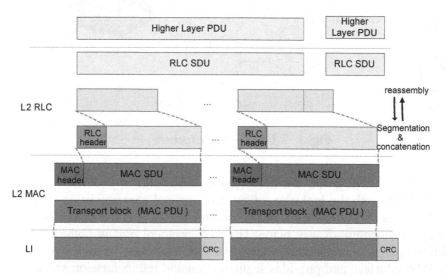

**Fig. 2  Data flow for DTCH or DCCH mapped to DCH**

In S-UMTS, the RLC layer provides segmentation and retransmission functionalities and it is capable of in-sequence delivery, duplication detection and piggyback control information. When it is working in AM, it uses a hybrid sliding window ARQ protocol with Selective ACKnowledgements (SACK) and Negative ACKnowledgements (NACK). Segmentation is performed when the RLC layer receives an RLC Service Data Unit (SDU) which is larger than the length of available space in AM mode data (AMD) Protocol Data Unit (PDU). The PDU size is conFigured by upper layers and can only be changed through re-establishment of the RLC-AM entry by the upper layer. If the receiver has not received the PDU successfully, it will use one the of the above ARQ mechanisms to send the STATUS PDU back to the sender. Acknowledge confirmation of received PDU will also be included in the STATUS PDU.

## 4.    MATHEMATIC MODELLING

In this section, we model the two scenarios for satellites working in transparent and relay modes. The previous work on TCP over wireless links mainly considers one hop networks only [10, 11]. Here we consider both one-hop and two-hop networks. The definitions and assumptions we use in our model are shown in Table 1.

**Table 1. Parameter Definitions**

| Parameter | Definition |
|---|---|
| $P_P$ | Point-to-point connection RLC packet loss probability. Here the point-to-point connection means the connection between two neighboring nodes with RLC protocol stack. |
| $M$ | Maximum number of RLC packet transmission attempts |
| $N$ | Number of RLC packets per TCP packet |
| $P_T$ | The probability of losing one TCP packet |
| $P_1$ | The up-link RLC packet loss probability |
| $P_2$ | The down-link RLC packet loss probability |
| $T_T$ | End-to-end delay of one TCP packet |
| $T_R$ | Delay of one RLC packet over point-to-point connection |

We assume $P_1$ and $P_2$ are independent. We only consider the satellite segments, i.e., uplink and downlink, while terrestrial segments are out of our discussion scope herein. We discuss these two scenarios from three aspects: end-to-end TCP packet loss rate, end-to-end TCP packet delay and TCP throughput.

## 4.1    Modelling of Transparent Mode

In this scenario, a satellite works as a transponder. The protocol stack in this scenario is depicted in Figure 3. Signals have gone up in one beam, been received at satellite, and the frequency has been shifted, amplified and transmitted down again. The connection between the source ground station and the end user can be considered as one point-to-point connection. When a TCP packet is transmitted, the source ground station fragments it into $N$ equal sized RLC packets which are transmitted via satellite to the end user. If a RLC packet lost or corrupted, it is retransmitted again using a certain ARQ mechanism. When all the RLC packets belong to one TCP packet are successfully received by the end user, they are reassembled into a TCP packet. If, after exhausting the retransmissions, some RLC packets are still missing, all the RLC packets belonging to a given TCP packet are dropped and this TCP packet is retransmitted.

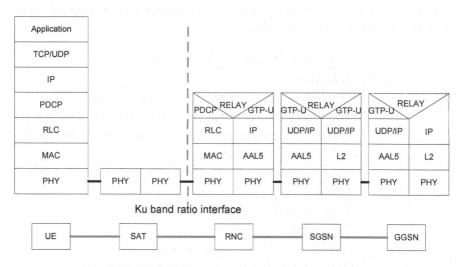

**Fig. 3    Protocol stack of transparent mode**

As for the performance metrics, first we derive the end-to-end TCP packet loss rate. In S-UMTS specification, when a TCP packet is fragmented to $N$ RLC packets, every RLC packet has maximum $M$ chances to be transmitted from the source ground station to the end user if it is lost or corrupted in the link. We assume one RLC packet needs $i$ times to be transmitted successfully. So the probability of successfully transmit a RLC packet after $i$ attempts is $P_P^{i-1} \times (1 - P_P)$, with $i \geq 1$. Therefore, probability of successfully transmitting an RLC packet is $\sum_{i=1}^{M} P_P^{i-1}(1-P_P)$, where $M$ is the maximum number of transmissions i.e. first transmission and subsequent retransmissions of one RLC packet. Thus, the probability of losing a TCP packet where it is fragmented into N RLC packet is

$$P_T = 1 - (\sum_{i=1}^{M} P_P^{i-1}(1-P_P))^N = 1 - (1 - P_P^M)^N \qquad (1)$$

In this scenario, as the RLC packet loss probabilities on the uplink and downlink, $P_1$, $P_2$, are independent, we have

Substituting equation (2) for $P_P$ in equation (1), we get the TCP packet loss rate as equation (3).

$$P_T = 1 - \{1 - [P_1 + (1 - P_1) \times P_2]^M\}^N \qquad (3)$$

The next performance metric to be modelled is the end-to-end TCP packet delay. The end-to-end TCP packet delay is the time spent by all the $N$ RLC packets transmitted successfully from the source ground station to the end user; this is given by $T_T = N \times M_{avg} \times T_R$, where $T_R$ is the round trip time of one RLC packet transmitted from the source ground station to the end user and $M_{avg}$ is the average times of one RLC packet transmission. We can derive as equation (4).

$$M_{avg} = \frac{1 - P_P^{M+1}}{1 - P_P} - (M+1) \times P_P^{M+1} \qquad (4)$$

Thus using equations (2) and (4), we can get the end-to-end TCP packet delay as equation (5).

$$T_T = N \times [(\frac{1 - (P_1 + (1 - P_1) \times P_2)^{M+1}}{1 - (P_1 + (1 - P_1) \times P_2)} - (M+1) \times (P_1 + (1 - P_1) \times P_2)^{M+1}] \times T_R \qquad (5)$$

We use Padhye's TCP model [12] in our studies to analyze the end-to-end TCP throughput. Padhye's model is based on TCP Reno. For the duration of the data transfer, the sender sends full-sized segments as fast as the congestion window allows, and the receiver has a normal delayed acknowledgement implementation, whereby it sends an acknowledgement for every $b$ data segments. The model considers the packet loss due to triple-duplicate (TD) loss indication and time-out (TO) indication. Then it computes duration of TD and TO period and the number of data packets transmitted in the respective periods. The throughput formula of TCP throughput is $B(p)$, which is based on packet loss rate $p$, round trip time $RTT$, retransmission timeout $T_O$, and the maximum receive window $W_{max}$.

$$B(p) = \begin{cases} \dfrac{(1-p)/p + E[W] + Q(E[W])/(1-p)}{RTT \times (E[W]) \times b/2 + 1) + Q(E[W]) \times T_0 \times f(p)/(1-p)} & \text{if} \quad E[W] < W_{max} \\ \dfrac{(1-p)/p + W_{max} + Q(W_{max})/(1-p)}{RTT \times (W_{max} \times b/2 + (1-p)/(p \times W_{max}) + 2) + Q(W_{max})T_o \times f(p)/(1-p)} & \text{otherwise} \end{cases} \quad (6)$$

Using equations (3) and (5) in equation (6), we can obtain the equation of TCP throughput considering RLC packet retransmission.

## 4.2   Modelling of Relay Mode

In this scenario, a satellite is doing the relay function we proposed. Unlike transparent mode, the satellite here is equipped with an onboard processor and RLC protocol stack functionalities. The protocol stack on board is depicted in Figure 4. The connection between the source ground station and the end user via satellite can be considered as two point-to-point connections. The first point-to-point connection is the uplink and the other one is the downlink link. When a TCP packet is about to be transmitted, the source ground station fragments it into RLC packets that are transmitted to the satellite. When the satellite receives the RLC packets, it uses buffer to store the RLC packets received. After all the RLC packets belonging to the same TCP packet are received at the buffer, they are transmitted again to the end user. In this case, the satellite provides a relay function and provides reliable RLC transmission on both the uplink and downlink. If one RLC packet is lost on the uplink, a certain ARQ mechanism is invoked to ask the source ground station to resend the RLC packet. If after several retransmissions, the satellite still cannot receive the RLC packet, all the RLC packets in the buffer are dropped and all the RLC packets belonging to this TCP packet will be retransmitted again from the source ground station. When all the RLC packets belonging to one TCP packet arrive at the satellite, they are transmitted to the end user via downlink. If there are some RLC packets lost or corrupted, the end user exercises a specified ARQ mechanism to ask the satellite to resend the RLC packets from the buffer. If the end user still cannot receive all the RLC packets from the satellite, it drops all the RLC packets received and asks the satellite to resend all the RLC packets belong to the TCP packet again.

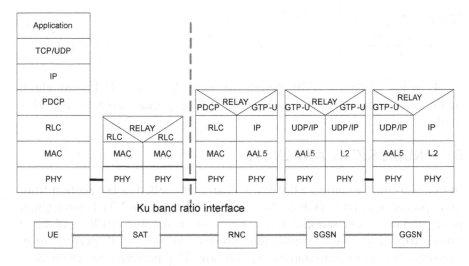

**Fig. 4  Protocol stack of relay mode**

In this scenario, we also derive the end-to-end TCP packet loss rate first. As the RLC packet loss rate on the uplink and downlink are independent, the probability of successful transmission of a given RLC packet is $\sum_{i=1}^{M} P_1^{i-1}(1-P_1)$ for the uplink and $\sum_{i=1}^{M} P_2^{i-1}(1-P_2)$ for the downlink. Thus the probability of successful transmission of a given RLC packet from the source ground station to the end user is $[\sum_{i=1}^{M} P_1^{i-1}(1-P_1)] \times [\sum_{i=1}^{M} P_2^{i-1}(1-P_2)]$. The probability of losing a TCP packet where it is fragmented into $N$ RLC packet is given by equation (7).

$$P_T = 1 - \{[\sum_{i=1}^{M} P_1^{i-1}(1-P_1)] \times [\sum_{i=1}^{M} P_2^{i-1}(1-P_2)]\}^N$$
$$= 1 - (1 - P_1^M)^N \times (1 - P_2^M)^N \tag{7}$$

Regarding the end-to-end TCP packet delay, we can consider it from the uplink and downlink separately. One successful TCP packet transmission requires all the RLC packets belong to this TCP packet successful transmission both on the uplink and downlink. So the end-to-end TCP packet delay consists of the total RLC packets transmission delay on the uplink and downlink as equation (8). Here $T_R$ is the RLC round trip time on uplink or downlink.

$$T_T = T_{T_{up}} + T_{T_{down}} \tag{8}$$

$$= N \times [\frac{1 - P_1^{M+1}}{1 - P_1} - (M + 1) \times P_1^{M+1}] \times T_R + N \times [\frac{1 - P_2^{M+1}}{1 - P_2} - (M + 1) \times P_2^{M+1}] \times T_R$$

By using Padhye's TCP model, we can obtain the TCP throughput while substituting equations with different RLC packet loss rates for relay mode.

## 5.    NUMERICAL ANALYSIS

In this section, we compare the two scenarios modelled in last section from TCP packet loss rate, TCP packet end-to-end delay and TCP throughput point of views. On satellite links, high bit error rates (BER) and large round trip time have significant impact on the TCP performance. Consequently, our discussion centres on how TCP performance changes as BER changes. In the following discussion, BER means BER on downlink. The TCP performance metrics are the functions of BERs on both uplink and downlink and the Figure plotted is a three dimensional. In order to make results clearer, we only change BER on downlink and fix the uplink bit error rate ($BER_{UP}$). With equations derived in last section, we plot some typical Figures to discuss the results.

Figure 5 and Figure 6 show the TCP packet loss rate versus BER. We set the RLC fragment number, $N$, to 5 and vary the maximum number of transmission attempts, $M$, with 1, 5 and 10 in Figure 5. We can see when BER increases from $10^{-8}$ to $10^{-4}$, the TCP packet loss rate remains stable and are almost the same in both two scenarios. When BER is over $10^{-4}$, TCP packet loss rate in both scenarios starts to increase rapidly but the performance in relay mode is better than in transparent mode. When BER is really high, reaching $10^{-1}$, the TCP packet loss rate in both scenarios becomes close to 1, which means almost all the TCP packets are lost in very bad channels. Figure 6 is TCP packet loss rate when the number of fragments per TCP packet changes while the maximum number of transmission attempts is fixed. We can see there is not much difference between the two satellite modes for BER values up to $10^{-4}$ beyond which the TCP packet loss rate starts to increate in both scenarios but the TCP packet loss rate in relay mode is still lower than in transparent mode. When the channel condition becomes very poor, all the TCP packets will get are lost in both scenarios. In both Figure 5 and Figure 6, we also find that the TCP packet loss rate decreases when we increase the transmission attempts or fragmentation numbers.

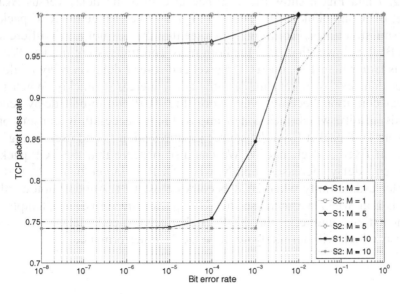

**Fig. 5  TCP packet loss rate, N = 5, M varying, $BER_{UP} = 10^{-2}$**

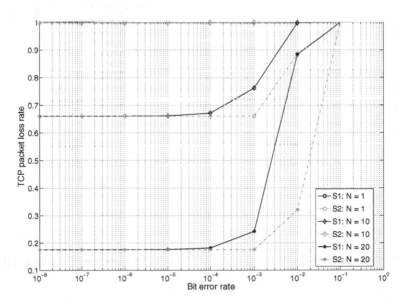

**Fig. 6  TCP packet loss rate, M = 5, N varying, $BER_{UP} = 10^{-2}$**

Fig. 7 and Fig. 8 show the TCP packet end-to-end delay versus BER. We set BER on uplink to $10^{-4}$ here. In Figure 7, we change the RLC packet retransmission times. From Fig. 7, we see that there is not much difference when BER is lower than $10^{-5}$ for both relay and transparent modes. When BER is larger than $10^{-5}$, the TCP packet end-to-end delay in relay mode is shorter than in transparent mode although it increases quickly. When the channel condition becomes very poor, the TCP end-to-end delay tends towards infinity, which means it is impossible to successfully transmit one complete TCP packet from the source ground station to end user. In Fig. 8, we set $M$ fixed and change $N$. We can also observe that the TCP packet end-to-end delay increases rapidly when BER is larger than $10^{-5}$ and it tends towards infinity when BER becomes close to 1. Another noteworthy point is that when we increase the RLC packet transmission attempts or fragmentation numbers, the TCP packet end-to-end delay will also increase, which will definitely degrade the TCP performance.

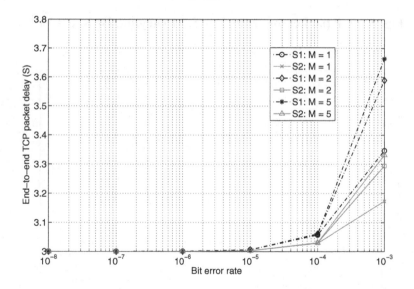

**Fig. 7  End-to-end TCP packet delay, N = 5, M varying, BER$_{\text{UP}}$ = $10^{-4}$**

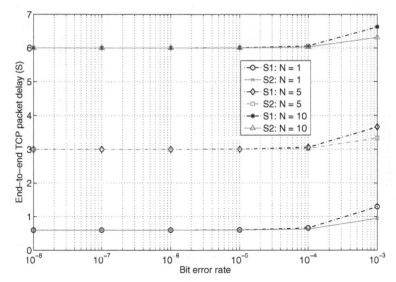

**Fig. 8  End-to-end TCP packet delay, M = 5, N varying, BER$_{UP}$ = 10$^{-4}$**

Fig. 9 and Fig. 10 show the TCP throughput versus BER. We set BER on uplink to 10$^{-2}$ here. The RLC packet fragmentation number, $N$, is set to 5 and RLC retransmission times, $M$, is varying with 1, 5 and 10. It can easily be seen that TCP throughputs in both relay mode and transparent mode are the same when BER is lower than 10$^{-5}$ in Fig. 9. The throughput decreases as the channel condition becomes poorer. When BER increases to around 10$^{-2}$, the TCP throughput becomes almost zero. Fig. 10 shows that the TCP throughput starts to decrease when BER increases to about 10$^{-5}$. As RLC packet transmission attempts and number of RLC fragments increase, the TCP throughput will increase in both relay and transparent modes.

From the above three different metrics, we can say that RLC packet fragmentation and retransmission mechanism enhance some aspects of TCP performance. For example, when we apply these two mechanisms, the TCP packet loss rate decreases and throughput increases; but at the same time, they incur an increase in the TCP packet end-to-end delay, which may degrade the TCP performance as it may cause the TCP sender to timeout. It is also very clear that the TCP performance in relay mode is much better than in transparent mode. We are sure this could be a possible way to enhance TCP performance in satellite networks when onboard processing technology is applied in the future.

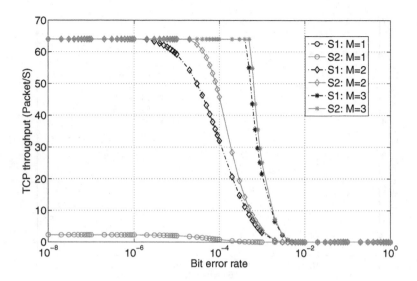

**Fig. 9 TCP throughput, N = 15, M varying, $BER_{UP} = 10^{-4}$**

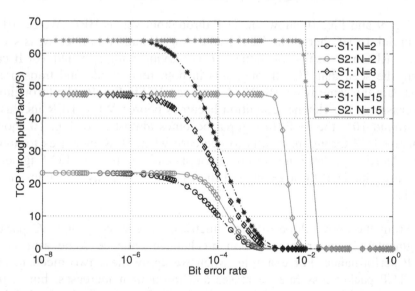

**Fig. 10 TCP throughput, M = 2, N varying, $BER_{UP} = 10^{-4}$**

## 6.    SIMULATION AND RESULT ANALYSIS

In this section, we will simulate these two scenarios and discuss the simulation results. In this work we have extended the networks simulator ns2 v2.1b7a [13] to assess the performance of RLC relay mechanism and compare it with transparent mode in S-UMTS. ns2 is a widely used open-source simulator in research area. It supports flexibly configurable and programmable simulations of different telecommunication network scenarios, satellite networks, wireless ad hot networks, local area networks and wide area networks. It also supports many communication protocol simulations from the physical layer to application layer. If some algorithms are not supported, users can develop it by themselves because it is a kind a open source simulator. In our work, we implement the RLC relay function with SR-ARQ in ns2. In the simulation, we use TCP NewReno. TCP packet size is set to 1024 bytes. The transport channel bandwidth is set to 64 kb/s. We choose ARQ-SR in AM mode. The propagation delay for uplink and downlink is 125ms respectively. FTP is used as application and each simulation runs 2500 seconds.

Fig. 11 and Fig. 12 show the TCP throughput versus different $BER_{UP}$ with different RLC packet segmentation in one TCP packets while the maximum RLC transmission attempt is set to 5. When $BER_{UP}=10^{-2}$, which means the channel condition is very poor on downlink, we can see that the maximum TCP throughput increases from 1.45 kb/s to 29.33 kb/s and 42.26 kb/s with 1, 5 and 10 RLC packet segmentations in one TCP packet using transparent mode. When we deploy the RLC relay mode, the maximum TCP throughputs are around 2.34 kb/s, 38.64 kb/s, and

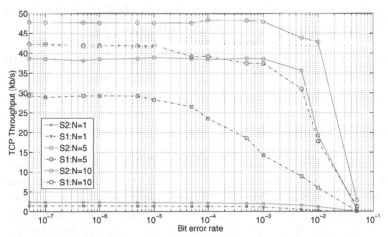

**Fig. 11 TCP throughput, M = 5, N varying, $BER_{UP}= 10^{-2}$**

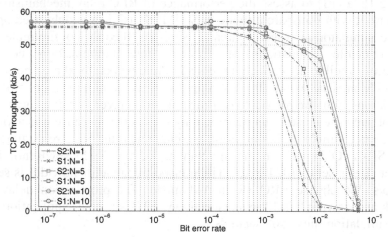

**Fig. 12  TCP throughput, M = 5, N varying, $BER_{UP}= 10^{-4}$**

47.78 kb/s, respectively, which are 61%, 31%, and 13% better than transparent mode. When downlink channel conditions become better, e.g., $BER_{UP}=10^{-4}$, we can find that the maximum TCP throughput is around 55 kb/s when BER is around $10^{-7}$ for both transparent mode and relay mode in Figure 12. But when uplink channel conditions is getting worse, e.g., $10^{-2}$, the TCP throughput of relay mode is clearly larger than of transparent mode regardless of the number of maximum RLC transmissions. From both Figure 11 and Figure 12, we see that the TCP throughput increases significantly when the RLC transmission times increase.

Fig. 13 and Fig. 14 show the TCP throughput versus different $BER_{UP}$ with different maximum RLC packet transmission attempts. We can find that the maximum TCP throughput is larger when the RLC relay is deployed compared with transparent mode, especially when the channel condition is poor, e.g., $BER=10^{-2}$.

From the simulation results, we also find the average TCP packet end-to-end delay also decreases when RLC relay is deployed. For example, when the RLC packet maximum transmission attempts is 5 and one TCP packet is segmented to 5 RLC packets, the average TCP packet end-to-end delay is decrease from around 1700 ms to 1300 ms in poor channel condition, e.g., $BER_{UP}=10^{-3}$.

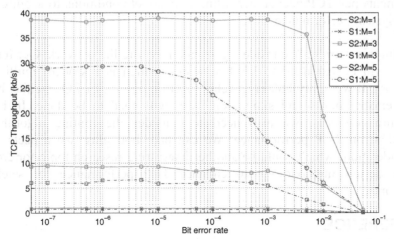

**Fig. 13 TCP throughput, N = 5, M varying, $BER_{UP} = 10^{-2}$**

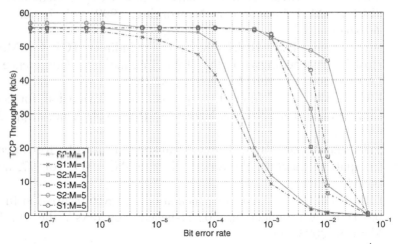

**Fig. 14  TCP throughput, N = 5, M varying, $BER_{UP} = 10^{-4}$**

## 7.    CONCLUSION AND FUTURE WORK

In this work, we study the TCP performance with link layer retransmission and fragmentation for S-UMTS networks. We provided an analytical model to study the system performance for both transparent mode and the RLC relay mode. Both the analytical and simulation results indicate that deploying RLC relay in S-UMTS networks offers significant gains in TCP throughput and end to end delay, particularly at high bit error rates. Our future work will be on how to dynamically set parameters, such as RLC fragments per TCP packet, according to channel conditions to acquire the best system performance.

But this work only considers geostationary satellite network. Our future work will be extended to LEO networks, which is a kind of multi-hop network. If we apply link layer relay function on every LEO satellite, both mathematic model and simulation work will need to be done. In LEO satellite networks, we also need to consider the routing algorithm's affection on TCP performance. We can take both this two aspects into consideration, which could be another interesting research topic for cross-layer design methodology to enhance TCP performance for satellite networks.

## REFERENCE

[1]    H. Chaskar, T.V. Lakshman, U. Madhow, "TCP over Wireless with Link Level Error Control Analysis and Design Methodology", IEEE/ACM Transaction on Networking, 1999, vol. 7, no. 5, pp. 605-615.

[2]    Ajay Bakre, B.R. Badrinath, "I-TCP: Indirect TCP for Mobile Hosts", Proceedings of the 15th International Conference on Distributed Computing Systems, May, 1995.

[3]    R.C. Durst, G.J. Miller, E.J. Travis, "TCP Extension for Space Communications", Wirless-Networks, 1997, vol. 3, no. 5, pp. 389-403.

[4]    T.R. Henderson, R.H. Katz, "Transport Protocols for Internet-Compatible Satellite Networks", IEEE JSAC 1999, vol. 17, no. 2, pp. 345-359.

[5]    Fethi Filali, "Link-Layer Fragmentation and Retransmission Impact on TCP Performance in 802.11-based Networks", the 7th IFIP MWCN, 2005.

[6]    Jing Zhu, S. Roy, "Improving Link Layer Performance on Satellite Channels with Shadowing via Delayed two-copy Selective Repeat ARQ", IEEE JSAC, vol. 22 , no. 3 , pp. 472-481, 2004.

[7]    Zhili Sun, "Satellite Networking Principles and Protocols", John Wiley & Sons, Ltd, 2005.

[8]    Victor Yong Hwa Kueh, "Session Establishment over an IP-based Satellite UMTS Network", Ph.D thesis, University of Surrey, 2004.

[9]    "Satellite Earth Stations and Systems (SES); Satellite Component of UMTS/IMT-2000; General aspects and principles", ETSI Technical Report, September, 2002.

[10]   A. Chockalingam, Zorzij Michele, "Wireless TCP Performance with Link Layer FEC/AKQ", In Proceedings of IEEE International Conference on Communications, 1999.

[11]   Chadi Barakat, Alaeddine AL FAWAL, "Analysis of Link-level Hybrid FEC/ARQ-SR for Wireless Links and Long-lived TCP Traffic", Performance Evaluation Journal, vol. 57, no. 4, pp. 423-500, August, 2004.

[12]   J. Padhye, V. Firoiu, D.F. Towldy, J.F. Kurose, "Modeling TCP Reno Performance: a Simple Model and Its Empirical Validation", IEEE/ ACM Transaction on Networking, 2000, vol. 8, no.2, pp. 133-145.

[13]   The Network Simulator (ns), http://www.isi.edu/nsnam.

# CHAPTER 8

## The Design of a FPGA-Based Traffic Light Control System: From Theory to Implementation

Ramón Martínez Rodríguez-Osorio, Miguel Á. Fernández Otero,
Miguel Calvo Ramón, Luis Cuéllar Navarrete,
Leandro de Haro Ariet

Grupo de Radiación. Dpto. de Señales, Sistemas y
Radiocomunicaciones. Universidad Politécnica de Madrid
ETSI de Telecomunicación. Ciudad Universitaria s/n. 28040
Madrid – SPAIN

**Abstract.** *Most software-defined radio (SDR) prototypes make use of FPGA (Field Programmable Gate Array) devices such as digital filtering that perform operations at high sampling rates. The process from specifications and design to the implementation in FPGA requires the use of a large number of simulation tools. In the first stages of the design, the use of high-level tools such as Matlab, are required to perform intensive simulations. Results will help us to select the best specifications. Once the main design parameters have been established, the overall design is divided into modules following a hierarchical scheme. Each module is defined using a hardware description language (HDL) such as VHDL or Verilog.*

*In the process of FPGA development, the design is simulated at multiple stages. Initially, each VHDL module is simulated individually by creating test benches to simulate the subsystem and observe the results. After each individual module has been tested, the complete design is integrated and mapped into a netlist which is translated to a gate level description. Once the design is laid out in the FPGA, a simulation stage takes place considering hardware aspects such as propagation delays.*

*Finally, it is very important to perform cosimulations for the final hardware verification. Cosimulation consists in applying input signals from numerical simulators such as Matlab to hardware components from hardware-based simulators such as ModelSim. Only the inputs and outputs of the hardware component are analyzed to check the performance.*

*In this paper, we discuss the overall simulation process involved in the implementation of a FPGA-based modem used in a traffic light control system using LEDs (Light Emitting Diodes). The application of LEDs in traffic lights has several advantages with respect to incandescent bulbs in terms of lower power consumption and a number of functions can be implemented: modification of lighting condition depending on climatic conditions, change in the crossing time for pedestrians, failure detection, generation of alarms, etc. In order to implement these applications, the installation of modems in the regulator and traffic lights sites is required.*

*In our proposal, these modems are implemented in FPGA boards. As an additional innovation, the physical transmission medium is formed by the powerlines connecting the regulator and traffic lights in a star topology. The communication system is based on the EchoNet standard for powerline communication. This specification proposes the use of the CDMA multiple access scheme, which makes the system very robust against impulsive noise interference oftenly found in traffic scenarios.*

*We have focused on the design flow, making special emphasis on the simulation tools required and the main parameters that must be taken into account to perform an efficient design. In the paper, performance results obtained by simulation and cosimulation will be presented, including parameters of the communication system (BER, frame detection probability) and also result from the hardware simulation tool (power consumption, delays, use of physical resources).*

## 1.    INTRODUCTION

Since the beginning of traffic signalling as a tool for traffic control, traffic lights have worked by means of incandescent lights, with a power supply of 220 V, in conjunction with a crystal diffuser or tinted methacrylate with the appropriate colour (red, green or amber) and a front reflector.

A traffic light group is defined as a set of traffic lights which are controlled by the same regulator, which acts as a master or coordinator.

The regulator operates under an intelligent system that allows for controlling the lights status depending on time, traffic conditions, etc.

In the last 70 years, several innovations on the original concept of traffic light control have been introduced. These innovations consist in the introduction of complex routines such as macro-and micro-regulation, redundancy to increment the security, more efficient and economical reflectors, etc. However, one aspect that remains the same in all the cases is the use of incandescent lights as the lighting element.

During the 80s, a new lighting technology was introduced: Light Emitting Diodes, most commonly known as LED. LEDs can be power supplied with a dc voltage and are able to emit light in a specified wavelength. LED technology is commonly used in displays, panel indicators, remote controls, television screens, etc.

LED technology has experienced a great evolution in the last few years, having a lower fabrication cost with the possibility of having LED with different illumination colour. LEDs are specially constructed to release a large number of photons outward. Additionally, they are housed in a plastic bulb that concentrates the light in a particular direction.

The application of LEDs in traffic lights has several advantages with respect to incandescent bulbs:

- LEDs do not have a filament that burn out, so that they do not get especially hot in contrast to incandescent bulbs;
- LEDs last much longer than incandescent lamps, which means that the long term operation and maintenance costs are significantly lower than for incandescent bulbs;
- Light production process is significantly more efficient than in incandescent bulbs, where a huge portion of the available power supply is used to heat the filament and is not directly used in the production of light;
- A large number of applications can be implemented with LEDs as traffic lighting elements: modification of lighting condition depending on climatic conditions, change in the crossing time for pedestrians, failure detection, generation of alarms, etc.

In order to implement these applications, a certain level of intelligence is required in both the traffic light and the regulator. Therefore, a communication link must be established, so that a transceiver must be installed in both sites of the link (traditional traffic control systems are unidirectional from regulator to traffic lights, without any response from the status of the traffic lights).

There are different transmission media than can be used. Physical layers based on radio technology are likely to receive the disturbances provided by impulsive noise from car engines, which is a significant interference contribution in different frequency bands. Wired technologies such as fiber, coaxial or copper lines are not available between traffic light and regulator, so that a significant deployment cost is required. Therefore, the use of power lines as transmission media is foreseen as the most appropriate technology as there is no need of deploying new infrastructure.

The scope of this contribution is to present a PLC-based smart traffic light control, where the communication link is established using the power lines used to feed the traffic light groups.

The structure of the paper is as follows. Section 2 describes the system and details the specifications of he communication system. Section 3 focuses on the implementation, in particular, hardware details, resources consumed and strategies to optimize the design are included. Section 4 is the core part of the paper, as it deals with the role of simulation along the design: the project is divided in three stages which corresponds to different simulation levels, design, hardware verification and cosimulation. Finally, section 5 concludes the paper.

## 2.    SYSTEM ARCHITECTURE AND SPECIFICATIONS

The architecture of the communications system must take into account the topology of the power lines that supply power to each traffic light. In typical situations, low voltage power lines are installed from the regulator to the traffic lights, resulting in a star topology.

According to the deployment of traffic light groups, the topology of the communication system from the regulator to the traffic lights follows a point-to-multipoint architecture. This means that a regulator controls several of traffic lights in a number that depends on each particular situation. Usually, a regulator controls all the traffic lights used to manage the traffic in a street crossing, as it can be seen in Fig. 1 Distances between the regulator and the traffic light groups typically vary in a range from 70 to 400 m.

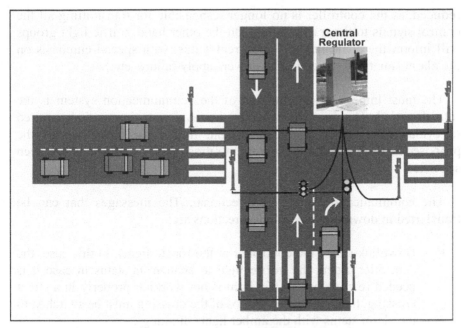

**Fig. 1 Typical traffic regulation scenario.**

In a traffic light control system, the required bit rate is low enough to be transmitted through power lines. Furthermore the conditions of the propagation channel are favourable to establish the link as typical conducted interference that appear in a PLC-based system is not found in traffic control scenario (dedicated low voltage lines to power supply the traffic lights are used). On the other hand, the star based topology reduces channel impairments such as impedance mismatching, echoes and multipath propagation.

There are different architectures to implement the control system. In present traffic control systems, the intelligence of the system is completely installed in the controller, so that the regulator is in charge of switching lights, generate alarms, etc. This is carried out by means of a power interface board composed of triacs and optocouplers between the traffic lights and the controller.

The architecture of the proposed system is based on the installation of a PLC modem in both the traffic light group and in the controller. Apart from the communications tasks, the PLC modem installed in the traffic light takes charge of the light operation. This new concept means that the information flow between traffic light and regulator is significantly reduced, as the controller is no longer responsible for transmitting all the control signals to the traffic lights. On the other hand, traffic light groups will inform the controller of the current status, with special emphasis on the alarm situations (fused lights, power supply failure, etc.).

The most important specification of the communication system is the refresh period. This interval indicates the maximum time period required to evaluate the status of a traffic light. In the particular case of the proposed traffic light control system, a refresh period of 100 ms has been specified.

The communication link is bidirectional. The messages that can be transferred in downlink and uplink directions are:

- Downlink (from the controller to the traffic light): in this case, the controller orders the traffic light to change its status in case it is needed (e.g., if one traffic light is not working properly in a street crossing, then the rest of groups of the crossing must be switched to the alarm status with the amber lights blinking);
- Uplink (from the traffic light modem to the controller): the traffic light group sends information about the current status of the lights (normal operation, fusing, etc.).

Normally, one traffic controller takes charge of more than one traffic group. In our application, each traffic controller is able to control up to 8 traffic light groups.

The transmission is organized in time frames of 100 ms. Each frame is divided in 9 time slots, following a TDD duplex scheme: the first time slot is for the downlink transmission, where the information for all the traffic lights groups is sent simultaneously using CDMA (one code per traffic light group). In the uplink, each traffic light group transmits in a different time slot with its corresponding code. The reason for choosing CDMA resides in the electromagnetic environment that appears in a traffic control scenario, where there is a number of impulsive noise sources coming from motor ignition [2][3]. Therefore, the multiple access scheme is TDMA/CDMA in the uplink, and CDMA for the downlink. Fig. 2 shows the system architecture with a description of multiple access and duplex schemes.

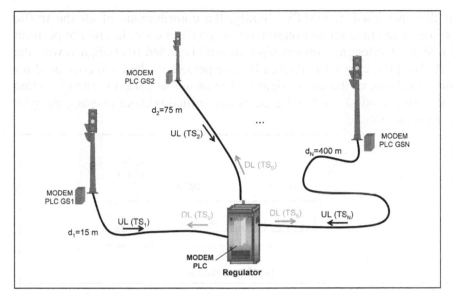

**Fig. 2  Point-to-multipoint topology of the communication network.**

Carrier frequency has been selected taking into account two factors. First, the signal must avoid spectral contributions in the 50 Hz band, as they would be filtered out by the coupling unit. Secondly, carrier frequency must be low enough to allow the implementation of most of the subsystems in the FPGA.

The configuration of each time slot has been adapted from the Echonet specifications for the powerline transmission media [4]. Each time slot is divided in three fields: preamble (8 bits), synchronization (16 bits) and data (16 bits).

Fig. 3a shows the structure of a frame in the downlink. Guard intervals are inserted between time slots to account for the propagation delays between different traffic lights paths. Typical propagation delays that appear in a real scenario are in the range of 0.23 to 1.66 µs.

The transmission scheme in the downlink is shown in Fig. 3b. The preamble is a period of a Gold code with good autocorrelation properties [5]. Gold codes can be implemented with a minimum number of resources in the selected hardware platform [6]. The preamble interval is used for the detection of a transmission. The synchronization and data fields are concatenated and then spread by a family of 32-chip Walsh codes, similar to the ones used in UMTS. Finally, the contributions of all the traffic groups is summed up and scrambled by the Gold code. In order to perform the slot detection, a common pilot channel is added time-aligned with the slot. The pilot channel is formed by five periods of the Gold code used for the scrambling of the users' signals. The preamble period is empty, so that only one period of the Gold code is transmitted without overlapping with other contributions.

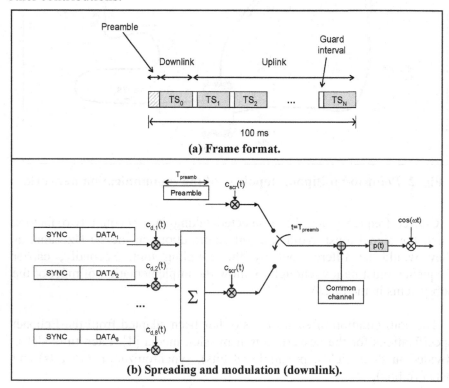

(a) Frame format.

(b) Spreading and modulation (downlink).

Fig. 3  Features of the communication system.

## 3.    IMPLEMENTATION

The block diagram of the prototype for the modem in the traffic light is shown in Figure 7. It is formed by an FPGA (Field Programmable Gate Array) connected to an interface board with the lighting element, a digital-to-analog and analog-to-digital converter. Then, the signal is injected in the power line using a commercial coupling unit. In the regulator, the block diagram is similar except for the interface with the light elements (as an application, the modem in the controller can be connected with a PC through the RS232 or USB interfaces).

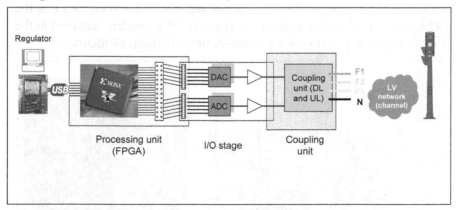

**Fig. 4  Block diagram of the system.**

The FPGA board selected for this prototype is a Spartan 3-E evaluation board [7]. The selection of an FPGA as the device for controlling the system is motivated for its flexibility and because the number of I/O ports (pins) is large enough to connect several lighting element. The clock of the FPGA is 100 MHz [8].

The available bit rate depends on the spreading factor, the time slot duration and the FPGA clock. With 40 bits per slot, a spreading factor of 32 and a guard interval of 6.8 ms, the maximum bit rate is 12.5 kbit/s. However, the bit rate can be halved in situation where the guard interval can be reduced up to 3.4 ms. Therefore, the chip rate can be easily obtained dividing the FPGA clock rate by 250 or 500.

Using an oversampling of 4 for the root-raised cosine filtering, the base band sample rate is 800 or 1600 ksamples/s. With this sample rate and taking into account the FPGA clock, we can think of a sigma-delta ($\Sigma\Delta$) modulation to implement the digital-to-analog conversion [9]. Thanks to the noise shaping produced by the oversampling factor and low-pass filtering, the number of required resolution bits is reduced in comparison with a uniform quantization. Implementing one-bit $\Sigma\Delta$ modulator included in the FPGA, the number of hardware devices of the prototype is reduced (note that for the digital-to-analog conversion, a fast comparator is required [10]). The selected oversampling rate must be much higher than twice the maximum signal frequency. The carrier is centered in 400 KHz.

Fig. 5(a) shows the connection of the interface board with the FPGA module in the traffic light position. The interface provides an indication of the status of LEDs, measuring the voltage reduction due to the fact that the LED light is fused. In the initial prototype, the PLC modem installed in the traffic light site is prepared for the monitoring of 8 light elements.

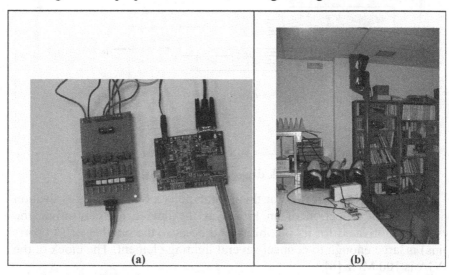

(a)                                          (b)

**Fig. 5  (a) Interface board connected to the modem in the traffic light group. (b) Testbed for the smart traffic light control based on PLC.**

In the following sections, we will describe the role and use of simulation on the design process.

The implementation for the MODEM has been divided in two phases: transmitter and receiver. We have begun with the transmission side, taking into account that some module will be replicated in the receiver side. Moreover, the implementation of the transmitter modules has taught us about the number of FPGA resources consumed by each module, so that the optimization phase will focus on the most complex sections.

Fig. 6(a) shows the block diagram of the transmitter. It is formed by three subsystems: GEN_SLOT, which generates the data to be transmitted according to the traffic light status, the digital upconverter (DUC), and the clock manager (CLOCK_GEN). In the design, four clocks are required to process bits, chips and samples rates.

The core of the transmitter is DUC, as it includes the operations of interpolation, baseband signal conditioning with a square root raised cosine filter of 19 taps, interpolation, BPSK-modulation, and digital-to-analog conversion.

Cascaded integrated-comb (CIC) filters are used in the DUC for the interpolation and sample-rate increase before filtering and modulation [11]. CIC digital filters are computationally efficient implementations of low pass filters without multipliers that are often embedded in digital hardware implementations. The generation of the 400 KHz carrier is implemented storing the samples of the cosine function in an internal RAM block from the FPGA device.

Fig. 6(b) shows the number of slices consumed in the FPGA by the transmitter. The percentage of device utilization is 35% of the 960 slices, where CLOCK_GEN, GEN_SLOT and DUC consume 19 (1%), 112 (11%) and 216 (22%), respectively. The CIC is composed of two taps, consuming the 7% of the slices. It is important to mention that the DAC based on a $\Sigma\Delta$ structure consumes less than 1%. Along with the receiver, the complete modem with interfaces occupies 90 % of one FPGA.

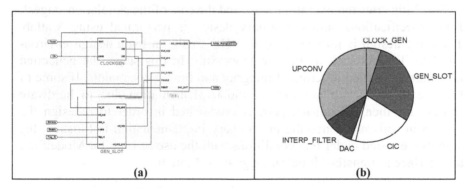

**Fig. 6 (a) Block diagram for the transmitter implementation.**
**(b) Device utilization: number of consumed slices**
**(Spartan 3-E evaluation board).**

## 4. THE ROLE OF SIMULATION IN THE DESIGN PROCESS

One of the most difficult stages of the system implementation is the verification and debug stages. In order to achieve success in this stage, we have used many tools that are able to implement simulations at different levels of our system in order to define the features and performance of the modem. Simulations have been a critical part in the initial stages of the project.

These tools are Mentor Graphics ModelSim 6.0, Matlab, and another tool from Mathworks: Link for ModelSim, that we have used to do cosimulations between ModelSim and Matlab simultaneously. With Link for ModelSim, we can do simulations with ModelSim in order to obtain a signal, then we can use Matlab on this signal to analize it or to use this treated signal on a ModelSim simulation.

The simulation tools that have been required during the research project can be divided in two groups:

- Numerical simulators, such as Matlab, that are used in the design process to define the characteristics of the signal (modulation), and also to estimate the performance limits of the prototype;
- Simulators to verify the hardware implementation, such as ModelSim: these tools help to validate the correct timing of clock signals, debug and optimize the design, etc.

Fig. 7 illustrtes the overall process and the role of the simulation stages[1]. First, specifications and preliminary design is performed using Matlab. Then, the design is implemented in VHDL using a logic design environment for FPGAs such as ISE or ModelSim. In this stage, the generated hardware is verified in terms of integrity and timing constraints. If some of the specifications are not met in the implementation due to hardware limitations, then a feedback path is established in order to redesign the system in software. Once the preliminary implementation is finished, the signals are tested under real conditions with the use of Link for ModelSim, an interface to transfer ModelSim signals to Matlab.

Let us start with the description and application of Matlab to the system under study.

---

[1]  Matlab/Simulink, ISE and MoodelSim are trademarks of The Mathworks, Xilinx and Mentor Graphics, respectively.

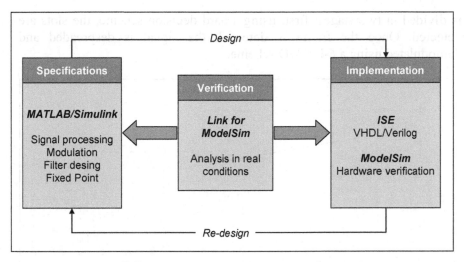

Fig. 7  Design scenario with simulation tools.

## 4.1  Simulation Stage for Design

Matlab is, probably, the most popular and powerful simulation tool available to perform simulations and design. This software environment can carry out simulations of multiple aspects of the system. First of all, Matlab has been a fundamental tool on the specification stage of the communication system of the project. Extensive simulations have been done to analyze which communication system best fits, to study the performance of the CDMA codes used, to evaluate how the system works in noisy scenarios, etc.

Matlab has been useful to design the communication system in the following terms:

- Selection of the most appropriate modulation, multiple access and duplex schemes, as well as the frame format to decide the information transmitted in uplink and downlink;
- Once CDMA has been chosen, the group of CDMA codes and its spreading gain has been defined;
- Test the modem under real conditions, such as noise, interference, etc.;
- Design of the receiver scheme (correlation, synchronization, etc.).

As an example, Fig. 8 shows the simulations performed to design the receiver based on correlations. As a result of the simulations, the reception is divided in two stages: first, using a hard decision scheme, the slots are detected. Once the frame is detected, the signal is despreaded and demodulated using a 6-bit A/D scheme.

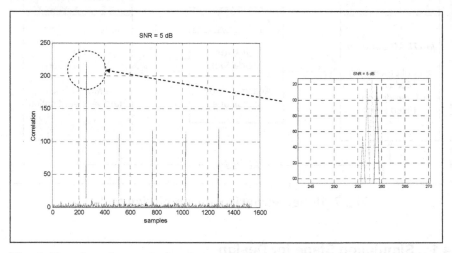

**Fig. 8  Results of correlation based on hard decision for detecting the slot (SNR=5 dB).**

The receiver scheme is shown in Fig. 9. The motivation for implementing the proposed receiver is to reduce the resources consumed by the correlator, whose computations are rather intensive in terms of multiplications and sums when words of more that one bit are used. The complete system would require a more advanced FPGA, if the correlation would have been performed on the received 6-bit words.

Results obtained with Matlab have also been important for selecting the appropriate hardware platform. As an example, consider the features of the D/A converter: its resolution (i.e., number of bits per quantized sample) has to do with a number a aspects such as the number of users present in the system, noise level, etc. The wider the word is, the better performance will be obtained at the cost of expending more hardware resources.

Thanks to these preliminary simulations, the system has been designed and the implementation in VHDL starts, according to the specifications obtained from the design phase. Matlab has also been used for making cosimulations with ModelSim, using the Link for ModelSim tool.

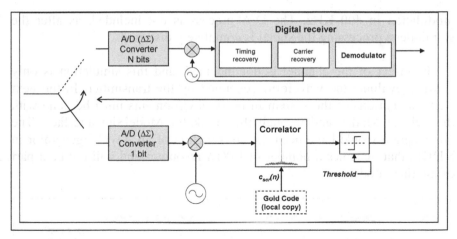

**Fig. 9 Receiver structure.**

## 4.2    Simulation Process for Hardware Verification

Once the implementation is ready, the signals taking part in the process must be analyzed. The only way to go insight the physical hardware platform is by means of hardware simulators. One of these tools is the Mentor Graphics hardware description language (HDL) simulator, named ModelSim SE/PE.

ModelSim SE has been shown to be a fundamental tool in the VHDL implementation stage. Using ModelSim, it has been possible to perform simulations to verify all the modules that form each subsystem of our modem. These simulations consist essentially of the stimulation of the in-ports of the module with the suitable signals, so that we can test the operation of the module under simulation. In order to check it, we must specify a *testbench* file with proper clock and input signals (enable, reset, data, etc.). This file can be created using the assistant included in ModelSim SE, or programming it with a hardware description language like VHDL. The last option gives us flexibility and control over the tests, so that this has been the option most used in the project.

In order to illustrate this situation, we have included several figures obtained from the simulation of most important subsystems of our modem, like transmitter, correlator, descrambling module and despreading module.

Fig. 10 shows the simulation of the whole transmitter. The figure shows the signal that the FPGA board sends to the powerline channel after modulation in 400 KHz. The D/A process is not included, as after the sigma-delta processing the signal is completely distorted.

The effect of the channel is not included, and this simulation is only valid to evaluate the waveform generated by the transmitter. In the next step, simulations of the system in noisy environments must be done with the help of Matlab and through thee Link for ModelSim interface. The other option would have been the construction of an AWGN generator in VHDL, that occupies a number of FPGA resources and will not be a part of the final modem.

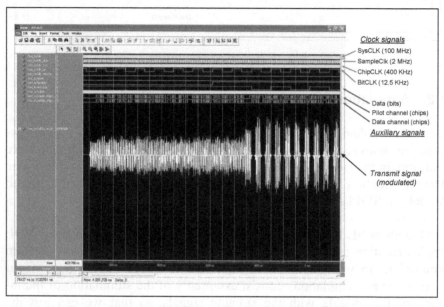

**Fig. 10   Process of signal generation in the transmitter side (clock, auxiliary and transmit signals).**

As an example of why hardware verification through simulations is required follows. In the process of design, the receiver must correlate the received signal with a copy of one Gold period formed by 256 chips. Therefore, the maximum value of the correlation after hard decision, considering a perfect time alignment between the local copy of the Gold code and the received samples, is 256.

However, during the implementation, it has been shown that a correlation during 256 cycles of the chip period would consume a large number of resources, due to the relation between different clocks. The correlation is implemented through LFSRs (Linear Feedback Shift Register) structures available in the FPGA architecture.

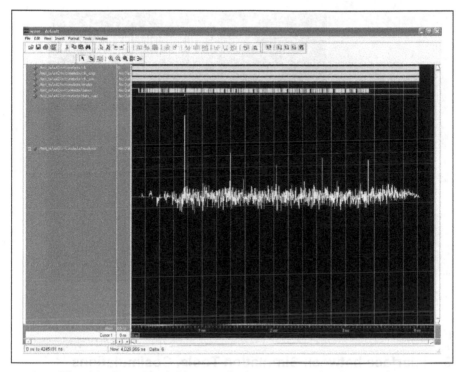

**Fig. 11   Result of the correlation process in the receiver.**

After analyzing several alternatives, a correlation with 250 clock cycles was found to give a huge saving in the hardware resources. Precisely, 250 is the relation between system and chip clocks (2 MHz and 400 KHz, respectively). In case of using 256 chips, we would need another shift register to store the 6 final chips of the code to complete the correlation, therefore consuming additional memory resources.

Because of that, we need to go back to Matlab to analyze the effect of the new correlation process on the slot detection process, and calculate the new threshold to optimize the probability of detection and probability of false alarm under different channel realizations.

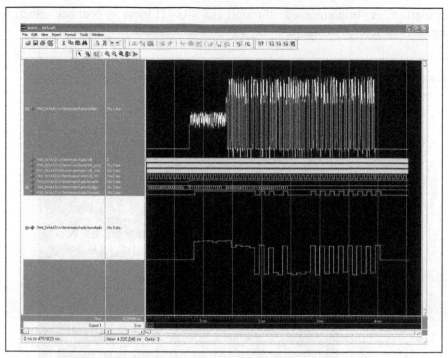

**Fig. 12  Result of the demodulation in the receiver.**

## 4.3    Interface between Simulation Tools, Cosimulations

So far, we have seen how the signals are generated through hardware verification. In order to test the signals in a noisy scenario or evaluate the signal filtered by a multipath time-variant propagation channel, we must transfer signals to Matlab in the form of a vector of samples, where the channel is easily simulated. The process of using a mix of simulation tools, being software and hardware-oriented, can be denoted as cosimulation.

Fig. 13 shows the cosimulation scheme. The interface between ModelSim and Matlab is made through Link for ModelSim, a cosimulation interface that integrates MathWorks tools into the Electronic Design Automation (EDA) workflow for field programmable gate array (FPGA) and other devices. The interface provides a fast bidirectional link between the ModelSim and Matlab for direct hardware design verification and cosimulation [12].

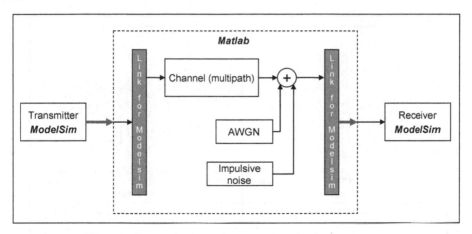

**Fig. 13   Description of the cosimulation process.**

Now, we can process this signal generated by the hardware platform with Matlab and add white Gaussian noise (with the predefined "awgn" function) or any other channel impairment present in the low-voltage powerline. The signal distorted by the channel is sent back to the receiver implemented in VHDL in order to evaluate the performance in different scenarios. Results are shown in the next plots. First, Fig. 14 shows the received signal for different SNR levels. The figures show a time interval slightly longer than one slot.

Fig. 15 shows the signals in different points of the receiver obtained from ModelSim for different SNR values. From top to down, the following five signals can be seen: received signal, demodulated waveform, result of the correlation during one slot, signal before dispreading (chips) and demodulated bits.

As it can be seen, the system fails to detect the slot for SNR under -12.5 dB. The correlator does not detect any valid correlation peak to trigger the descrambling and despreading modules. When noise power is significantly higher than signal power, the correlation peak is reduced, and in case of using a hard decision on the received samples, the degradation is even more important. In these scenarios, if the detection threshold is reduced, then the probability of detecting a slot in a wrong position (probability of false alarm) is increased.

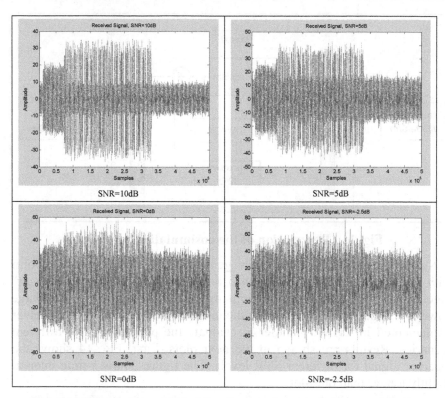

**Fig. 14  Signals transmitted by the hardware platform with the AWGN added in Matlab.**

It is to be noted that, the correlator implemented in the FPGA is not perfect, as not all the chips are considered in the correlation in order to economize hardware resources and improve the occupied area on the FPGA. For this reason, the maximum correlation peak that can be obtained is lower than the theoretical maximum, implying an additional degradation of 0.3 dB in the correlation level.

Finally, in the simulations for SNRs under -10 dB, the receiver is saturated due to the high noise level added. This saturation event causes a negative effect on the system performance in noisy environments. As a consequence, the SNR of -10 dB is considered as the preliminary limit of operation of the system.

In order to choose an appropriate threshold for detecting a slot, a detailed study on the statistics of the maximum correlation values for different scenarios is required. The result of the analysis will be a threshold value to ensure a given probability of detection. Fig. 16 shows the cumulative distribution functions (CDF) obtained from the histograms of the correlation peak for a wide range of possible SNR levels.

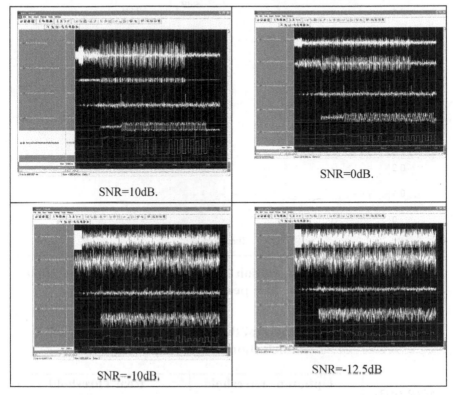

**Fig. 15   Demodulation results in the receiver for different SNR.**

Table 1 shows the threshold required to obtain a probability of detection over 95%. Results show the theoretical optimum threshold in case of using one entire Gold code period (256 chips) for carrying out the correlation, and the real value that comes from the implementation, where only 250 chips are correlated.

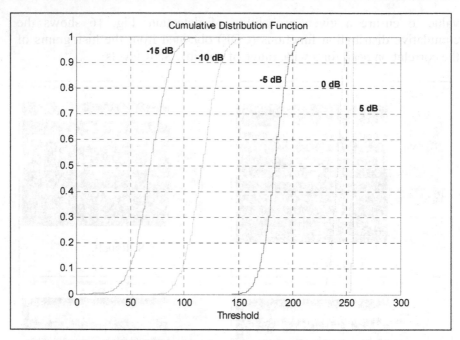

**Fig. 16  Cumulative distribution functions for the first correlation peak.**

**Table 1 Optimum and real thresholds for a probability of detection of 95%.**

| SNR (dB) | Optimum Threshold $P_D = 0.95$ | Real Threshold $P_D = 0.95$ |
|---|---|---|
| -15 | 45 | 39 |
| -12.5 | 65 | 59 |
| -10 | 95 | 89 |
| -7.5 | 127 | 121 |
| -5 | 166 | 160 |
| -2.5 | 202 | 196 |
| 0 | 232 | 226 |
| 2.5 | 247 | 241 |
| 5 | 254 | 248 |
| 7.5 | 256 | 250 |
| 10 | 256 | 250 |

One technique to improve the detection process consists in analyzing the subsequent correlation peaks along the slot. During one slot interval, the pilot channel is formed by five periods of the Gold code. The last four periods provide a good correlation peak, but smaller than the first one due to the presence of synchronization and data fields. The resulting CDF for these peaks is shown in Fig. 17. It can be seen how the average peak value is reduced as compared with the first one, so that a lower threshold must be used (between 41 and 115 for a probability of detection of 95%, depending on the SNR).

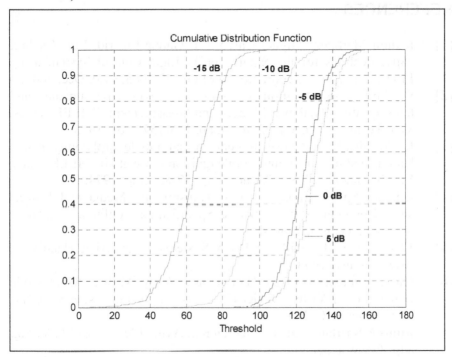

**Fig. 17  Cumulative distribution functions for the rest of correlation peaks.**

## 5.    CONCLUSIONS

In this contribution, we have presented the design of a smart system for traffic light control, using low-voltage powerline communications as transmission media. The specifications and architecture of the prototype have been shown.

The core part of the contribution is the description of the design process with a special emphasis on the simulation stages required to prototype a first version if the modem. The impact of different simulation processes in the design has been fully described including the tools used for that purpose.

Different simulation stages lead to solve the limitations that may appear during the design and implementation. In this research work, it has been found justifiable to evaluate the impact of reducing the correlation window on system performance, as a consequence of optimization.

## REFERENCES

[1]    Ramón Martínez, Miguel Calvo, F.J. García-Madrid, Luis Cuéllar, "Specifications for the Smart Traffic Light Control System using LED technology," Report No. UPM/GR/27/2005, v1.0, Dec. 2005.

[2]    D. Middleton, "Man-made noise in urban environments and transportation systems: Models and measurements," IEEE Trans. Veh. Technol., vol. VT-22, no. 4, pp. 148-157, Nov. 1973.

[3]    R. A. Shepherd, "Measurements of amplitude probability distributions and power of automobile ignition noise at HF," IEEE Trans. Veh. Technol., vol. VT-23, no. 3, pp. 72-83, Aug. 1974.

[4]    Echonet Specifications, Part 3: Transmission Media and Lower-layer Communication Software Specification [online]. Available: www.echonet.gr.jp/english.

[5]    J. S. Lee, L. E. Miller, CDMA Systems Engineering Handbook, Artech House, 1998.

[6]    Maria George, Mujtaba Hamid, and Andy Miller, "Gold Code Generators in Virtex Devices," Xilinx Application Note xapp217, v1.1, January 10, 2001.

[7]    Xilinx® Spartan™-3E Evaluation Kit, Avnet Electronics Marketing, http://www.avnet.com.

[8]    Xilinx Spartan™-3E FPGAs, Reference Documentation [online]. Available: http://www.xilinx.com/spartan3e.

[9]    Steven R. Norsworthy, Richard Schreier, and Gabor C. Temes, Delta-Sigma Data Converters: Theory, Design, and Simulation, IEEE Press, 1997.

[10]   "Demystifying Sigma-Delta ADCs," Maxim Application Note AN1870, January 2003.

[11]   E. B. Hogenhauer, "An economical class of digital filters for decimation and interpolation," IEEE Trans. on Acoustics, Speech and Signal Processing, vol. 29, no. 2, pp. 155-162, April 1981.

[12]   Link for ModelSim, Data sheet, The Mathworks, 2006.

# CHAPTER 9

# Distributed Multihop Clustering Approach for Wireless Sensor Networks

Nauman Israr, Irfan Awan

Mobile Computing Networks and Security Research Group
School of Informatics
University of Bradford, UK

**Abstract.** *Prolonging the life time of Wireless Sensor Networks (WSNs) has been the focus of current research. One of the issues that needs to be addressed along with prolonging the network life time is to ensure uniform energy consumption across the network in WSNs especially in case of random network deployment. Cluster based routing algorithms are believed to be the best choice for WSNs because they work on the principle of divide and conquer and also improve the network life time considerably compared to flat based routing schemes. In this paper we propose a new routing strategy based on two layers clustering which exploits the redundancy property of the network in order to minimise duplicate data transmission and also make the intercluster and intracluster communication multihop. The proposed algorithm makes use of the nodes in a network whose area coverage is covered by the neighbouring nodes. These nodes are marked as temporary cluster heads and later use these temporary cluster heads randomly for multihop intercluster communication. Performance studies indicate that the proposed algorithm solves effectively the problem of load balancing across the network and is more energy efficient compared to the enhanced version of widely used Leach algorithm.*

**Keywords.** Distributed Clustering, efficient cluster based routing, energy efficient routing, multilayer clustering.

## 1.  INTRODUCTION

Wireless Sensor Networks (WSNs) generally consist of nodes with sensing, computing and communication capability connected according to some topology and to a sink for external communication. The network is capable of monitoring activities and phenomenon which can not be easily monitored by humans such as the site of a nuclear accident, some chemical field monitoring, or environmental monitoring for a longer period of time. The general characteristics of WSNs include continuously changing topology [1] due to nodes in different states and dying nodes as the network evolves, dense deployment of the network, autonomous network management, multihop communication, limited node energy [2] and limited bandwidth. Because of the short range of the radio communication and since consumption of energy is proportional to the square of the distance [3], making communication multihop instead of direct communication will save energy in WSNs. Since computation is less expensive than data transmission in WSNs, each node tries to perform computation on data locally, thus resulting in a reduced amount of data to be forwarded. For example, to calculate the median of a data sample at a node is much more efficient than to transmit the sample data and calculate the median at the sink. WSNs are data centric networks and because of the sheer number of nodes it is not efficient to give unique identification numbers (ID) to sensor nodes. The nodes are usually referred to with respect to the type or the range of data they are dealing with [4]. These networks are highly application specific so the architecture of protocol operation varies from application to application. One routing algorithm might be good for periodic monitoring, but may not perform well where it will have continuous data sensing.

WSNs have tremendous applications in different areas such as civil, agriculture, environment, health and military. The WSNs can be used to automate the environment of large civil structures to report the conditions within an area where human presence for a longer period of time is not feasible. Engineering applications include maintenance in a large industrial plant or monitoring of civil structures, regulation of modern buildings in terms of temperature, humidity etc. Other applications include forest fire detection, flood detection [5] etc.

The rest of the paper is organised as follows. Section 2 includes the challenges and issues in WSNs. Section 3 is an overview of related work.

Section 4 describes the algorithm, Section 5 includes simulation and discussion and Section 6 concludes the paper.

## 2.   CHALLENGES AND ISSUES IN THE WSNs

Despite the tremendous potential and numerous advantages like distributed localised computing, communication in which failure of one part of the network does not affect the operation in other parts of the network, longer area coverage, on-the-fly network setup, and extreme environment area monitoring, WSNs pose various challenges to the research community. This section briefly summarizes some of the major challenges faced by researchers in the field of WSNs.

♦   *Limited Resources*

The primary challenge in WSNs is that they have limited resources in terms of battery power, computation, memory and limited bandwidth to communicate .Other constraints of WSNs are directly or indirectly related to limited resources in WSNs.

♦   *Network Deployment*

Node deployment in WSNs is either fixed or random depending on the application. In fixed deployment the network is deployed in predetermined locations, whereas in random deployment the resulting distribution may not cover the area completely. In such a case, careful management of the network is necessary in order to ensure entire area coverage and also to make sure that the energy consumption is also uniform across the network.

♦   *Heterogeneous Network*

WSNs are not always uniform. In some cases a network is heterogeneous, consisting of nodes with different energy levels. Some nodes are less energy-constrained than others. Usually the fraction of nodes which are less energy-constrained is small. In such types of networks, the least energy-constrained node is chosen as cluster head of the cluster and the energy-constrained nodes are the worker nodes of the cluster. A problem arises in such networks when the network is deployed randomly and all cluster heads are concentrated in a particular part of the network, resulting in an unbalanced cluster formation and also making some parts of the network unreachable. Even if the resulting distribution of the cluster heads is uniform and we use multihop communication, the nodes which are close to the cluster head are under heavy load as all the traffic is routed from different areas of the network to the cluster head via the neighbours of the cluster head .This will cause quick dying of the nodes in the vicinity of the cluster heads, resulting in holes near the cluster heads and decreasing the network connectivity and also increasing the network energy consumption. Heterogeneous sensor networks require careful management of the clusters in order to avoid the problems resulting from unbalanced cluster head formation, as well as to ensure that the energy consumption across the network is uniform.

♦   *Network Scalability*

When WSNs are deployed, sometimes new nodes need to be added to the network in order to cover more area or to prolong the lifetime of the current network. In both cases the clustering scheme should be able to adapt dynamically to changes in the topology of the network. The key point in designing the management scheme is that it should be local and distributed in nature.

♦   *Uniform Energy Consumption*

Transmission in WSNs is more energy-consuming compared to sensing and computing, therefore the cluster heads which perform the function of transmitting the data to the base station consume more energy compared to the rest of the nodes. Clustering schemes should ensure that energy dissipation across the network is balanced and the cluster heads should be rotated in an efficient way in order to balance the network energy consumption.

♦   *Multi Hop or Single Hop Communication*

The communication model that wireless sensor networks use is either single hop or multihop. Since energy consumption in wireless systems is directly proportional to the square of the distance, single hop communication is expensive in terms of energy consumption. Most of the routing algorithms use a multihop communication model because it is more energy efficient in terms of energy consumption. However, with multihop communication the nodes nearer to the cluster head are subjected to heavy traffic intensity and can create holes near the cluster head when their energy expires. Multihop communication can cause delay; so there is a tradeoff between delay and energy consumption.

♦ *Attribute Based Addressing*

Because of the sheer number of nodes it is not possible to assign IDs to individual nodes in WSNs. Data is accessed from nodes via attributes, and not by IDs. This makes intrusion into the system easier and implementing a security mechanism difficult.

♦ *Cluster Dynamics*

Cluster dynamics addresses how the different parameters of the cluster are determined, for example, the number of clusters in a particular network. In some cases the number might be preassigned whereas in other cases it might be dynamic. The cluster head performs the function of compression as well as transmission of data. The distance between cluster heads is an open research issue. It can be dynamic, or can be set in accordance with some minimum value. If dynamic, there is a possibility of forming unbalanced clusters. Limiting it by some preassigned minimum distance can be effective in some cases. Cluster head selection can either be centralised or decentralised. Both have advantages and disadvantages. The number of clusters might be fixed or dynamic. A fixed number of clusters causes less overhead in that the network will not have to go again and again through the set up phase in which clusters are formed. In terms of scalability it is poor.

♦ *Security Issues*

The use of wireless links makes WSNs susceptible to attacks. So far there exist few algorithms that implement security in wireless sensor networks. The sheer number of nodes in a sensor network makes it difficult to implement any centralised scheme for the network, which includes security and any other central-based administration tasks.

♦ *Common Platform*

One of the important open research issues in wireless sensor networks is the design of different architectures of WSN networks for different purposes. A periodic data sensing algorithm may not be able to perform efficiently on a continuous data sensing algorithm.

♦ *Robustness*

The network should be robust enough that the death of some nodes does not affect the functionality of the entire network, and route configuration should be such that failure of one route should not affect routine data transmission. In heterogeneous networks, nodes which are near the cluster heads die faster, making unbalance energy consumption in the network. In such a case the sensor network should be able to cope.

## 3.    RELATED WORK

This Section provides a brief introduction to various clustering-based routing algorithms for WSNs. Leach [3] was one of the first hierarchal routing approaches for sensor networks. Most of the clustering algorithms are based on this algorithm. This protocol uses only two layers for communication. One is for communication within the clusters, and the other is between the cluster heads and sink. The cluster head selection is random and the role of cluster heads rotates so as to balance the energy consumption throughout the network. Clusters are formed depending upon the signal strength of the cluster head advertisement message each node receives. Nodes will go for the one which has the strongest signal to it. The algorithm also calculates the total number of cluster heads for the network, which is 5% of the entire network. Simulation results show that Leach performs over a factor of 7 reductions in energy dissipation compared to flat base routing algorithms such as direct diffusion [6]. The main problem with the Leach protocol lies in the random selection of cluster heads. There exists a probability that the cluster heads formed are unbalanced and may be in one part of the network, making some parts unreachable.

An extension of the Leech protocol (Leach-C [7]) uses a centralized cluster formation algorithm. The algorithm execution starts from the base station. The base station first receives all the information about each node's location and energy level. The base station runs the algorithm for the formation of cluster heads and clusters. The number of cluster heads is limited and the selection of the cluster heads is also random, but the base station makes sure that a node with less energy does not become a cluster head. However Leach-C is not feasible for larger networks because nodes far from the base station will have problems sending their states to the base station, and since the role of cluster heads rotates, the far nodes will not reach the base station in enough time, increasing the latency and delay.

The routing algorithm in Leech is based on two phases: the setup phase of cluster head selection and cluster formation. Since the cluster head role is rotated, both steps are rotated every time new cluster heads are selected. Leach-F [7] uses the idea that if the cluster remains fixed and only rotates the cluster head role within the cluster, this will save of energy and increase the system throughput. The disadvantage is a lack of scalability within the network, meaning that new nodes cannot be added.

Teen [5] is for time critical applications that respond to sudden changes in sensed data. Here the nodes continuously sense data but occasionally transmit data when the data is in the interest range of the user. The cluster head uses two value thresholds. One is a hard threshold and the other is a soft threshold. The hard threshold is the minimum value of the attribute that triggers the transmission from node to cluster head; the soft threshold is a small change in the value of the sense attribute. The node will transmit only when the value of the attribute changes by an amount equal to or greater than the soft threshold. The soft threshold reduces transmissions further if there is no significant change of the value of the sense attribute. The advantage of this scheme is its suitability for time critical applications and that it significantly reduces the number of transmission and gives the user control in the accuracy of the value of the attribute collected, by varying the value of the soft threshold (see Fig.1).

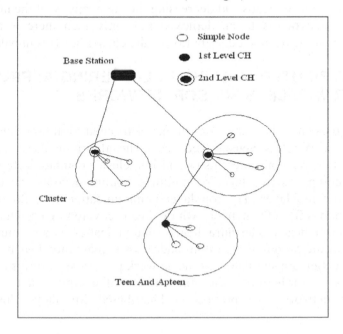

**Fig. 1 Clustering in TEEN and APTEEN**

Apteen [8] is an extension to Teen, and is a hybrid protocol for both periodic data collection and for time critical events data collection. The cluster head broadcasts several types of messages to the node: values of the threshold, attributes' values, and a TDMA scheduling scheme allowing every node a single slot for transmission. Simulation shows that Teen and Apteen perform better than Leach in terms of energy consumption, and Teen performs better than the other two. The disadvantage is that since there is multilevel clustering in Teen and Apteen, they result in complexity and overhead. (see Fig.1)

Energy-aware routing for cluster based sensor networks [9] is a multi-gateway architecture to cover large areas of interest without degrading the service of the system. The algorithm balances the load among different clusters at clustering time to keep the density of the cluster uniform. The network incorporates two types of nodes: sensor nodes which are energy constrained, and gateway nodes which are less constrained. Gateways maintain the state of the sensors as well as setting up multihop routes for collecting sensor data. The nodes use a TDMA-based Medium Access Control (MAC) for communication with cluster heads. The disadvantage is that since the cluster heads are static and less energy constrained than the rest of the nodes and are fixed for the lifetime of the network, the nodes close to the cluster head die quickly compared to other nodes, thus creating holes near the cluster heads and decreasing the connectivity of the network Also if the network is to be deployed randomly then there is a high probability that the resultant distribution of the cluster heads is unbalanced.

## 4.   DISTRIBUTED MULTIHOP CLUSTERING APPROACH FOR WIRELESS SENSOR NETWORKS

In [10] we presented the framework of the Distributed Multihop Clustering Approach for Wireless Sensor Networks. The algorithm uses multihop communication for both intercluster and intracluster communication. The algorithm comprises two layer of multihop communication, the bottom layer and the top layer. The top layer communication is multihop and comprises nodes from the network whose area is covered by its neighbours and the cluster heads. The intracluster communication is also multihop. The problem the proposed algorithm addresses is that when Leach and its enhanced version are simulated, as the network progresses it forms clusters of dead nodes; furthermore, the consumption of energy is not uniform across the network. We propose a Distributed Multihop Clustering

Approach for intercluster communication in order to solve the uneven energy consumption of Leach and its enhanced version.

The proposed algorithm comprises three distinct phases. The initialization phase in which the network starts for the first time and each node broadcasts its location, range and area it covers; after this the nodes build a table of neighbours; following the setup phase, the steady phase is similar to Leach. In the initialization phase, the algorithm selects those nodes in the network whose sensing area is covered by its neighbours using the method discussed in [11] in which each node calculates its sensing area and compares it with that of its neighbours. If the sensing area of one node is fully embraced by the union set of its neighbours such that its neighbours can cover the current node's sensing area, the node becomes a temporary cluster head without reducing the system's overall sensing coverage and later uses a preassigned percentage of nodes from the temporary cluster heads in multihop intercluster communication. All the nodes in the network follow the same procedure. After the cluster heads are selected randomly, the cluster heads broadcast an advertisement message. Depending on the message strength, each node makes the decision to join a cluster. This phase uses Code Division Multiple Access Medium Access Control (CSMA MAC) protocol, and during this period all nodes are listening. The selection of the cluster head depends on probability, and is similar to Leach. During each cycle the cluster head selection is random and depends on the amount of energy left in the node and its probability of not being a cluster head during the last n rounds. A sensor node chooses a random number between 0 and 1. If this number is less than the threshold T (n), the sensor node becomes a cluster head.

$$T (n) = P / \{1 - P[r \bmod (1/P)]\} \text{ if n is element of H} \qquad (1)$$

◆   P is the desired percentage of cluster head (5%).
◆   r is the current round.
◆   H is the set of nodes that have not been cluster heads in the last 1/P rounds.

Once the cluster heads are selected and a cluster is formed, the algorithm forms two network layers – the top layer which will comprise the temporary cluster heads and the bottom layer which will comprise member nodes of the clusters. After the set up phase, the steady phase (transmission phase) starts in which all nodes transmit data using TDMA scheduling. When all the nodes in the cluster finish, the cluster head performs computations and sends results to the base station via multihop using the temporary cluster heads. The role of the cluster head is rotated randomly after some predefined time. Figure 2 depicts the general operation of the protocol.

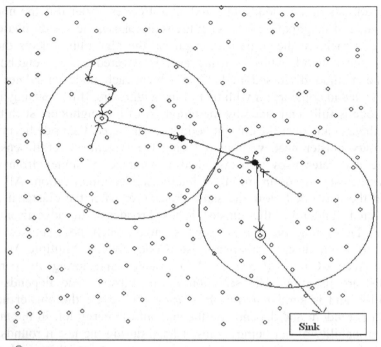

⊙    Cluster Head
●    Temporary cluster head

**Fig. 2 General operation of the proposed Algorithm**

We model the network as a directed weighted graph S=(N,L) with N as a set of nodes and L as set of edges. An edge l belonging to L from nodes n1 to N and n2 to N is represented as l(n1,n2).The path to the cluster head followed by a node can be a sequence of <n1,n2,n3,...,nk> of the nodes such that edge (Lk-1,Lk) belongs to L for k=1,2,3,..k, the path containing nodes n1,n2n3,...,nk, and links (L0,L1),(L1,L2),...(Lk-1,Lk).

The nodes in the network are of three types

♦ Sensing Nodes
These nodes are assigned the task of sensing the data in particular region and, depending upon the protocol, if necessary try to perform computations on the data locally and forward it to the cluster head.

♦ Cluster Heads
The cluster head is responsible for collecting the data from a cluster and performing computations on it if possible, and forwarding the data to the sink or gateway either via single hop or multihop.

♦ Temporary Cluster Heads
Are nodes in the network whose sensing area is covered by its neighbouring nodes. The algorithm eliminates these nodes as sensing nodes and makes them temporary cluster heads, so they serve as a relay station during the intercluster communication. The energy consumption model is given below.

For node transmission the energy consumption is based on the following two equations: to transmit n bits across a distance d the total energy will be the sum of energy for transmission plus the energy used to run transceiver circuitry. Etenergy is the transmission energy and Etcir is the energy to run the transmission circuit.

$$Energy\ (n, d) = Etenergy*n + Etcir*n*d*d \qquad (2)$$

To receive the message the energy consumption is calculated as below

$$Erecp = Etcir*d. \qquad (3)$$

## 5.   SIMULATION AND DISCUSSION

We make the following assumptions about the simulated network.

♦ The network comprises 200 sensor nodes.
♦ All the nodes are homogeneous with the same battery power and architecture.
♦ Energy of a node is 3 Joule.
♦ The network is deployed randomly in an area of 500 by 500 meters square.
♦ The energy consumption for a node is 50 nJ/bit to run the circuitry of both transmitter and receiver and 100 PJ/bit to transmit.

◆    Each node knows its location via some GPS system or by using
     some localization algorithm [12] [13]; each node also has the
     information about neighbors.
◆    Message size is 2000 bytes.
◆    Nodes have information regarding their area coverage.

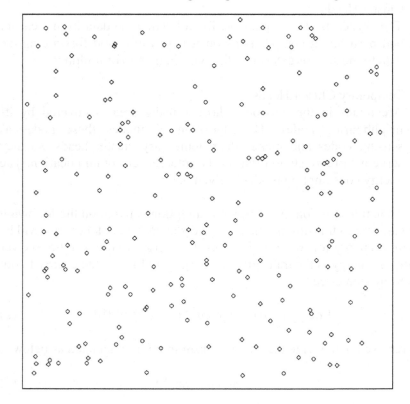

**Fig. 3 Random Deployment of the Network in 500 by 500 meter square
area**

We have not made any assumptions about network synchronization and
radio transmission range. Fig. 3 depicts the random deployment of network
in an area of 500 by 500 meters square.

Fig. 4 depicts the process of formation of temporary cluster heads. In
Figure 3, node 5's sensing area is covered by nodes 1, 2, 3 and 4 so it will
be marked as a temporary cluster head and will not take part in the
intracluster communication, nor will it be a member of any cluster. After
the elimination of temporary cluster heads from the network, the two

layers formed are shown in Fig. 5 and Fig. 6. Fig. 5 depicts the bottom layer of the network which will comprise the sensing nodes, whereas Figure 6 depicts the top layer of the network.

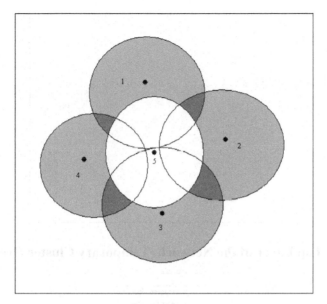

**Fig. 4 Formation of Temporary Cluster Head**

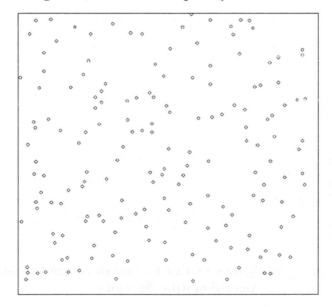

**Fig. 5 Sensing Layer of the Network**

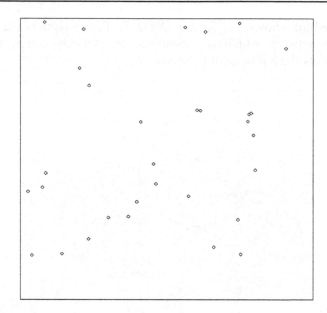

**Fig. 6 Top Layer of the Network (Temporary Cluster Head)**

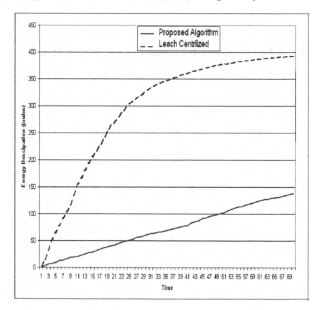

**Fig. 7 Energy Dissipation by Leach Centralised and Proposed
Algorithm with 200 nodes**

The simulation was run for 2500 iterations. The setup phase ran after every 30 iterations in order to rotate the cluster heads' role for both algorithms. Figure 7 shows the energy dissipation by Leach-C and the proposed algorithm. The proposed algorithm performs very well in terms of energy dissipation compared to Leach-C. The reason for better performance is the formation of temporary cluster heads which eliminates duplicate transmissions as well as using temporary cluster heads nodes in order to make the intercluster communication multihop. Fig. 8 depicts the energy dissipation when the proposed algorithm is simulated for 100 nodes. The simulation was run for 5000 iterations using an area of 500 by 500 meters square and the same message size. In Fig. 8 the energy dissipation by the proposed algorithm is much more steady compared to Fig. 7. The reason is the increase of density of the network in Fig. 7 – i.e., we have more nodes in Fig. 7 – 200 vs. 100.

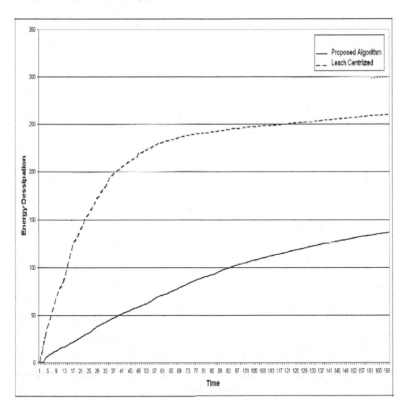

**Fig. 8 Energy Dissipation by Leach Centralised and Proposed Algorithm 100 nodes**

For the temporary cluster heads in Figure 8, there were about 27 nodes participating in the top layer vs. about 42 nodes in Figure 7. The top layer included the cluster head nodes and a more dense network which made the multihop communication cheaper.

Fig. 9 shows the distribution of dead nodes in the proposed algorithm when half of the network is dead and the sink is at position (250,250) vs. in Fig. 10 shows when half the network is dead and the sink is at (450,450) which is centre of the network. From both Figures it is obvious that even if the sink is located at one corner or at the centre of the network, the two layer architecture is still able to balance the dead nodes' distribution across the network compared with Leach-C dead node distribution when the sink position was (250,250) (Fig. 11) and at (450,450) (Fig. 12).

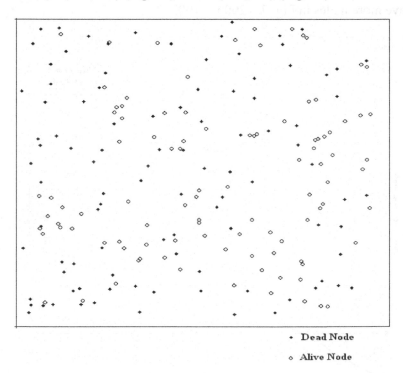

• Dead Node

○ Alive Node

**Fig. 9 Dead nodes distribution with sink at 250,250 in the proposed algorithm**

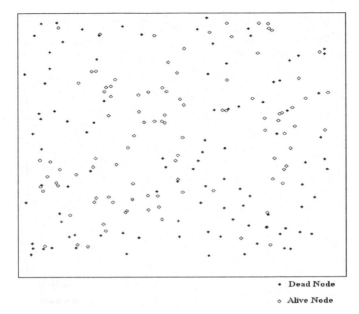

Fig. 10 Dead nodes distribution with sink at 450,450 in the proposed algorithm

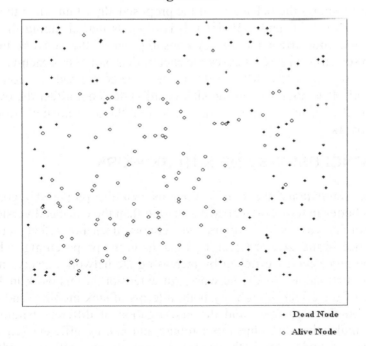

Fig. 11 Dead nodes distribution in leach-c when sinks is at 250,250

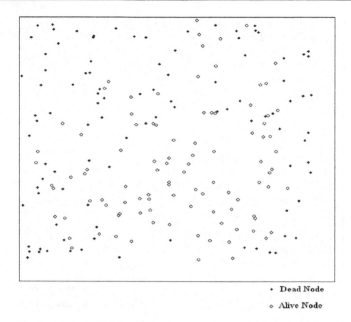

**Fig. 12 dead nodes distribution in Leach-C when sink is at 450,450**

Figure 13 shows the behaviour of the proposed algorithm when the sink position is (250,250) and (450,450). It is obvious that changing the sink position does not affect the energy consumption of the network in this multihop scenario. Figure 14 gives the energy dissipation in Leach-C when the sink is placed at two different locations – the centre and at a corner in the network. It is obvious that the sink position does not affect the overall lifetime in this scenario, but does have effect on the dead node distribution in the network.

## 6.    CONCLUSIONS AND FUTURE WORK

From the simulations above it is obvious that the proposed algorithm performs better in terms of energy dissipation than the enhanced version of Leach. An increase in density in the network does not affect network performance in the case of Leach-C, whereas in the proposed algorithm it makes the more energy efficient by increasing the network density and by balancing the load across the network. An extension of this work includes the study of the effect of mobility both in terms of sink mobility and node mobility on the algorithm, and the investigation of different parameters that will make the algorithm more robust and energy efficient (e.g., the percentage of nodes for both layers). Future studies will also address scalability issues in the two layer architecture.

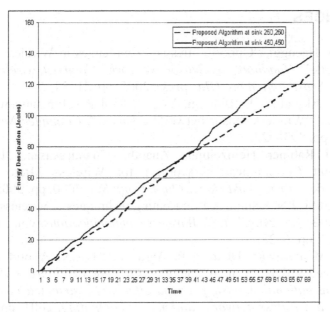

**Fig. 13 Energy Dissipation by proposed algorithm when the sink is at 250,250 and 450,450**

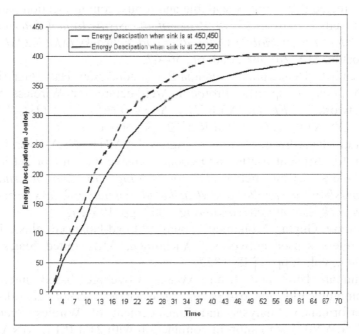

**Fig. 14 Energy Dissipation by Leach-c when the sink is at 250,250 and 450,450**

# REFERENCES

[1]    Martin Haenggi, "Opportunities and Challenges in Wireless Sensor Network", *Handbook of Sensor Networks Compact wireless and Wired Sensing Systems, CRC press*, 2005, pp. 21–34.

[2]    Ian F. Akyildiz, WellJan Su, Yogesh Sankarasubramaniam, Erdal Cayirci, "Wireless sensor network: a survey", *Computer Networks*, 2002, pp. 393–422.

[3]    Wendi Rabiner Heinzelman, Anantha Chandrakasan, "Energy-Efficient Communication Protocol for Wireless Micro sensor Networks," *Proc. 33rd Hawaii Int'l. Conf. Sys,* 2000. pp. 3005-3014

[4]    Al-Karaki, J.N. Kamal, A.E., "Routing techniques in wireless sensor networks: A survey," *IEEE Wireless Communications*, vol. 11, issue 6, 2004, pp. 6–28.

[5]    Arati Manjeshwar, Dharma P. Agrawal, "TEEN: A protocol for enhanced efficiency in wireless sensor networks," *proceedings of 1st international workshop on parallel and distributed computing issues in wireless networks and mobile computing*, 2001, pp. 2009-2015.

[6]    Chalermek Intanagonwiwat, Ramesh Govindan, Deborah Estrin, "Directed diffusion: A scalable and robust communication paradigm for sensor networks," *In Proc. of the Sixth Annual International Conference on Mobile Computing and Networks (MobiCOM 2000)*, Boston, MA, August 2000, pp. 56–67.

[7]    Wendi B. Heinzelman, Anantha P. Chandrakasan, Hari Balakrishnan "Application specific Protocol Architecture for Wireless Sensor Network," *IEEE TRANSACTIONS ON WIRELESS COMMUNICATIONS*, VOL. 1, OCTOBER 2002 , pp. 660–670.

[8]    Arati Manjeshwar, Dharma P. Agrawal, "APTEEN: A Hybrid protocol for efficient routing and comprehensive information retrieval in wireless sensor networks," *proceedings of 2nd international workshop on parallel and distributed computing issues in wireless networks and mobile computing*, 2002, pp. 195-202.

[9]    Gaurav Gupta, Mohamed Younis, "Load-balanced clustering of wireless sensor networks," Anchorage, AK, United States, May 2003., vol. 3, pp. 1848–1852.

[10]   Nauman Israr and Irfan Awan, "Coverage based intercluster communication for load balancing in wireless sensor networks" 2nd Performance Analysis and Enhancement of Wireless Networks (PAEWN07) workshop in conjunction with 21st IEEE AINA 2007, Nigra Falls, Canada.

[11] D. Tian and N. D. Georganas, "A node scheduling scheme for energy conservation in large wireless sensor networks", *Wireless Communication and Mobile Computing*, (2003), pp. 271–290.

[12] Andreas Savvides, Chih-Chieh Han, Mani B. Strivastava, "Dynamic fine-grained localization in ad hoc Networks of sensors", *Proceeding of ACM International Conference on Mobile Computing and Networking (MOBICOM'01)*, 2001. pp. 166–179

[13] N. Bulusu, J. Heidemann, D. Estrin, "Gps-less low cost outdoor localization for very small devices". *IEEE Personal Communications Magazine, 7(5)*, October 2000, pp. 28–34.

# CHAPTER 10

# Scenario Simulation
# for Network-Centric Technology Assessment

Osman Balci [1], William F. Ormsby [2]

[1] Department of Computer Science
660 McBryde Hall, MC 0106
Virginia Tech
Blacksburg, Virginia 24061, USA
[2] Naval Surface Warfare Center
Dahlgren Division, Code T12
17320 Dahlgren Road
Dahlgren, Virginia 22448, USA

**Abstract.** *Network-centric system technologies are assessed for a number of quality characteristics including readiness, interoperability, and effectiveness. This assessment is carried out under a demonstration, trial, exercise or experimentation using a specially set up global multinational communications network and services infrastructure. This paper addresses the simulation of the scenarios under which such technologies are assessed. Guidelines are given for scenario simulation model development and credibility assessment. Role players such as warfighters, operators, and subject matter expert evaluators are employed to carry out a technology assessment under simulated scenarios. Well defined technology intended uses guide the role players and the simulation of the scenarios. A case study is presented for the assessment of an unmanned aircraft system technology at the 2006 Coalition Warrior Interoperability Demonstration (CWID) annual event.*

**Key Words and Phrases:** Communications networks, input data modeling, network-centric systems, operational test and evaluation, scenario simulation, technology assessment.

## 1.   INTRODUCTION

We use the term "network-centric technology" to refer to the technology of a network-centric system intended for military, homeland defense, or homeland security purposes. A *network-centric system* is an interconnection of hardware, software, and humans that operate together over a communications network (e.g., Internet, mobile ad hoc network, virtual private network, wireless sensor network) to accomplish a set of goals.

The adjective "network-centric" has been coined in the United States Department of Defense (DoD) to refer to a class of systems, which is mandated for DoD components to build/use for transforming their operations and warfare capabilities to be network-centric. The terms "network-centric operations", "network-centric warfare", and FORCEnet currently constitute a common terminology in DoD. The major distinguishing characteristic of this class of systems is the fact that the components (or subsystems or modules) of this type of system communicate with each other over a network. For example, the space shuttle or an aircraft is a complex system, but it is not a network-centric system as its components do not work with each other over a communications network. A supply chain system operating over a company's virtual private network with geographically dispersed employees using the system with their handheld computers, cellular phones, laptop computers, and desktop computers is a network-centric system. The adjective "network-centric" is not just for DoD systems, but for any kind of system, which possesses the characteristics of this class of systems.

A network-centric system typically consists of a system of systems or a family of systems forming a complex infrastructure utilizing many technologies [Balci and Ormsby 2006]. Technology of a network-centric system goes through an evolution to mature and become acceptable for use. For example, Voice over Internet Protocol (VoIP) is a technology used to transmit voice conversations over an IP-based data network. The VoIP technology has been improving and evolving to be suitable for integration within many network-centric systems. Examples of network-centric technologies include: coalition and civil agency capable wireless information system, coalition command and control system, global satellite-based broadcast system, multi national coalition security system, and unmanned aircraft system for surveillance and reconnaissance.

Network-centric technologies are assessed under a demonstration, trial, exercise or experimentation for a set of quality characteristics such as effectiveness, functionality, interoperability, performance, and readiness. Such technology assessments are carried out by role players under simulated scenarios. Credibility of simulated scenarios affects the credibility of technology assessment. Development of sufficiently credible simulated scenarios poses significant technical challenges.

This paper deals with the simulation of the scenarios under which a network-centric technology is assessed. Network-centric technology assessment is introduced in Section 2. Section 3 describes scenario simulation within the context of technology assessment. Guidelines are provided for scenario simulation model credibility assessment in Section 4. A case study is presented for the assessment of an unmanned aircraft system technology in Section 5. Concluding remarks are given in Section 6.

## 2.    ASSESSMENT OF A NETWORK-CENTRIC TECHNOLOGY

A network-centric technology can be assessed for a number of quality characteristics including *readiness*, *interoperability*, and *effectiveness*. Technology *readiness* is characterized at nine levels as depicted in Fig. 1. Technology Readiness Level (TRL) is a measure used by DoD and some U.S. government agencies as an indication of maturity of evolving technologies. A technology originates in basic research and its feasibility is assessed before development. As the technology evolves, it is subjected to demonstration, experimentation, and refinement. Once it is sufficiently proven, it can be incorporated as part of an operational system.

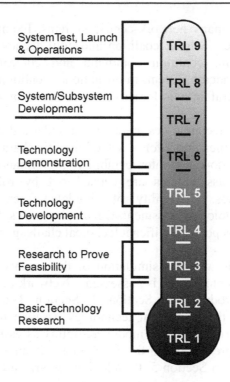

**Fig. 1 Technology Readiness Levels**

DoD [2005] provides guidelines, roles, responsibilities, and procedures for TRL assessment. A simulated operational environment is commonly used for TRL assessment. A technology can be subjected to operational test and evaluation under *simulated scenarios* representing operational requirements and specifications required of the final system.

*Interoperability* is considered to be one of the most important quality characteristics of a given network-centric technology. Therefore, Coalition Warrior Interoperability Demonstration (CWID) is organized annually by U.S. [CWID US 2006], U.K. [CWID UK 2006], and NATO [CWID NATO 2006]. CWID is an annual event, which enables the U.S. combatant commands and international community to investigate command, control, communications, computers, intelligence, surveillance, and reconnaissance (C4ISR) solutions that focus on relevant and timely objectives for enhancing coalition interoperability. CWID conducts demonstrations and trials of C4ISR capabilities, which can then be moved into operational use within a year following the execution period.

CWID provides an experimental global communications network and services infrastructure by integrating the C4ISR technologies under demonstration with each other and with coalition-standard core services under *classified* as well as *unclassified* modes of operation. A vendor's technology is interfaced/integrated with the experimental coalition communications network using the approved list of information exchange formats, messaging protocols, mapping and imaging protocols, and transport protocols. A technology under demonstration, trial or experimentation is assessed by Role Players under the prescribed technology Intended Uses (IUs) and *simulated scenarios* as depicted in Fig. 2.

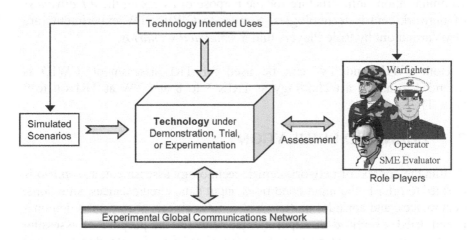

**Fig. 2 CWID Technology Assessment under Simulated Scenarios**

CWID objectives (e.g., Cross-Domain Data Sharing, Integrated Intelligence, Integrated Logistics) are created based on the need to share and exchange critical, time-sensitive information between military organizations, international coalitions and civilian agencies. A technology is demonstrated/tried under one or more of the CWID objectives. However, since each CWID objective is very high level, IUs of the technology under demonstration/trial are specified in a sufficiently detailed manner under each objective. Each IU should be specified to demonstrate a capability of the technology. IUs should drive the generation of simulated scenarios under which to demonstrate the technology. IUs can be categorized under Coalition Task Force (CTF) or Homeland Defense (HLD)/Homeland Security (HLS). IUs guide the Role Players in assessing a technology.

A *Role Player* is a person who uses the technology under demonstration/ trial according to the scripted events and activities of the simulated scenarios for the purpose of assessing the technology and its interoperability with respect to the prescribed IUs. A role player can be a warfighter, operator, and/or Subject Matter Expert (SME) Evaluator.

Network-centric technologies are assessed at another annual event called Trident Warrior (TW) [FORCEnet 2006]. TW is a multinational exercise/experimentation that seeks to accelerate the delivery of network-centric warfare capabilities to the warfighter. TW creates an experimental communications infrastructure for the purpose of assessing the *effectiveness* of network-centric technologies. Similar to CWID, TW experiments are also carried out by Role Players under *simulated scenarios*.

Both CWID and TW can be used for TRL assessment. CWID is intended to assess a technology at TRLs 3 to 8 and TW at TRLs 6 to 9 (Fig. 1).

## 3.    SCENARIO SIMULATION

Within the context of network-centric technology assessment, a *scenario* is defined to refer to the input conditions, input data, circumstances, situations, occurrences, and episodes under which a network-centric system is demonstrated, tried, exercised or experimented with for the purpose of assessing the technology of that system. Scenario simulation is intended to create sufficiently realistic inputs representing operational requirements and specifications required of the final or desired system.

Typically, a technology under assessment is integrated or interfaced with other technologies under assessment over a specially set up communications network. Scenarios are modeled and simulated for assessing multiple technologies and they describe the interactions among the technologies. A master scenario can be developed as an umbrella theme under which other scenarios can be created for specific technology assessments.

A scenario simulation model (SSM) represents a hypothesized chain of events, activities, and processes in a chronological order on a timeline, which may consist of days, hours, minutes, and seconds. The time scale is determined based on the fidelity, degree of representativeness, needed in the SSM. A SSM represents what might happen and should not be viewed as a model to use for predictions or forecasts of what will happen.

Events, activities, and processes form the foundation of a SSM. Fig. 3 illustrates the occurrences of events ($E_j$, j=1, 2, ..., 9) and activities ($A_k$, k=1, 2, ..., 8) of a process. An *event* is anything that occurs at a time *t* and changes the state of the system. For example, "Presidential Disaster Declaration at time 1100 on Day 3" is an event. An *activity* is an action that occurs over an interval of time. For example, "Analysis of environmental impact of a terrorist bomb explosion from time 1220 to 1350 on Day 2" is an activity. Each activity starts with an event and ends with another event. A *process* consists of a number of activities for accomplishing a mission or an objective. For example, "terrorist bomb explosion impact analysis and reporting" can be a process consisting of activities "environmental impact analysis", "human life impact analysis", "infrastructure impact analysis", and "report preparation" as depicted in Fig. 3. A process can be decomposed into other processes. A process or a set of processes can be viewed as an episode.

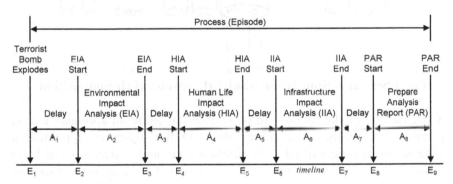

**Fig. 3 An Episode of Terrorist Bomb Explosion Impact Analysis and Reporting**

A SSM identifies the role players and represents their interactions with the technology under assessment. Execution of the model triggers directives to the role players based on the occurrences of events and actions in the scenario.

A SSM should be modularized with high cohesion and low coupling. Fig. 4 shows a hierarchical decomposition to accomplish such modularization. The top level contains a master scenario, which is decomposed into sub-scenarios at level 2. A level 2 sub-scenario can be decomposed into other sub-scenarios at level 3. A level 3 sub-scenario can be decomposed into other sub-scenarios at level 4. This decomposition is continued until sufficient modularization is achieved. A sub-scenario may refer to an episode and contain processes, activities, and events.

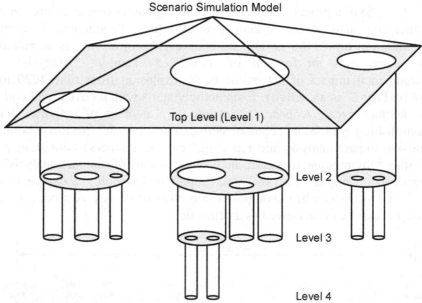

**Fig. 4 Scenario Simulation Model Hierarchical Decomposition**

Construction of the model can be carried out using an approach that is top-down, bottom-up, or a combination. In the top-down approach, a master scenario is identified at the highest level and is decomposed level by level from top to bottom. The decomposition can be vertical or horizontal. In vertical decomposition, a top-level scenario is decomposed all the way along a branch of the hierarchy. In horizontal decomposition, a top-level scenario is decomposed into all of its sub-scenarios first at level 2. Then, each level 2 sub-scenario is decomposed into its sub-scenarios at level 3. After completing all of the level 3 sub-scenarios, decomposition is continued at the next level in a horizontal manner.

In using a bottom-up approach, lowest level sub-scenarios are first identified and specified in accordance with the technology IUs. Then, some of the sub-scenarios are grouped together to make up a higher level sub-scenario. By combining sub-scenarios level by level in a bottom-up manner, the highest level master scenario is generated.

Scenario simulation modeling is an artful balancing of opposites; on the one hand, a model should not contain unnecessary details and become needlessly complex and difficult for the role players to follow, on the other hand, it should not exclude the essential details of what it represents. Successfully accomplishing the artful balancing of opposites requires significant experience and knowledge not only in modeling, but also in the problem domain.

Data are an integral part of a SSM. Data can be categorized into constant, random, trace (real), or hybrid. Scenario *constant data,* also called *parameters,* are fixed values that do not change during the system operation represented by a scenario. Examples of constant data include: number of ground-based interceptors, minimum weight, maximum temperature, payload capacity, number of network routers, and number of wireless sensors.

Scenario *random data,* also called *random variates,* are random values generated based on a probabilistic model such as a probability distribution (e.g., exponential, gamma, normal, weibull) of a random variable. A *random variable* is a real-valued function characterized with a probability distribution that maps a sample space into the real line. Example random variables include: bomb damage assessment time, inter-arrival time of missiles, target coordinates computation time, number of tanks in a combat zone, and report preparation time.

Random variables are either continuous or discrete. For example, "bomb damage assessment time" is a continuous random variable that may be characterized with an exponential probability distribution having a particular mean value. This characterization forms a probabilistic model of the random phenomenon "bomb damage assessment time". The random variable "number of tanks in a combat zone" is a discrete random variable that may be characterized with a Poisson probability distribution.

A *random variate* is a particular outcome or sample value of a random variable. For example, "24 minutes" can be a random variate for the "bomb damage assessment time" random variable. Random variates are generated by using Random Variate Generation (RVG) algorithms. Each RVG algorithm is designed to produce random variates that form a particular probability distribution. Sabah and Balci [2005] developed web services for RVG, which can be used for generating scenario random data. Scripted events of a scenario may reflect a snapshot of random variates.

Trace data can also be used in a SSM. Trace data are data extracted from the recording of a real-life happening of an event. For example, actual values recorded about the occurrences of events and activities during the actions of first responders for a real-life happening of a terrorist bomb explosion in a city can be used to make up a scenario.

Scenario data can be hybrid including both trace (real) values as well as random variates generated from a probability distribution representing a random phenomenon.

## 4.    SCENARIO SIMULATION MODEL CREDIBILITY ASSESSMENT

SSM *credibility* is the degree to which the scenarios represented in the SSM are believable. SSM credibility assessment is situation dependent and should be viewed as a confidence building activity.    The assessment outcome should not be considered as a binary variable where the credibility is either perfect or totally imperfect. Credibility should be judged on a scale for expressing confidence. A SSM is built for a prescribed set of IUs of the technology under assessment and its credibility must be judged with respect to those IUs. A hierarchy of indicators is presented below for SSM credibility assessment.

1.    *SSM Accuracy* is the degree to which SSM possesses sufficient transformational, behavioral, and representational correctness. SSM accuracy is judged by verity and validity.

   a)    *SSM Verity* is assessed by conducting SSM verification, which is substantiating that the SSM is transformed from one representation into another with sufficient accuracy. SSM verification addresses the question of "Are we building the SSM right?" Some example SSM verity indicators are given below.

   - How accurately are the SSM data converted from one measurement unit (e.g., meter, kilogram, centigrade) into another (e.g., inch, pound, Fahrenheit)?
   - How accurately are the SSM data converted from one type (e.g., real, integer, boolean, text, character, date) into another?
   - How accurately are the SSM data and scenario event descriptions translated from one language (e.g., French) into another (e.g., English)?

- How accurately are the SSM data transformed from one form (e.g., written, recorded voice, terrain data, binary, numeric, decimal) into another?
- How accurately are the SSM data retrieved from a database management system?
- How accurately are the SSM random data estimation techniques (e.g., maximum likelihood estimation technique) implemented?
- How accurately are the SSM data measured in the real-life system?
- How accurately is the random number generator algorithm implemented?
- How accurately are the random variate generation algorithms implemented?
- How accurate are the instruments (e.g., software monitors, hardware monitors, recording devices) used for recording the raw trace data?
- How accurately are the SSM trace data extracted from the real-life raw data?
- How accurately are the SSM trace data integrated into the SSM?

b) *SSM Validity* is assessed by conducting SSM validation, which is substantiating that the SSM possesses sufficient behavioral and representational accuracy. SSM validation addresses the question of "Are we building the right SSM?" Some example SSM validity indicators are given below.

- How well is *counterintuitive behavior* captured in the SSM representation?
- How accurately does the SSM represent the interrelationships among the scenario events, activities, and processes?
- How accurately does the SSM represent the reality in terms of the measurement units such as meter, kilogram, centigrade, inch, pound, Fahrenheit?
- How accurately does the SSM represent the reality in terms of the data types such as real, integer, boolean, text, character, and date?
- How accurately does the SSM represent the reality in terms of the language used?

- How accurately do the SSM constant data represent the reality?
- How accurately do the SSM random data represent the reality?
- How accurately do the SSM trace data represent the reality?

2.  *SSM Clarity* is the degree to which SSM is unambiguous and understandable.

    a) *SSM Unambiguity* is the degree to which each scenario event or activity and each directive given to a role player can only be interpreted by a role player one way. Role players should not interpret a scenario or a given directive in different ways and act differently.

    b) *SSM Understandability* is the degree to which the meaning of each scenario and each directive given to a role player is easily comprehended by all of the role players. Each event or activity in a scenario and each directive for a role player must be described in a way understandable by the role players. Technical jargon that may confuse role players and cause them to act erroneously should be avoided.

3.  *SSM Completeness* is the degree to which

    i. all essential elements of a scenario are specified with no missing information {e.g., phrases such as "as a minimum", "as a maximum", and "not limited to" are indications of incomplete specifications},
    ii. all parts of scenario data are provided {e.g., "radar frequency is 85" is an incomplete data specification since no unit (e.g., hertz) is given}, and
    iii. all operational requirements and specifications required of the final or desired system technology under assessment are represented in the SSM {e.g., an unmanned aircraft system technology is expected to be used during nighttime; however, if the SSM includes scenarios only for daytime, then it becomes incomplete}.

4.  *SSM Consistency* is the degree to which (a) SSM is specified using consistent measurement unit, uniform notation, and uniform terminology, and (b) any one scenario event or activity does not

conflict with any other. Once agreed on a time zone (e.g., Zulu) and time unit (e.g., minutes), all time values in a scenario must be specified accordingly. Once a measurement unit (e.g., meters, pounds, Fahrenheit) is selected for a particular data set, that unit must be used consistently throughout the entire SSM. A scenario event by itself may make sense, but in combination of other events it may be out of order or create conflicts. Consistency of events with each other must be examined.

5.   *SSM Fidelity* is the degree to which the SSM possesses sufficient level of detail or exactness. The level of granularity captured in SSM representation must be judged in accordance with the technology IUs.

# 5.   A CASE STUDY

We conducted a structured assessment of the Backpack Unmanned aerial vehicle Surveillance, Target acquisition, and Enhanced Reconnaissance (BUSTER) Unmanned Aircraft System (UAS) technology during the CWID 2006 annual event (June 12-22) at the Naval Surface Warfare Center Dahlgren Division (NSWCDD), Dahlgren, Virginia. The technology assessment was carried out with respect to 11 major quality characteristics under 17 IUs with associated simulated scenarios using an assessment methodology [Balci and Ormsby 2006; Orca 2003]. Details of the assessment are given by Ormsby et al. [2006].

## 5.1   Experimental Communications Network Set Up

An experimental multinational global communications network was set up at the CWID 2006 Dahlgren site incorporating the BUSTER UAS and Global Broadcast System (GBS) technologies as shown in Figure 5. All together more than 40 technologies were demonstrated, tried, exercised or experimented with under simulated scenarios at several CWID 2006 sites [CWID US 2006; CWID UK 2006].

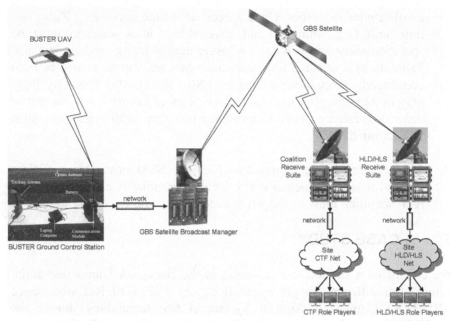

**Fig. 5 BUSTER UAS and GBS Network-Centric System of Systems**

BUSTER is classified as a mini/small UAS [OSD 2005] that can be transported by several men on foot and rapidly set up and deployed by a non-pilot. It is useful for military as well as HLD/HLS purposes. The BUSTER UAS enables the user/warfighter with enhanced situational awareness by providing the means for expanded reconnaissance/surveillance, coverage of marginal maneuver areas, and increased target acquisition capability. BUSTER UAS consists of an Unmanned Aerial Vehicle (UAV), a small catapult launcher, and a Ground Control Station (GCS), which includes a tracking antenna, a communications antenna, a communications module with battery, and a rugged touch screen laptop computer. The UAV can be loaded with a color daylight Electro Optical (EO) camera, black and white (B&W) nighttime thermal Infrared (IR) camera, or a High Definition TV (HDTV) digital camera. The UAV is recovered after its mission by a built-in parachute.

BUSTER UAS was interfaced with the GBS, also known as Global Broadcast Service. GBS is a wideband military satellite communications system. GBS consists of three segments as shown in Fig. 5: (1) Satellite Broadcast Manager (SBM) used for transmitting data (e.g., imagery, video, voice) in near real-time to coalition military forces around the world, (2) military satellites, and (3) a transportable receive suite, including a

Receive Broadcast Manager (RBM) connected to a Next Generation Receive Terminal (NGRT) with an Integrated Receiver Decoder (IRD), used to process and display broadcasts. [Raytheon 2006]

For the purpose of technology assessment, BUSTER UAV was flown to send video images in near real-time to the GCS. The video images received by the GCS are encoded and transmitted over the network to the GBS SBM, which uplinks the images to the GBS satellite for multi broadcasting to the receive suites. Two receive suites were set up at the Dahlgren site for CTF and HLD/HLS purposes. The images were received by the RBM and decoded by the IRD. The decoded images were transmitted over the network to the CTF and HLD/HLS role players.

## 5.2    Intended Uses and Simulated Scenarios

We conducted the BUSTER UAS technology assessment under 7 IUs for HLD/HLS concerns and 10 IUs for CTF concerns. The IUs guided the development of the SSM as well as the assessments by the role players. The IUs are listed below. A brief description of the simulated scenario associated with each IU is also given.

*1.    HLD/HLS IU 1: Surveillance of area of chlorine rail car explosion*

"A terrorist organization detonates an explosive device which ruptures a Chlorine Storage Tank in transport through Quantico, VA rail lines. A large quantity of chlorine gas is released downwind of incident site. When released, it quickly turns into a gas and stays close to the ground and spreads rapidly. Assuming a high-density area, as many as 700,000 people may be in the actual downwind area, which could extend as far as 25 miles. Of these, 5% (35,000) will receive potentially lethal exposures, and half of these will die before or during treatment." [CWID US 2006]

*2.    HLD/HLS IU 2: Surveillance of evacuation routes along the projected path of a tropical storm*

"In response to Presidential Disaster Declaration in anticipation of Tropical Storm Anna, Commander, Coast Guard Atlantic Area (LANTAREA) implements OPLAN-9700 to all Atlantic Area units. LANTAREA directs CGC GALLATIN and DALLAS to evacuate port." [CWID US 2006]

3.   *HLD/HLS IU 3: Surveillance of area of chemical weapon explosion via VBIED*

"Vehicle Borne Improvised Explosive Device (VBIED) used to deliver Chemical Weapon at the intersection of interstate roads I-10 and I-25 in the vicinity of Las Cruces Terrizona." [CWID US 2006]

4.   *HLD/HLS IU 4: Surveillance of the hazard area near tunnels where chemical weapons exploded via VBIED*

"Chemical weapons were exploded via VBIEDs in the Hampton Roads and Monitor Merrimac Bay Tunnels in Virginia." [CWID US 2006]

5.   *HLD/HLS IU 5: Surveillance of the bridge damaged by terrorist attack for damage assessment*

"Potomac River Harry E. Nice Bridge has been damaged by terrorist attacks." [CWID US 2006]

6.   *HLD/HLS IU 6: Surveillance of terrorist attack area to support rescue operations*

"CGC James Rankin arrives at Hampton Roads. Rescue operations continue. 43 survivors and 112 bodies have been recovered and are being processed through Fort Monroe, Norfolk Naval Station, and ISC Portsmouth in Virginia." [CWID US 2006]

7.   *HLD/HLS IU 7: Surveillance of the downtown Atlanta area, where a Radiological Dispersion Device detonated by terrorists, for bomb damage assessment*

"Radiological Dispersion Device detonated in downtown Atlanta, Georgia by terrorists. The contaminated region covers approximately thirty-six blocks and includes the business district (high-rise street canyons), residential row houses, crowded shopping areas, and a high school. Due to the size of the explosion, the radioactive contamination is blown widely. Variable winds of 3 to 8 miles per hour carry the radioactively contaminated aerosol throughout an area of approximately thirty-six blocks (the primary deposition zone). Complex urban wind patterns carry the contamination in unpredictable directions, leaving highly variable contamination deposition with numerous hot spots created by wind eddies and vortices." [CWID US 2006]

*8.    CTF IU 1: Reconnaissance of enemy troop movements*

"National and CTF Intelligence Assets report that Nevatah is preparing for open hostilities (invasion/TBM attack) of Terrizona and Wassegon within days." [CWID US 2006]

*9.    CTF IU 2: Surveillance of movements to staging areas*

"1 UK - North of MSR Gray (I-8), 3 UK - South of MSR Gray (I-8), US 101 - West of (I-15), ANZAC - East of (I-15), IT - Terrizona w/TSF." [CWID US 2006]

*10.   CTF IU 3: Surveillance of parachute assaults*

"Parachute assaults conducted by the 101st Airborne Division to secure Terrizona airheads at the Thermal Airport (Coacella) and the Phoenix Goodyear Municipal Airport. Launch from SPOD San Diego using C-130's and CAS overhead provided by US FA-15's and FA-18's." [CWID US 2006]

*11.   CTF IU 4: Surveillance of area of Non-combatant Evacuation*
    *Operation (NEO) from US Embassy*

"NEO from US Embassy in Phoenix, Terrizona." [CWID US 2006]

*12.   CTF IU 5: Surveillance of the theater ballistic missile (TBM) attack*
    *area for post attack (aftermath) analysis*

"Nevatah orders attack; their TBMs impact at 1216Z hitting CTF San Diego SPOD/APOD with mass TBM strike: chemical and HE." [CWID US 2006]

*13.   CTF IU 6: Surveillance of convoy movement along Military Supply*
    *Routes (MSRs)*

"CFLCC forces assume responsibility of AORs in Terrizona as they coordinate Transfer of Authority with TSF. CFLCC extends and secures MSR Blue through Flagstaff, Gallup and Albuquerque; MSR Gray Yuma to Tucson; MSR Rail Yuma, Phoenix and Tucson; MSR Green (Bullhead-Flagstaff)." [CWID US 2006]

*14.  CTF IU 7: Surveillance of large insurgent camp*

"CFLCC Forces initiate counterinsurgency strikes into Terrizona (large Insurgent camp hit 10 miles south of Prescott)." [CWID US 2006]

*15.  CTF IU 8: Reconnaissance of enemy buildup of forces*

"Reconnaissance of Terrizona detects buildup of Nevatah forces near Terrizona Boarder." [CWID US 2006]

*16.  CTF IU 9: Reconnaissance of airfield and surrounding terrain*

"Final Plan review of 1700Z raid on Nellis AFB, 1730Z STOM raid on Reno/Tahoe International Airport and TLAM strikes on Nevatah. CFLCC and SOF conducts assault on Nellis AFB (G-2's provide IPBS for SA) prior to launching Assault." [CWID US 2006]

*17.  CTF IU 10: Surveillance of shoreline and port facilities to support G-2/C-2 for planning purposes*

"CFMCC, MARFOR and CFACC finalize plans for opposed amphibious assault at Corpus Christi at 1500Z, C+30. Issue final orders. Develop and distribute integrated C2 systems' Common Operational Picture: Operational Areas, Boundaries, and Control Measures." [CWID US 2006]

## 5.3  Quality Characteristics Assessed

We used the Evaluation Environment (EE) web-based software system [Orca 2003] to apply our assessment methodology [Balci and Ormsby 2006]. We created a hierarchy of 227 quality indicators, of which 210 are leaf indicators and 17 are branch indicators, for assessing the BUSTER UAS technology with respect to the IUs and simulated scenarios described above. The higher-level indicators of the hierarchy are shown in the EE screen shot in Figure 6 and are presented below.

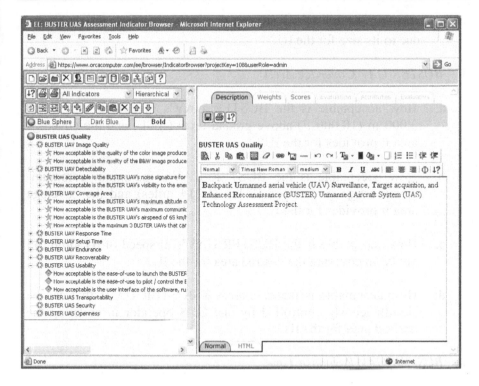

**Fig. 6 The EE Project for BUSTER UAS Technology Assessment**

*1.  BUSTER UAV Image Quality*

   a.  How acceptable is the quality of the color image produced by the
       BUSTER UAV's EO camera operating under the specified weather
       condition for the IU?

   b.  How acceptable is the quality of the B&W image produced by the
       BUSTER UAV's IR camera operating under the specified weather
       condition for the IU?

*2.  BUSTER UAV Detectability*

   a.  How acceptable is the BUSTER UAV's noise signature for the
       IU? How acceptable is the ease by which the enemy can detect the
       UAV by the noise it generates for the IU?

b.    How acceptable is the BUSTER UAV's visibility to the enemy due to its size for the IU?

3.   *BUSTER UAV Coverage Area*

a.    How acceptable is the BUSTER UAV's maximum altitude of 3,000 m (10,000 ft) above ground level (AGL) and the coverage area it provides for the IU?

b.    How acceptable is the BUSTER UAV's maximum communication range (radius) of 10 km (6.214 miles) and the coverage area it provides for the IU?

c.    How acceptable is the BUSTER UAV's airspeed of 65 km/h (35 knots) in covering the desired area for the IU?

d.    How acceptable is the maximum 3 BUSTER UAVs that can be simultaneously controlled by one GCS operator in covering the desired area for the IU?

4.   *BUSTER UAV Response Time*

How acceptable is the BUSTER UAV's Response Time for the IU?

Response Time     $=$   $T_{FirstImageReceived} - T_{Launch}$

where

$T_{Launch}$                $=$   the time at which the UAV is launched

$T_{FirstImageReceived}$     $=$   the time at which first image is received from the UAV

5.   *BUSTER UAS Setup Time*

How acceptable is the BUSTER UAS's Setup Time for the IU?

Setup Time        $=$   $T_{ReadyToUse} - T_{DecisionToUse}$

where

$T_{DecisionToUse}$         $=$   The time at which decision is made to use the BUSTER UAS

$T_{ReadyToUse}$            $=$   The time at which the BUSTER UAV is ready to launch and the laptop computer is ready to control/communicate with the UAV

*6.   BUSTER UAV Endurance*

How acceptable is the BUSTER UAV's endurance of 4 hours (maximum amount of time operational in air) for the IU?

*7.   BUSTER UAV Recoverability*

How acceptable is the BUSTER UAV's Recoverability with its built-in parachute for the IU?

*8.   BUSTER UAS Usability*

   a.   How acceptable is the ease-of-use to launch the BUSTER UAV using its small catapult?

   b.   How acceptable is the ease-of-use to pilot/control the BUSTER UAV using a laptop computer?

   c.   How acceptable is the user interface of the software, running on the laptop computer, used for piloting/controlling the BUSTER UAV?

*9.   BUSTER UAS Transportability*

How acceptable is the transportability of the entire BUSTER UAS?

*10. BUSTER UAS Security*

How acceptable is the security of the wireless communication between the GCS user and the UAV?

*11. BUSTER UAS Openness*

How acceptable is the BUSTER UAS's openness (interoperability with other systems)?

## 5.4   Assessment Results

Four role players participated in assessing the BUSTER UAS technology according to the nominal score set definition given in Table 1.

## Table 1. Nominal Score Set Definition for the BUSTER UAS Technology Assessment

| Nominal Score | Numerical Score | Description |
|---|---|---|
| Highly Acceptable | [95 .. 100] | Exceeds the capabilities/requirements expected for the IU |
| Acceptable | [80 .. 94] | Satisfies the capabilities/requirements expected for the IU |
| Somewhat Acceptable | [60 .. 79] | Partially satisfies the capabilities/requirements expected for the IU |
| Somewhat Unacceptable | [40 .. 59] | Partially fails to satisfy the capabilities/requirements expected for the IU |
| Unacceptable | [20 .. 39] | Fails to satisfy the capabilities/requirements expected for the IU |
| Highly Unacceptable | [0 .. 19] | BUSTER UAS is not created for the IU |

The overall assessment results are presented in a Kiviat graph shown in Fig. 7. Each radius of the circle in the graph represents an indicator with its name and interval score, [low score, high score], shown just outside of the circumference. The center of the circle represents a score of zero and the circumference intersection point represents a perfect score of 100. An indicator score is designated on its radius with its low, average, and high values.

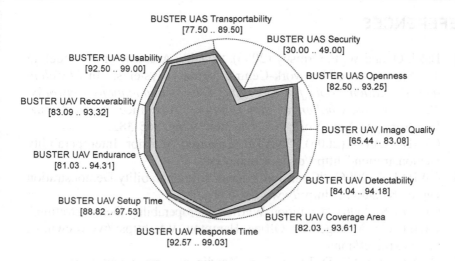

**Fig. 7  BUSTER UAS Technology Overall Assessment**

## 6.  CONCLUDING REMARKS

Scenarios are commonly employed for complex technology assessment without realizing that they are simulation models, the credibility of which should be substantiated against the technology's IUs. Scenario development and use should be carried out under the fundamentals of modeling and simulation. Credibility of the scenarios used significantly affects the credibility of technology assessment.

Technology assessment of a network-centric system of systems is a very complex process, involves the measurement and evaluation of qualitative and quantitative elements, mandates evaluations by warfighters, operators, and subject matter experts, and requires the integration of disparate evaluations. Planning and managing such measurements and evaluations require a unifying methodology and should not be performed in an ad hoc manner.

CWID enables effective planning and management of such measurements and evaluations and provides a multinational global communications network and services infrastructure for complex network-centric technology assessment. CWID's experimental infrastructure can also be used to produce trace data, validation data, performance data, and workload characterization data that can be used by modeling and simulation tools for communications networks and services.

# REFERENCES

[1] Balci, O. and W. F. Ormsby (2006), "Quality Assessment of Modeling and Simulation of Network-Centric Military Systems," In *Modeling and Simulation Tools for Emerging Telecommunications Networks: Needs, Trends, Challenges and Solutions*, A.N. Ince and E. Topuz, Eds, Springer, New York, NY, Chapter 19, pp. 365-382.

[2] CWID NATO (2006), "NATO Coalition Warrior Interoperability Demonstration," http://cwid.act.nato.int/

[3] CWID UK (2006), "Coalition Warrior Interoperability Demonstration United Kingdom," http://www.cwid.org.uk/

[4] CWID US (2006), "Coalition Warrior Interoperability Demonstration," CWID Joint Management Office, Hampton, VA. https://www.cwid.js.mil/c/extranet/home

[5] DoD (2005), "DoD Technology Readiness Assessment Deskbook," Deputy Under Secretary of Defense for Science and Technology, U.S. Department of Defense, May.

[6] FORCENet (2006), "Trident Warrior," Naval Network Warfare Command, Norfolk, VA, http://forcenet.navy.mil/tw/

[7] Orca (2003), "Evaluation Environment," Orca Computer, Inc., Blacksburg, VA, https://www.orcacomputer.com/ee/

[8] Ormsby, W. F., O. Balci, T. P. Lewis, C. G. Tua, and B. B. Driskell (2006), "Assessment of BUSTER UAS for Use in Operations in Response to CTF and HLD Events," Technical Report, Warfare Systems Department, Naval Surface Warfare Center Dahlgren Division, Dahlgren, VA, Aug. 7.

[9] OSD (2005), "Unmanned Aircraft Systems Roadmap 2005-2030," U.S. Office of the Secretary of Defense (OSD), Aug. 4.

[10] Raytheon (2006), "Global Broadcast Service," Raytheon Company, Waltham, MA, http://www.raytheon.com/products/gbs/

[11] Sabah, M. and O. Balci (2005), "Web-based Random Variate Generation for Stochastic Simulations," *International Journal of Simulation and Process Modelling 1*, 1-2, 16-25.

# CHAPTER 11

# Verification and Validation of Simulation Models and Applications:
# A Methodological Approach

Zhongshi Wang[1], Axel Lehmann[2]

[1] Institut für Technik Intelligenter Systeme (ITIS e.V.)
[2] Institut für Technische Informatik
Fakultät für Informatik
Universität der Bundeswehr München
D-85577 Neubiberg, Germany

**Abstract.** *Under pressure, time- and cost-constraints, the importance of modelling and simulation (M&S) techniques for analyses of dynamic systems behaviour is permanently increasing. With respect to the permanent increase of embedding and networking of computing and telecommunication systems, the complexity of real systems applications is permanently increasing. As a consequence, the complexity of models and simulation applications is also increasing, and the urgent demand for developing appropriate verification and validation methods, techniques, and tools to guarantee the models credibility is viable. The basic requirement for analysis of a model's credibility is to verify the model's correctness, and to validate its validity with respect to predefined application purposes and validity criteria. This requires that the different design, development and application phases of M&S are well specified, and the results of each phase are well documented.*

*This paper will present a refined M&S verification and validation (V&V) process based on a multi-phase M&S development and application concept already developed and presented in 2002 [5]. The extended and refined V&V approach will be demonstrated. In addition, we will show how this method can be applied in various application scenarios, and how it can be tailored according to credibility criteria under specified cost, time and application constraints.*

## 1.    INTRODUCTION

Considering rigorous analysis of divers existing concepts for verification and validation (V&V) of simulation applications, the collected experts experiences of model development, and experiences with V&V of models at our institute, we presented - within the scope of the previous COST 285 Symposium in 2002 - a refined, structured V&V approach [5] also referred to as V&V Triangle [3, 4]. That approach addressed the following essential issues of successful VV&A:

- following a structured and stepwise approach;
- conducting V&V during model development;
- examining intermediate products;
- building a chain of evidences based on V&V results;
- providing templates for documentation of V&V activities and results; and
- conducting V&V activities independently.

To achieve this purpose, our "classic" V&V triangle provides [3]:

- detailed documentation requirements of the well-defined inter-mediate products created during model development;
- a summary of error types, which are most likely to be hidden in the intermediate product on which the V&V activities are focused;
- V&V main-phases to assess the correctness and validity of each intermediate product individually;
- V&V sub-phases with generic V&V objectives to explore the potential of the examination of specific types of intermediate products and external information;
- guidance on how to apply V&V techniques, and on how to reuse previously created V&V products;
- an overview of the dependencies between different V&V objectives and the influence of repetitive examination on the credibility of the simulation model.

During model development, data modelling is a very time consuming and difficult task. Up to one third of the total time used in a simulation study can be spent on it [14]. In addition, the quality of data is also a crucial factor for the credibility assessment of simulation models and applications. As a consequence for the V&V process, correctness and accuracy of data acquisition, data analysis, data transformation, and data use must be estimated in each model development phase. However, within the scope of our "classic" V&V triangle, this aspect was not especially addressed as a separate issue, and not discussed in detail. In this paper, we attempt to improve the "classic" V&V approach by appending an extra consideration derived from the recommendation [9, 11], in which the V&V process of data modelling is explicitly handled. In addition, with an advanced tailoring concept, we will show how this approach can be adapted to the special requirements of any given M&S project.

The remainder of this paper is organized as follows: Section 2 briefly introduces the main problem fields of data modelling in M&S. In Section 3, a discussion on how to increase the credibility of a data model is given. Further in Section 4, the "extended" V&V approach is presented. Section 5 presents a multistage tailoring concept for the purpose of project-specific adaptation of V&V-processes. Finally, Section 6 concludes the contributions of the paper and points out the future research.

## 2. DATA MODELLING PROCESS IN M&S

Data modelling is of prime importance for conducting a simulation study, and typically, consists of the following steps and contents [2, 6, 7, 13]:

1. Data requirements analysis,
2. Data collection,
3. Data analysis,
4. Data transformation, and
5. Output analysis and interpretation.

**Data requirements analysis.** This step deals with identification of information and data necessary for model development and simulation experiments from the system being studied. Both quantitative and qualitative data which can be used as measurements to describe the system of interest should be considered. According to the given constraints within the underlying simulation study, for example, time or cost limitations, investigation shall be made to illustrate from what sources the desired data arise, what methods should be used, and what schedule should be followed, so that data can be collected more efficiently and accurately.

**Data collection.** Depending on the results of requirements analysis, data collection should be conducted in a planned and systematic manner. For some situations data gathering through simple direct observation and measurement of the attribute of interest seems sufficient for the present data requirements, but sometimes, documents must be used. Documents used for data modelling are usually in a form of tables, graphics, specifications, reports and the like. However, the existence of documentation does not automatically imply availability for data modelling. One of the major problems in regard to fact finding in documents is that the documents available in a simulation study could be rich in numbers, but poor in contents actually required for the investigation purpose. In addition, the documents may be only available in parts and even out of date. Therefore, the ability to discover and interpret the appropriate information and data contained in documents is of particular importance.

**Data analysis.** Raw data, derived from the variety of sources, are used for different aspects concerning simulation modelling. Basically, there are three types of data [12] for model input:

- Data for specifying the proposed model;
- Data for test; and
- Data for performing simulation experiments.

Based upon the given data the probability distributions should be determined, which are used to specify the behaviour of the random processes driving the system under consideration. In principle there are two alternatives [6] in selecting probability distributions: 1.) use the actual sample data to represent the probability distributions, or 2.) determine a theoretical probability distribution according to the data collected. A large number of statistical methods was discussed [6, 7], which could be applied for distribution selecting in different situations. Once this task has been completely performed, random samples used as input to the simulation model can be generated from the specified distribution function.

**Data transformation.** Both qualitative and quantitative data eventually need to be transformed into a computer processable form during model development. Some data are used to specify the model being built, and finally, become integrated into the model built; while the other data, which are used to compare with the simulation results or to perform simulation experiments, usually need to be managed separately from the model under study. Therefore, it is essential for data transformation not only to format data technically correctly in type, format, structure and amount, etc. which are required by some software systems used or certain standard followed, but also to establish a concept that facilitates the reliable data storing and data retrieving, and as well, the efficient data transfer between a simulation application and its cooperating data repository.

**Output analysis and interpretation.** Output data are generated as results of simulation experiments driven by supplying input data. Thereby, since random samples derived from the identified probability distribution functions are typically used, the model output is influenced by random factors consequently. If the output data are not analyzed sufficiently, they can easily be misinterpreted, so that false conclusions about the system of interest are drawn, regardless how well the model has been actually built. For analyzing output data, it is important to make certain whether the system being modelled is terminating or nonterminating, and further to distinguish between a steady state and a transient (nonsteady) state because different statistical methods should be used for each case.

## 3.  ESTABLISHING CREDIBLE DATA MODELS

### 3.1  Gathering "Good" Data

Obtaining appropriate data from the system of interest is a crucial premise to achieve a valid simulation model. The process for collecting data is however frequently influenced by a large number of subjective and objective factors. The issues discussed below address how to tackle the problems typically met in data collecting.

- **Collecting data manually or automatically.** Often, data are manually gathered through direct observation and measurement. However, since the person recording data could easily be disturbed by the system being measured or its environment, and in the same way, the system behaviour itself could also be influenced by the presence of an observer, it is impossible for a human observer to collect data just accurately and orderly as desired and planned. To tackle the problems derived from the manual nature, techniques to increase automatic portion in data collecting should be applied.

Recently, several new approaches for automatic data collection and data integration in simulation applications [10] have been employed, in which a data interface between a simulation application and a corporate business system is developed, which collects, stores and retrieves data, and also supplies data used for simulation experiments fully automatically. Because of the high technical requirements, however, these methodologies can only be applied in a limited number of applications, for example, in modelling manufacture industry.

- **No data available.** Unfortunately, there exist also some situations in reality where it is impossible or infeasible to gather data. For example, if the system under consideration does not remain in a real form, or if it is too complex and time consuming to gather data from an existing system. This difficulty can also occur by gathering data only in some certain processes of the system. In such cases, expert opinion and knowledge of the system and its behaviour are indispensable fundamentals to make assumptions about the system for the purposes for which the simulation study is intended. Moreover, wherever applicable, data gathered from different, but similar systems can also be considered.

- **Applying historical data.** Historical data from the system being studied can be used for a purpose of model validation, in which outcomes of the real system and the model are compared by using the same historical input data [7]. However, the comparison of this manner is only reasonable, when the actual state of the model can be considered to be equal to the then state of the system, from which the historical data arose. The identical input variables can not ensure yet the model and the system are driven exactly on the same condition, because the historical data normally used for model validation cover only just a limited range of influencing factors on the original system.

- **Collecting information by interviewing.** There is no doubt that interviews are significant means for information gathering. With the aid of interviews the experts' knowledge not yet documented in some real form could be thus communicated to another. In the case discussed above, where data are not available from the current system, interviews could be the only way to get some information about the system to be modelled. It should be noted that interviewing is a process of obtaining both objective and subjective information. Shannon [13] stated: "It is always important to distinguish between facts and opinions; both are necessary and valuable but must be handled differently."

## 3.2    Integrating Data Verification and Validation

Although some part of activities in data gathering and data analyzing can be conducted concurrently with model development, data modelling at large is by no means an independent process, but closely coupled within the underlying simulation study, and therefore, should be considered as an integral part of the overall simulation modelling. And just like the nature of model building, conducting data model evolves also in a modular and iterative manner. As illustrated in Figure 1, which is here presented in a form following the literature [11], the outcomes of each data modelling phase provide additional knowledge about the system of interest to drive the model progress, whereas the model under construction returns the feedbacks which prompt further data modelling effort or a new iteration. Finally, the simulation conclusion is reached at the last intersection of the both processes.

Data V&V is intended to reveal any quality deficiencies that involved in each intermediate result of date model being conducted from data requirements analysis to output analysis and interpretation [1]. Data verification is defined to assure that data are transformed during the modelling process accurately in form and content; while data validation is concerned with determining whether the use of data model sufficiently satisfies the intended purpose of the simulation objectives. As Spieckermann [11] stated, data V&V should be performed in accordance with model V&V throughout the entire development process of a simulation study.

## 4.    THE "EXTENDED" V&V TRIANGLE

As Figure 2 shows, the improved V&V process, which is extended by including an exact consideration of data modelling, consists of two closely associated parts of V&V activities: model V&V and data V&V. The main emphasis in this section is placed on describing data V&V and the relationship between the two parts. More details about the basic principle of the V&V triangle can be found in the former paper [5] and literature [3, 4].

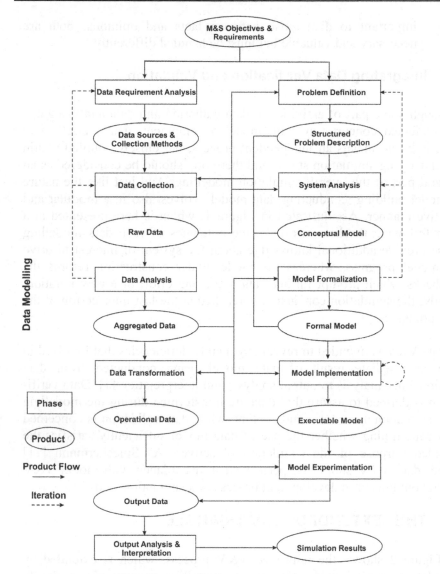

**Fig. 1  Data Modelling in M&S**

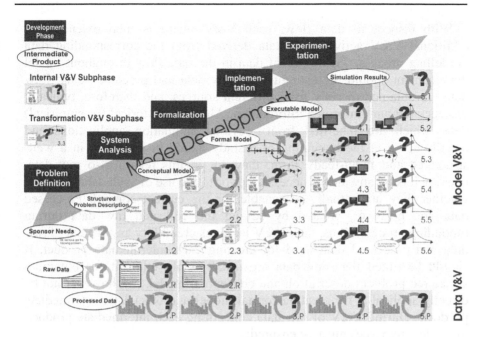

**Fig. 2  The "Extended" V&V Triangle (based on [3, 4, 9, 11])**

In model V&V, each well-defined intermediate product created during model development from "structured problem description" to "model results" is input to a V&V phase, numbered 1 through 5. Each V&V phase is again split into more sub-phases, each with a defined sub-aim to detect the internal errors or transformation errors. In the sub-phases numbered as x.1, the absence of product internal errors in each particular intermediate product should be demonstrated. For example, in sub-phase 1.1 it should be ensured that the problem description is free of misunderstanding and inconsistence, and in sub-phase 3.1 a syntax check can be applied to the formal model comparison of the chosen formalism. In any other sub-phases, the pairwise comparison between the current intermediate product and each previous intermediate product can be made to confirm the absence of transformation errors. Such as in sub-phases 3.2, 3.3, and 3.4, the formal model could be compared with the conceptual model, the structured problem description, and the sponsor needs one by one. By repeating the comparison vs. an intermediate product in this manner, more intensity of V&V activities is reached, and so, the credibility established so far can also be increased accordingly.

With respect to data flow, each V&V phase is then extended by additional V&V activities of data derived from the corresponding data modelling process. Two types of data in the data flow throughout model development should be distinguished: raw data and processed data. Raw data are obtained directly from different sources, and therefore, typically unstructured and unformed information. Although historical (or empirical) data, which are inherited from previous simulation applications and usually given at the beginning of a study, could be available in a well-structured and input-ready form, they are in this regard also raw data, because it is by any means necessary prior to the use of such data to ensure whether they are actually reasonable for the current context. Processed data are, however, created by editing the collected raw data during modelling process. Thus, data V&V involves credibility assessment of raw data and processed data used for creating each intermediate product. It should be noted that raw data are usually only relevant for obtaining structured problem description and conceptual model, can however not be directly applicable for creating formal model and other later intermediate products. During V&V of raw data concerning each intermediate product, the following issues must be ensured:

- data sources are reasonable for the intended purpose of the model. It is especially critical if the data are derived from a different system,
- both quantitative and qualitative data have been measured precisely enough, and
- the amount of data gathered is adequate for the further investigation.

V&V of processed data focus on ensuring that all data used for each intermediate product are correct and accurate in their transformed form during the model development, including the following typical issues:

- to evaluate the assumptions of independence and homogeneity made on the gathered data sets;
- to ensure that the probability distribution used and the associated parameters are reasonable for the data collection, for example, by using a goodness-of-fit test;
- to determine that data have been transformed in required form and structure; and
- to ensure that enough independent simulation runs have been executed for a stochastic model.

For documentation purposes, the contents of data V&V in the single phases are added to the V&V plan and V&V report, according to the well-defined document structures.

## 5.   MULTISTAGE TAILORING

As mentioned above, executing V&V activities in V&V sub-phases redundantly, such as comparing the formal model individually with the conceptual model, the structured problem description and the sponsor needs, takes more viewpoints of model assessment into consideration, so that the concluded V&V results in this way are more reliable. However, for many simulation applications in practice it is impossible to fully conduct all V&V activities recommended in the V&V triangle due to time and budge constraints. In such cases, a slim set of V&V activities, which conducts the credibility assessment still in a certain acceptable level in spite of the limitations, should be tailored.

Based on the detailed documentation requirements of M&S and VV&A [8], in which project constraints, intermediate products and their dependencies, VV&A acceptance criteria, V&V activities, and project roles are well defined and specified, a multistage tailoring process is proposed not only for model development, but also for conducting VV&A, including the following stages:

1.  Tailoring at the process level,
2.  Tailoring at the product level, and
3.  Tailoring at the role level.

At the beginning of an M&S project, tailoring of the model development process used in the simulation study is of prime importance for preparing M&S and VV&A plan. According to the determinations of the M&S project constraints, project-specific products (intermediate products or parts of them) and the associated V&V activities can be identified, and the irrelevant products are therefore ignored. For example, if it is determined that the formal model is not essential for the current project, the related products of the formal model and its defined V&V activities remain hence out of consideration. By considering the specified product dependencies, the project adaptation to the product level is conducted. This is the reason that during the model development further products to be developed may be selected, whereas the products existing in the M&S plan may be removed because the obligations between the products are identified. Moreover, tailoring is conducted at the role level. It means each project role has only the access according to its authority issued in the M&S project.

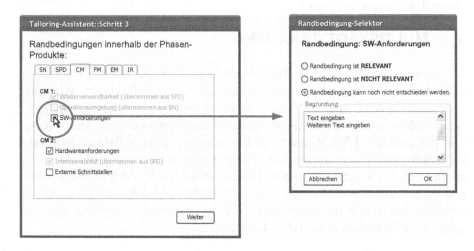

**Fig. 3  M&S Tailoring Assistant (German version)**

Based on this concept, a supporting tool, so-called M&S Tailoring Assistant, is prototypically implemented. Figure 3 shows an example for identifying an internal product dependency when developing the intermediate product "conceptual model" (abbr. to CM in this figure).

## 6.   CONCLUSION AND FUTURE RESEARCH

On the basis of our "classic" V&V concept, we present in this paper an improved approach for planning and conducting V&V of models and simulation results. By integrating the additional data V&V activities for each V&V phase, this concept extends the consideration range of the V&V triangle and refines the associated documentation requirements of intermediate products and V&V results consistently. Within the scope of project planning, a multistage tailoring concept for the purpose of project-specific adaptation is introduced. By arranging the tailoring efforts respectively at the levels of process, product and role, this generic tailoring concept offers a high degree of flexibility and feasibility for conducting M&S and VV&A under different constraints.

Further research will concentrate on (1) applying our proposed concepts of V&V and tailoring process in a real M&S project in practice, and (2) extending the tool support for conducting V&V activities, for instance, developing a V&V tool to support selecting and applying appropriate V&V techniques in different V&V contexts.

## REFERENCES

[1]   Balci, O.: Verification, Validation and Testing, in the Handbook of Simulation, Chapter 10, ed. Banks, J., John Wiley & Sons, 1998.

[2]   Banks, J., Carson II, J., Nelson, B., and Nicol, D.: Discrete-Event System Simulation. Forth Edition, Pearson Education International, 2005.

[3]   Brade, D.: A Generalized Process for the Verification and Validation of Models and Simulation Results, Dissertation, Universität der Bundeswehr München, 2003.

[4]   Brade, D.: Enhancing Modeling and Simulation Accreditation by Structuring Verification and Validation Results. In Proceeding of the 2000 Winter Simulation Conference, 2000.

[5]   Brade, D., and Lehmann, A.: Model Validation and Verification. In Modeling and Simulation Environment for Satellite and Terrestrial Communication Networks – Proceedings of the European COST Telecommunication Symposium, Kluwer Academic Publishers of Bosten, USA, 2002.

[6]   Hoover, S., and Perry, R.: Simulation: a problem-solving approach. Addison-Wesley Publishing Company, 1989.

[7]   Law, A., and Kelton, W.: Simulation Modelling and Analysis. Second Edition, McGraw-Hill, 1991.

[8]   Lehmann, A., Saad, S., Best, M., Köster, A., Pohl, S., Qian, J., Walder, C., Wang, Z., and Xu, Z.: Leitfaden für Modelldokumentation. Abschlussbericht (in German). ITIS e.V., 2005.

[9]   Rabe, M., Spieckermann, S., and Sigrid, W. (Hrsg.). Verifikation und Validierung für die Simulation in Produktion und Logistik. Springer, Berlin, to be published in 2007.

[10]  Robertson, N., and Perera, T.: Feasibility for Automatic Data Collection. In Proceedings of the 2001 Winter Simulation Conference, 2001.

[11]  Spieckermann, A., Lehmann, A., and Rabe, M.: Verifikation und Validierung: Überlegungen zu einer integrierten Vorgehensweise. In: Mertins, K and Rabe, M. (Hrsg.): Experiences from the Future (in German). Fraunhofer IRB, Stuttgart, p. 263-274, Stuttgart, 2004.

[12]  Sargent, R.: Verification, Validation, and Accreditation of Simulation Models. In Proceeding of the 2000 Winter Simulation Conference.

[13]  Shannon, R.: Systems Simulation: the art and science. Prentice-Hall, Inc, 1975.
[14]  Shannon, R.: Introduction to the Art and Science of Simulation. In Proceedings of the 1998 Winter Simulation Conference, 1998.

# CHAPTER 12

# Extending OPNET Modeler with External Pseudo Random Number Generators and Statistical Evaluation by the Limited Relative Error Algorithm

Markus Becker, Thushara Lanka Weerawardane,

Xi Li, Carmelita Görg

Communication Networks, TZI ikom, University of Bremen 28334
Bremen, Germany

**Abstract.** *Pseudo Random Number Generators (PRNG) are the base for stochastic simulations. The usage of good generators is essential for valid simulation results. OPNET Modeler a well-known tool for simulation of communication networks provides a Pseudo Random Number Generator. The extension of OPNET Modeler with external generators and additional statistical evaluation methods that has been performed for this paper increases the flexibility and options in the simulation studies performed.*

## 1. INTRODUCTION

Simulative analysis of complex systems is generally regarded as a scientific method. Stochastic simulations are based on sources of randomness. The randomness can be truly random [2, 3], but is usually created using algorithms called Pseudo Random Number Generators (PRNG). These algorithms do not create true random numbers. Many algorithms for PRNGs have been proposed and have been implemented [5]. Depending on the properties of the PRNGs [7], some of them are more or less suited for usage in simulations [8]. There are many different tests for PRNGs. Good PRNGs and their correct usage is essential for good and valid simulation results [3]. Every simulation environment provides PRNGs for the usage in simulation. In this paper the focus is on the well-known and often used simulation environment OPNET Modeler for communication networks and its Pseudo Random Number Generators.

In the following sections the OPNET Modeler PRNG and its limitations are introduced, other available PRNG implementations and statistical evaluation libraries are introduced and an integration of those into the OPNET Modeler is described. An application of the PRNGs and statistical evaluation algorithm into an M/M/1 model is evaluated with regard to the simulation time needed to fulfill the requirements of a given certain maximum relative error.

## 2.    OPNET PRNG

According to the documentation of the OPNET Modeler [15] the PRNGs in use in the tool are based on the operating systems random() implementation as shown in Table 1.

**Table 1: Random Number Generators**

| Operating System | Random Number Generator |
|---|---|
| Sun Solaris | random() |
| Microsoft Windows | random() (an OPNET port from the UNIX BSD source distribution) |

The usage in simulations is provided by the kernel procedures op_dist_uniform() and op_dist_outcome(). The underlying PRNG is initialized using the seed environment variable, which can be changed in the *'Configure/Run DES'* dialog. In order to create new instances of the PRNG the kernel procedure op_prg_random_gen_create() can be used.

### Limitations of the Provided PRNG

The PRNG provided by the OPNET Modeler has at least four limitations as described in the following paragraphs.

## Uncertainty of the PRNG

Although, as stated in the previous paragraph OPNET is using the BSD random() PRNG, it seems to be a customized version of the BSD random() PRNG. Additionally, it is not clear which version of the BSD random() PRNG it is based on as according to [18] there are at least 3 different versions (SunOS4, libc5, glibc2), which differ in the seeding procedure of the PRNG.

## The PRNG Fails Tests

According to [16] the BSD PRNGs fails at least the p-value test, which checks the uniformity of the values the PRNG outputs. PRNGs which fail tests should not be used, as several others are passing the test suites [2].

## Limited Number of Provided PRNGs

The OPNET Modeler provides only one PRNG. However, simulation results are doubtful if created with only one type of PRNG according to [19].

## No Independence of Sequences

If there is a need for complete independence of random number sequences, which is usually the case, an external PRNG needs to be used, according to the tools' documentation [15]. The kernel procedure op_dist_outcome_ext() can be used to get non-uniformly distributed random numbers using an external PRNG. However, the OPNET Modeler's documentation does not specify how to include external PRNGs into the models.

## Available PRNG Implementations

Implementations of PRNG algorithms can be found in many locations of the Internet. Two sources of implementations of PRNGs are introduced in more detail: the Communication Networks Class Library (CNCL) [12] and the GNU Scientific Library (GSL) [13].

## Communication Networks Class Library

The CNCL is a C++ library created by Communication Networks, Aachen University of Technology, Germany. It provides universal classes, event driven simulation classes, Pseudo Random Number Generators and distribution classes.

The PRNGs have the common super class CNRNG. Currently the CNCL provides the following PRNGs: additive random number generator

(CNACG), Fibonacci random number generator (CNFiboG), data file random number generator (CNFileG), linear congruential generator (CNLCG), multiple linear congruential generator (CNMLCG), Tausworthe generator (CNTausG).

Additionally the CNCL provides statistical evaluation classes, which are derived from CNStatistics: batch means, various limited relative error (LRE) algorithms, histograms and moments. It has been compiled using the GNU compiler collection (gcc) [20] on UNIX operating systems.

## GNU Scientific Library

The GNU Scientific Library (GSL) is a powerful and extensive numerical library for C and C++ programmers. Included in the library are algorithms for complex numbers, vectors and matrices, fast Fourier transforms, histograms, statistics and differential equations among many others. Additionally there are also algorithms for the generation of pseudo random numbers and distributions. The random number generators included are Mersenne Twister, RANLUX, CMRG, MRG, Tausworthe, GFSR, the UNIX PRNGs and many others. A Windows version of the GSL is available at [22].

## Approaches to the Integration of External PRNGs and Statistical Evaluation

In order to diminish the drawbacks of the OPNET Modeler's PRNG and to add functionality with respect to the statistical evaluation, the coupling of external libraries and OPNET Modeler is investigated in this paper. As a first step the integration of the library CNCL and the GSL into OPNET Modeler has been performed. There are different possibilities of integrating external PRNGs and statistical evaluation into OPNET Modeler. In the following we are detailing four approaches.

## Approach 1

The first approach is to use the source code of the CNCL or GSL and integrate it into OPNET process models. For this approach the code needs to be cumbersomely copied and adopted. When integrated into the process models it is compiled and linked in conjunction with the process models. This approach is viable for OPNET on Linux as well as for Windows operating system.

## Approach 2

OPNET Modeler provides a way to use other compilers than the usual Microsoft Visual Studio tools. This second approach uses OPNET External Compiler Interface (ECI) as described in [22] and GCC/mingw. ECI is a specification for interfacing OPNET with third-party compilers and linker programs. This approach is viable for OPNET on Linux as well as for Windows operating system.

## Approach 3

The Linux version of the OPNET simulator could be used. PRNGs and statistical distributions of CNCL could be integrated into the OPNET simulator as a link library. In this case, the task is rather direct because, CNCL, GSL and OPNET are compiling with the GCC compiler. However, this approach is fixed to the operating system Linux.

## Approach 4

The compilation and linking of the libraries is done using Microsoft Visual Studio tools on the Windows platform in the fourth approach. In order to do so, the CNCL library needs to be slightly adapted as until now it has been compiled using the GNU compiler tools. The GSL is available as a Windows library [22].

## Integration of External PRNGs and Statistical Evaluation

As a first way to get independent PRNGs into OPNET approach 1 was chosen. During this research progress was made with regard to approach 4. In the following details on the inclusion of PRNGs using approach 4 are given. The advantages of approach 4 are that it does not involve adaptation of source code by hand, a different operating system and the creation of an external compiler interface. The following steps need to be performed to integrate CNCL/GSL and OPNET:

## 1. Compilation of the CNCL with the Visual C++ Compiler and Creation of a Link Library of the CNCL

In order to create a link library, the Configuration Type needs to be set to Static Library (.lib), in the general project properties. Additionally the usage of the Microsoft Foundation Class needs to be specified as a shared library in the properties. The definitions - DCNCL_CC_GCC32 - DCNCL_HAS_BOOL need to be set. A binary library of the CNCL has been made available at [24].

## 2. Inclusion of the Header Files and the Library into the OPNET Simulation Models

Include the following in the source code header block of the process model to indicate to OPNET to use the C++ compiler:

```
OPC_COMPILE_CPP
```

Furthermore, the inclusion of the PRNGs header file and the definition of the variables are needed. Here is an example for the CNCL and GSL PRNG and distributions:

```
#include <CNCL/TausG.h>
#include <CNCL/NegExp.h>

#include <gsl/gsl_rng.h>
#include <gsl/gsl_randist.h>

CNTausG* t_rng;
CNNegExp* cncl_negexp;

gsl_rng* gsl_opnet_rng;
```

In the init enter execs the pseudo random number generators and distributions need to be created.

```
t_rng = new CNTausG();
t_rng->seed(seed);
cncl_negexp = new CNNegExp(1, t_rng);

gsl_opnet_rng = gsl_rng_alloc (gsl_rng_taus2);
gsl_rng_set(gsl_opnet_rng, seed);
```

The following code block shows the usage of the different PRNGs:

```
if (rng_type == OPNET) {
     next_intarr_time       =       oms_dist_outcome
(interarrival_dist_ptr);
} else if (rng_type == CNCL) {
     next_intarr_time = (*cncl_negexp)();
} else { //GSL
     next_intarr_time       =       gsl_ran_exponential
(gsl_opnet_rng, 1);
}
```

For the usage of the LRE algorithms the following additions to the header code block need to be made:

```
OPC_COMPILE_CPP

#include <CNCL/DLREF.h>

CNDLREF*  delay_lre  =  new  CNDLREF(0.0,  100.0,  1,
0.05);
CNDLREF*  size_lre   =  new  CNDLREF(0.0,  100.0,  1,
0.05);
```

To use the LRE, the values need to be put into the object:

```
size_lre->put(op_subq_stat (0, OPC_QSTAT_PKSIZE));
```

## 3. Changes to the Preferences Need to be Made to Enable Compilation and Binding of the Simulator

Edit the preferences to meet the settings listed in Table 2 adapted to the paths on your system. After changing the preferences all files need to be saved and compiled by executing 'DES -> Configure/Run Discrete Event Simulation'. At the advanced tab the model recompilation needs to be forced.

**Table 2: Preferences Settings**

| comp_flags_common | -IC:\Docume~1\mab\MyDocu~1\src\cncl-2.8\include  -IC:\Progra~1\GnuWin32\include<br>-DCNCL_CC_GCC32 -DCNCL_HAS_BOOL |
|---|---|
| bind_shobj_libs | C:\Docume~1\mab\MyDocu--1\Visual~1\CNCL_M~1\Debug\CNCL_M~1.lib<br>C:\Progra~1\GnuWin32\lib\libgsl.a |
| bind_static_flag | /LIBPATH:C:\PROGRA~1\OPNET\10.0.A\sys\pc_inte l_win32\lib /NODEFAULTLIB:library |
| repositories | (Empty) not (stdmod) |

## Limited Relative Error

The limited relative error has been described in several publications [25], [26], [27], [28]. There are three different versions of the algorithm. LRE I is used for an independent, continuous x-sequence; LRE II for a correlated, continuous x-sequence and the LRE III is for a correlated, discrete x-sequence.

The algorithm uses local mappings to 2-node Markov Chains to calculate the local correlation coefficients and thus the relative error. Shown below is exemplary output of the algorithm. It calculates the cumulative distribution function (CDF), the relative error and correlation coefficient.

```
#LRE RESULT (THIS IS A MAGIC LINE)
#-----------------------------------------------------
--------------------------
#    Discrete Lre --- distribution function
#-----------------------------------------------------
--------------------------
#Name: No name
#Text: No description
#Default values: max.rel. error =    5%  X_min: 0
X_max: 100
#trials: 24983  mean: 10.84       variance: 96.62
#trials < X_min: 0     trials > X_max: 0
#All levels calculated.
#-----------------------------------------------------
--------------------------
#F(x)              x                 rel.error
rho               sigrho
0.0000000e+000    0.0000000e+000    0.0000000e+000
0.0000000e+000
3.8426130e-002    0.0000000e+000    4.6821223e-002
3.7277310e-001    1.5821438e-002
3.8426130e-002    1.0000000e+000    4.6821223e-002
3.7277310e-001
1.1431774e-001    1.0000000e+000    3.9807701e-002
6.7266369e-001    8.5854153e-003
1.1431774e-001    2.0000000e+000    3.9807701e-002
6.7266369e-001
1.8196374e-001    2.0000000e+000    3.9791740e-002
7.9590151e-001    5.6872325e-003
1.8196374e-001    3.0000000e+000    3.9791740e-002
7.9590151e-001
2.4692791e-001    3.0000000e+000    3.7231946e-002
8.3812994e-001    4.4035090e-003
2.4692791e-001    4.0000000e+000    3.7231946e-002
8.3812994e-001
```

## Application of the External PRNGs and the LRE in Simulations

In order to show the impact of using external PRNGs and external statistical evaluation tools, an M/M/1 model as described in the Tutorial of the OPNET Modeler's documentation [29] is used. The model is depicted in Fig. 1 and consists of a source of packets, a queue and a sink, which models the serving process. All settings are according to the tutorial, the changes that where introduced are the usage of different PRNGs, and the evaluation of the number of packets and the delays using the limited relative error (LRE) algorithm. The PRNGs in use are the original OPNET PRNG, the CNCL Tausworthe PRNG and the GSL Tausworthe PRNG.

**Fig. 1  M/M/1 OPNET Model**

The cumulative distribution function (CDF) of the packet delay is shown in  (a) OPNET, while the number of packets in the queue is shown in Fig. 3. Additionally, the relative error is shown in the Figures. The simulations were run with a fixed seed of 128 for all PRNGs. The model time simulated is 7 hours as described in the tutorial. When comparing Figures 2(a)-(c), it can be seen that the OPNET PRNG has a higher relative error at low packet delay times, where the error is in high regions for all PRNGs. This region would determine the time needed to simulate with a limited relative error. In the preset time of 7 hours model time, the relative error could not go below a value of 0.05. This means, that the model time has not been long enough to be statistically sound with respect to an error level of 0.05. With respect to the number of packets in the queue, all PRNGs could limit the relative error to 0.05 in the given model time.

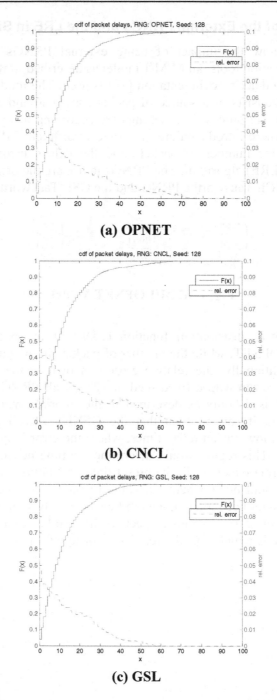

(a) OPNET

(b) CNCL

(c) GSL

**Fig. 2  CDF and relative error of packet delays**

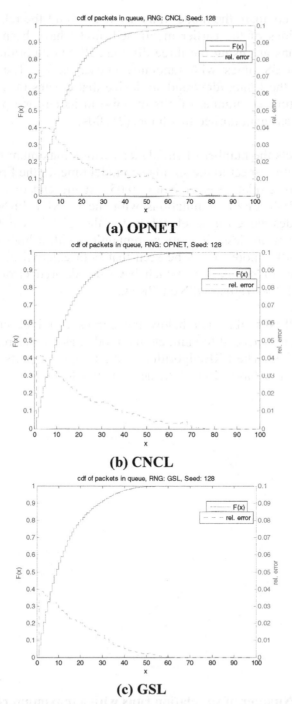

**(a) OPNET**

**(b) CNCL**

**(c) GSL**

**Fig. 3  CDF and relative error of number of packets in the queue**

In order to compare the model time needed to limit the relative error to 0.05, simulations of the earlier mentioned model have been undertaken. The simulations are using the three different PRNG algorithms and each PRNG is run 88 times with randomly chosen seeds. The seeds were created using the Linux /dev/random device that creates random numbers within the estimated number of bits of noise in its entropy pool [23].The model time was again limited to 7 hours (25200s).

Fig. 4 depicts the number of simulations with a maximum relative error below 0.05 with respect to the simulated model time. In the first 10000s no simulation has a relative error below 0.05. At the end of the simulated model time 10% of the simulations with the OPNET PRNG have not reached the desired error level, while for the CNCL and GSL PRNG algorithms there are less simulations remaining with a higher error level than 0.05. Furthermore, it can be seen that both external PRNGs have a higher amount of simulations which have the desired error level when compared with the original OPNET PRNG.

With all PRNGs the area below the curves could be employed for reducing the time needed to simulate the model, as the desired error level has been reached. The LRE algorithm in the CNCL supports the stopping of simulations that have reached the desired error level.

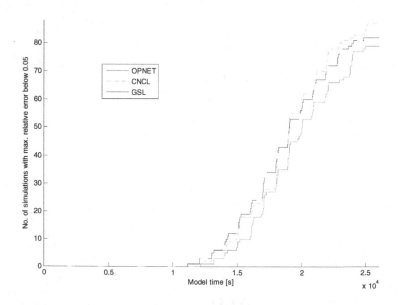

**Fig. 4  Number of simulation runs with a maximum relative error of 0.05**

## CONCLUSION AND OUTLOOK

In this paper the PRNG used in the well-known simulation tool OPNET Modeler was presented. The limitations of using only one PRNG in this tool were discussed. As a way to overcome these limitations 4 different approaches are proposed in this paper and detailed information is provided on how to integrate external algorithms, including PRNGs and the LRE statistical evaluation, into the tool. The results by the different PRNGs are evaluated using the LRE algorithm. It was shown that the usage of external PRNGs in combination with the LRE algorithm can reduce the computation time for simulations.

In future the external PRNG and additional statistical evaluation methods will be used in simulations of UMTS radio network simulations as well as simulations that evaluate the usage of mobile radio communications for logistical processes.

## ACKNOWLEDGEMENTS

This research was supported by the German Research Foundation (DFG) as part of the Collaborative Research Centre 637 "Autonomous Cooperating Logistic Processes".

## REFERENCES

[1]    Krzysztof Pawlikowski, Hae-Duck Joshua Jeong, Jong-Suk Ruth Lee: On credibility of simulation studies of telecommunication networks. IEEE Communications Magazine, vol. 40, no. 1, Jan 2002 pp. 132–139.

[2]    P. L'Ecuyer: Random Number Generation. Chapter 4 of the Handbook on Simulation, Jerry Banks Ed., Wiley, 1998, 93–137.

[3]    P. L'Ecuyer: Software for Uniform Random Number Generation: Distinguishing the Good and the Bad. Proceedings of the 2001 Winter Simulation Conference, IEEE Press, Dec. 2001, 95-105.

[4]    P. Hellenek: Vorsicht: Zufallszahlen!, International Mathematische Nachrichten, Nr. 180, April 1999.

[5]    M. Matsumoto and T. Nishimura: Mersenne Twister: A 623–dimensionally equidistributed uniform pseudorandom number generator. ACM Trans. on Modeling and Computer Simulation Vol. 8, No. 1, January pp. 3–30 (1998).

[6]    Webpage: Theory and Practice of Random Number Generation. http://random.mat.sbg.ac.at/

[7]    Webpage: Random Number Generation and Testing. http://csrc.nist. gov/rng/

[8]    Webpage: True Random Numbers. http://www.random.org/

[9]    Webpage: True Deterministic Numbers. http://www.noentropy.net/

[10]   M. Junius, M. Steppler, M. Büter, D. Pesch, and others, Communication Networks Class Library, Edition 1.10, 1998.

[11]   Webpage: GNU Compiler Collection (gcc). http://gcc.gnu.org/

[12]   Webpage: Communication Networks Class Library (CNCL). https:// www.comnets.uni-bremen.de/typo3site/index.php?id=31

[13]   Webpage: GSL - GNU Scientific Library http://www.gnu.org/ software/gsl/

[14]   OPNET technologies Inc., OPNET Modeler Accelerating Networks R&D, www.opnet.com

[15]   OPNET Modeler Product Documentation Release 10.0, pages MC-11–26 – MC–11–27.

[16]   Pierre L'Ecuyer, Richard Simard: TestU01: A C Library for Empirical Testing of Random Number Generators. May 2006, Revised November 2006, ACM Transactions on Mathematical Software, to appear.

[17]   GNU Scientific Library Reference Manual - Revised Second Edition, http://www.gnu.org/

[18]   M. Galassi et al: GNU Scientific Library Reference Manual. Revised Second Edition, Section 17.10: Unix random number generators, ISBN 0954161734.

[19]   P. Hellekalek: Good random number generators are (not so) easy to find. In Mathematics and Computers in Simulation (1998).

[20]   Webpage: GNU compiler collection: http://gcc.gnu.org

[21]   OPNET Modeler Product Documentation Release 10.0, pages MC-11–26 – MC–11–27. OPNET Modeler Product Documentation Release 10.0, external reference manual, pages E–6–1 to E–6–5.

[22]   Webpage: Windows Version of the GSL: http://gnuwin32.sourceforge. net/packages/gsl.htm

[23]   Linux Programmer's Manual RANDOM(4), 2003–10–25.

[24]   Webpage: Windows binary of the Communication Networks Class Library: http://www.comnets.uni-bremen.de/~mab/opnet/cncl/

[25]   F. Schreiber, C. Görg: Rare Event Simulation: A Modified RESTART-Method using the LRE-Algorithm. Teletraffic and Datatraffic, Proceedings 14th ITC, Antibes, Juan-Les-Pins, France, June 6–10, 1994, 787–796, 1994.

[26]  F. Schreiber, C. Görg: Stochastic Simulation: a Simplified LRE-Algorithm for Discrete Random Sequences. AEU, 50:233–239, 1996.

[27]  C. Görg, F. Schreiber: Der LRE - Algorithmus für die statistische Auswertung korrelierter Zufallsdaten. In F. Breitenecker, I. Troch, P. Kopacek, (Eds.), Simulationstechnik, 170–174, Wiesbaden, 1990. 6. ASIM - Symposium, Wien 1990, Vieweg.

[28]  C. Görg, F. Schreiber: The RESTART/LRE Method for Rare Event Simulation. In 1996 Winter Simulation Conference, 390–397, Coronado, California, USA, December 1996.

[29]  OPNET Modeler Product Documentation Release 10.0, General Tutorials, M/M/1 Queue, pages 1 – 42.

# CHAPTER 13

## Towards Flexible, Reliable, High Throughput Parallel Discrete Event Simulations

Richard Fujimoto, Alfred Park, Jen-Chih Huang

Computational Science and Engineering Division
College of Computing
Georgia Institute of Technology

**Abstract.** *The excessive amount of time necessary to complete large-scale discrete-event simulations of complex systems such as telecommunication networks, transportation systems, and multiprocessor computers continues to plague researchers and impede progress in many important domains. Parallel discrete-event simulation techniques offer an attractive solution to addressing this problem by enabling scalable execution, and much prior research has been focused on this approach. However, effective, practical solutions have been elusive. This is largely because of the complexity and difficulty associated with developing parallel discrete event simulation systems and software. In particular, an effective parallel execution mechanism must simultaneously address a variety of issues, such as efficient synchronization, resource allocation, load distribution, and fault tolerance, to mention a few. Further, most systems that have been developed to date assume a set of processors is dedicated to completing the simulation computation, yielding inflexible execution environments. Effective exploitation of parallelization techniques requires that these issues be addressed automatically by the underlying system, largely transparent to the application developer.*

*We describe an approach to execute large-scale parallel discrete event simulation programs over multiple processor computing resources that automates many of the tasks associated with parallel execution. Based on concepts utilized in volunteer distributed computing projects, an approach is proposed that supports execution over computing platforms shared with other users. This approach automatically adapts as new processors are added or existing processors taken aware during the course of the execution. The runtime environment based on a master-worker approach is used to automatically distribute simulation computations over the available processors to balance workload, and to automatically recover from processor failures that may occur during the computation. Synchronization, a particularly important problem for parallel discrete-event simulation computations, is handled automatically by the underlying runtime system.*

## 1.    INTRODUCTION

Simulation is widely recognized as an essential tool to analyze complex systems such as large-scale telecommunication networks. In telecommunications, analytic methods are useful in many situations, however, the complexity of many networks combined with the inability to apply simplifying assumptions such as Markovian traffic limit the applicability of purely analytic approaches. Simulation is often used to gain insight into the behavior of particular protocols and mechanisms under a variety of network conditions. In some cases, simulations of small to medium sized networks may be sufficient to gain critical insights into the behavior of the network. However, if one is concerned with scalability issues or the impact of design decisions on the Internet as a whole, large-scale network simulations are often required. Such simulations are problematic on desktop machines and workstations because the memory requirements and computation time required to complete large-scale simulations is prohibitive. For such simulations, parallel discrete event simulation (PDES) techniques that distribute the execution of the simulation over many processors can be useful.

Several efforts in recent years have been aimed at harnessing the massive potential computing power afforded by the Internet through large-scale public distributed computing projects. Successful volunteer distributed computing projects include distributed.net, World Community Grid, and SETI@home [1]. These projects utilize spare processor cycles to execute portions of a larger task that could potentially take many years if attempted on even the largest supercomputers. The Aurora Parallel and

Distributed Simulation System (Aurora) attempts to bridge the gap between general distributed computing projects such as these and parallel discrete event simulation PDES field. Like the other systems mentioned above, Aurora is designed as a vehicle for *high throughput computing* where the goal is to harness available computing cycles from large numbers of machines rather than strictly achieving high speedups on dedicated hardware.

Parallel discrete event simulation systems have traditionally been developed "from scratch" for execution on high performance computing platforms. However, these systems typically offer relatively low tolerance for dynamic client behavior and node failures. The latter is becoming increasingly problematic; as new machines emerge containing hundreds of thousands to millions of processors, the likelihood of a failure during a long simulation run is becoming a greater concern.

By contrast, the master/worker approach allows distribution of work to any clients that request it, greatly reducing the reliance on dedicating machine resources. Clients can be easily added or removed during the execution of the simulation as new resources become available, or must be removed for use by other computations. There are no restrictions placed upon the client other than proper configuration and the ability to contact the server to download simulation state and data. Client failures are easily handled by reissuing pending computations to other clients, and server failures can be handled by maintaining state information on secondary storage.

## 2.    RELATED WORK

There has been a significant amount of work leveraging the World Wide Web for simulations. Work in this area includes web-based simulations using Java RMI [5], self-managing web-based simulations [6], and use of Object Request Brokers for web-based simulation [7]. The Extensible Modeling and Simulation Framework is a collection of software and tools that promotes interoperability and the use of standards in the context of modeling and simulation [8]. There has been work done using grid-based technologies such as Globus [9] to execute HLA-compliant simulations over the grid through efforts such as IDSim [10] and HLAGrid [11]. PIRS is an effort to speed up parallel simulation on machines with varying workloads using a scheduling policy [12]. The work presented here is fundamentally different than these efforts in that the Aurora framework employs a master/worker paradigm to allow parallel and distributed simulations to be run on a variety of clients but without guarantees that the client may ever return a result. Moreover, the Aurora system allows simulations to be run nearly anywhere, where resources do not have to be designated as part of a grid, a supercomputer, or a computational cluster.

Several distributed computing systems share similar goals as the Aurora system. Condor [13], Parallel Virtual Machine (PVM) [14], and Condor MW [15] are systems that pool processing power from various machines into a single computing resource. More recent work referred to as "public" or "volunteer" computing has attempted to harness computers on a massive scale. Examples include Unicorn [16], InteGrade [17], and Berkley Open Infrastructure for Network Computing (BOINC) [18]. The Aurora system utilizes a similar master/worker style of work distribution as employed by Condor MW combined with the features of BOINC-enabled projects like SETI@home. The important difference is that the Aurora system is specifically tailored for PDES execution, offering services such as time and logical process (LP) management.

## 3.    BACKGROUND AND MOTIVATION

Node failure can be problematic for large-scale simulations over super-computers or grids unless a checkpoint/recovery system is implemented. The Aurora system, through the master/worker design, allows a level of robustness for parallel and distributed simulations for dealing with node failure as well as distributing simulation load across the available client pool. Another major feature of the Aurora system is the ability to run simulations in the "background." Machines with Aurora clients can be processing other jobs. This allows simulations to be run on non-dedicated or unreserved machines without significant overhead, while contributing to the overall distributed simulation computation.

Aurora is best adapted for applications where a significant amount of computation can be handed to a client for execution. Tightly coupled simulations with much global communication or low amount of para-llelism may be better suited for traditional PDES or sequential execution mechanisms. This is an area of future research.

An initial version of the Aurora system is described in [19]. Although the main principles of the original system have carried over to the Aurora2 system described here, there were some shortcomings that the system architecture presented as simulations began to scale. The motivation for this next generation Aurora system was a culmination of ideas for improvements over its predecessor while maintaining high performance and scalability as a paramount concern.

## 4.   PARALLEL DISCRETE EVENT SIMULATION AND NETWORK SIMULATION

The programming model in Aurora mirrors that used in traditional PDES systems. Specifically, the application is assumed to consist of a collection of logical processes, or LPs. Each LP maintains its own local state variables. Global state variables that are shared between LPs are not allowed. Rather, LPs communicate by exchanging time stamped events. Here, we use the terms "event" and "message" synonymously. In essence, each LP can be viewed as a sequential discrete event simulation program with a list of pending events that it must process. LPs can schedule events for other LPs by sending a time stamped message.

For example, in a telecommunication network simulator that is performing a packet-level simulation of a large network, each LP might model a router or an end host (computer). Events within each LP might correspond to the arrival or generation of new packets. For example, the transmission of a packet from one router to another could be simulated by one LP scheduling a packet arrival event at the second, where the two LPs models the sending and receiving router, respectively. The time stamp reflects the time of arrival at the latter router. The state variables within each LP might include message queues and tables necessary to correctly route packets.

## 5.   MASTER/WORKER AND PDES: AN OVERVIEW

The master/worker paradigm is a mechanism in a distributed computing environment for dividing up a potentially large computation into smaller portions of work which can be tasked out to a pool of workers operating under the direction of a master controller. Although this concept has been well-studied in the general distributed computation literature, it has not been explored fully when coupled with the requirements of parallel discrete event simulations.

General distributed computing programs do not have the same requirements as those of PDES programs and thus infrastructure must be specifically designed to support this simulation environment. Traditional master/worker systems lease "work units" to clients for execution. For example, SETI@Home divides received radio telescope data into portions which clients can download for analysis. These work units are time-independent from other clients and require no communication between clients as they perform computations as leased by the master. These conditions simplify the runtime requirements of the underlying master/worker infrastructure and are inadequate to support PDES.

In conventional PDES systems, a simulation consists of many logical processes that communicate by exchanging time-stamped messages as the simulation progresses. The first important difference in a master/worker PDES system is that the LP state must be tracked and stored. Some general distributed computing projects only require a simplifying result at the end of their computation, however, a PDES system must maintain the state of the LP which may be leased to a different client at a later time. Furthermore, the PDES system must ensure that these time-stamped messages are delivered in the correct order to the proper destination LP to preserve the local causality constraint (LCC). Therefore, in addition to correctly ordering messages sent between LPs, these messages must be maintained for future delivery to any LP or collection of LPs that are leased as a work unit to an available client. Moreover, work units must be properly constrained for execution as processing events and messages arbitrarily into the future may violate the LCC. Therefore conservative or optimistic time management schemes must be employed alongside LP and work unit management in a master/worker PDES system.

These key differences and requirements between general distributed computing programs and PDES in a master/worker paradigm is the impetus for the Aurora system. However, the need for highly scalable and high performance distributed simulations drive the architecture for the system, which is described next.

## 6.   AURORA2 ARCHITECTURE

The Aurora2 architecture is a complete re-engineered effort over the previous generation Aurora Master/Worker Parallel and Discrete Event Simulation system. Although the first generation Aurora system showed good performance through the use of web services, there were various issues impeding the scalability and thus high performance in large-scale simulations, the paramount goal for this PDES system while maintaining the benefits of a master/worker style computation. The Aurora2 system design incorporates new features and novel concepts to further improve performance over its predecessor.

The first generation Aurora system utilized the gSOAP toolkit [20] to provide most of the communications infrastructure. gSOAP provides high performance web services for C and C++ applications which can be bridged to other languages. The document-centric nature of web services provides an architecture neutral computing platform but incurs performance penalties due to the encoding of any data that is sent over the wire including encoding binary data in Base64 which is performed frequently under a master/worker style system due to state saving.

The Aurora2 architecture incorporates several important changes over its predecessor to further performance, scalability, and robustness of the computing platform. The major changes include multiple concurrent simulation and simulation replication support, multiple work unit servers, multiple message state servers, sockets-based communication, multi-threaded execution, and support for caching mechanisms to improve performance.

## 6.1    Conceptual Overview

The master/worker paradigm promotes a clear separation between the controller and workers that perform computation on the work unit passed to them by the master. The Aurora2 (henceforth referred to as simply Aurora) architecture divides the master infrastructure into three main back-end services as shown in Fig. 1. These services include a proxy, one or multiple work unit state servers, and one or multiple work unit message state servers. The distributed nature of the back-end services helps to ensure scalability and robustness of the Aurora system. These back-end services communicate with each other over TCP/IP sockets.

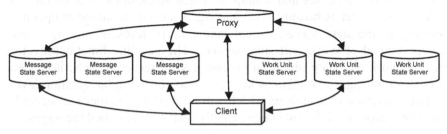

**Fig. 1  General overview of interaction between different back-end services and a client during a typical simulation**

The Aurora clients perform the actual simulation computation by contacting the proper back-end services to download simulation state and associated messages per work unit lease. Computation is done locally, independent of other clients. Once the computation completes, the final state and messages are uploaded to the work unit state and message state servers. This process can repeat for a specified number of times or until the simulation reaches its end time. As illustrated in Fig. 1, the client will only contact back-end services pertinent to its own execution as directed by the proxy.

Due to the addition of multiple concurrent simulation support, Aurora uses the concept of simulation packages (SimPkg). These simulation packages contain all of the runtime parameters of the simulation such as number of work units, a lookahead connectivity graph, simulation begin and end times, wallclock time deadlines per work unit lease, and possible initial states. These specifications are uploaded to the proxy service where necessary metadata and allocation of resources is done prior to starting the simulation and allowing clients to begin execution.

## 6.2   Aurora Proxy

The Aurora Proxy service is the central core controller that oversees the simulation and the other two back-end components. The management of the other services is handled by internal managers. The work unit state and message state servers are controlled by independent managers within the proxy that keep track of metadata such as client keys, server IP addresses, and simulation package to work unit storage allocation. The proxy currently contains three major managers: state server manager, message state server manager, and a simulation package manager as shown in Fig. 2.

The work unit state server manager contains control information such as state server IP addresses and a map of which work units of a simulation package the server is hosting. The message state server manager operates similarly to the state server, except that it keeps track of message state servers instead of work unit state servers. The baseline functionality for both the work unit state server and message state server are inherited from a common manager class, but is kept separate at the implementation level for future caching mechanisms which will be distinct whether the server is supporting atomic work unit states or individual time stamped messages.

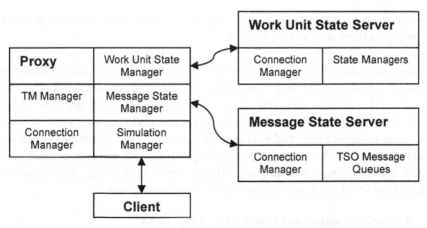

**Fig. 2  Internal metadata and state management**

The simulation manager stores the metadata of a simulation package and performs any work related to simulation packages and work units associated with simulation packages. For example, when a simulation package is uploaded, the simulation manager finds available space onto where work unit state and future message state can be stored on available servers. Client requests for work are passed to the simulation managers for leasing duties as well as keeping track of which work units have been leased or locked down to prevent further leasing.

The simulation managers instantiate time managers as specified by the simulation package definition. Time managers contain information regarding leased work unit simulation times for time management. These managers are responsible for computing safe processing bounds for any given work unit. Additionally, time managers may employ conservative or optimistic time management schemes or a possible combination of both. The current implementation of Aurora contains a centralized conservative time management mechanism.

## 6.3  Aurora Work Unit and Message State Services

The other components of the Aurora back-end service are the work unit and message state servers. The work unit server contains the current values of state vectors for each work unit in the system and its associated simulation time for which this state is valid. These work unit states are application-defined contiguous blocks of memory and are handled by pack and unpack procedures overwritten by the Aurora clients. The message state server is similar to the state server except that instead of storing state of work units, future messages are stored in increasing timestamp order according to their destination work unit.

These services can be easily adapted for optimistic and caching routines by simply storing state and message state histories instead of discarding previous values upon state and message updates. Although distribution of the workload among the proxy, work unit state and message state servers has increased scalability and performance, much of the future performance potential of the Aurora system lies in exploiting optimistic execution and employing caching mechanisms. These services include the baseline architecture for these types of performance enhancements.

## 6.4  Aurora Clients and Work Unit Lifecycle

The Aurora clients perform work as dictated by the master comprised of the proxy and associated state servers. The Aurora client will perform iterations of a work unit lifecycle as specified at run time. This lifecycle is comprised of four major steps:

1. Initialization
2. Work unit setup
3. Application-defined simulation execution
4. Work unit finalization

The initialization step is typically done only one time when the client starts up. This step includes thread initialization, signal handler setup, and command-line parsing. After this step completes, the work unit begins the setup and download phase to populate the client with the proper state variables and messages to process for the leased simulation execution time. The steps for the work unit setup are performed in the following chrono-logical order:

1. Client key request
2. Request work unit and associated metadata
3. Populate internal metadata structures and create a work unit manager if necessary
4. Contact state server and download state
5. Contact message state server and download messages
6. Unpack work unit state
7. Unpack work unit messages and populate the incoming message queue in time-stamp order

Client keys are unique identifiers issued to the clients upon first contact to the proxy and is used by the client to identify itself in future communications. Once a unique client key is issued, the client performs a work unit request where the proxy may or may not lease a work unit to the requesting worker. If a work unit is available to be leased, associated metadata about the work unit is downloaded from the proxy service. Internally, the client will then set up supporting data structures for the impending work unit. Once this step has completed, the client will then contact the proper work unit state and message state servers and download the packed information. The work unit state is then processed by the application-defined unpack method to load current state variables. The message states are automatically unpacked by the Aurora client into a time-stamp ordered priority queue for processing by the client during the simulation execution.

After the work unit setup has completed, the application-defined simulation execution method is invoked and the simulation runs until the end time as specified during the work unit metadata download (step 2 of the work unit setup). During the simulation execution, if the work unit detects a message that is destined for another work unit, it will perform a destination message server lookup. This is performed in a separate thread from the main execution loop and the result is cached for future use. When the simulation reaches the end time as specified by the proxy, work unit finalization begins which is the final step in the work unit lifecycle. This process is comprised of seven steps:

1. Pack final state
2. Pack future messages destined for itself
3. Contact proxy to begin consistency convergence
4. Collate and pack future messages destined for other work units by message state server keys; deliver collated messages to the proper message state servers
5. Upload work unit state to state server
6. Upload messages packed in step 2 to message state servers
7. Receive consistency convergence verification from proxy

The first step calls an application-defined method for packing the final state into a contiguous area of memory for upload to the state server. Next, the client packages any remaining unprocessed messages on the time-stamp ordered message queue which may have been created by sending messages during simulation execution by the work unit to itself. The client then initiates a consistency convergence to the proxy.

A consistency convergence locks down the work unit so it may not be leased again or updated in multiple lease scenarios. This allows atomic commits and prevents inconsistent updates of updated work unit and message states. The client then begins a message collation process where future messages destined for work units which reside on the same physical message state server are packed together. This reduces the frequency of smaller message updates and allows the clients to update groups of messages at one time. After this process completes, the final state and future messages destined for the work unit are uploaded to the appropriate servers. The final step is a verification of consistency convergence from the proxy that the process was completed successfully without errors on the back-end. During steps 4-6, the Aurora state and message state servers send messages to the proxy indicating updates to their respective states. The proxy acknowledges these messages and keeps track of the consistency convergence process with the final result of the update returned to the client.

## 6.5    Aurora Application Programmer's Interface

The Aurora C++ API consists of two major parts: the simulation package definition interface and the Aurora client interface. The simulation package definition contains all of the information necessary to load a simulation instance on to the Aurora back-end services for leasing to clients.

### Simulation Package Definition Interface

The simulation package inherits most of the functionality from the base AuroraSimPkg class.

The `CreateConnectionMatrix` method must be overwritten which provides a reference to the connectivity matrix. This matrix is a simple two-dimensional array of lookahead values representing the connectivity graph of work units in the simulation.

**TestSimPkg.h**

```
#include "AuroraSimPkg.h"

class TestSimPkg : public AuroraSimPkg {
  public:
    TestSimPkg() {}
    ~TestSimPkg() {}
    double **CreateConnectionMatrix(void);
};
```

**TestSimPkg.cc**

```
#include "TestSimPkg.h"

double **CreateConnectionMatrix() {
  double **la_table;
  // fill connectivity matrix with lookahead values
  return la_table;
}

int main(int argc, char *argv[]) {
  TestSimPkg simpkg;
  simpkg.Initialize(numwu, AURORA_TM_CONSERVATIVE, memperlp,
                    deadline, begintime, endtime, "testsim");
  simpkg.UploadSimPkg("127.0.0.1");
  // upload any initial state
  for (aurora_int_t i = 0; i < numwu; i++) {
    simpkg.UploadLPState(i, initialstatesize, packedstate);
  }
  return AURORA_SUCCESS;
}
```

**Fig. 3  Simulation Package Definition API**

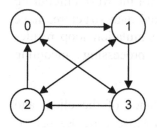

|   | 0   | 1   | 2   | 3   |
|---|-----|-----|-----|-----|
| 0 | 0   | 1.0 | -1  | 0.7 |
| 1 | -1  | 0   | 0.8 | 0.1 |
| 2 | 0.5 | 0.9 | 0   | -1  |
| 3 | 0.4 | -1  | 0.3 | 0   |

**Fig. 4  Example four work unit connectivity graph and associated lookahead table**

A simple four work unit connectivity graph and its associated lookahead connection matrix is shown in Fig. 4. Work units which do not communicate with each other are indicated by a lookahead value of less than zero.

The simulation package definition interface offers three other method calls for simulation setup. The `Initialize` method is called indicating various initial values such as total number of work units, simulation begin and end times, wallclock deadlines per lease, etc. The `UploadSimPkg` method is called when the definition is ready to be uploaded to the Aurora back-end, where the parameter for the method is the dotted-quad IP address of the Aurora proxy service. The final method is optional which the application programmer may use to populate initial work unit states via `UploadLPState`.

### Client Interface

The Aurora Client API provides interfaces for creating a simulation worker client that downloads work unit state, messages, processes events for its leased time window, and returns finalized state vectors and output messages. Fig. 5 shows an example implementation of the Aurora Client API. The TestClient inherits the base AuroraClient class which provides most of the internal routines for contacting the Aurora back-end services for leasing and work unit finalizing. Three pure-virtual methods must be overwritten to provide application-dependent routines specific to the simulation. These methods are `Run`, `PackState`, and `UnpackState`. `UnpackState` is called by the client to unpack and populate the various application-dependent state vectors upon receiving a valid work unit lease and after the work unit state has been successfully downloaded. `PackState` is the logical inverse of `UnpackState` and is called during the finalization procedure is invoked. The `Run` method is called by the client after `UnpackState`, all messages destined for the work unit during the leased simulation time window, and all internal data structures have been initialized. This `Run` method is where the simulation loop resides performing the simulation computation and processing incoming messages.

The client's `main` routine instantiates an instance of the client and hands execution to the AuroraClient class through `Execute`. `Execute` performs command-line parsing on Aurora-specific parameters such as –i for maximum client iterations.

**TestClient.h**

```
#include "AuroraClient.h"

class TestClient : public AuroraClient {
  public:
    TestClient() {}
    ~TestClient() {}
    void Run(void);
    aurora_data_t *PackState(aurora_int_t *);
    void UnpackState(aurora_int_t, aurora_data_t *);
};
```

**TestClient.cc**

```
#include "TestClient.h"

aurora_data_t  *TestClient::PackState(aurora_int_t  *size)
{
  aurora_data_t *packedstate;
  // perform application-dependent state packing routine
  *size = packedstate_size;
  return packedstate;
}

void       TestClient::UnpackState(aurora_int_t       size,
aurora_data_t *data) {
  //   perform   application-dependent   state   unpacking
routine
}

void TestClient::Run(void) {
  AuroraMessage *msg;
  while (CanRun()) {
    msg = GetNextMessage();
    if (msg != NULL) {
      // Process Event
      IncEventCounter();
    }
    if (terminating_condition == true) {
      EndRun();
    }
  }
}
int main(int argc, char *argv[]) {
  TestClient client;
  client.Execute(argc, argv);
  return AURORA_SUCCESS;
}
```

**Fig. 5  Client API**

## 7.    FAULT TOLERANCE SYSTEM

The Aurora system provides a transparent fault tolerance system for simulations that exploits the inherent state and message saving that is necessary in a master/worker paradigm. By leveraging this mechanism, most of the support and modifications are only needed on the back-end services. The two major approaches used in the Aurora system for fault tolerance are replication and checkpointing.

### 7.1    Resilience to Client Failure

Due to the assumption that clients are not guaranteed to return a result, one of the requirements of creating a simulation package definition is to specify a *deadline*. These deadlines are essentially wallclock runtime limits for any leased work unit for that particular simulation. If the back-end services do not receive a work unit return within this time limit, it is assumed that the client has failed whether this is due to the client crashing or the computation exceeding the stated wallclock time limit. If a work unit return is not received by the deadline, this work unit is re-issued to another client. If the client attempts to return the work unit after their deadline period, the results are simply ignored and discarded.

Although the data of the simulation is distributed on the back-end, the metadata for the simulation is not. Thus client failures or the appearance of failure due to clients unable to perform their designated computation within the deadline have no direct impact on critical services such as time management as what would normally occur in conventional PDES executions.

A total reliance on deadlines for client failure and recovery can lead to less than optimal performance in certain situations due to wait times and possible lease failures due to the unavailability of work units. A simple solution to this problem is to utilize a heart-beat mechanism where the client periodically provides a progress report to the back-end at application-defined time intervals. This option may be detrimental to performance in situations where the amount of computation per work unit lease is low and the addition of more service requests can degrade back-end responsiveness.

### 7.2    Resilience to Server Failure

Server failure is a more difficult problem to address than client failure due to the back-end possessing the simulation state and possible transient nature of the system at the time of failure. Due to the distributed hierarchy of the new Aurora back-end services, work is ongoing to implement a robust, high-performance fault tolerance system. We describe the approach used in the first generation Aurora system in the following sections.

### Checkpointing and Restoration

The internal metadata and states must be saved in case of a server side crash. There are two logical times at which this can be done: checkpoint after each work unit return or checkpoint after a lower bound on timestamp (LBTS) advance. Checkpointing after each work unit return can incur high overhead due to frequent checkpointing but has the advantage of being able to store the latest computational results. The latter has the advantage of lower overhead at the cost of possibly sacrificing recent computational results. Checkpoint on LBTS advance was implemented in the first generation Aurora system.

In addition to work unit and message state checkpoints, metadata has to be stored as well. Information such as key tables and time information has to be serialized and written to a hard store such as a common file on disk. Recovery from a failure is handled by reading this information from the file, and re-populating metadata tables and saved state.

### Replication

To augment the robustness of the Aurora system to handle runtime failures, replication is used where the Aurora server was mirrored to different machines. One server was designated as the primary server, while the other servers were secondary servers forming a cyclic ring based on a specified sequence. Clients are also given this information on the availability of servers. If the primary server is unresponsive, the clients will attempt to contact the next server in the ring. If a secondary server receives a work unit request, it broadcasts a vote to the other servers in the ring for promotion as the primary server. If during this phase the primary server did not actually crash and provided a delayed vote return, perhaps due to a network issue, the secondary server that issued the vote will assume the primary server has crashed. The newly designated primary server will then periodically send messages to the previous primary server indicating leadership change in cases where the primary server did not actually crash but is experiencing slowdown issues.

The new primary server will use the common checkpoint store to populate metadata and state upon promotion. Once the simulation state has been restored, execution can continue and work units can be leased. Since the simulation has a possibility of rollback, work units that may be returning that are out-of-sync are simply discarded. In the first generation Aurora fault tolerance system, no transient server failure is assumed on the client side, therefore, once the client assumes the server has crashed, it will no longer try to contact it in the future.

## 8.   BENCHMARKS

For a performance evaluation of the Aurora system, a torus queuing network was used to compare the impact of work unit granularity and the amount of work per work unit lease on overall system throughput. In this simulation, servers can be aggregated into subnets which can then be mapped to single work units. In this study, the coarse-grained queuing network was configured as a 250,000 server 500x500 closed torus network with 625 partitions of 25x25 torus subnets. The fine-grained queueing network was configured as a 22,500 server 150x150 closed torus network partition into 225 10x10 torus subnets which can be leased as work units. The coarse-grained simulation had internal links within each work unit with a delay of 10 microseconds and external work unit-to-work unit delays of 1 millisecond. The fine-grained simulation had the external delay set at 0.1 milliseconds while the internal delay remained unchanged. Both simulation scenarios generated 10,000 jobs destined for internal servers and 10,000 jobs destined for servers external to the work unit. Additionally, both scenarios had job service times exponentially distributed with a mean of 5 microseconds. The differences in simulation parameters ensured that the amount of work per work unit lease differed significantly.

A total of 42 processors consisting of heterogeneous architectures were used in this performance evaluation. 16 processors in two compute nodes were comprised of 8-way 550MHz Pentium III machines with 4 GB of memory per node and the remaining 26 processors were Pentium Xeon 3.06GHz Hyperthreading-enabled processors across 13 nodes with 1 GB of memory per node. The Aurora back-end was run on three hyperthreaded Pentium Xeon 2.8GHz machines with 4 GB of memory each. All machines were running RedHat Linux and had Fast Ethernet among each set of similar processors, but on disparate LANs between machine types. The back-end setup for the *Coarse* and *Fine* scenario contained 1 work unit state server and 1 message state server whereas the *Fine (2)* scenario contained 1 work unit server and 2 message state servers.

For the figures below, *deferred* refers to the amount of wallclock time (seconds) a client spends waiting for a valid work unit lease from the back-end. *Import* indicates to the amount of time the client spends downloading work unit metadata, work unit state vectors, messages and the associated time spent in the application-dependent deserialization routine. *Finalize* is the time to perform the logical inverse of *import* where the work unit state and messages are serialized and consistency convergence is achieved on the back-end services for the returning work unit. *Application* denotes the time spent executing application-dependent simulation code.

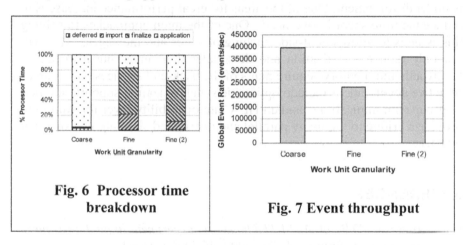

**Fig. 6  Processor time breakdown**

**Fig. 7 Event throughput**

The total overhead for the coarse and fine grained simulations are detailed in Fig. 6. As expected, the coarse-grained simulation incurred the least amount of relative overhead than the fine-grained simulations. For the fine-grained simulations, we see that the majority of the time spent is in the work unit overheads, most notably the work unit finalization and import. With an additional message state server available, we can observe a reduction in overhead time in the *Fine (2)* scenario. Figure 7 details the global event throughput for each of the scenarios. Although the coarse-grained simulation was expected to have higher event throughput than the fine-grained simulations due to overhead, the *Fine (2)* scenario showed notable gains through the addition of only one more message state server; an event throughput boost of more than 50%.

## 9.    CONCLUSIONS AND FUTURE WORK

The Aurora system provides a unique approach to providing flexibility and reliability to large-scale parallel and discrete event simulations without compromising high throughput. This application independent framework builds upon the first generation Aurora system delivering higher performance without the scalability limitations for applications suitable for the master/worker style of parallel workload distribution and execution.

The Aurora system can be extended and enhanced in a variety of areas, many of which are under active development at this time. As mentioned previously, the fault tolerance system for the distributed back-end services is under development. One of the areas for great performance increase is to reduce the time spent in overhead. One of the main approaches to solving this issue is to allow client-side caching of states and messages. This will not only reduce serialization and de-serialization times, but also reduce bandwidth and memory requirements of the back-end services. Other areas of active development include optimistic synchronization support, addition of group communications, and an HLA interoperability layer for Aurora to provide a bridge to the many parallel and distributed simulations using that interface.

## REFERENCES

[1]    Anderson, D.P., et al., *SETI@home: an experiment in public-resource computing.* Commun. ACM, 2002. **45**(11): p. 56-61.

[2]    Nicol, D. and P. Heidelberger, *Parallel execution for serial simulators.* ACM Trans. Model. Comput. Simul., 1996. **6**(3): p. 210-242.

[3]    Riley, G.F., et al., *A federated approach to distributed network simulation.* ACM Trans. Model. Comput. Simul., 2004. **14**(2): p. 116-148.

[4]    *IEEE standard for modeling and simulation (M&S) high level architecture (HLA) - framework and rules.* IEEE Std 1516-2000, 2000: p. i-22.

[5]    Page, E.H., J. Robert L. Moose, and S.P. Griffin, *Web-based simulation in Simjava using remote method invocation,* in *Proceedings of the 29th conference on Winter simulation.* 1997, ACM Press: Atlanta, Georgia, United States.

[6]   Huang, Y., X. Xiang, and G. Madey, *A Self Manageable Infrastructure for Supporting Web-based Simulations*, in *Proceedings of the 37th annual symposium on Simulation*. 2004, IEEE Computer Society: Arlington, VA.

[7]   Cholkar, A. and P. Koopman, *A widely deployable Web-based network simulation framework using CORBA IDL-based APIs*, in *Proceedings of the 31st conference on Winter simulation: Simulation–a bridge to the future - Volume 2*. 1999, ACM Press: Phoenix, Arizona, United States.

[8]   Pullen, J.M., et al., *Using Web services to integrate heterogeneous simulations in a grid environment*. Future Gener. Comput. Syst., 2005. **21**(1): p. 97-106.

[9]   Foster, I. *Globus Toolkit Version 4: Software for Service-Oriented Systems*. in *IFIP International Conference on Network and Parallel Computing*. 2005: Springer-Verlag LNCS 3779.

[10]  Fitzgibbons, J.B., et al. *IDSim: an extensible framework for Interoperable Distributed Simulation*. in *Proceedings of the IEEE International Conference on Web Services*. 2004. San Diego, CA.

[11]  Xie, Y., et al., *Servicing Provisioning for HLA-Based Distributed Simulation on the Grid*, in *Proceedings of the 19th Workshop on Principles of Advanced and Distributed Simulation*. 2005, IEEE Computer Society: Monterey, CA.

[12]  Lin, Y.-B., *Parallel independent replicated simulation on a network of workstations*, in *Proceedings of the eighth workshop on Parallel and distributed simulation*. 1994, ACM Press: Edinburgh, Scotland, United Kingdom.

[13]  Litzkow, M.J., M. Livny, and M.W. Mutka. *Condor - A hunter of idle workstations*. in *Proceedings of the 8th International Conference on Distributed Computing Systems*. 1988. San Jose, CA.

[14]  Sunderam, V.S., *PVM: a framework for parallel distributed computing*. Concurrency: Pract. Exper., 1990. **2**(4): p. 315-339.

[15]  Goux, J.-P., J. Linderoth, and M. Yoder, *Metacomputing and the Master-Worker Paradigm*. 2000, Mathematics and Computer Science Division, Argonne National Laboratory.

[16]  Ong, T.M., et al., *Unicorn: voluntary computing over Internet*. SIGOPS Oper. Syst. Rev., 2002. **36**(2): p. 36-51.

[17]  Goldchleger, A., et al., *InteGrade: object-oriented Grid middleware leveraging the idle computing power of desktop machines*. Concurr. Comput.: Pract. Exper., 2004. **16**(5): p. 449-459.

[18]  Anderson, D.P. *BOINC: a system for public-resource computing and storage*. in *Proceedings of the Fifth IEEE/ACM International Workshop on Grid Computing*. 2004. Pittsburgh, PA.

[19]    Park, A. and R.M. Fujimoto, *Aurora: An Approach to High Through-put Parallel Simulation*, in *Proceedings of the 20th Workshop on Principles of Advanced and Distributed Simulation*. 2006, IEEE Computer Society.

[20]    van Engelen, R.A. and K.A. Gallivan. *The gSOAP toolkit for Web services and peer-to-peer computing networks*. in *Proceedings of the 2nd IEEE/ACM International Symposium on Cluster Computing and the Grid*. 2002. Berlin, Germany.

# CHAPTER 14

# Design and Performance Evaluation
# of a Packet-Switching Satellite Emulator

Tomaso de Cola [1], Mario Marchese [2], Giancarlo Portomauro[1]

[1] CNIT - Italian National Consortium for TelecommunicationsGenoa
Research Unit University of Genoa, Via Opera Pia 13, 16145,
Genoa, Italy
[2] DIST - Department of Communication, Computer and System
Science University of Genoa Via Opera Pia 13, 16145, Genoa, Italy

**Abstract.** *The increasing interest for the satellite technology as suitable means for transporting multimedia applications has fostered several research investigations aimed at identifying proper algorithm tunings and exploring the performance of communication protocols in general. To this end, the support of analysis and research tools is of primary importance to assess performance of data communication and, hence, to provide the satellite system designers with proper indications suited to develop effective satellite networks.*

*From this standpoint, a satellite emulation tool is presented, showing the features it provides and a large set of applications in which it might be employed to asses the performance of data communication.*

## 1. INTRODUCTION

Satellite technology has many advantages with respect to terrestrial one in terms of area coverage, high availability of bandwidth and intrinsic multicast capability. On the other hand, it presents critical aspects such as high delay of propagation and non-negligible packet loss, which have to be taken into account in the design of satellite architecture. As a consequence, within this framework, there is the need of developing new instruments and schemes to improve the efficiency of the communications along with the testing of the proposed solutions.

A satellite system may be hardly studied on the field. It is expensive and it often concerns only software components for earth stations. Alternatives are necessary to investigate new systems and to evaluate the performance. The first one is the analytical study. It is very attractive but complex; moreover it often requires simplifications and approximations. The second alternative is the simulation of the system behaviour via software, in order to by-pass the complexity of real systems and to test solutions not yet technically feasible, in view of future evolutions. In this case, there is the need of modelling effort, even if a model, often, is not accurate enough to consider all the aspects of a real system.

A third alternative, which seems to summarize most of the advantages of the solutions mentioned, is emulation, which is composed of hardware and software components that behave as a real system. An emulator allows using real traffic and it is similar to the real system also from the point of view of the physical architecture.

The paper presents the design and implementation of an emulator concerning on-board satellite packet switching. This proposal takes as reference the emulation system developed within a wider Project called "Emulation of on-board satellite switching systems" (ACE - ASI CNIT Emulator) [1], and extends its main functionalities, in order to have a powerful instrument for performance analysis of data communication achieved in satellite networks [2].

The paper is structured as follows. The need for a real-time simulator is discussed in Section 2 together with a presentation of the related works that can be found in the literature. Section 3 shows the proposal concerning the architecture and specifies the modules, embedded within the emulation core, needed to perform the satellite channel emulation together with the real-time issue and the transport of information. In Section 4, the performance analysis and the response of such system in presence of bulk transfer and multimedia traffic are given, in order to show the robustness and the capabilities of the proposed emulation system. Finally, Section 5 contains the conclusions.

## 2.    BACKGROUND AND RELATED WORKS

Due to network complexity, simulation plays a vital role in attempting to characterize both the behaviours of the current Internet and the possible effects of proposed changes to its operations [3]. However, simulation and analysis are restricted to exploring a constructed, abstract model of the world while measurement and experimentation provide an effective instrument for exploring the real world. In this perspective emulator allows creating network topologies, conditions and to perform real-time tests with various prototype protocols and products.

NIST Net is implemented [4] as a kernel module extension for the Linux operating system and an X Window System-based user interface application. It provides parameters such as delay, packet drop probability, fraction of duplicated packets and link bandwidth. Dummynet [5], implemented as a FreeBSD UNIX kernel patch in the IP stack, works by intercepting packets on their way through the protocol stack. The NRL Mobile Network Emulator (MNE) performs real-time simulations in wireless environment by extending network capabilities implemented on the IP stack in Linux kernel and exploiting IPTABLES capabilities [6]. EGPRS system [7] allows emulation of GPRS environments by means of a virtual network device, which allows the definition of a proper radio link control operating at the MAC level. Finally, EMPOWER system [8] distributes the emulation core in several nodes and performs the real-time simulation by means of virtual devices modules linked to the network stack.

Likewise EGPRS and EMPOWER approaches, our proposal (ACE) is based on the employment of network virtual devices, which allow implementing specific MAC functionalities running on the top of the network device driver. In the following, the description of the proposed emulation architecture is presented together with the presentation of the software modules necessary to interface the emulated environment with the rest of the architecture.

## 3.    EMULATION SYSTEM

A satellite system is constituted by a certain number of ground stations (each composed of a satellite modem that acts both at the physical and at the data link layer) and a satellite that communicates with the ground station over the satellite channel. The emulator should allow testing various kinds of protocols of TCP/IP suite and switching systems, in order to evaluate suitable solutions to be adopted. In the following subsections, particular attention is devoted to the description of the ACE architecture and then to the implementation of the emulation core in terms of software modules and interaction between "emulated" and "real" world.

## 3.1    Overall Architecture

In a real satellite system, it is possible to identify the following main parts. The satellite channel, characterized by its own peculiarities (e.g. bandwidth, propagation delay, bit error rate, etc.) connects the ground stations with the satellite platforms, supporting on-board switching capabilities [9]. On the other hand, it is worth noting the role played by the satellite modem, mounted within the ground stations, which provides an interface towards the upper layers (namely the network layer) and performs operation of framing, access to the medium, and channel coding for example, through the data link protocol.

In the ACE system, two main units are required to reproduce effectively the behaviour of a real system, as shown in Figure 1:

- Emulator Unit (EU): it has a powerful elaboration capacity, carries out most of the emulation, as the decisions about each PDU (i.e. the loss, delay and any statistics of each PDU regards the EU).
- Gateway (GTW): it operates as interface among the Emulator Unit (EU) and the external PCs, and it is responsible of managing the specific functionalities of a satellite modem in the real system. For this purpose, the interface between the modem at the ground station and the protocols of the upper network layers has been implemented in the ACE system by creating a virtual device.

The aforementioned units communicate by means of control packets, carrying notifications about the emulation. The data transportation is achieved exploiting the capabilities of TAP device [10], provided by Linux kernel, which allows the emulator to behave exactly as a broadcast link that connects more stations. Concerning the traffic traversing the emulation system and managed by its modules, we have:

- the real traffic, (the information coming from the external PCs) transported from a GTW (input GTW) to the other (output GTW) and then forwarded to the upper layer (or discarded) through notification from the EU.

- The control traffic, exchanged among the EU and the GTWs, carrying the notifications generated by the emulation core, i.e. delivery instant, packet corruption and so on.

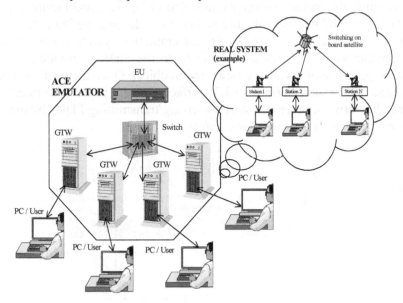

**Fig. 1  Overall Emulator Architecture and Real System**

## 3.2    Software Modules

The software implementation of the emulation core is composed of several modules, which are responsible of the real-time simulation as well as the generation of the control traffic and the data communication among the different GTWs. The emulation core is organized in two levels, as depicted in Figure 2:

- Low Level (LL): it is responsible for providing the functions needed to the communication and the interaction among the physical units (GTWs and EU).
- High Level (HL): it is responsible for the emulation processing. It allows the emulation of the main transmission characteristics (e.g. bit error ratio, channel fading, loss and packet delay), the implementation of various media access control protocols and the on-board switching architecture.

In order to make the architecture modular and flexible to further evolutions, an Object Oriented Programming paradigm has been considered. A particular attention has to be reserved to the main operations performed by the High Level, namely the emulation of the data communication and the behaviour of the satellite channel.

Concerning the former aspect, as indicated in Figure 2 and Figure 3, two objects play a fundamental role, the Station Provider and the Station. When a new station needs to register itself to the emulation system, a notification is communicated (by *setStationProvider()*) to the Station Provider, which will be responsible of creating a new Station object. Once the operation has completed, the Station defines an L3interface in order to have an interface towards the network layer and starts receiving/transmitting PDUs by means of the methods *put_pdu()* and *fetch_pdu()*.

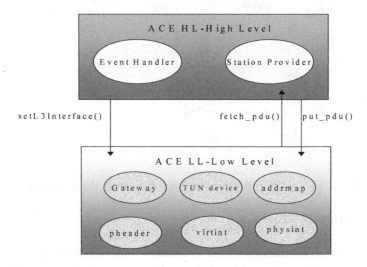

**Fig. 2  Software architecture of the ACE system**

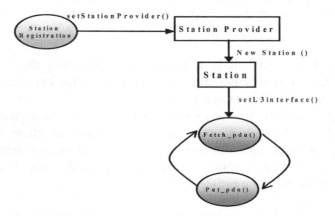

**Fig. 3  Objects involved in the data communication**

Concerning the emulation of the satellite channel, a coupled interaction between the objects characterising the station and the satellite channel itself is required.

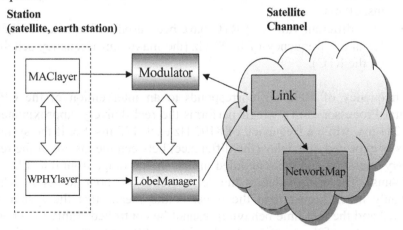

**Fig. 4  Objects involved in the channel emulation**

On one hand, as indicated in Figure 4, the station components involved in the emulation are the *MAClayer* (MAC Layer) and the *WPHYlayer* (Physical Layer) and on the other hand, the elements necessary to the characterisation of the channel are the objects *Link* and *NetworkMap*, which maintain the information about the network topology and the physical link peculiarities. The communication between the channel and the station is realised by means of the *Modulator* object, which performs also operations of access to the medium, encoding and digital modulation, and of the *LobeManager* that effectively manages the satellite channel.

# 4.  VALIDATION TESTS

## 4.1  Measure of Gateway Delivery Accuracy

This measure is dedicated to test the accuracy of the developed code in delivering the PDUs to the upper network layer at a given time instant. The difference between the instant of the real delivery and the scheduled instant is the performance index in order to evaluate the delay in PDU delivery operation to the upper layers. The tests have been composed as follows:

- The overall number of packets delivered in each test is 1000;
- The dimension of the packets delivered to the upper network layer is fixed at 1500 bytes (the Ethernet MTU);

- The scheduled time interval between the delivery of two consecutive packets is not time variant within the same test, especially, the following values have been tested: 20ms, 200 ms, 2 ms, 20 ms;
- Two different values of RTC have been used: a frequency of 4096 Hz and a frequency of 8192 Hz (the maximum frequency settable on the RTC).

A frequency of 4096 Hz corresponds to an intervention of the CPU (Central Processor Unit), which performs the real delivery, approximately each 244 ms, while a frequency of 8192 Hz each 122 ms. So, if the system works as expected, the delay (the difference) between the instant of the real delivery operation and the scheduled instant should range from 0 to 122 ms (or 244ms). The mean value of the delay should be about 60 ms. A delay constantly much higher than the upper bound means that the system is saturated and the real time behaviour cannot be controlled. Table I contains the mean value of the mentioned delay for the different scheduled delivery interval and RTC. Actually, the results obtained respect the expected values. Only the case apparently more critical (20 ms) behaves better than expected. The behaviour is explained in Figure 5 and in Figure 6, where the events occurring in the emulator for the 20 ms and the 200 ms case, respectively, are reported over the time. In the first case, when the CPU time needed to process and deliver a packet is over, it is probable there is another packet scheduled to be served before the CPU returns to the sleep status, waiting for the next RTC signal. On the contrary, in the second case, when the service time is over, the process returns immediately to the sleep status because there is no packet scheduled to be sent. The overall effect, in the first case, is a drastic reduction of the delay value. Figure 7 contains the mentioned delay versus time in the case of a RTC frequency of 8192 Hz and a scheduled delivery of 20 ms. The figure allows checking the real behaviour over time and to verify that not only the mean value is under the upper bound but that each single packet has been delivered with a low delay. Similar considerations may be done concerning the other tests (200 ms, 2 ms and 20 ms), not reported. It is important to observe that the results provided by adopting a RTC frequency of 4096 Hz are also satisfying when they are compared with the mean delay of satellite systems. The advantage of a lower RTC frequency is a CPU less loaded. Anyway, the measures about the CPU load performed during the tests have shown an acceptable load level even in the case of a RTC frequency of 8192 Hz.

## Table 1  Mean value of the delay

| Delivery interval | Mean delivery delay [µs] | |
|---|---|---|
| | **4096 Hz** | **8192 Hz** |
| 20 µs | 57.656 | 25.559 |
| 200 µs | 112.840 | 70.024 |
| 2 ms | 130.460 | 69.850 |
| 20 ms | 129.870 | 70.284 |

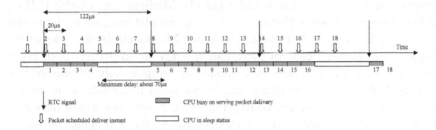

Fig. 5 Emulator events - 20 ms

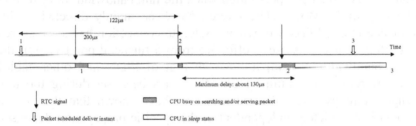

Fig. 6 Emulator events - 200 ms

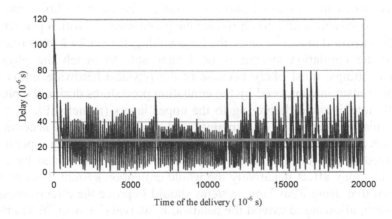

Fig. 7 Delay vs. time, 8192 Hz, 20 ms

## 4.2   Performance Limits of the Emulation System

In order to identify the possible scenarios and applications, in which it would be possible to employ such a tool as a research instrument, the system effectiveness has been checked also by varying the emulated link bandwidth and propagation delay. In practice, the aim of this validation has been to see which are the emulation limits of the system and hence to draw the edges of this emulation framework. In more detail, different propagation values have been considered in order to reproduce common satellite scenarios including Low Earth Orbit (LEO), Medium Earth Orbit (MEO) and Geostationary Earth Orbiting (GEO) satellite platform, each giving rise to delays of 5, 100 and 260 ms, respectively. Moreover, for the sake of the completeness, also the case of propagation delay set to 0 s has been taken under consideration in order to evaluate the responsivity of the system when the link propagation delay can be assumed negligible as in cabled networks or in some wireless configurations (e.g. wireless sensor networks and short-range WLANs). In correspondence to these propagation delay settings, also several emulated bandwidth values have been considered. In particular, tests have been performed when the link bandwidth ranged from 64 kbit/s up to 26 Mbit/s. The interest has been mainly directed to this performance interval because, when a satellite connection has to be shared among different users its use is effective from a financial point view if the available bandwidth is comparable with that of ISDN and other cabled systems. moreover, the limit of 26 Mbit/s has been set during the trial campaign. Actually, the collected measures have shown that the system robustness is completely independent of the specific propagation delay set. On the contrary, the impact of the emulated link bandwidth plays a more important role and can negatively affect the overall data communication. In practice, when the emulated bandwidth ranges between 64 kbit/s and 24 Mbit/s, the system is able to reproduce the given scenario with a percentage deviation lower than 0.5%. Once the bandwidth gets over 24 Mbit/s (e.g. 26 Mbit/s) the emulation system is no longer able to match the physical channel settings, most likely because of the physical hardware limits and the time constraints imposed by the emulation procedures during the phases of PDU fetching and delivering to the upper layers (namely IP). In more detail, this behaviour can be explained and clarified by taking account the inner network architecture and the fetching and delivering operations performed at the ACE layer. In particular, the delay introduced by these operations may affect negatively the whole emulation system. Finally, it is expected that using Real Time systems should improve the effectiveness of the system, allowing to extend the bandwidth interval (i.e. over 26 Mbit/s).

In Table 2, the most significant results are summarised. For the sake of clarity, the first column represents the reference bandwidth values, while the second one shows the values actually set on the emulation system.

## Table 2  Emulated Link Bandwidth Performance

| Reference Bandwidth [Kbit/s] | Emulation System | | Measurements |
| --- | --- | --- | --- |
| | Bandwidth [Kbit/s] | Propagation Delay. [ms] | Bandwidth [Kbit/s] |
| 64 | 65.28 | 0 | 64 |
| | | 5 | 64 |
| | | 100 | 64 |
| | | 260 | 64 |
| 512 | 522.24 | 0 | 512 |
| | | 5 | 512 |
| | | 100 | 512 |
| | | 260 | 512 |
| 1000 | 1020.00 | 0 | 1000 |
| | | 5 | 1000 |
| | | 100 | 1000 |
| | | 260 | 1000 |
| 4000 | 4080.00 | 0 | 4000 |
| | | 5 | 4000 |
| | | 100 | 4000 |
| | | 260 | 4000 |
| 10000 | 10200.00 | 0 | 9970 |
| | | 5 | 9960 |
| | | 100 | 9990 |
| | | 260 | 9990 |
| 16000 | 16320.00 | 0 | 15900 |
| | | 5 | 15900 |
| | | 100 | 15700 |
| | | 260 | 15900 |
| 20000 | 20400.00 | 0 | 19800 |
| | | 5 | 19800 |
| | | 100 | 19800 |
| | | 260 | 19800 |
| 24000 | 24480.00 | 0 | 24000 |
| | | 5 | 24000 |
| | | 100 | 23900 |
| | | 260 | 23900 |
| 26000 | 26520.00 | 0 | Failed Test |
| | | 5 | Failed Test |
| | | 100 | Failed Test |
| | | 260 | Failed Test |

The slight difference between the values reported in the two columns is due to the fact that the measures have been performed at the application layer, while bandwidth setting refer to the datalink layer; consequently, the overhead introduced by layers operating between application and datalink layers has to be accounted for.

## 4.3    Comparison with a Real System

In this section, a particular emphasis is given to the comparison of the ACE behaviour with a real satellite system.

The real system taken as reference employs the satellite ITALSAT II (13° EST). It provides coverage in the single spot-beam on Ka-band (20-30 GHz), providing an overall bandwidth of 36 MHz. The satellite station has a full-duplex channel with a bit-rate of 2 Mbit/s.

In order to test the effectiveness and the response of the proposed emulation system, the performance analysis has been accomplished considering two different patterns of data traffic.

On one hand, we have taken as reference bulk transfers, generated by FTP-like applications, when different versions of TCP are mounted on the PCs, in order to see the emulator response, in presence of aggressive TCP flows, with respect to the real system behaviour. On the other hand, we have considered the case in which multimedia traffic mixed with FTP transfers traverses the system, in order to show the effectiveness of ACE when TCP and UDP connections are multiplexed together on the same satellite channel.

The application used to get the result is a simple ftp-like one, which allows transferring data between the two remote sites. In order to extend the effectiveness of our analysis we have considered modified [11] NewReno TCP versions [12]. In more detail, the robustness of the system in presence of a slow-start phase more aggressive (as indicated in Table 3) has been tested to evaluate the emulator response. In this perspective, we have taken as main parameter the transmission instant for each data packet released to the network and the tests are achieved by performing a data transfer of about 3 Mbytes.

The testbed employed in this case is composed of two PCs communicating through the ACE system configured with two gateways (GTW1 and GTW2 respectively in Figure 8).

## Table 3  Different TCP Implementations Tested

| TCP version | Initial Window (IW) | TCP buffer (bytes) | Congestion Window Increase (k) |
|---|---|---|---|
| IW2-64Kbytes | 2 | 64K | 1 |
| IW4-256Kbytes | 4 | 256K | 1 |
| IW6-k2-256Kbytes | 6 | 256K | 2 |
| IW6-k8-64Kbytes | 6 | 64K | 8 |
| IW6-k4-320Kbytes | 6 | 320K | 4 |

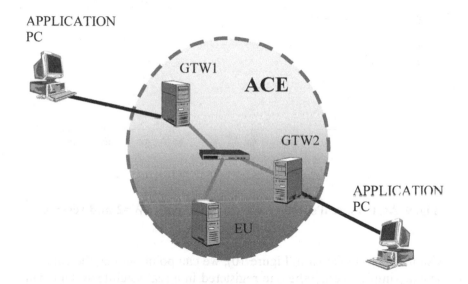

**Fig. 8  Configuration of ACE emulation system**

In the first instance, we may consider the case of standard TCP employment, when an initial transmission window (IW) equal to 2 segments and a TCP Receiver Buffer of 64 Kbytes are assumed (IW2-64Kbytes in Table I). The comparison between ACE and a real system is depicted in Figure 6 where, for the sake of simplicity, only the first 144 packets are reported. It can be seen that the difference between the two cases is really minimal: the curves, describing how the packet transmission instant changes during the data transfer, just overlap.

As a second instance, a more aggressive implementation of TCP is considered in order to investigate the response of proposed emulation system in presence of high burst of data. For this purpose a TCP buffer of 320Kbytes with IW equal to 6 packets and congestion window increase k equal to 4 is assumed (IW6-k4-320Kbytes in Table 3).

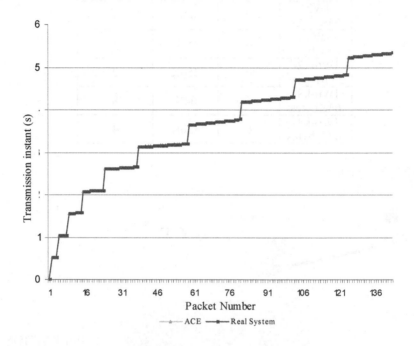

**Fig. 9  ACE vs. real satellite system: TCP with IW=2 and receive buffer=64Kbytes**

Also in this test (shown in Figure 10), we can point out that the emulator behaviour simply overlap the one registered in a real satellite system. This further test thus verifies emulator capabilities of reflecting the overall performance of real systems and following the behaviour of different TCP implementations. It is also important to highlight that ACE system respects real time constraints and then the time dedicated to the emulation elaboration does not affect the overall performances since it does not involve a hard delay in the data packets processing.

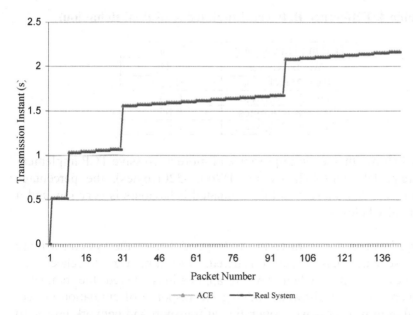

**Fig. 10  ACE vs. real satellite system: TCP with IW=6, k=4 and receive buffer=320Kbytes**

For the sake of simplicity, we omit the analysis of other TCP versions (i.e. IW4-256Kbytes, IW6-k2-256Kbytes and IW6-k8-64Kbytes in Table 1), which lead to similar conclusions.

The next step is represented by the comparison of the performed tests in order to show the accuracy of the emulator with respect to the real behaviour. In particular, we consider as a main parameter the average value of the difference $\xi$ between the transmission instants in the emulation and in the real cases, defined as:

$$\xi = \frac{T_{real} - T_{emul}}{T_{real}}$$

where $T_{real}$ and $T_{emul}$ represent the transmission instants respectively in the cases of the emulation and of the real behaviour (Table 4).

**Table 4  Difference Between Emulated And Real Behaviours**

| TCP implementations | $\xi$ (%) |
|---|---|
| IW2-64Kbytes | $9.7 \cdot 10^{-3}$ |
| IW4-256Kbytes | 0.01 |
| IW6-k2-256Kbytes | 0.03 |
| IW6-k8-64Kbytes | 0.05 |
| IW6-k4-320Kbytes | 0.09 |

Table 4 shows that, even in presence of more aggressive TCP implementations (e.g. IW6-k8-64Kbytes and IW6-k4-320Kbytes), the percentage difference between the real and the emulated behaviours is very low and it is numerically below 0.1%.

Finally, in order to evaluate the full operability of the system, a more complex scenario has been considered. The aim was to check the effectiveness of ACE when several applications shared the emulator. Furthermore, this test allowed studying the response of emulation system when different protocols were operating at transport and network layers. In more detail, we have taken as reference UDP/TCP based applications such as videoconference and transfer file processes and an ICMP packet traffic generated by a PING application. Summarizing, the following applications have been employed:

- FTP (File Transfer Protocol);
- SDR (Session Directory Tool) for multicast conferences on the Mbone;
- Ping.

The general architecture employed is depicted in Figure 11.

Four PCs are connected to gateways belonging to the emulation system; a further PC within the emulator is responsible of the emulation functionalities. The processes considered in the test-bed are resident on the PCs shown in the figure. It is also important to say some more words about the application employed. The three processes act at the same time and are considered to analyse how the whole system behaves when different real data communications are performed. In more detail, FTP is considered in order to evaluate the emulator performance when a big transfer of data ruled by the TCP protocol is accomplished. SDR allows showing the ACE behaviour when a real – time service is required. PING is employed to verify that a correct RTT value, proper of geostationary link, is experienced.

A snapshot of the overall behaviour is presented in Figure 12, where different windows show the applications considered.

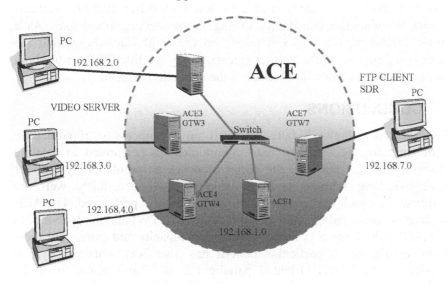

**Fig. 11 Test-bed general architecture**

**Fig. 12 Traffic patterns involved in the test**

The windows on the left side describe the FTP session, while the ones on the top reproduce a webcam application (employed by the videoconference tool). The RTP–based real–time service (videoconference application) and the TCP-based communication are accomplished at the same time. The tests show that emulation system is able to deal with different traffic patterns without introducing extra delays during the processing operations. As a further validation, the PING window, on the right side, shows that the system performs as in the correct Geostationary satellite RTT, set to about 520 ms, even if multiple flows enter in the emulation system.

## 5.    CONCLUSIONS

The analysed framework puts emphasis on the necessity of emulation instruments for the study of data communication performed in satellite networks. For this purpose, the paper proposes an emulation system for packet-switching satellite systems, able to reproduce fairly well the conditions in which real communications are usually performed. The ACE emulator is composed of units called Gateways (GTW) and the Elaboration Unit (EU), which has a powerful elaboration capacity and carries out most of the emulation. A particular benefit has also been optained by the adoption of the Object Oriented paradigm in the implementation of the emulation core. It has allowed a flexible definition of a real-time environment that may be extended to different satellite scenarios, simply by acting on the objects resident in the High Level implementation, without care of how the transmission is physically performed.

The results have been used to test the accuracy of the emulation in order to show the effectiveness of such an instrument when traffic of different flavours, i.e. bulk transfer and multimedia communication is analysed. In the former case (i.e. bulk transfer), reported results have highlighted that the emulation system is able to reflect very fairly the real behaviour even when aggressive TCP flows are entering in the system. In particular, we have registered a maximum relative error with respect to real behaviour of about 0.1%. In the latter case, emulation tool has shown its capability of supporting different traffic flows (TCP mixed with UDP), ratifying the robustness and the flexibility of the proposed system, even if a hard load is driven throughout the satellite network under investigation.

## REFERENCES

[1]    G. Albertengo, T. Pecorella, M. Marchese, "The ACE project: a Real Time Simulator for Satellite Telecommunication Systems," Proc. Sixth Ka-Band Utilization Conference, Cleveland, OH, Jun. 2000, pp. 571-576.

[2]    M. Allman, D. Glover, L. Sanchez, "Enhancing TCP Over Satellite Channels using Standard Mechanism," IETF, RFC 2488, Jan. 1999.

[3]    Sally Floyd, Vern Paxson, "Difficulties in simulating the internet," IEEE/ACM Transactions on Networking, no. 4, pp. 392-403, Aug. 2001.

[4]    NIST Interworking Technology Group. NIST Net network emulation package. http://snad.ncsl.nist.gov/ itg/nistnet/

[5]    L. Rizzo, "Dummynet: a simple approach to the evaluation of network protocols," ACM Computer Communication Review, no. 1, vol. 27, pp. 31-41, Jan. 1997.

[6]    Naval Research Laboratory January 24, 2003 NRL/FR/5523–03-10,054 NRL Mobile Network Emulator, Washington, DC 20375-5320.

[7]    X. Qiu, K. Chawla, L. F. Chang, J. Chuang, N. Sollenberger, J. Whitehead, "An enhanced RLC/MAC design for supporting integrated services over EGPRS", IEEE WCNC 2000, no. 1, Chicago, IL, Sep. 2000, pp. 907-912.

[8]    P. Zheng, L. Ni , "EMPOWER: A Network Emulator for Wireless and Wireline Networks," IEEE INFOCOM 2003, no.1, San Francisco, CA, Mar. 2003, pp.1933-1942.

[9]    M. Marchese, M. Perrando, "A packet-switching satellite emulator: A proposal about architecture and implementation", IEEE ICC 2002, no. 1, New York City, NY, Apr. 2002, pp. 3033-3037.

[10]   Universal TUN/TAP Device Driver http://vtun.sourceforge.net/tun/index.html.

[11]   M. Marchese, "TCP Modification over Satellite Channels: Study and Performance Evaluation", International Journal of Satellite Communications, Special Issue on IP, Vol. 19, Issue 1, pp. 93-110, Jan./Feb. 2001.

[12]   S. Floyd, T. Henderson, A. Gurtov, "The NewReno Modification to TCP's Fast Recovery Algorithm", IETF RFC 3782, Apr. 2004.

REFERENCES

[1]

[2]

[3]

[4]

[5]

[6]

[7]

[8]

[9]

[10]

[11]

[12]

# CHAPTER 15

## Simulation Techniques for Peer-to-Peer Information Sharing Networks

Gergő Buchholcz, Tien Van Do

Telecommunications Department, Budapest University
of Technology and Economics
Budapest, Hungary

**Abstract.** *In recent years p2p file sharing networks have become extensively widespread in terms of popularity and the number of applications. Besides free file sharing software new commercial p2p based products arise as well to share large amount of information through the Internet. These trends make performance issues – in addition to scalability and robustness – come forward. Despite the growing demand simulators available for public focus only on the protocol aspects of p2p technologies and disregard performance related issues. In this paper we introduce simulation techniques to evaluate the performance of p2p information sharing applications with respect to scalability, accuracy and speed. We also tested our proposed solution and compared it to analytical results.*

**Keywords.** Simulator, p2p networks, file-sharing

## 1.    INTRODUCTION

In the past years due to the fast-developing data transfer technologies subscribers' network access capabilities improved significantly. DSL, cable net and 3G mobile systems provide high speed up and downloading for users that service providers can hardly keep step with. To satisfy the constantly growing user demands adequately p2p systems have become the fastest-growing communication technology in the IT sector.

p2p systems proved to be efficient in resource sharing and they also served as a new model for information controlled systems. While conventional network services like web browsing or FTP transfer have to deal with not only the required information but also the location of the information, P2P services are content driven. Users do not need to be concerned with the location of information; p2p systems satisfy the requests on a content basis. In order to provide a suitable platform for content based services several large international companies have developed free and commercial p2p software products (like Sony, Yahoo or Microsoft) mostly for file distribution. However these p2p systems cannot exploit the potential of the p2p concept. New emerging services like grid computing, mobile agent based operating systems, network node managers, and reliable multicast services need efficient information driven distribution methods that can be based on the new generation of p2p systems. In contrast with file-sharing approaching p2p based products deployed in industrial environments have different characteristics. Distribution performance is more independent of node behavior and capacities since they are more independent of human needs and a wide range of operational parameters can be set as a requirement and so be known prior to any communication. In this paper we introduce new methods of simulating p2p information-sharing networks. Our work is focused on the performance of distribution and neglects user interaction and search capabilities that have a well established literature from both analytical and simulation aspects.

Several papers were published related to p2p file-sharing systems, however these publications did not distinguish between p2p functionalities (search, distribution), system-operation and user level behavior. In [1] the detailed measurement results of an operating Kazaa system are given. These results show clearly the relation between user characteristics and the experienced throughput. Other measurement and analysis based results on user characteristics can be found in [2] and [3]. Many publications focus on the searching methods of p2p systems [4, 5]. Searching is a major factor of the distribution performance of file-sharing systems however in p2p information-sharing networks the sources of information are available prior to communication. On the simulation side several works are concerned with the searching performance of p2p networks like PeerSim [10] and p2psim [11] however these simulators are unable to measure the distribution performance of p2p systems. General simulation techniques are presented in [9] with a detailed description of both high and low level simulation methods but without the validation against analytical or measured results.

The paper is organized as follows. First the simulation model and the rationale behind it are introduced in addition to the major factors that influence simulation results. The next section gives a brief description of simulation techniques with respect to accuracy and simulation speed. Then we present our simulation results and examine how well they fit analytical results. Finally we conclude the paper.

## 2.    SIMULATION MODEL

A p2p system consists of a large number of network nodes that share information in a scalable and efficient way using a dynamic communication-role model. The types and capacities of nodes are highly heterogeneous in addition to their connections and types of information they are to share.

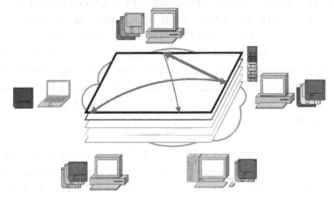

**Fig. 1  The boundaries of the simulated system**

Our simulation model is based on the projection of p2p systems to a certain file or information. That is, only peers interested in the same infor-mation − namely a file − are included in the model as shown in Fig. 1. Interested peers can be sources or demanding clients or both in accordance with the p2p behavior. Since peers can take part in multiple sharing processes simultaneously it is assumed that a priority of interest exists for each participant. Thus in case of multiple parallel communication-flows resources like bandwidth can be evaluated.

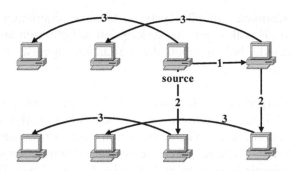

**Fig. 2  The growth of an unrestricted p2p system**

The rationale behind the simulation techniques is that, the size of p2p systems could grow exponentially if no restrictions existed. The size growth is illustrated in Fig. 2. In the first time interval the source shares the information with one peer. In the second interval both the source and the peer with the received information keep on sharing; thus at the end of interval 4 peers will own the information. At the end of the third interval 4 new peers will acquire the information increasing the number of sources up to 8. The network is unrestricted in terms of bandwidth, since in a real network as the load of communication increases the size of consecutive time intervals increases as well decelerating the network growth. Network size is also limited due to the peers' behavior. Peers in a real environment do not stay in the system forever; they leave the system with variable departure intensity.

However, even in restricted networks taking uncooperative peers into account the growth rate can grow exponentially until a certain saturation point. After reaching the saturation point the growth rate is limited to a linear increase in time.

The derivative of the network size shows the growth rate that determines how fast a set of peers can share information. Fig. 3 shows a p2p system with an exponential growth rate. At time 180 the network size is 36 peers and the growth rate is 0.73. That is, during a time unit 0.73 peers can acquire the information assuming 36 peers in the system with the given amount of information.

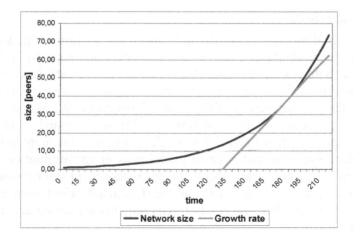

**Fig. 3   The network size and its derivative tangent at a given point versus time**

In information sharing systems contrary to file-sharing systems peers reside at least as long as they acquire the needed data. Free-riding and other user related phenomena do not influence the distribution performance. Thus, a rational peer behavior can be assumed. The rational peer enters the network, takes part in the communication – uploads and downloads – and leaves the network as the information arrives. As a consequence peers' departure rate is directly affected by the growth rate and the network size.

Using the simulation model distribution performance can be determined in steady-state where the arrival rate equals the departure rate. In equilibrium state the network size remains statistically the same keeping the growth rate fixed. To sum up, operational p2p systems have a certain arrival rate that increases the network size directly and the strongly related growth rate indirectly. When the departure rate reaches the growth rate the network size stops increasing and the system gets to an equilibrium state. At this point the departure rate equals to the arrival rate and the steady-state distribution performance can be evaluated neglecting user behavior and information look up methods.

There are multiple parameters affecting the model and the operation of p2p systems. In the following we give a description of the major parameters.

- Arrival process

  The arrival rate can be hardly determined for operational p2p systems since all communication flow between peers and strongly influenced by user behavior. In file-sharing systems the arrival rate depends on the popularity of files, on the users' behavior, information visibility and other factors that are out of the scope of this paper. We assume that the arrival process is a Poisson process; that is, inter-arrival times are exponentially distributed. We neglect information popularity and visibility since the behavior of participants of an information sharing system – like network routers sharing management information – can be predicted. They all know that the demanded information exists in the system and their information requirements are set-up according to known functions.

- Information representation

  Information is represented as files in computer networks. These files are segmented before transfer and these segments are sent thorough the p2p connections. Segmentation is important to exploit the power of the p2p communication model. Peers acquiring a segment become uploaders with their limited parts of information. That is, peers can utilize their upload capacity even before the whole information arrives. There are two major segmentation methods used in p2p applications. Simple segmenting is done by dividing the file into equal size parts. Network coding [6] is a more sophisticated method that increases the randomization of segment sequences to ease the scheduling of segment propagation and thus, make the distribution more efficient.

- Structural parameters

  There are two major factors that affect the structure of p2p systems. The maximum number of simultaneous uploads determines how many uploading connections a peer can have. This limitation is to overcome performance issues that arise when there are a high number of ongoing TCP connections over a low bandwidth channel. The other structural parameter is the number of peers that a connecting peer obtains knowledge of. The information that the connecting peer acquires includes the addresses of other neighboring peers and the sequence numbers of segments owned by those peers. This information changes in time and it is the responsibility of the p2p protocol to keep peers up-to-date.

- Information acquirement

  As a peer gets informed on other peers, that is, it collects information on the segments and peer addresses, it starts acquiring data. This process has two factors. The uploader must choose whom it wants to upload, and the downloader must make a choice which segment it wants to get. It is possible that the segment choice is also the responsibility of the uploader, however in operational p2p systems like BitTorent this is not the case. Downloading peers acquire the segment which is present at the least number of neighbor peers. As a consequence the distribution of segments become more homogeneous keeping the availability of all segments high.

## 3.    SIMULATION TECHNIQUES

An efficient simulation technique provides accurate results within a reasonable simulation run-time. Typically it is difficult to achieve both goals at the same time, thus it is important to find the right balance between accuracy and run-time.

Packet-level simulators can provide very accurate results, however there are multiple disadvantages of using them. First, packet-level simulators need distribution algorithms to be implemented at protocol level. This can increase development time and it can also make difficult to compare different algorithms since fine-grained and coarse-grained implementations can give different results. Packet-level simulators also need a well specified configuration to be built up prior to simulation. Links must be deployed so that the bandwidth and latency of each link between a peer pair can be different as shown in Fig. 1. In general this means $O(n^2)$ links assuming that the number of peers in the system is $n$. If possible active connections are limited and evaluated before a peer joins the network the number of links can be reduced to $O(c*n)$.

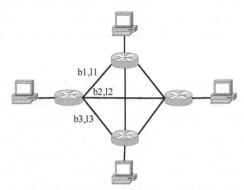

b1,l1
b2,l2
b3,l3

**Fig. 4  A possible configuration of packet-level simulation**

The major factor that affects simulation speed is the size of information; that is, the size of the file to be shared. A file – with size of *s Mbytes* – will be fragmented into about *s\*1000* IP packets. Each IP packet will generate an event at departure and arrival. If during a simulation run *n* peers are to acquire the information before leaving the network then the run-time of simulation will be proposal to *O(1000\*s\*n)* neglecting the complexity of switching on links and additional computation time needed for link and peer configuration.

Time complexity of packet-level simulators scales very well however if the information size is high the simulation run-time can be very high even in case of small size networks. Difficulties arise also when configuring the network. Queue size, latency and bandwidth values can be hardly determined to model real environments. Their obvious choice, setting them to the same level on every link, makes packet-level simulation needless since other simulation methods can produce faster results under the same circumstances.

The simulation speed cannot be upgraded since decreasing information size – the major factor of run-time – would make the accuracy of results unpredictable. TCP, that is the carrier protocol in most of the cases, needs long bursts to saturate to the given bandwidth. Lower number of segments in a TCP stream could produce a fluctuation in the throughput decreasing the accuracy.

To ease the difficulties related to packet-level simulators the fair-share throughput method (FST) can be used. The fundamental idea behind FST is that peers with their fixed upload and download bandwidth share bandwidth fairly when communicating. Prior to transferring an information segment the fair share bandwidth for each communicating peer pair can be calculated and using the results the arrival time of a segment can be determined.

The fair share bandwidth for a single downloader and multiple uploaders can be calculated as follows. Each uploader offers a certain amount of bandwidth for the downloader. The downloader accepts an offer if it is less or equal to the fair bandwidth share, that is the upload capacity divided by the number of uploaders. Certain offers might be less than the fair-share; in that case the unused bandwidth is reallocated between the unfulfilled offers. The algorithm stops when all offers are fulfilled or no offers can be fulfilled. In the later case unfulfilled offers are restricted by the proportional download capacity of the peer. The same algorithm can be used at both uploader and downloader side.

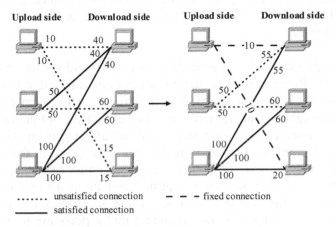

Fig. 5  **Fair-share throughput technique**

Contrary to the simplicity of the algorithm the method to calculate fair-shares of a system is more burdensome. This is due to the fact that the algorithm does not guarantee convergence at the system level. To avoid fluctuation in bandwidth allocation the targets of the algorithm must be chosen in the right sequence.

First uploading and downloading peers are grouped as illustrated in Fig. 5. Every downloader and uploader calculates the theoretical fair-share of their connections according to their capacities. Then all connections are classified. Connections where the upload offer is higher than the download offer are marked as satisfied otherwise marked as unsatisfied. If all the connections of a downloader are satisfied then the bandwidth shares can be fixed to the download share. If all the connections of an uploader are unsatisfied then the shares can be fixed to the upload share as shown in Fig. 5. In the next phase fair-shares are recalculated neglecting the fixed connections. Peers with all connections fixed are skipped in the algorithm that continues with the reclassification of links. Finally all peers will have fixed connections. Thus, the algorithm stops with the fair-share bandwidth of connections determined. The algorithm assumes that after the classification phase there will be at least one uploader with only unsatisfied connections or one downloader with only satisfied connections. This can be easily proved. Take the uploader with the lowest fair-share per connection. If all of its connections are unsatisfied then it is a suitable peer.

Otherwise take a downloader peer that is connected to the uploader with a satisfied connection. Since even the lowest upload share can saturate the downloader's connection, all of the downloader connections must be satisfied in accordance with the definitions. That is, the downloader is suitable for the choice.

The complexity of the algorithm does not depend on the information size directly. Recalculation of bandwidth is done only after a connection gets closed or a new connection gets initiated. This happens after an information segment transfer terminates or starts. Thus not the information size but the number of information segments affects the run-time. Other complexity factors can be determined by the description of the algorithm. Each link must be classified and each node must be examined. This classification and examination is repeated as long as all of the peers get set. In general this happens $n$ times where $n$ denotes the number of concurrent peers in the system. Assuming that $k$ peers are to acquire the information during a simulation run and there are $l$ concurrent connections the complexity of the algorithm is at least $O((l+n)*s*k)$. Since the value of $l$ is typically proportional to $n$, the complexity can be simplified to $O(c*n*s*k)$.

The fair-share throughput technique does not scale as fine as the packet level simulators. However if the concurrent number of peers and the proportion between the number of links and peers is low then the fair-share throughput algorithm's performance can be much better. This algorithm eliminates the need for determining topological parameters like link latency and queue length making the results less accurate. But despite the disadvantages it can be suitable for raw performance measurement.

The third technique that we applied for simulations is the unrestricted upload method. The fundamental idea is simple; it assumes that every peer has an unlimited download bandwidth capacity. Thus, when calculating the arrival time of an information segment, there is no need to take down-loader capacities into account. The uploader prior to initiating a transfer calculates the fair-share according to its capacity and using the fair-share bandwidth it also calculates the arrival time of a segment. Using the arrival time a new event is generated that is received by the downloader. Every time a new transfer is started or a transfer is finished fair-share bandwidth must be recalculated for all ongoing transfers. This means that the complexity of the algorithm is $O(s^2 n)$, where $s$ denotes the number of information segments and $n$ denotes the total number of peers that are to acquire the information during a simulation run.

Despite the low complexity compared to the fair-share throughput method and the decent scalability the algorithm has the disadvantage of neglecting download bandwidth resources. In case of file-sharing simulations this disadvantage can be easily overcome since typical internet access types have a very limited upload capacity compared to the download rate. In information-sharing systems this disadvantage is more difficult to handle. Possible solutions are to take it into account that reasonable network accessing nodes have at most as high upload bandwidth as download. Thus in a homogeneous distribution system it is more unlikely that a transfer is limited by the download rate. Another solution is the "a priori" setup of connection priorities allowing the communicating peers to agree on the transfer speed before starting the transfer. These features must be integrated into a high performance distribution algorithm making the algorithm highly efficient for testing and measurements.

The great advantage of this solution is the low complexity, the simplicity of implementing new distribution methods and the power of efficient testing the raw performance of distribution. Distribution methods are still under heavy research; thus, there is no standard expectation of simulation techniques. The flexibility of the algorithm allows testing new technologies and as the requirements become well established the algorithm can be modified to be more suitable keeping the advantages of high performance.

## 4.    SIMULATION AND ANALYTICAL RESULTS

Using the unrestricted upload method we developed a simulator to investigate the raw distribution performance of BitTorent system. During a simulation run we measured the departure rate and segment distribution of the system that can be experienced when sharing a 500Mbytes large file segmented into 500 pieces. One seed was used in the simulated system; that is, only one peer was present in the network permanently having the whole file. Other peers joined the network with exponential inter-arrival time with two different intensity parameters. Peers behaved according to the rational behavior, they remained in the network as long as they got the whole file; after that they quitted immediately. To build up the system structure a server was present in the simulated network with the responsibility of informing joining peers on other nodes. Peers joining the network acquired other peer's address from the server and the server returned a fixed number of addresses. Using the addresses all peers had a clear picture of which segment their neighbors possess. Segment and peer choosing before initiating a download was done as described in the specification of BitTorent [7]. The least frequent segment was queried from the neighbor peers; in case of multiple choices the decision was made randomly. The maximum number of simultaneous uploads and the maximum upload rate was set to a fixed value in all the simulation runs except run no. 7 where multiple types of peers could join the network with different probabilities simulating a real network environment.

### Table 1 Simulation parameters

| Run no. | Arrival rate | Max. upload rate | Acquired peers | Max parallel upload |
|---------|--------------|------------------|----------------|---------------------|
| 1 | 0.002 | 10 | 10 | 10 |
| 2 | 0.002 | 10 | 20 | 10 |
| 3 | 0.002 | 10 | 20 | 20 |
| 4 | 0.004 | 10 | 10 | 10 |
| 5 | 0.004 | 10 | 20 | 10 |
| 6 | 0.004 | 10 | 20 | 20 |
| 7 | 0.004 | 10 (80%) / 40 (15%) / 120 (5%) | 20 | 20 |

A simulation run finished after 20000 peers quitted the network. All simulation runs were repeated 5 times to acquire more accurate results. The parameters of simulation runs are presented in Table 1.

### Table 2 General simulation results

| Test no. | Average inter-arrival time | Average inter-departure time | Average network size |
|----------|----------------------------|------------------------------|----------------------|
| 1 | 500 | 500.13±4.64 | 100.45±0.89 |
| 2 | 500 | 495.95±7.82 | 101±1.56 |
| 3 | 500 | 500.14±4.97 | 100.15±1.03 |
| 4 | 250 | 249.06±1.68 | 201.77±1.19 |
| 5 | 250 | 248.57±3.31 | 201.57±2.54 |
| 6 | 250 | 250.78±1.74 | 199.82±1.38 |
| 7 | 250 | 248.46±1.55 | 20.36±0.17 |

In case of simulation runs 1, 2 and 3 the average inter arrival time was 500s in case 4, 5, 6 and 7 the inter-arrival time was 250s as the arrival rate was halved in these cases. Inter-departure times were analyzed and the confidence interval was determined with $\alpha=0.05$. The measured average inter-departure time – taking the confidence intervals into account – fitted the inter-arrival time in all the cases as expected; thus, the simulation could capture the steady-state behavior of the system adequately. Average network size that is in strong relation to the arrival rate also doubled in accordance with the arrival rate.

Our analytical approach is derived from the method presented in [8]. The basic idea of the analysis is to approximate the segment distribution of the steady-state p2p system using simulation parameters presented in Table 1 and Table 2. The approximation is done by calculating the probability of that, a peer owning $i$ segments can upload to a peer owning $j$ segments.

First, it is assumed that the initial segment distribution of the steady-state system is uniform. That is, the same number of peers owns $i$ segments and $j$ segments independently of the value of $i$ and $j$. Let $k$ denote the total number of segments and $n$ denote the number of peers present in the steady-state network. In this case $l_i$ is the number of peers owning $i$ segments. Note that, if $i$ equals to the total number of segments the value of $l$ is 1 since there is exactly one seed in the network.

$$l_i = \begin{vmatrix} 1 \; if \; i = k \\ \dfrac{n}{k} \; otherwise \end{vmatrix}$$

Let $a$ denote the number of initial acquired peers and $f_{i,j}$ be the number of segments that a peer with $j$ segments uploaded to a peer owning $i$ segments. It is assumed that every peer received equal amount of segments from their neighbor peers. Thus,

$$f_{i,j} = \left\lfloor \frac{i}{a} \right\rfloor$$

independently of the value of $j$. Using these results the probability can be calculated by combinatorial methods as follows

$$p_{i,j} = \begin{vmatrix} 1 \; if \; i > j \\ 1 - \dfrac{\left( \dfrac{j - f_{i,j}}{i - f_{i,j}} \right)}{\left( \dfrac{k - f_{i,j}}{i - f_{i,j}} \right)} \; otherwise \end{vmatrix}$$

where $p_{i,j}$ is the probability of that, a peer owning $i$ segments can upload to a peer owning $j$ segments. Note, that if the value of $i$ is greater than $j$ then the probability is 1. That is, a peer can always upload to another having fewer segments. Next the number of simultaneous uploads is calculated. This value is important when calculating the download speed that a peer experiences since a peer's download rate depends on the upload rate of neighboring peers that is determined by the number of simultaneous uploads of neighboring peers. It is obvious that statistically the maximum number of parallel uploads is less than $a$. The value must be weighted by the number of peers having a given number of segments. Thus, the number of parallel uploads is

$$un_i = \frac{a}{n} * \left[ \sum_{j=0}^{k} (l_j * p_{i,j}) - p_{i,i} \right]$$

The download speed a peer with $i$ segments can be calculated using the results above.

$$sp_i = \frac{a * uspeed}{n} * \left[ \sum_{j=1}^{k} \left( l_j * \frac{p_{j,i}}{un_j} \right) - \frac{p_{i,i}}{un_i} \right]$$

The time that a peer spends in a network owning exactly $i$ segments is inversely proportional to the download speed it experiences. Let $t_i$ be the time spent by a peer in the steady-state network having exactly $i$ segments.

$$t_i = \frac{1}{sp_i}$$

Now, the distribution of segments in the steady-state system can be determined by normalizing the values of $t$.

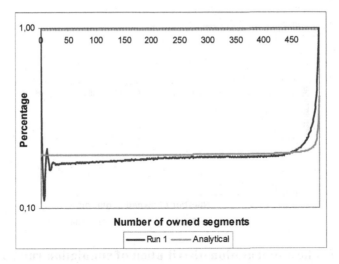

**Fig. 6 The segmentation distribution of simulation run 1 compared to the analytical result**

For each simulation run the distribution of segments was measured and analyzed. The boundaries of the confidence interval using $\alpha=0.05$ was very close, less than 1% of the absolute value. Thus; it is not presented on the charts.

The segment distribution shows how many percent of peers owns a given number of segments in a steady-state system. If the segment distribution were uniform then its value would be equal to the reciprocal of the total number of segments that is 0.02. Both simulation and analytical results differ from uniform distribution. They show that peers having a high number of segments need more time to acquire new segments. This is due to the fact, when a peer has many segments it is less likely that another peer has and can upload a new segment.

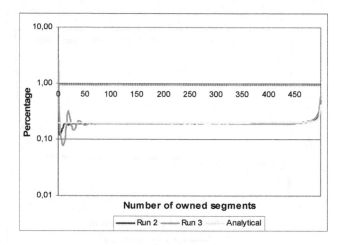

**Fig. 7  The segmentation distribution of simulation run 2 and 3 compared to the analytical result**

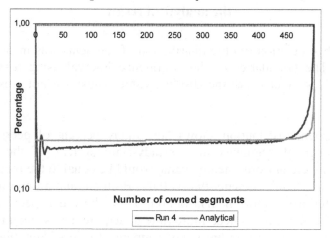

**Fig. 8  The segmentation distribution of simulation run 4 compared to the analytical result**

In all figures the simulation results follow the analytical results. However the curve of simulation run 1 is less sheer compared to run 2 and 3. The reason for this is that our analytical method is an approximation of distribution. The value of $f_{i,j}$ depends only on the value of $i$ neglecting the effect of that peers spending more time in the system can upload more segments for other peers. Despite this slight difference the measured and calculated curves still show convergence. The convergence becomes stronger as the number of initial acquired peers increases. Thus, when peers have a clearer picture of the system our approximation becomes more accurate. The same phenomenon can be seen on Fig. 8 and Fig. 9.

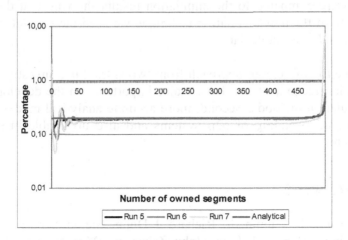

**Fig. 9  The segmentation distribution of simulation run 5, 6 and 7 compared to the analytical result**

Note that the number of maximum simultaneous uploads has less affect on the convergence. It has a greater influence on the initial fluctuation that can be clearly seen in Fig. 7. The reason of fluctuation comes from the difference of the initial waiting time, the time spent before acquiring the first segment. As the initial waiting time increases the number of possible ongoing downloads increases as well. Higher number of maximum parallel uploads allows a waiting peer to acquire more connections in the initial waiting state. After the initial waiting period peers having more ongoing downloads will spend less time having a few number of segments. The reason for this is that segments under download in the initial waiting state will arrive in a batch.

## 5.    CONCLUSIONS AND FUTURE WORK

In this paper we introduced a new p2p model to investigate the performance of p2p information-sharing systems. We presented simulation techniques that can be used to simulate p2p systems efficiently and also introduced a new but simple technique – the unrestricted upload method – to investigate the raw performance of p2p networks.

We implemented a simulator that uses the unrestricted upload method. Several number of simulation runs were used to validate the results. We also introduced an analytical method for performance evaluation. Analytical results were compared to the simulation results showing that despite the simplicity of the new simulation technique we used the simulator delivers accurate and reasonable data.

We are to enforce our approach from two sides. First, investigating new distribution techniques can have major importance in the development of the simulation methods. Second, more accurate analytical models provide a better understanding of p2p systems and also invaluable in simulator validation.

## REFERENCES

[1] Krishna, P. Gummadi, Richard J Dunn, Stefan Saroiu, Steven D. Gribble, Henry M. Levy, John Zahorjan, "Measurement, Modeling, and Analysis of a Peer-to-Peer File-Sharing Workload", SOSP'03, 2003, New York

[2] R. Bhagwan, S. Savage, G. M. Voelker, "Understanding availability", IPTPS'03, 2003, USA

[3] M. Feldman, C. Papadimitriou, J. Chuang, I. Stoica, "Free-Riding and Whitewashing in Peer-to-Peer Systems", IEEE Journal on Selected Areas in Communications, Vol. 24, No. 5, May 2006.

[4] Brian, F. Cooper, Hector Garcia-Molina, "SIL: Modeling and Measuring Scalable Peer-to-Peer Search Networks", International Workshop on Databases, Information Systems and Peer-to-Peer Computing, Berlin, 2003.

[5] D. Liben-Nowell, Hari Balakrishnan, D. Karger, "Analysis of the Evolution of Peer-to-Peer Systems", PODC 2002, USA

[6] C. Gkantsidis and P. Rodriguez. *Network coding for large scale content distribution.* In Proc. IEEE Infocom'2005.

[7] Official BitTorent Specification, accessible at http://www.bittorrent. org/protocol.html

[8] Qiu D. and Srikant R., Modeling and performance analysis of bittorrent like peer-to-peer networks. Technical report, University of Illinois at Urbana-Champaign, USA, 2004.

[9]  T. Hoßfeld, A. Binzenhöfer, D. Schlosser, K. Eger, J. Oberender, I. Dedinski, G. Kunzmann, Towards Efficient Simulation of Large Scale P2P Networks, Research Report 371, University of Würzburg, 2005.

[10] PeerSim simulator, available at http://peersim.sourceforge.net/

[11] p2psim  simulator, available at http://pdos.csail.mit.edu/p2psim/

# CHAPTER 16

# Repair Strategies on the Operation of MPLS Routing

Dénes Papp[1], Tien Van Do[1], Ram Chakka[2],
Xuan Mai Thi Truong[1]

[1]Department of Telecommunications
Budapest University of Technology and Economics
[2]Rajeev Gandhi Memorial College of Engineering & Technology
(RGMCET), Nandyal, India

**Abstract.** *Efficient operation of multipath routing is considered as one of the important aspects in MPLS traffic engineering. Multipath routing has an advantage over the traffic routing based on single shortest path because single path routing may lead to unbalanced traffic situations and degraded QoS (Quality of Service). The adequate strategy for the order of repairing failed links can greatly influence performance characteristics of an MPLS network.*

*In this paper we propose a new repair strategy for MPLS multipath routing. We compare our repair strategy with several existing repair strategies, by way of comparing the associated performance measures. Numerical results show that our scheme performs better than many other repair schemes.*

## 1.  INTRODUCTION

Recently, there has been intensive research dealing with MPLS multipath routing. In [4], the authors proposed two multipath bandwidth-constraint based routing algorithms in MPLS networks. In case there is no single path satisfying the whole constraint, these algorithms can divide the bandwidth-constraint into two or more sub-constraints and find an adequate path for each of the sub-constraints. Simulation results therein [4] show that the proposed algorithms can enhance the success probability of path setup and the utilization of network resources compared to the case of single-path routing algorithms. A dynamic multipath traffic engineering mechanism called LDM (Load Distribution over Multipath) has been proposed in [10]. This mechanism enhances the network utilization as well as the network performance perceived by users. This enhancement is gained by adaptively splitting traffic load among the multiple paths. The simulation results confirm that LDM performs better than hop-count based, as well as the traffic-load based routing mechanisms. However, no theoretical or mathematical analysis has been performed to explicitly point out the benefits of multipath routing.

In [6] the authors compare different multi-path routing algorithms in respect of mixing both load balancing and DiffServ prioritizing approach in MPLS networks, evaluating thus their scalability and efficiency. The results therein have been derived theoretically by comparing the complexities of the examined algorithms. The authors also propose a real adaptive multi-path routing mechanism, which is essentially a modified LDM indeed.

In [11] multipath routing algorithms are investigated at flow-level, and a flow-level routing mechanism is proposed. Despite being a heuristic, this routing algorithm appears to be efficient and easy to implement. However, the performance results have been obtained only by simulation [11].

Multipath routing is not only a great solution for load-balancing, but also for fault-tolerance. In [9], Seok et al investigate the MPLS multipath routing from this enhanced point of view. The proposed scheme consists of determining the maximally disjoint multipath configurations and appropriate traffic rerouting mechanism for fault recovery. Whenever a linkfailure occurs, the traffic can be rerouted in polynomial time. Through case studies by simulation, it has been shown that the traffic engineering using the maximally disjoint multipaths recovers effectively when some link-failures occur.

The performance evaluation of multipath routing in IP/MPLS networks has also been done in several other works [10][2][8]. In [2] the authors provide performance analysis of a burst - level bandwidth allocation algorithm based on multipath routing to efficiently allocate resources for real time traffic. This is done by comparing the performance of multipath reservation algorithms to single path reservation algorithms, both with reattempt-allowed and without. Numerical results have been presented but without validation by simulation.

In this paper we present some investigations regarding the repair strategies that can be applied in multipath routing. As we show later in this paper, the order of repairing failed links can influence the performance characteristics of an MPLS network very considerably and hence it is crucial to find an appropriate and adequate repair strategy. We first compare repair strategies based on the arrival time of failure-events (e.g. the FCFS, LCFS strategies), and then make effort to bring out certain promising new, priority-based repair strategies, the priorities dependent on network link parameters, such as failure, repair rates and the link bandwidth.

The rest of the paper is organized as follows. In Section 2 the overview of the operation of MPLS multipath routing is presented. The model is discussed in Section 3. Numerical results are presented in Section 4. Section 5 concludes the paper.

## 2. MPLS MULTIPATH ROUTING

MPLS are often used in the backbone of IP networks, and it consists of MPLS routers and links between MPLS nodes. Traffic demands traversing the MPLS domain are conveyed along pipes, or in the MPLS terminology, Label Switched Paths (LSPs). When a packet arrives at the ingress router called Label Edge Router (LER) of the MPLS domain, a short fixed-length label is appended to it. The packet will be assigned to a specific LSP. The criteria for the assignment are the destination IP address of the incoming packet and some additional considerations concerning the current resource availability in the domain. After that, the packet is forwarded along the assigned LSP in the core of the MPLS domain. At each core router called Label Switched Router (LSR), the label is simply swapped instead of interrogating the IP header, significantly increasing packet-forwarding efficiency, which results in tremendous gains in traffic forwarding speed, performance and QoS.

Source-based routing is also supported in MPLS besides the shortest path routing based on the routing protocols such as the OSPF (Open Shortest Path First) [7]. That is, an explicit LSP for a given traffic flow from the ingress LER to the egress LER can be established and maintained based on the operation of constraint based routing (CBR) algorithms and signaling protocols such as Resource Reservation Protocol–Traffic Engineering (RSVP-TE). These two components allow MPLS to decide upon the LSP, based not only on the link metric (as the OSPF does) but also on the currently available resources along the links. By doing this way, traffic may be routed not along the shortest path but along the most adequate path that has enough resources to meet a given target QoS (e.g. sufficient bandwidth, low delay). Moreover, traffic may also be split and routed simultaneously along several LSPs. All of these features make MPLS traffic engineering able to distribute the traffic rather evenly inside the domain, along with many other benefits as well.

## 3.    MODEL OVERVIEW

In this Section we provide the overview of the base-model presented in [5]. Let us assume that there are c LSPs built between source and destination nodes in the MPLS domain. Ingress router will demultiplex IP packets travelling to the egress router into these LSPs. From the viewpoint of source-destination nodes, LSPs are considered as servers (i.e., equivalent to servers in the queuing model) which are responsible for conveying IP packets between the two endpoints.

As shown in figure 1, each LSP is thus mapped to a server in the model. Since we use one-to-one relationship between LSPs and servers, there would be c number of servers that serve incoming requests.

The arrival intensity of requests to the servers in the model is the same as the arrival intensity of the incoming IP packets. Different IP packets may have differing sizes, which translates into different requests having different service times at servers, and these service time parameters can be derived from the packet sizes. Also different LSPs can have different bandwidths.

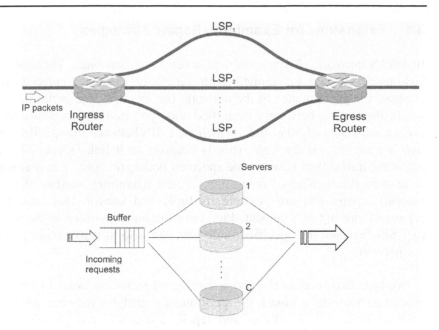

**Fig. 1  Mapping LSPs to servers**

A server can serve only one request at the maximum, at any given time. If another request arrives while serving a request, then the new request has to wait in the buffer until the server becomes free again. If more than one request are waiting in the queue, then these will be served in the order of their arrival. The buffer size is assumed finite, hence a new request would be discarded, if all the places in the buffer are engaged (i.e., the buffer is full) at its arrival instance. The buffer size parameter in the model is derived from the buffer sizes assigned to the LSPs in MPLS edge routers.

In order to evaluate the performance of parallel LSPs between two specific MPLS nodes, a source and destination node, the methodology presented in detail in [5] can be applied. We have used the same methodology to obtain the performance measures such as probability of packet-loss and average number of customers waiting in the queue (buffer). This analysis and information is essential for the planning and dimensioning process of an MPLS network and also for controlling the operation and maintenance of the network, that is by the realization of traffic engineering functionalities adequately. These goals can be achieved through a number of investigations in which performance measures versus specified network parameters are thoroughly examined.

## 3.1   Extensions for Examining Repair Strategies

In MPLS networks, LSPs consist of several physical links. Therefore, the base-model should be applied with necessary care and correctness to evaluate the performance of the network. For example, the performance of multipath routing between a specified node-pair can also depends on the failure and repair of other links which the LSPs between the specific node-pair are not routed through. This is because such link-failures also can affect the traffic flow between the specified node-pair. Also, it is reasonable to assume the number of repairmen, i.e. the maximum number of simultaneous repairs that are possible, is finite and known. However, these repairmen are not only allocated to repair the links involved in the routing of LSPs between the specified node-pair, but also to repair other links in the network.

We take into account the above mentioned factors in order to make our model possible to evaluate the performance analysis between arbitrarily selected nodes while failures and repairs are considered globally in the whole network. Such investigations are very useful for network design, maintenance or control of the operation.

## 3.2   Repair Strategies

Link-failures may affect the operation of LSPs and cause network breakdowns. When the failed link is repaired, the repaired LSP can be used again. Repair strategy defines the order of repairing failed links, when they are more than one. A number of alternative repair-strategies exist when there are failures of links. Since repair strategies can influence the performance of the network, choosing an adequate or nearly optimal repair strategy can be crucial since that can enhance the performance to meet QoS constraints. Repair strategies can be preemptive or non- preemptive. Though we have used only the latter, we believe preemptive-priority based repair strategies can be better than non-preemptive ones, in cases where the repair time distributions are exponential or they are done in phases of exponential times.

In this paper we present investigations and results regarding some repair strategies that can be applied in MPLS traffic engineering. We would also show quantitatively, how various repair strategies can influence the performance characteristics of an MPLS network, considerably.

The simplest and trivially arising repair policies are Last-Come- First-Serve (LCFS) and First-Come-First-Serve (FCFS), in which the order of repairs depends on the order of link failures. As the names indicate, always the latest and the earliest link failure will be repaired respectively in these two strategies.

The key element regarding the strategies based on link-priorities is that links withhigher priority should be set into repair sooner, even if these failures have occurred later. The priority list of links should be constructed on a greedy way, with a view to repair first the link which would result the biggest gain (that is, having highest sensitivity).

A comparison between LCFS, FCFS and priority-based repair strategies in [5] shows clearly that it is worth to apply priority-based strategy for link repairs, because better performance characteristics can be gained this way.

In this paper we present further investigations mainly regarding the priority-based repair strategies. A new function would be introduced for deciding the repair priorities of the links, which balances the repair order and causes higher utilization of the network.

## 3.2.1 Developing Efficient Decision Function for Priority Strategy

A decision function is developed here for obtaining near optimal repair order in a priority strategy to obtain best possible performance characteristics. The decision function is based on three parameters, the failure, repair rates and the bandwidth of the optical links.

Simple performance-observations and explanations are sufficient to state that it is worth to repair the link with:

- smaller failure rate,
- larger repair rate,
- larger bandwidth,

if only one of these parameter is changing while the other two are fixed.

The real issue emerges when more than one of these parameters differ among the failed links when comparing link characteristics. Since all these factors influence the performance, we would need a decision function to decide upon the priorities of the failed links, that decision function should involve all these 3 factors.

Let us assume that failure rate of link i is $f_i$, repair rate is $r_i$ and bandwidth is $b_i$. The bandwidth of a link is computed from the summation of the LSPs bandwidths passing through this particular link. This approach ensures that links used by several LSPs may get higher priority, over the links used only by one LSP, when the former has more bandwidth contribution.

The $w_i$ weight of link i is set to:

$$w_i = \frac{r_i}{f_i} * b_i \qquad (1)$$

constructed, This formula can be divided into two parts, the ratio of the repair and failure rates, and the bandwidth parameter. Thus, repair rates may have larger influence on the priority function ($w_i$) through the repair rate, failure rate ratio than failure rate. The second part of the formula assures that links with higher bandwidth deserve higher priority.

### 3.3    Solution of the Model

The model simplifies the real world with the assumption that the source node notices the breakdown of an LSP immediately. In truth, many packets get into the failed LSP until the router at the end of the failed link detects the link failure and notifies the source router. We should also take this phenomenon into consideration. It is reasonable to assume that the sum of the times for failure detection and notification are constant for all LSPs.

Both simulation and analytical solutions are developed for solving our model. The analytical model [3] is capable of generating results rather much faster which is a vital factor by network design process.

## 4.    NUMERICAL RESULTS

In order to validate the accuracy of the proposed model, some case studies are carried out to determine the performance of a multipath routing scenario depicted in Figure 2. We assume that the IP/MPLS topology is overlaid on the optical DWDM (Dense Wavelength Division Multiplexing) network. That is, the interconnection of IP/MPLS routers is realized by the DWDM network.

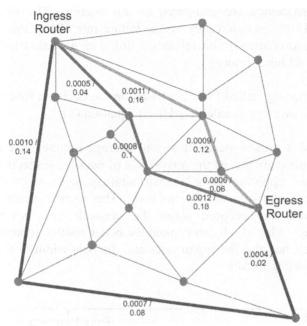

**Fig. 2  Network topology**

Traffic to be carried between the ingress and egress nodes follows the ON-OFF process with two states (ON − OFF). The ON and OFF periods are exponentially distributed with mean 0.4 and 0.5 respectively. The distribution of inter-arrival times in state ON is generalized exponential with parameters ($\sigma$ = 110, . . . , 190, $\theta$ = 0.526471). In state OFF no packets arrive. These parameters of arrival stream derive from the interarrival times of recorded samples of the real Bellcore traffic trace BC-pAug89 [1].

A reference network which contains 18 nodes and 38 optical links is used in our investigations. Assume that there are three LSPs established between ingress and egress nodes of the IP/MPLS network as shown in Figure 2. Failure/repair rate parameters and link IDs are indicated next to the links in the network. Thus, we have c = 3 servers with GE exponential distribution parameters ($\mu_i$, $\varphi_i$): $\mu_1$ = 96, $\mu_2$ = 128 $\mu_3$ = 160; $\varphi_1$ = $\varphi_2$ = $\varphi_3$ = 0.109929. Note that, these parameters have been obtained based on the service capacity of the LSPs and the packet lengths from the trace, as stated earlier.

Two repair strategies are compared in this section. The first repair strategy called Prior1 is based only on the failure rate of the links (that is, when there are simultaneous link failures, a link with a smaller failure rate is repaired with a higher priority).

The second strategy called Prior2 is based on the decision function ($w_i$). That is the repair strategy is calculated from equation (1).

Figures 3 and 4 present packet loss and average number of customers waiting in the queue are versus the arrival rate of packets, respectively. We can observe that applying Prior2 repair strategy will result in better performance characteristics in the network. The second strategy takes more information into account about the network links towards the decision of repair order which can explain the better results. It balances not only failure rates, but also the repair rates and the bandwidth of links used by the passing-through LSPs.

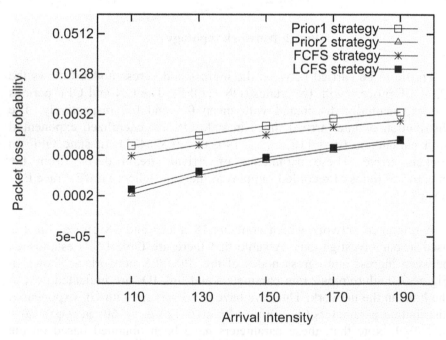

**Fig. 3  Packet loss probability versus arrival intensity**

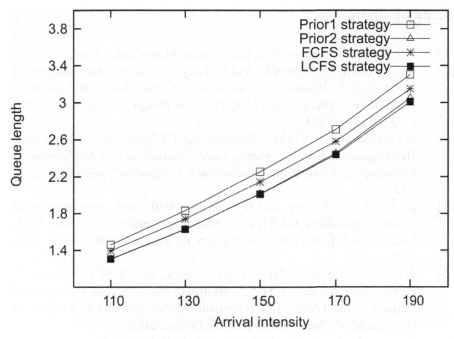

**Fig.4  Queue length versus arrival intensity**

## 5.    CONCLUSIONS

We have computed the MPLS performance when link-failures and repairs are involved. We have illustrated how a number of repair strategies can exist and how considerably they can influence the performance of the MPLS. This does imply that selecting an appropriate repair strategy is indeed crucial top performance- gain. We have compared the impacts on performance by few repair strategies for link-failures and repairs, in the MPLS multipath routing. Numerical results show that our proposal scheme can outperform other schemes.

Though we have used non-preemptive priority based strategies, in future, we will attempt preemptive priority based strategies too since the latter would be better than the former, when the repair time distributions are exponential or when the repairs are done in phases of exponential times.

## REFERENCES

[1]     The Internet traffic archive. http://ita.ee.lbl.gov/index.html.

[2]     M. Ashibani, D. Mashaob, and B. Nleya. "Performance Analysis of Burst Level Bandwidth Allocation Using Multipath Routing Reservation." *International Conference on Trends in Communications*, 1:70–76, July 2001.

[3]     R. Chakka and T. V. Do. "The MM $\sum_{k=1}$CPP$_k$/GE/c/L G-Queue with Heterogeneous Servers: Steady State Solution and an Application to Performance Evaluation. Performance Evaluation", 64(3):191–209, 2007.

[4]     H. Y. Cho, J. Y. Lee, and B. C. Kim. "Multi-path constraint-based routing algorithms for MPLS traffic engineering." ICC '03. IEEE International Conference on Communications, 3:1963–1967, May 2003.

[5]     Tien V. Do, Denes Papp, Ram Chakka, and X.M.T. Truong. A Performance Model of MPLS Multipath Routing with Failures and Repairs of the LSPs". In Performance Modelling and Evaluation of Heterogeneous Networks (HET-NETs '06), 2006.

[6]     K. Lee, A. Toguyeni, A. Noce, and A. Rahmani. "Comparison of Multipath Algorithms for Load Balancing in a MPLS Network", volume 3391. Springer Link, 2005.

[7]     J. Moy. Ospf version 2. Technical Report RFC2328, Internet Engineering Task Force, 1998.

[8]     S. Nelakuditi and Z. L. Zhang. "On selection of paths for multipath routing." In IWQoS '01: Proceedings of the 9th International Workshop on Quality of Service, pages 170–186, London, UK, 2001. Springer-Verlag.

[9]     Y. Seok, Y. Lee, N. Choi, and Y. Choi. "Fault-tolerant Multipath Traffic Engineering for MPLS Networks." Communications, Internet, and Information Technology, 2003.

[10]    J. Song, S. Kim, and M. Lee. "Dynamic Load Distribution in MPLS Networks", volume 2662. Springer Link, 2003.

[11]    Z. Zhao, Y. Shu, L. Zhang, H. Wang, and O. W. W. Yang. "Flow-level multipath load balancing in MPLS network." IEEE International Conference on Communications, 2:1222 – 1226, June 2004.

# CHAPTER 17

# Incorporating Uncertainties into Traffic Simulators

M. J. Bayarri, J. O. Berger, G. Molina

University of Valencia/SAMSI/Duke University

**Abstract.** *It is possible to incorporate uncertainty in model inputs into analyses of traffic simulators, and incorporating this uncertainty can significantly improve the predictions made with these simulators.*

*CORSIM is a microsimulator for vehicular traffic, and is being studied with respect to its ability to successfully model and predict the behavior of traffic in a large vehicular network. However, the developments described herein will also be useful in dealing with general discrete network structures, such as traffic in telecommunications networks. In these types of networks, 'vehicles' are analogous to packets or ATM cells or messages, 'streets' to communications channels or links, 'highways' to high capacity trunks, and 'turning proportions' to routing and switching decision probabilities made within network elements – routers, switches, etc.*

*Inputs to the simulator include information about network topology, traffic behavior, turning probabilities at each point of intersection, and distributions of traffic ingress into the system. Data are available concerning the turning proportions in a sub-network, as well as counts of vehicular ingress into the sub-network and internal system counts, during a day in May 2000. Some of the data are based on direct measurements and are quite accurate, while some other data are quite inaccurate. Traffic data from telecommunications networks also varies from accurate (when high-performance line-rate monitors are used) to coarse estimates – e.g., in wireless networks, and in all-optical networks in which monitoring is typically done only at endpoints and in the optoelectronic control plane.*

*Previous utilization of the full data set was to 'tune' the parameters of CORSIM – in an ad hoc fashion – until CORSIM output was reasonably close to the actual data. This common approach, of simply tuning a complex computer model to real data, can result in poor parameter choices and will completely ignore the often considerable uncertainty remaining in the parameters.*

*To overcome these problems, we adopt a Bayesian approach, together with a measurement error model for the inaccurate data, to derive the posterior distribution of turning probabilities and of the parameters of the CORSIM input distribution. This posterior distribution can then be used to initialize runs of CORSIM, yielding outputs that reflect that actual uncertainty in the analysis. Determining the posterior via Markov Chain Monte Carlo methodology is not directly feasible because of the running-time of CORSIM. Fortunately, the turning probabilities and parameters of the input distribution enter CORSIM through a probability structure that can almost exactly be described by a stochastic network that does allow an MCMC analysis.*

## INTRODUCTION

Computer simulators are very useful 'surrogates' of reality. However, they are not perfect. Appropriate use should include a discrepancy term (Kennedy and O'Hagan, 2001; Bayarri et al 2007), viz.:

$$Reality = Model + Discrepancy$$

The discrepancy (or bias) term is a function of the model inputs, so a model can be good in some parts of the parameter space, but not as good in others. One can use field data (physical experiments) to learn more about simulator inputs and to 'tune' the model (calibration), and to assess the model's discrepancy/bias vis-à-vis reality (validation). To avoid over-tuning and to increase the model's predictive power, it is essential to learn simultaneously about both – unknown parameters and model deficiency.

In doing so, one must take various uncertainties into account and combine them in an appropriate ways; uncertainties appear:

- In the inputs;
- In the discrepancy term itself;
- In the simulator (if stochastic);
- For slow simulators, in the surrogate emulator used for several purposes (design, sensitivity analysis, optimization, Bayesian computations, etc.);
- In field data (bias, missing values, etc.); and
- As measurement errors in the field data, which is usually the only source acknowledged by simulation practitioners.

Extrapolation is often required, which leads to still more uncertainty. All of these can be taken into account globally, but it is a very difficult statistical challenge.

Calibration, that is using field data to determine the inputs to the simulator (also called the "inverse problem"), is only one component of this global analysis. In the past, this was often done by tuning. However, there are uncertainties in the data, and these must be accounted for in the analysis. In this paper, we limit ourselves to treating this specific aspect of the global analysis in isolation.

A Bayesian approach allows us to view quantities about which we are uncertain (including the inputs and the random simulator output for given inputs) as random quantities endowed with a (prior) probability distribution, and to relate them to the actual observations through a measurement error model. When data is observed, this prior distribution (for the inputs and other unknowns) gets revised using Bayes' Theorem to produce their posterior distribution, given the observations. This distribution automatically incorporates all the uncertainties, including the ones in the simulator inputs.

Uncertainty in simulator predictions can then be assessed by treating the posterior distribution as the 'random input distribution' for the simulator, and making repeated runs of the simulator initialized by draws from this posterior distribution. This is not significantly more expensive than running the basic simulator. It is a stochastic simulator so its predictions can only be ascertained through repeated runs, and starting each run with inputs chosen from the posterior distribution is no more expensive that starting each run with fixed inputs.

To illustrate, we describe experiments using the CORSIM traffic simulator, a computer model (microsimulator) of vehicular street and highway traffic. However, the concepts are directly applicable to traffic in telecommunication networks, and especially in networks in which switching or routing decisions are not static (in that they depend on resource availability, queue size, priority, etc.), and in which there is a street/highway dichotomy – viz., lines/trunks, access links/core links, wireless/wireline, etc. The dichotomy is due to the carrying capacities of 'streets' vs. 'highways'.

## THE SIMULATOR

### Characteristics

The traffic simulator's main characteristics are (Fig. 1):

- It is stochastic, as vehicles enter and turn in intersections randomly and independently; in networks, packets enter and are routed or switched more or less randomly and independently;
- It has many inputs, so one focuses on a subset – e.g., demand (entering rate) and turning probabilities; note the parallels with networking queuing systems postulated by Kleinrock and others in the early days of packet switched networks;
- It was used to model traffic in rush hours; in telecommunications networks, one focuses almost exclusively on 'peak' traffic periods;
- Key assumptions are that arrivals are Poisson, and that turning movements are multinomials.

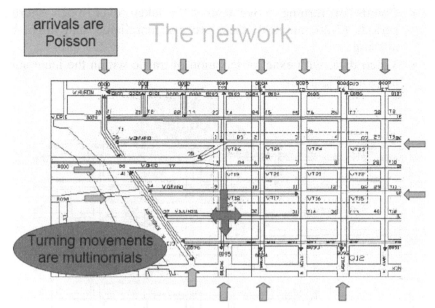

**Fig. 1 Reference model used in the CORSIM traffic simulator.**

## Uncertainties

The key uncertainties come from:

- Vehicles (or packets or ATM cells or messages or ...) entering each street (link) at the specific (unknown) rate $\lambda_{street}$ per hour;
- Turning (routing/switching) unknown probabilities $p_{left}$, $p_{through}$, $p_{right}$ at each intersection (switch/router) in each direction;
- The key uncertainties in this problem are the $\lambda$'s, and the p's which are estimated (based on physical data) and fed into CORSIM.
- Other uncertainties (type of drivers (packets), percentages of trucks and cars (comparable to the 'mice vs. elephants' issue in networking)) were set at default values, but could have been tuned.

## Data

Data consists of:

- One hour counts $C^{street}$ of vehicles entering the network at each street; this is very unreliable, with errors up to 50%;

- Counts of turning movements $C^{turn}$ taken over much shorter periods (7-20 minutes); these are also unreliable, and might be missing;
- Video data, with exact observation of traffic within the inner sub-network (Figure 2);

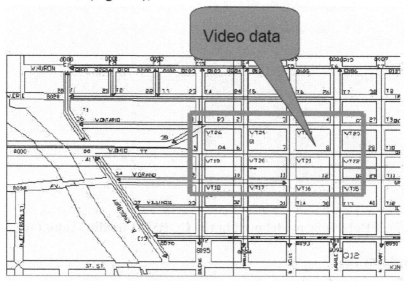

**Fig. 2 Exact observations (e.g., from video monitors for vehicular traffic, or packet monitors for telecommunication networks) may be restricted to a small part of the network.**

In telecommunications networks, arrivals are often difficult to measure. This is especially the case in very large networks, where having monitors at each point of ingress is impossible. 'Turning' measurements may have to be obtained from router MIBs, whose counters cannot keep pace with high traffic loads. 'Video' in the vehicular example corresponds to telecommunications traffic monitors, which may only be used in limited situations due to their cost. Network traffic monitors for all-optical networks are not commercially available, and are not widely used in wireless networks.

Traditional solutions often find that manual counts are incompatible with video counts, which leads to ad-hoc "adjustments" of some of the manual counts (Figure 3). This approach then estimates $\lambda$ (the vector of all of the $\lambda$'s) and $p$ (the vector of all of the p's) from the ad-hoc adjusted counts and feeds them into CORSIM; among other difficulties, this treats estimates as known values, ignoring inherent (and important) uncertainties. Manual 'tuning' is also questionable, in that it imposes a double use of the data.

## Example of a tuning adjustment

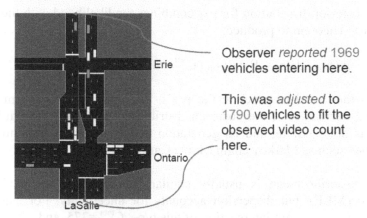

Erie

Ontario

LaSalle

Observer *reported* 1969 vehicles entering here.

This was *adjusted* to 1790 vehicles to fit the observed video count here.

**Fig. 3  Traditional approach to adjustments.**

### A Bayesian Approach for Accurate Counts

A simple way to account for and combine uncertainties is through Bayesian analysis. Bayesian analysis requires the *likelihood function*, a *prior distribution* for unknown parameters, and computational resources to deal with the *posterior distribution*. Each is described below.

Let us assume first that counts $C^{street}$ and $C^{turn}$ are free of errors (which is true in some networks with automatic monitoring). Here, we use the adjusted counts as if they were true counts, and instead of feeding CORSIM with fixed values for the $\lambda$'s and p's, we generate them from a distribution that reflects the uncertainty – i.e., the Bayesian *posterior distribution*.

To illustrate, consider an analysis for turning probabilities. We assume that a given intersection only has two possibilities, going left or continuing straight, so that $\mathbf{p} = (p_{left} , p_{through} )$. We then only need to determine the distribution for $p_{left}$, (since $p_{through} = 1 - p_{left}$ ). For observed data $C^{left}$ out of $C^{total}$ , the *likelihood function* of $p_{left}$ is Binomial($C^{left} \mid C^{total}$, $p_{left}$). Standard Bayesian analysis also requires a *prior distribution* for $p_{left}$. This can incorporate genuine prior information, and/or be chosen in an objective fashion, that is, chosen so that it alters little the likelihood while having desirable (statistical) properties. We use an objective prior; the Uniform(0,1), that is, all values of $p_{left}$ equally likely a priori would be a reasonable choice, but a better one is $\pi(\ p_{left}) = Beta(p_{left}\ |0.5,\ 0.5)$., using a Beta distribution; (note that the Uniform(0,1) is the Beta(1,1) distribution).

The posterior distribution for $p_{left}$ combines the likelihood with the prior via Bayes' Theorem to produce:

$$\pi\ (p_{left}\ |\ data) = Beta(p_{left}\ |\ C^{left} + 0.5,\ C^{total} - C^{left} + 0.5),$$

which is then used to generate the $p_{left}$'s. Note that in complex models, analytical derivation of the posterior distribution and/or direct simulation from it is not possible, and its generation needs sophisticated simulation techniques such as Markov chain Monte Carlo (MCMC).

The posterior mean is usually similar to the maximum likelihood estimator (MLE), but dispersion accounts for uncertainty. For example, assume that at a certain intersection of this type, $C^{tota} = 375$, and $C^{left} = 50$, so that MLE = .118. The Posterior Distribution is a Beta (50.5, 375.5), whose mean=.118, but it has an SD=.0156. Then, if 10 runs from CORSIM are required, instead of running it 10 times with the same value .118 of $p_{left}$ for the 10 runs, 10 generations from this Beta posterior distribution will be used, for example, .142, .152, .117, .131, .109, .110, .126, .129, .101, .153.

One can perform a similar analysis for the more general case $\mathbf{p} = (p_{left}, p_{through}, p_{right})$ based on Dirichlet prior/posterior distributions, and a multinomial for data model.

Analysis of demand rates for a given input location (street or network trunk) is as follows: For each specific input street we have

- $\lambda_{street}$ = true rate of cars, packets, etc. entering per hour.
- For the observed count $C^{street}$ of cars entering, the likelihood of $\lambda_{street}$ is $Po(C^{street}\ |\ \lambda_{street})$.
- Objective prior ➔ $\pi(\lambda_{street}) \propto \lambda_{street}^{-1/2}$
- Posterior ➔ $\lambda$street $|\ C^{street} \sim Ga(C^{street} + 1/2,\ 1)$ with mean and mode $\cong$ MLE of $\lambda_{street}$
- Example – if $C^{street} = 540$ is observed, the posterior has mean 540.5, and standard deviation 23.24. If 10 runs of CORSIM are required, one uses 10 simulations with 10 independent values simulated from the Gamma posterior Ga(540.5, 1), for example

516.41, 534.07, 557.4, 506.03, 553.95, 544.05, 532, 551.43, 541.51.

## Running CORSIM:

- The joint posterior is the product of all posteriors for all input locations and all turning probability vectors;
- Generate the $\lambda$'s and p's from their (independent) posteriors and feed into CORSIM instead of fixed values;
- This provides a simple yet objective way to incorporate uncertainties into the models; note that since uncertainties are incorporated rather than ignored, distributions describing the system are expected to be less precise. In particular, the analysis results in longer tails in the distributions of the measures of congestion, thus properly accounting for uncertainties (Figure 4).

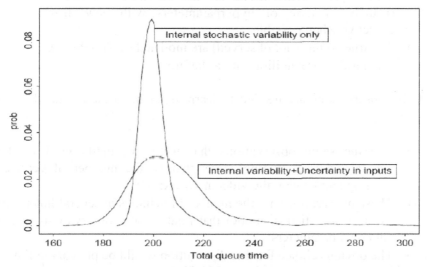

**Fig. 4  Uncertainty produces longer tails in the queuing time distribution.**

## Incorporating Errors in Counts

The previous approach, although very simple, was based on the assumption that we had 'good' counts free of error; however, we instead used 'tuned', manually adjusted counts, and this is not entirely satisfactory for several reasons:

- Too few inputs were tuned, and those may be over-tuned;
- It ignores uncertainties in the tuned (erroneous) inputs, so there may be not only an overly optimistic assessment of output variance (which is the usual result of ignoring uncertainties) but, what is worse, in these models it can produce biased inferences, as we see later.

Bayesian analysis can handle the additional uncertainty. Conceptually, the analysis remains basically the same. The numerical implementation is much more difficult.

Biases are handled as follows:

- The (observed) manual counts are modeled as $C_i^D \sim Po\,(b_i\,N_i)$, where $N_i$ is true counts, and $(b_i - 1)$ is bias of observer at entry $i$;
- Assess prior distributions for the unknowns vectors $\mathbf{b}$ and $\mathbf{N}$ (usually in term of hyperparameters with new distributions, objective when possible);
- The true counts (not observed) are modeled as $N_i \sim Po(\lambda_i)$;
- The turning probabilities are as before.

Extra observations are needed to learn about $\mathbf{b}$. These are handled as follows:

- Use the same observations that were informally used in the manual, ad hoc, 'tuning' case; that is, the number of vehicles entering and leaving the video network: $N^v$;
- These observations are the number of vehicles in several links, and we need a statistical model that relates these observations to the unknown parameters;
- The obvious choice for this distribution would be p(# cars in links | inputs) as computed from CORSIM runs, but we cannot use it because the analysis would require thousands of runs, which is infeasible.

However, key stochastic features (for $\lambda$ and $\mathbf{p}$) can be represented by a simple stochastic network (Figure 5), which:

- Has the same nodal structure as CORSIM;
- Has the same inputs $\lambda$ (vehicle inter-arrival rates) and $\mathbf{p}$ (turning probabilities) as in CORSIM;

- Assumes 'instantaneous' vehicles, that (i) enter the network; (ii) turn appropriately; (iii) exit.

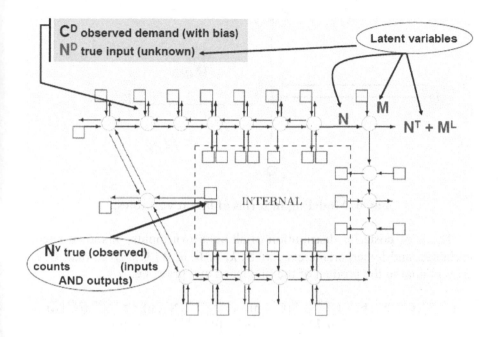

**Fig. 5 Stochastic network.**

This approach mimics the probabilistic structure of CORSIM, but introduces many non-observed (latent) variables – the number of cars in links (which behave like multinomials) – viz., Fig. 6.

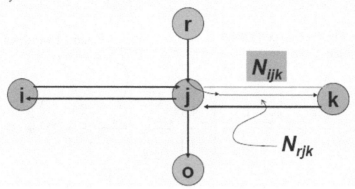

Fig. 6  **Modeling in terms of latent variables.**

The joint posterior distribution of all unknown inputs, unknown latent variables, and hyperparameters , $\pi(\ \mathbf{N}, \boldsymbol{\lambda}, \mathbf{p}, \mathbf{b}, \alpha, \beta \mid \mathbf{C})$, given data $\mathbf{C}$, is proportional to the product of the likelihood and prior; i.e.,

$$\mathrm{f}^{\text{Poisson}}(\mathbf{C}^{\mathrm{D}} \mid \mathbf{N}^{\mathrm{D}}, \mathbf{b}) \times \mathrm{f}^{\text{multinomial}}(\mathbf{C}^{\mathrm{T}} \mid \mathbf{p}) \times \pi^{\text{multinomial}} (\mathbf{N}^{\mathrm{T}} \mid \mathbf{p}) \times \pi^{\text{Poisson}} (\mathbf{N}^{\mathrm{D}} \mid \boldsymbol{\lambda})$$
$$\times \pi^{\text{Objective}} (\mathbf{p}, \boldsymbol{\lambda}) \times \pi^{\text{Gamma}} (\mathbf{b} \mid \alpha, \beta) \times \pi^{\text{mild Inform}} (\alpha, \beta ),$$

where $\mathbf{C}^{\mathrm{D}}$ is the vector of observed demand counts, $\mathbf{N}^{\mathrm{D}}$ the vector of true (unobserved) demand counts, $\mathbf{N}^{\mathrm{T}}$ the vector of true turning counts, $\mathbf{b}$ are biases, $\mathbf{p}$ turning probabilities, $\boldsymbol{\lambda}$ input rates, and $(\alpha,\beta)$ are hyperparameters of the prior distribution for $\mathbf{b}$. There are 16 demand N's, 16 b's, 16 $\lambda$'s, 84 p's, and 74 inside N's so the posterior has 208 unknowns.

Introduction of the latent variables results in a highly dimensional and highly constrained parameter space. Non standard and imaginative procedures are needed to handle these constraints and carry out the required numerical (MCMC) analysis (see details in Molina et al., 2005). The analysis again produces simulations from the posterior distribution of $\lambda$ and $\mathbf{p}$ which are then fed into CORSIM, along with simulations from the bias (and the rest of unknowns).

**Some Results**

We next present some of the results we obtained for the analyzed network in Chicago.

## Posterior Distributions of Demand Rates

In Figure 7, we present the posterior distribution of a couple of demand rates ($\lambda$'s) corresponding to two adjacent entries into the network, here denoted R1 and F1. We also indicate the raw counts ($C^D$'s) for these two entries along with the manually adjusted counts (the ones used in the preliminary analysis). The histograms represent the reliable posterior distributions from the complete Bayesian analysis of the previous section, while the smooth curves are the (inadequate) posteriors based on taking the 'adjusted counts' as if they were the true, observed counts. It can be immediately seen that both counts get adjusted (the one for R1 upwards, and the one for F1 downwards), and also the remarkable uncertainty remaining about the rates after data is observed. The manual adjustment did not adjust the counts for R1 at all, and it can be seen that entries for F1 are over-tuned to compensate.

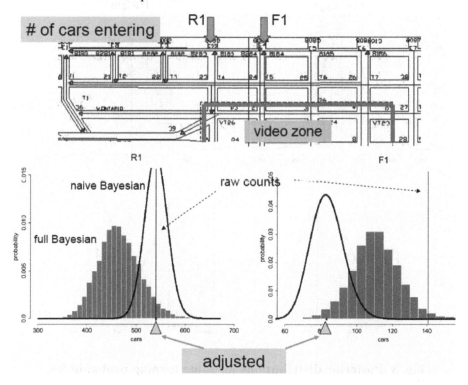

**Fig. 7 Posterior distributions of demand rates ($\lambda$) for two specific entry streets.**

## Posterior Distributions of Turning Probabilities

The turning probabilities are not affected as much by errors in the demand counts as the demand rates are; most posterior distributions change very little whether or not we acknowledge the possible errors in the demand counts; only some few of them get noticeably altered by the error in the counts. In Figure 8 we present the (correct) posterior distributions of turning probabilities for a couple of intersections with only two possible choices (go through or turn right); these are the histograms. The smooth curves correspond to the analysis using the adjusted counts and ignoring the uncertainties in the demand counts. We present an example in which both distributions differ somewhat and another for which there are almost no changes.

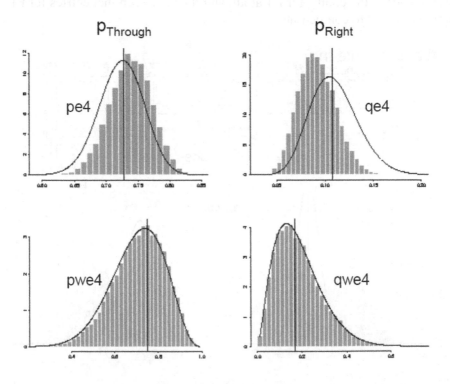

**Fig. 8 Posterior distributions for some turning probabilities.**

**Posterior distributions of bias on the counts**

The bias on the counts turned out to be significant, much larger than expected, and, surprisingly, many of them were in the direction of over counting instead of under counting as expected. This was a significant conclusion of this analysis, and of great interest to traffic engineers. In Figure 9 we present the histograms corresponding to some of the biases. Recall that the value 1 corresponds to no bias. The manual counts of intersections R1, L1 and G1 all present positive bias, some very remarkable, as for example G1; UF6 seems to have a slight negative (under count) bias. The uncertainties are important, and differ from entry to entry; for instance, the distribution corresponding to L1 is reasonably tight (but still reflecting a lot of uncertainty) while the one for UF6 is very disperse.

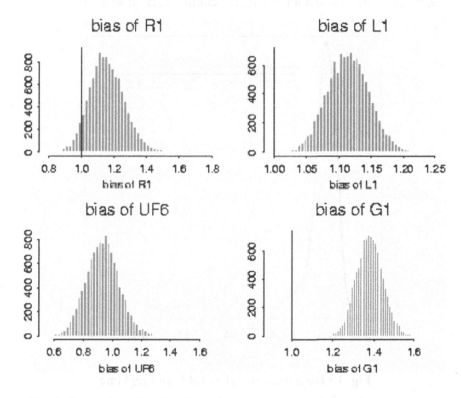

**Fig. 9 Posterior distributions for some count biases. 1 represents no bias.**

## Measures of Congestion of the Network

By feeding CORSIM with simulation from the posteriors for the inputs, it is possible to get appropriate distributions of the measures of congestion of the system (as computed by CORSIM) that do take into account all the uncertainties in the problem. Notice that feeding CORSIM with a fixed estimate only takes into account the internal variability due to the stochasticity of CORSIM. The differences can be remarkable.

In Fig. 10 we present the distributions of the total queuing time (in hours) both, when inherent uncertainties (in the inputs and in the counts) are accounted for, along with the one obtained when these uncertainties are ignored. Notice that, the later is not only more dispersed, but also gives the wrong estimate, the distribution being noticeably switched to the left in comparison to the one obtained with the complete, right analysis.

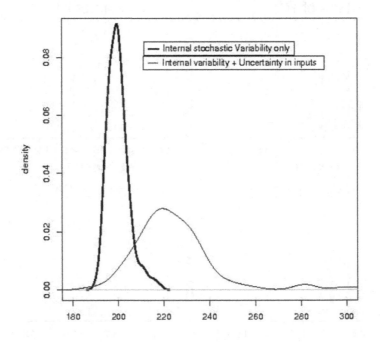

**Fig. 10 Distributions of Total QueuingTime.**

## CONCLUSIONS

- Full Bayesian analysis accounts for and combines uncertainties in stochastic networks.
- An implementation might require the help of a simple probabilistic network (which is feasible for many interacting stochastic networks).
- A solution exists for handling highly constrained parameter spaces. The technique should be applicable to many other discrete networks – e.g., telecommunications networks.
- Calibration/tuning of inputs parameters is only one aspect of the global Bayesian validation of computer simulators.

## ACKNOWLEDGEMENTS

This paper was mainly prepared by Arnold Bragg from the slides presented at the Cost 285 final symposium. His invaluable help is gratefully acknowledged. Full details of the analysis can be found in Bayarri et al. (2004) and Molina et al. (2005). This work was supported in part by the Spanish Ministry of Science and Technology, under Grant MTM2004-03290.

## REFERENCES

[1] Bayarri, M.J., Berger, J., Molina, G., Rouphail, N.M., and Sacks, J. (2004). "Assessing uncertainties in traffic simulation: a key component in model calibration and validation." *Transportation Research Record* **1876**, pp 32-40.

[2] Bayarri, M.J., Berger, J.O., Paulo, R., Sacks, J., Cafeo, J.A., Cavendish, J., Lin, C.H., and Tu, J. (2007). "A Framework for Validation of Computer Models." *Technometrics* **49**, pp.138-154.

[3] Molina, G., Bayarri, M.J., and Berger, J.O. (2005). "Statistical inverse analysis for a network microsimulator." *Technometrics* **47**, pp 388-398.

[4] Kennedy, M. C. and O'Hagan, A. (2001). "Bayesian calibration of computer models (with discussion)." *Journal of the Royal Statistical Society B* **63**, pp 425-464.

# CHAPTER 18

## Effects of Bursty and Correlated Traffic on the Performance of Active Queue Management Schemes

Lan Wang, Geyong Min, Irfan Awan

Department of Computing, School of Informatics,
University of Bradford, Bradford, BD7 1DP, UK

**Abstract.** *Motivated by the need of performance analysis of Active Queue Management (AQM) schemes under highly bursty and correlated traffic in multi-service networks, this paper develops an analytical model for a finite capacity queueing system with an AQM scheme subject to two heterogeneous classes of traffic which are modeled, respectively, by the bursty Markov-Modulated Poisson Process (MMPP) and non-bursty Poisson Process. The well-known MMPP is adopted for modelling bursty traffic owing to its ability to model the time-varying arrival rate and capture the important correlation between inter-arrival times while still maintaining analytical tractability. We derive the aggregate and marginal performance metrics including the mean queue length, response time, system utilization, throughput and loss probability. The accuracy of the model is validated by comparing analytical results with those obtained from simulation. We further focus on the evaluation of the effects of traffic burstiness and correlation of inter-arrival time on the aggregate performance metrics of AQM with different thresholds.*

## 1.   INTRODUCTION

In high-speed communication networks, traffic congestion caused by sources competing for bandwidth and buffer space while being unaware of the current state of the system resources can result in serious problems, such as high packet loss rates, increased delays, degraded Quality-of-Service (QoS), and even break the whole system due to congestion collapse. However, end-to-end congestion control mechanisms are not sufficient to prevent congestion collapse in the Internet. It is therefore necessary to employ buffer management schemes at intermediate routers which drop packets when necessary or appropriate in order to effectively control and reduce traffic congestion. Two critical issues for these schemes are when and how to drop packets. Both have significant impacts on the system performance metrics, such as the queue length, average delay, system throughput, and packet loss probability.

Tail-drop (TD) [3] is a traditional scheme that can be easily implemented to manage the buffer space. The activity of packet dropping does not start until the buffer space is exhausted. However, TD has three drawbacks, namely, global synchronization, lock-out, and full queues, and thus leading to poor network performance in terms of utilization, fairness and per-packet delays as well as jitter [3]. "Drop front on full" and "Random drop on full" [3] are two improved TD schemes which can solve the lock-out problem only, but not others. The Internet Engineering Task Force (IETF) has recommended the deployment of Active Queue Management (AQM) schemes at gateways [2], which can tackle all these drawbacks. AQM aiming to ensure high network utilization and low end-to-end delay is a pro-active approach of explicitly/implicitly notifying Transmission Control Protocol (TCP) about incipient congestion by marking/dropping packets before congestion actually occurs.

Random Early Detection (RED) with two thresholds initially proposed and analyzed in [11] is the first generation of AQM. The network is considered to be congested when the exponentially-weighted moving average of the queue length monitored by an RED-enabled router exceeds the lower threshold. To inform TCP sources of the degree of congestion, the forthcoming packets are randomly dropped with a linearly growing dropping probability when the average queue length increases from the lower threshold to the upper threshold. All coming packets are dropped as long as the average queue length exceeds the upper threshold. RED is able to eliminate global synchronization and minimize the bias against bursty traffic. However, the existing studies [4, 6, 8-10, 12, 17-19] have shown that the performance of RED is highly sensitive to its parameter settings and it is extremely difficult to tune the parameters in order to balance the trade-off between various performance metrics under different traffic conditions. With the aim of further enhancing the efficiency and performance of RED, many substantial AQM mechanisms have been proposed. For instance, May *et al.* [17] have proposed GRED-I mechanism, which uses an instantaneous queue length instead of the average queue length. Moreover, it adopts a dropping probability varying from 0 to 1 between the threshold and the queue size. [3] and [17] have concluded that GRED-I outperforms RED in terms of throughput, loss probability, packet delay, and number of consecutive losses due to avoiding the interaction between the average queue length and the sharp edge in the dropping function.

There have been active research and increasing interests in the area of performance modelling and analysis of AQM schemes over the past decade. The study [15] has derived the marginal mean queue length for each traffic class in a queuing system with RED mechanism subject to two traffic classes modelled by non-bursty Poisson processes, respectively. Lee, Seo and Yoon [16] have derived the Laplace-Stieltjes transform of the distribution of waiting time for a multiple-class M/G/1 queueing system. Kuusela *et al.* [14] have analyzed the dynamic behavior of a single RED controlled queue interacting with a large population of idealized TCP sources. With the aim of capturing the bursty property of network traffic, Bonald *et al.* [1] have developed an analytical model of RED under two classes of traffic modeled by Poisson process and batch Poisson process, respectively. Motivated by the need of performance analysis of Active Queue Management (AQM) schemes under highly bursty and correlated traffic, this study develops a new analytical queueing model for AQM mechanisms based on the GRED-I method [17] with two traffic classes which are modeled, respectively, by two different arrival processes: bursty Markov-Modulated Poisson Process (MMPP) [7] and non-bursty Poisson process.

The rest of this chapter is organized as follows. Section 2 describes a queueing system model with AQM mechanisms for two classes of traffic. The aggregated and marginal performance measures are presented in Section 3. The performance results are validated and analysed in Section 4. Finally, Section 5 concludes the study.

## 2. THE ANALYTICAL MODEL

We consider two classes of traffic in a single-server queueing system with threshold $th_k$ for each class $k$ ($k = 1, 2$) under FIFO service discipline. The first traffic class follows a two-state MMPP process for modeling bursty data traffic and the second follows a Poisson process with an average arrival rate $\lambda$ for modelling non-bursty traffic. The traffic source of class one can be seen as voice and class two as text data.

The two-state MMPP (denoted by MMPP-2) is a doubly stochastic Poisson process where the arrival rates are determined by an irreducible continuous-time Markov chain consisting of two different states [7]. As shown in Fig. 1, two states $S_1$ and $S_2$ of MMPP-2 correspond to two different traffic arrival processes with rate $\lambda_1$ and $\lambda_2$, respectively. $\delta_1$ and $\delta_2$ are the intensities of transition between $S_1$ to $S_2$. They are independent of the arrival process. MMPP-2 is generally parameterized by the infinitesimal generator $\mathbf{Q}$ of the Markov chain and the rate matrix $\mathbf{\Lambda}$, as given below.

$$\mathbf{Q} = \begin{bmatrix} -\delta_1 & \delta_1 \\ \delta_2 & -\delta_2 \end{bmatrix} \tag{1}$$

$$\mathbf{\Lambda} = \begin{bmatrix} \lambda_1 & 0 \\ 0 & \lambda_2 \end{bmatrix} \tag{2}$$

The duration of state $i$ ($i = 1,2$) is in accordance with an exponential distribution with mean $1/\delta_i$. The mean arrival rate, $\lambda$, of an MMPP-2 is $(\lambda_1\delta_2 + \lambda_2\delta_1)/(\delta_1 + \delta_2)$.

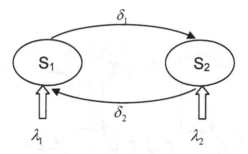

**Fig. 1  Two-state MMPP.**

The packet service time of both traffic classes is exponentially distributed with mean $1/\mu$. The total system capacity is $L$. As shown in Fig. 2, the packets of class $k$ ($k = 1, 2$) will be dropped randomly based on a linear dropping function when the number of packets in the system exceeds threshold $th_k$. As data traffic can tolerate lower packet loss rate than voice, the traffic of class one is dropped earlier in the presence of the sign of congestion.

The dropping process can be seen as a decrease in the arrival rate with function $d_i^k$, where $i$ represents the number of packets in the system. The state transition diagram of the queueing system with the AQM mechanism is shown in Fig. 3.

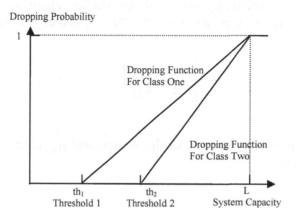

**Fig. 2  Dropping functions for two traffic classes.**

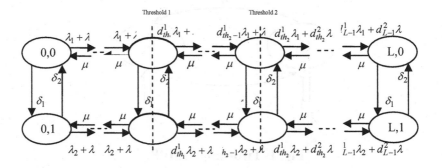

**Fig. 3  A state transition rate diagram.**

The parameters $d_i^k$ for each class $k$ are given by

$$d_i^k = \begin{cases} 1 & 0 \le i < th_k \\ 1 - \dfrac{i - th_k + 1}{L - th_k + 1} \times d_{\max k} & th_k \le i \le L \end{cases} \tag{3}$$

The probability, $p_{ij}$ $(0 \le i \le L, j = 0,1)$, of each state in the state transition diagram can be derived as follow. Let $\mathbf{P} = (p_{00}, \cdots, p_{L0}, p_{01}, \cdots, p_{L1})$ denote the steady state probability vector of this Markov chain. Its infinitesimal generator matrix, $\mathbf{Z}$, is of size $(2L+2) \times (2L+2)$ and can be written as

$$\mathbf{Z} = \begin{bmatrix} \mathbf{A}_{11} & \delta_1 \mathbf{I} \\ \delta_2 \mathbf{I} & \mathbf{A}_{22} \end{bmatrix} \tag{4}$$

where $\mathbf{I}$ is an $(L+1) \times (L+1)$ identify matrix, and $\mathbf{A}_{ii}$ is an $(L+1) \times (L+1)$ matrix given by:

$$
\mathbf{A_{ii}} =
\begin{bmatrix}
-\alpha_{i1} & \gamma_{i1} & 0 & \cdots & 0 \\
\mu & -\alpha_{i2} & \gamma_{i2} & \cdots & 0 \\
0 & \mu & -\alpha_{i3} & \cdots & 0 \\
\vdots & \ddots & & \ddots & \vdots \\
\vdots & & \ddots & & \ddots & \vdots \\
\vdots & & & \ddots & & \ddots & \vdots \\
0 & 0 & 0 & \cdots & -\alpha_{i(L+1)}
\end{bmatrix}
\tag{5}
$$

$$
\alpha_{im} =
\begin{cases}
\delta_i + \gamma_{im} & (i = 1,2; \ m = 1) \\
\delta_i + \gamma_{im} + \mu & (i = 1,2; \ 2 \le m \le L) \\
\delta_i + \mu & (i = 1,2; \ m = L+1)
\end{cases}
\tag{6}
$$

$$
\gamma_{ij} = d_j^1 \lambda_i + d_j^2 \lambda \qquad (i = 1,2; 1 \le j \le L)
\tag{7}
$$

The steady-state probability vector $\mathbf{P}$ satisfies the following equations

$$
\begin{cases}
\mathbf{PZ} = 0 \\
\mathbf{Pe} = 1
\end{cases}
\tag{8}
$$

where $\mathbf{e} = (1,1,\cdots,1)^T$ is a unit column vector of length $(4L+4) \times 1$. Solving Equations (8) using the approach presented in [7] yields the steady-state probability vector, $\mathbf{P}$, as

$$
\mathbf{P} = \alpha(\mathbf{I} - \mathbf{X} + \mathbf{e}\alpha)^{-1}
\tag{9}
$$

where matrix $\mathbf{X} = \mathbf{I} + \mathbf{Q}/\beta$, $\beta \le \min\{\mathbf{Q}_{ii}\}$, and $\alpha$ is an arbitrary row vector of $\mathbf{X}$.

## 3.    DERIVATION OF PERFORMANCE METRICS

In what follows, we will derive the aggregate system performance metrics including the mean queue length ($\overline{L}$), mean response time ($\overline{R}$), system utilization ($U$), throughput ($T$), packet loss probability ($\overline{P_l}$) and relevant marginal performance metrics of traffic each class.

### 3.1    The Aggregate Performance Metrics

The system utilization ($U$) is equal to the probability that the server is not empty and can be given by

$$U = 1 - \sum_{j=0}^{1} p_{0j} \tag{10}$$

As the probability that there are $i$ packets in the system is $\sum_{j=0}^{1} p_{ij}$, ($0 \le i \le L$), the aggregate mean queue length is clearly given by

$$\overline{L} = \sum_{i=0}^{l} (i \times \sum_{j=0}^{1} p_{ij}) \tag{11}$$

When the system is not empty, the average rate of traffic across the system is $\mu$. Therefore the throughput can be written as

$$T = U \times \mu \tag{12}$$

The expression for the mean response time can be derived using Little's Law [13]

$$\overline{R} = \frac{\overline{L}}{T} \tag{13}$$

The ratio of the average packet loss rate of aggregate traffic to its average arrival rate is the packet loss probability. Therefore, the loss probability, $\overline{P_l}$, can be written as

$$\overline{P_l} = \frac{\overline{\lambda_A^1} + \overline{\lambda_A^2} - T}{\overline{\lambda_A^1} + \overline{\lambda_A^2}} \tag{14}$$

where $\overline{\lambda_A^k}$ is the average traffic arrival rate of class $k$

$$\overline{\lambda_A^k} = \begin{cases} \dfrac{\lambda_1\delta_2 + \lambda_2\delta_1}{\delta_1 + \delta_2} & (k=1) \\ \lambda & (k=2) \end{cases} \tag{15}$$

## 3.2   The Marginal Performance Measures

The average number of packets for class $k$ ($k = 1, 2$) in the system, can be approximated by

$$\overline{L^k} = \frac{\overline{\lambda_I^k}}{\overline{\lambda_I^1} + \overline{\lambda_I^2}} \overline{L} \tag{16}$$

where $\overline{\lambda_I^k}$ is the mean actually injecting rate of class $k$ and is given by:

$$\overline{\lambda_I^k} = \begin{cases} \displaystyle\sum_{i=0}^{L} d_i^1 (p_{i0}\lambda_1 + p_{i0}\lambda_2) & (k=1) \\ \displaystyle\sum_{i=0}^{L} (\sum_{j=0}^{1} p_{ij} d_i^2 \lambda) & (k=2) \end{cases} \tag{17}$$

For a system in the steady state, the mean actually injecting rate equals to its throughput. So the marginal throughput of each class can be expressed as Eq. (18):

$$T^k = \overline{\lambda_l^k} \tag{18}$$

Also the expression for the marginal mean response time can be derived using Little's Law [13].

$$\overline{R^k} = \frac{\overline{L^k}}{T^k} \tag{19}$$

The ratio of the average packet loss rate of class $k$ to its average arrival rate is the probability of packet loss for class $k$. So the marginal packet loss probability can be solved by

$$\overline{P_l^k} = \frac{(\overline{\lambda_A^k} - T^k)}{\lambda_A^k} \tag{20}$$

## 4.    VALIDATION AND ANALYSIS

We developed a discrete-event simulator using JAVA programming language to evaluate the accuracy of the above analytical model. The effects of traffic burstiness and correlation of the inter-arrival time on the aggregate performance metrics with varying threshold, $th_1$, are presented in this section.

The Squared Coefficient of Variation (SCV) of the inter-arrival time, $c^2$, and the one-lag correlation coefficient, $r_1$, of an MMPP are given by [5].

$$c^2 = 1 + \frac{2\delta_1\delta_2(\lambda_1 - \lambda_2)^2}{(\delta_1 + \delta_2)^2(\lambda_1\lambda_2 + \lambda_2\delta_1 + \lambda_1\delta_2)} \tag{21}$$

$$r_1 = \frac{\delta_1\delta_2\lambda_1\lambda_2(\lambda_1 - \lambda_2)^2}{c^2(\delta_1 + \delta_2)^2(\lambda_1\lambda_2 + \lambda_2\delta_1 + \lambda_1\delta_2)^2} \tag{22}$$

We consider a two-state MMPP with the rate matrix $\Lambda = \begin{bmatrix} 0.1 & 0 \\ 0 & 5.9 \end{bmatrix}$ which implies that the traffic arrival rate at the second state is much higher than that at the first state. Furthermore, in order to focus on the evaluation of the effects of SCV and one-lag correlation coefficients, we keep the average arrival rate $\lambda_A^1 = (\lambda_1 \delta_2 + \lambda_2 \delta_1)/(\delta_1 + \delta_2)$ of the MMPP unchanged. Therefore, the state transition rates $\delta_1$ and $\delta_2$ are set to be identical, i.e., $\delta_1 = \delta_2 = \delta$. With the given SCVs or one-lag correlation coefficients, we can derive the state transition rate $\delta$ using Eqs. (21) and (22). Table 1 presents a group of the SCVs $(c^2)$ and the corresponding transition rates while Table 2 reveals the correlation coefficients $(r_1)$ and the corresponding transition rates.

**Table 1. SCVs $(c^2)$ and the corresponding state transition rates**

| $c^2$ | 4 | 8 | 12 | 16 | 20 | 24 | 28 |
|---|---|---|---|---|---|---|---|
| $\delta$ | 0.836 | 0.302 | 0.157 | 0.089 | 0.049 | 0.024 | 0.005 |

**Table 2. One-lag correlation coefficients $(r_1)$ and the corresponding state transition rates**

| $r_1$ | 0.1 | 0.2 | 0.3 | 0.4 |
|---|---|---|---|---|
| $\delta$ | 0.328 | 0.129 | 0.057 | 0.02 |

Class-2 traffic is generated by a non-bursty Poisson process with the average arrival rate $\lambda = 1$. The service rate $\mu$ is set to 5 in order to make certain that the queueing system is stable. With the aim of investigating the impacts of different AQM parameters (e.g., threshold), we assign the threshold of MMPP traffic $th_1 = 1$, 6, and 19, respectively and the threshold of Poisson traffic $th_2 = 19$.

Figs. 4-7 depict the utilization and throughput versus the different SCV and correlation, respectively, with $th_1 = 1$, 6, and 19. It can be seen from the figures that the utilization and throughput decrease as the result of the growth of the SCV or correlation. Such a trend becomes more remarkable when threshold $th_1$ is bigger. Furthermore, for $th_1 = 19$, utilization and throughput decrease almost linearly when the SCV and correlation increases. However, for $th_1 = 1$ and 6, utilization and throughput decrease more sharply when the SCV increases from 4 to 12 and the correlation increases from 0.1 to 0.2, respectively. On the other hand, a smaller threshold $th_1$ results in a lower utilization and throughput when the SCV or correlation is fixed because the decrease of threshold $th_1$ increases the dropping rate.

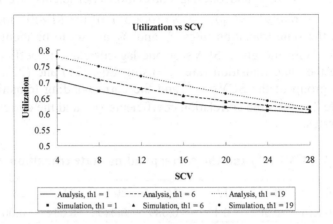

**Fig. 4  The utilization vs SCV with $th_1$ = 1, 6, and 19.**

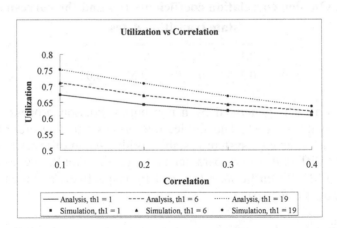

**Fig. 5  The utilization vs correlation with $th_1$ = 1, 6, and 19.**

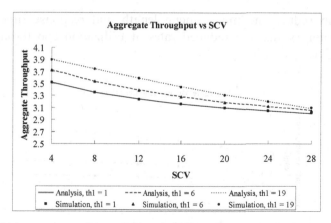

Fig. 6  **Aggregate throughput vs SCV with** $th_1$ **= 1, 6, and 19.**

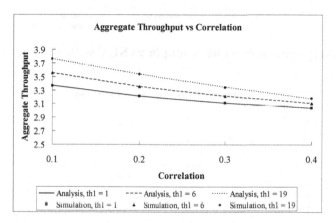

Fig. 7  **Aggregate throughput vs correlation with** $th_1$ **= 1, 6, and 19.**

Figs. 8-11 illustrate the mean aggregate queue length and response time versus the SCV and correlation, respectively. As the SCV or correlation increases, the mean aggregate queue length and response time tends to increase. Also a remarkably increasing trend can be seen from each of these figures when threshold $th_1$ is 19. Figures 7 and 10 show that the mean queue length and response time increase more quickly when the SCV increase from 4 to 8. However, they grow smoothly as the correlation varies from 0.1 to 0.4.

Moreover, the mean queue length and response time becomes smaller when $th_1$ is reduced in that fewer packets can inject into the system. Especially, when the SCV or correlation is higher, a smaller threshold $th_1$, say 6, can reduce the mean queue length and response time by 50% approximately whilst the reduced rates of utilization and throughput are less than 5%.

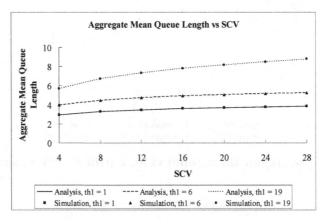

**Fig. 8  Aggregate mean queue length vs SCV with $th_1$ = 1, 6, and 19.**

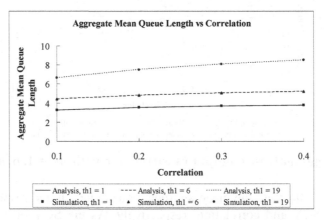

**Fig. 9  Aggregate mean queue length vs correlation with $th_1$ = 1, 6, and 19.**

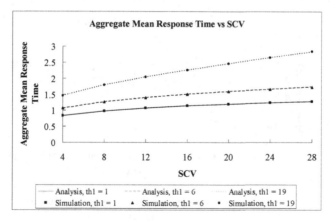

**Fig. 10  Aggregate mean response time vs SCV with** $th_1$ **= 1, 6, and 19.**

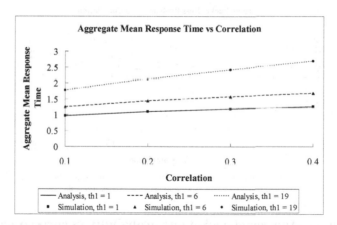

**Fig. 11  Aggregate mean response time vs correlation with** $th_1$ **= 1, 6, and 19.**

Finally, the effects of the SCV and correlation on the aggregate packet loss probability are presented in Figs 12 and 13. It is clear that higher SCV or correlation results in higher packet loss probability. Furthermore, as threshold $th_1$ decreases, the aggregate packet loss probability increases because more packets are dropped before the queue overflows.

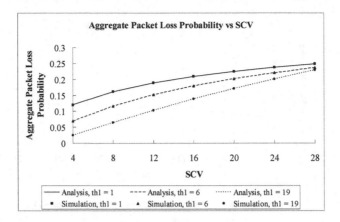

**Fig. 12  Aggregate packet loss probability vs SCV
with $th_1$ = 1, 6, and 19.**

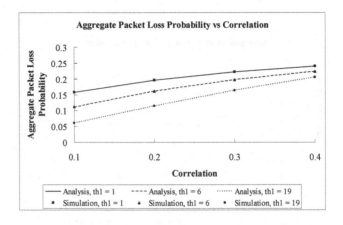

**Fig. 13  Aggregate packet loss probability vs correlation
with $th_1$ = 1, 6, and 19.**

## 5.    CONCLUSIONS

In this chapter, an analytical model has been developed and validated for evaluating the aggregated and marginal performance measures, including mean queue length, response time, utilization, throughput, and packet loss probability of a queueing system with two individual thresholds subject to heterogeneous traffic in an AQM-enabled router. This study has modeled the voice and data sources, respectively, by non-bursty Poisson Process and bursty MMPP Process. The validity of the model has been demonstrated through extensive simulation experiments. Although our analysis is based on the well-known GRED-I method for AQM [18], the derivation of the model is general and can be easily extended to deal with other AQM methods.

Analytical results have shown that, using the same way to drop packets of both traffic classes, the aggregate performance metrics change significantly as the burstiness and correlation of class-1 traffic varies. For instance, the utilization, throughput and aggregate packet loss probability tend to decrease while the mean queue length and response time tend to increase as the SCV or correlation coefficient of traffic increases.

# REFERENCES

[1]     Bonald T, May M, Bolot JC (2000) Analytic evaluation of RED performance, In: Proc. IEEE INFOCOM. Tel Aviv, Israel, pp 1415-1424.

[2]     Braden B, Clark D, Crowcroft J, Davie B, Deering S, Estrin D, Floyd S, Jacobson V, Minshall G, Partridge C, Peterson L, Ramakrishnan K, Shenker S, Wroclawski J, Zhang L (1998) Recommendations on queue management and congestion avoidance in the Internet. In: IETF RFC 2039.

[3]     Brandauer C, Iannaccone G, Diot C, Ziegler T, Fdida S, May M (2001) Comparison of tail drop and active queue management performance for bulk-date and web-like Internet traffic. In: Proc. ISCC. ENIT/ENSI, Tunisia, pp 122-129.

[4]     Christiansen M, Jeffay K, Ott D, Smith FD (2001) Tuning RED for web traffic. J IEEE/ACM Trans. Networking. 9(3): 249-264.

[5]     Cui Z, Nilsson AA (1994) The impact of correlation on delay performance of high speed networks. In: Proc. Southeastern Symposium on System Theory. Ohio University, pp 371-374.

[6]     Feng WC, Kandlur DD, Saha D, Shin KG (1999) A self-configuring RED gateway. In: Proc. IEEE INFOCOM. New York, USA, pp 1320-1328.

[7]     Fischer W, Meier-Hellstern K (1993) The markov-modulated poisson process (MMPP) cookbook. J Performance Evaluation. 18(2): 149-171.

[8]     Floyd S (1997) RED: discussions of setting parameters. http://www.icir.org/floyd/REDparameters.txt.

[9]    Floyd S, Fall K (1999) Promoting the use of end-to-end congestion control in the Internet. J IEEE/ACM Trans. Networking. 7(4): 458-472.

[10]    Floyd S, Gummadi R, Shenker S (2001) Adaptive RED: an algorithm for increasing the robustness of RED's active queue management. http://www.icir.org/floyd/papers/adaptiveRed.pdf.

[11]    Floyd S, Jacobson V (1993) Random early detection gateways for congestion avoidance, J IEEE/ACM Trans. Networking. 1(4): 397-413.

[12]    Jiang K, Wang X, Xi Y (2004) Nonlinear analysis of RED - a comparative study, In: Proc. American Control Conference. Boston, pp 2960-2965.

[13]    Kleinrock L (1975) Queueing Systems: Compute Applications, vol. 1, John Wiley & Sons, New York.

[14]    Kuusela P, Lassila P, Virtamo J, Key P (2001) Modeling RED with idealized TCP sources. In: Proc. IFIP Conference on Performance Modelling and Evaluation of ATM & IP Networks. Budapest, Hungary, pp 155-166.

[15]    Kuuela P, Virtamo JT (2000) Modeling RED with two traffic classes. In: Proc. NTS-15. Lund, Sweden, pp 271-282.

[16]    Lee HW, Seo WJ, Yoon SH (2001) An analysis of multiple-class vacation queues with individual thresholds. J Operations Research Letters. 28(1): 35-49.

[17]    May M, Diot C, Lyles B, Bolot J (2000) Influence of active queue management parameters on aggregate traffic performance. In: INRIA RR 3995.

[18]    Ott TJ, Lakshman TV, Wong LH (1999) SRED: stabilized RED. In: Proc. IEEE INFOCOM. New York, USA, pp 1346-1355.

[19]    Ryu SW, Rump C, Qiao C (2003) Advances in Internet congestion control. J IEEE Communications Surveys and Tutorials. 5(1).

# CHAPTER 19

# Quality-of-Service Analysis of Priority Queueing Systems under Long-Range Dependent and Short-Range Dependent Traffic

Xiaolong Jin, Geyong Min

Department of Computing, School of Informatics,
University of Bradford, Bradford, BD7 1DP, UK

**Abstract.** *Priority queueing is an important and popular traffic scheduling mechanism for the provisioning of network Quality-of-Service (QoS) which has received numerous research efforts. Realistic traffic in multi-service networks exhibits heterogeneous Long-Range Dependent (LRD) and Short-Range Dependent (SRD) properties. This chapter presents an efficient and comprehensive performance model for investigating the QoS of priority queueing systems in the presence of heterogeneous LRD and SRD traffic. We derive and validate the closed-form expressions of the queue length and loss probability distributions for individual traffic flows. The analytical model is used to evaluate the impact of LRD traffic on system performance under different working conditions and investigate the buffer management and allocation in priority queueing systems with QoS constraints.*

## 1. INTRODUCTION

The provisioning of Quality-of-Service (QoS) in modern communication networks has been an issue of great interest in recent years. Traffic scheduling mechanism is responsible for determining the order in which packets are forwarded through the internal multiplexes of communication networks and plays a crucial rule in achieving differentiated QoS. Priority queueing becomes an important and popular scheduling mechanism due to its simplicity and high efficiency. Many research efforts have been made on performance analysis and evaluation of the priority queueing mechanism [1, 2, 9, 14, 16, 20, 22], as well as its development and applications [6, 12, 24].

Realistic traffic in multi-service networks has been convincingly demonstrated to exhibit heterogeneous Long-Range Dependent (LRD) and Short-Range Dependent (SRD) properties. The LRD property (i.e., large-lag correlation and scale-invariant burstiness) of traffic has been shown to be a ubiquitous phenomenon in a variety of contexts, from local-area networks [13] to wide-area networks [19] to World Wide Web [5] to wireless networks [23]. This fractal-like feature of network traffic is significantly different from those of the conventional SRD processes (e.g., Poisson process). Although packet loss probability, as one of the most important QoS metrics, plays an important role in the design and performance of traffic scheduling mechanisms, no efforts have been reported in the open literature to analytically investigate the loss probability of priority queueing systems in the presence of heterogeneous LRD and SRD traffic.

This chapter presents an efficient and comprehensive performance model for investigating the QoS of priority systems subject to LRD fractional Brownian motion (fBm) traffic and SRD Poisson traffic. Specifically, we derive the closed-form expressions of the queue length and loss probability distributions for individual traffic flows. We investigate the accuracy of the analytical model through comparison between analytical and simulation results. Besides, we evaluate the performance of priority queueing systems under different working conditions. The performance results demonstrate that the increase of the Hurst parameter and variance coefficient of fBm traffic as well as the server utilization can significantly arise the loss probabilities of both traffic flows. Furthermore, we use the model to study the buffer allocation problem with the aim of meeting the specific QoS requirements of individual traffic flows.

The rest of the chapter is organized as follows: Section 2 introduces the characteristics and mathematical modelling of LRD fBm traffic and SRD Poisson traffic, respectively. Section 3 presents the analytical model and derives the distributions of queue length and loss probability. Through comparison between analytical and simulation results, we validate the accuracy of the model in Section 4. We investigate the performance and the issue of buffer allocation of priority queueing systems under different working conditions in Section 5. Finally, Section 6 concludes the chapter.

## 2.    MODELLING LRD AND SRD TRAFFIC

In this section, we briefly review the modelling issues of LRD and SRD traffic. In general, LRD processes can be used to model traffic generated by multimedia applications (e.g., VBR video), while SRD Poisson processes are applied to model traffic generated by the traditional non-bursty text communication. As compared to the text counterpart, multimedia applications have more stringent QoS constraints. Therefore, the high priority is assigned to LRD traffic.

Generally speaking, a traffic flow[1] can be modelled as a stochastic process and denoted in a cumulative arrival form as $A = \{A(t)\}_{t \in N}$ where $A(t)$ is the cumulative number of traffic arrivals at time $t$. Consequently, $A(s,t) = A(t) - A(s)$ denotes the amount of traffic arriving in time interval $(s,t]$. Traffic flow $A$ can also be denoted in an increment form, i.e., $A = \{B(t)\}_{t \in N}$, where $B(t)$ is the traffic arriving in time interval $(t-1,t]$ with $B(0) = 0$. $A(t)$ and $B(t)$ have the following relationship: $A(t) = \sum_{i=0}^{t} B(i)$ and $B(t) = A(t) - A(t-1)$.

Note that for the sake of clarity of the model derivation, hereafter we will use subscripts $f$ and $p$ to distinguish a given quantity of fBm and Poisson traffic, respectively.

### 2.1    LRD fBm Traffic

Since the innovative study on LRD traffic [13], many models and techniques have been developed to characterize and generate LRD traffic traces. Among the existing models, fractional Brownian motion (fBm) is identified as an efficient way for modelling and generating LRD traffic [17]. An fBm traffic flow can be expressed as $A_f = \{A_f(t)\}_{t \in N}$ [17]:

$$A_f(t) = \lambda_f t + Z_f(t), \tag{1}$$

---

[1] All traffic flows are modelled in discrete time in this chapter.

where $\lambda_f$ is the mean arrival rate and $Z_f(t) = \sqrt{a_f \lambda_f} \, \overline{Z}_f(t)$. $\overline{Z}_f(t)$ is a centered (i.e., $E(\overline{Z}_f(t)) = 0$) fBm with variance $Var(\overline{Z}_f(t)) = t^{2H_f}$. The variance and covariance functions of $A_f$ can be given as follows:

$$Var(A_f(t)) = a_f \lambda_f t^{2H_f}, \tag{2}$$

$$\Gamma_f(s,t) = \frac{1}{2} a_f \lambda_f \left( t^{2H_f} + s^{2H_f} - (t-s)^{2H_f} \right), \tag{3}$$

where $H \in (\frac{1}{2}, 1]$ is Hurst parameter indicating the degree of long-range dependence.

In the increment form, traffic flow $A_f$ can be expressed as $A_f = \{B_f(t)\}_{t \in N}$ with mean arrival rate $E(B_f(t)) = \lambda_f$ and variance $Var(B_f(t)) = a_f \lambda_f$.

## 2.2   SRD Poisson Traffic

Using the similar notation of fBm, a Poisson traffic flow can be denoted as $A_p = \{A_p(t)\}_{t \in N}$:

$$A_p(t) = \lambda_p t + Z_p(t), \tag{4}$$

where $\lambda_p$ is the mean arrival rate of $A_p(t)$ and $Z_p(t)$ is a stochastic process with expectation $E(Z_p(t)) = 0$. The variance and covariance functions of $A_p$ are as follows:

$$Var(A_p(t)) = \lambda_p t, \tag{5}$$

$$\Gamma_p(s,t) = \lambda_p \min(s,t). \tag{6}$$

Similarly, the Poisson traffic flow can be expressed in the increment form as $A_p = \{B_p(t)\}_{t \in N}$ with mean arrival rate $E(B_p(t)) = \lambda_p$ and variance $Var(B_f(t)) = \lambda_p$.

## 3.    THE ANALYTICAL MODEL

In this section, we present the approximations of the queue length distributions of both fBm and Poisson traffic flows, based on which we further derive their loss probabilities. For the clarity of the model derivation, we denote the service capacity of the priority queueing system as $C$, and the queue lengths of fBm and Poisson traffic at time $t$ as $Q_f(t)$ and $Q_p(t)$, respectively.

### 3.1    Queue Length Distributions

In [14, 15], an approach based on a large deviation principle was developed to derive the upper and lower bounds of the aggregate queue length distribution of priority queueing systems subject to general Gaussian traffic. By approximating a Poisson traffic flow as a Gaussian process, the above approach was extended to deal with heterogeneous LRD fBm and SRD Poisson traffic in [10]. More specifically, the analytical upper and lower bounds for the queue length distributions (i.e., $P(Q > x)$) of individual traffic flows were developed.

The high priority traffic in a priority queueing system is served in a manner as if the low priority traffic does not exist. Consequently, the upper and lower bounds of the queue length distribution of the high priority fBm traffic can be given as follows [10]:

$$P(Q_f \geq x) \leq \exp\left(-\frac{1}{2}Y_f(t_x)\right), \tag{7}$$

$$P(Q_f \geq x) \geq \overline{\Phi}\left(\sqrt{Y_f(t_x)}\right), \tag{8}$$

where

$$Y_f(t) = \frac{(-x + (C - \lambda_f)t)^2}{\Gamma_f(t,t)}, \tag{9}$$

and $t_x = \operatorname{argmin}_t Y_f(t)$. $C$ is the service capacity of the priority queueing system. $\overline{\Phi}(\cdot)$ is the residual distribution function of the standard Gaussian distribution. A commonly adopted approximation is $\overline{\Phi}(x) \approx \exp(-\frac{1}{2}x^2)/\sqrt{2\pi(1+x)^2}$.

The upper and lower bounds corresponding to the low priority Poisson traffic are derived with the aid of the well-known empty buffer approximation (EBA) [3]. The total queue in a priority queueing system is almost exclusively composed of the low priority traffic. Therefore, the EBA suggests that the queue length distribution of the low priority traffic can be reasonably approximated by the total queue length distribution of the priority queueing system. Following this approximation, the upper and lower bounds of the queue length distribution of the low priority Poisson traffic can be calculated by [10]:

$$P(Q_p \geq x) \leq \exp\left(-\frac{1}{2}Y_p(s_x)\right),$$    (10)

$$P(Q_p \geq x) \geq \overline{\Phi}\left(\sqrt{Y_p(s_x)}\right),$$    (11)

where

$$Y_p(s) = \frac{(-x + (C - \lambda_f - \lambda_p)s)^2}{\Gamma_f(s,s) + \Gamma_p(s,s)},$$    (12)

and $s_x = \text{argmin}_s\, Y_p(s)$.

Given $\overline{\Phi}(x) \approx \exp(-\frac{1}{2}x^2)/\sqrt{2\pi(1+x)^2}$, the difference between the upper and lower bounds for the queue length distribution of the high priority fBm traffic is the coefficients of $\exp(-\frac{1}{2}Y_f(t_x))$ (see Equations (7) and (8)). Examining the upper and lower bounds corresponding to the low priority Poisson traffic reveals the same phenomenon (see Equations (10) and (11)). This finding inspires us to take a certain mean (e.g., arithmetic mean, geometric mean) of the upper and lower bounds of the queue length distribution as its approximation. In this chapter, we employ the geometric mean as this method has been proven effective in [20]. As a result, we obtain the following approximations to the queue length distributions of fBm and Poisson traffic, respectively:

$$P(Q_f \geq x) \approx \frac{\exp\left(-\frac{1}{2}Y_f(t_x)\right)}{\sqrt[4]{2\pi\left(1 + \sqrt{Y_f(t_x)}\right)^2}},$$    (13)

$$P(Q_p \geq x) \approx \frac{\exp\left(-\frac{1}{2}Y_p(s_x)\right)}{\sqrt[4]{2\pi\left(1+\sqrt{Y_p(s_x)}\right)^2}}. \tag{14}$$

## 3.2    Loss Probability Distributions

We estimate the loss probabilities, $P_L(x)$, of fBm and Poisson traffic in the priority system based on the individual queue length distributions (i.e., $P(Q > x)$) presented in Section 3.1. Given that the system is stable (i.e., $\lambda_f + \lambda_p < C$), the relationship between the distributions of loss probability and queue length can be described as follows [11]:

$$\frac{P_L(x)}{P(Q > x)} = \frac{P_L(b)}{P(Q > b)}, \tag{15}$$

where $b$ is an arbitrary constant. Let $\alpha = P_L(b)/P(Q > b)$. Equation (15) can be rewritten as

$$P_L(x) = \alpha P(Q > x). \tag{16}$$

In what follows, we will calculate the corresponding $\alpha_f$ and $\alpha_p$ for fBm and Poisson traffic, respectively, in order to obtain their loss probabilities, $P_{L,f}$ and $P_{L,p}$.

It is shown in [11] that for a Gaussian traffic flow $\mathbf{A} = \{B(t)\}_{t \in N}$ with mean arrival rate $E(B(t)) = \lambda$ and variance $Var(B(t)) = \sigma^2$, the constant $\alpha$ for the case $b = 0$ can be calculated as follows:

$$\alpha = \frac{1}{\lambda\sqrt{2\pi}\sigma}\exp\left(\frac{(c-\lambda)^2}{2\sigma^2}\right)\int_c^\infty (z-c)\exp\left(-\frac{(z-\lambda)^2}{2\sigma^2}\right)dz. \tag{17}$$

where $c$ is the service rate received by the traffic flow.

Since the fBm traffic flow is essentially a Gaussian process with mean arrival rate $\lambda_f$ and variance $a_f\lambda_f$, and is served with the full service capacity $C$ of the priority queueing system, we can calculate $\alpha_f$ by substituting $c = C$, $\lambda = \lambda_f$, and $\sigma = \sqrt{a_f \lambda_f}$ into Equation (17) as follows:

$$\alpha_f = \frac{1}{\lambda_f \sqrt{2\pi a_f \lambda_f}} \exp\left(\frac{(C - \lambda_f)^2}{2a_f \lambda_f}\right) \int_C^\infty (z - C) \exp\left(-\frac{(z - \lambda_f)^2}{2a_f \lambda_f}\right) dz. \tag{18}$$

A Poisson traffic flow is approximated as a Gaussian process to derive the upper and lower bounds of its queue length distribution in [10]. Actually, the feasibility of such an approximation has been widely proven [4, 7, 8, 21]. When the mean arrival rate of the Poisson traffic flow is large or the process time tends to infinity, the approximation is considerably exact. Therefore, in this chapter we approximate the Poisson traffic flow $\mathbf{A}_p$ as a Gaussian process with mean arrival rate $E(B_f(t)) = \lambda_p$ and variance $Var(B_f(t)) = \lambda_p$. As a result, the aggregate traffic flow, $\mathbf{A}_{\{f,p\}} = \{B_{\{f,p\}}(t)\}_{t \in N}$, of fBm and Poisson traffic can be regarded as a Gaussian process, which has the mean arrival rate

$$E(B_{\{f,p\}}(t)) = E(B_f(t)) + E(B_p(t)) = \lambda_f + \lambda_p, \tag{19}$$

and variance

$$Var(B_{\{f,p\}}(t)) = Var(B_f(t)) + Var(B_p(t)) = a_f \lambda_f + \lambda_p. \tag{20}$$

Obviously, the service rate obtained by the aggregate traffic flow $\mathbf{A}_{\{f,p\}}$ is equal to the service capacity, $C$, of the priority queueing system. Therefore, by substituting $c = C$, $\lambda = \lambda_f + \lambda_p$ (Equation (19)), and $\sigma = \sqrt{a_f \lambda_f + \lambda_p}$ (Equation (20)) into Equation (17), we obtain $\alpha_p$:

$$\alpha_p = \frac{1}{(\lambda_f + \lambda_p)\sqrt{2\pi(a_f \lambda_f + \lambda_p)}} \exp\left(\frac{(C - (\lambda_f + \lambda_p))^2}{2(a_f \lambda_f + \lambda_p)}\right) \times$$
$$\int_C^\infty (z - C) \exp\left(-\frac{(z - (\lambda_f + \lambda_p))^2}{2(a_f \lambda_f + \lambda_p)}\right) dz. \tag{21}$$

Upon obtaining $\alpha_f$ and $\alpha_p$ and following Equation (16), the loss probabilities, $P_{L,f}$ and $P_{L,p}$, of fBm and Poisson traffic can be derived by integrating Equations (13) and (18), and Equations (14) and (21), respectively.

## 4.    MODEL VALIDATION

In this section, we investigate the accuracy of the analytical model derived for the priority queueing system subject to heterogeneous fBm and Poisson traffic. For this purpose, we developed a simulator for the queueing system using the C++ programming language. We compared the analytical results of the queue length and loss probability distributions with those obtained from extensive simulation experiments. In our simulation, the conditionalized Random Midpoint Displacement algorithm $(RMD_{3,3})$ [18] was adopted to generate fBm traffic traces owing to its ability of producing real-time fBm traffic without prior knowledge of simulation trace length. Moreover, the computational complexity of this algorithm is linear as the trace length increases, thus keeping the time complexity of simulation at a reasonable level.

We have conducted extensive simulation experiments for various scenarios. In what follows we will present the results of two typical scenarios, which correspond to two representative values of Hurst parameter $H_f$ of fBm traffic, i.e., $H_f \in \{0.85, 0.75\}$, of the priority queueing system with service capacity $C = 120$. Under each scenario, we further test three cases where the mean arrival rates, $\lambda_f$, of fBm traffic and, $\lambda_p$, of Poisson traffic are set as follows:

- Case I: $\lambda_f = 90$ and $\lambda_p = 20$;
- Case II: $\lambda_f = 55$ and $\lambda_p = 55$;
- Case III: $\lambda_f = 20$ and $\lambda_p = 90$.

In Case I, the mean arrival rate $\lambda_f$ of fBm traffic is 4.5 times larger than the rate $\lambda_p$ of Poisson traffic. Therefore, fBm traffic dominates the input of the priority queueing system. On the contrary, Poisson traffic dominates the input in Case III. In Case II, fBm traffic and Poisson traffic are comparative. Analytical and simulation results are shown in Figures 1 and 2, where subfigures (a), (b), and (c) correspond to queue length distributions, whilst subfigures (d), (e), and (f) represent loss probabilities.

## 4.1  Scenario I: $H_f = 0.85$

Above all, it can be found from Figure 1 that in all cases, the simulation results of queue length and loss probability distributions of both fBm traffic (i.e., the solid curves with sign 'o') and Poisson traffic (i.e., the dashed curves with sign 'o') closely match the corresponding analytical results (i.e., the solid curves with sign '*' for fBm traffic and the dashed curves with sign '*' for Poisson traffic). This important finding suggests that the developed analytical model has a good degree of accuracy in predicting the queue length and loss probability distributions of both traffic flows.

We can also find that the analytical and simulation results for both fBm and Poisson traffic appear in Figures 1 (a) and (d), corresponding to Case I. However, only the results for Poisson traffic are plotted in Figures 1 (b) and (c), as well as (e) and (f), which correspond to Cases II and III, respectively. This phenomenon is due to the following reason: The arrival rates of fBm traffic in Cases II and III are much smaller than the system service capacity. As a result, the arrivals of the high priority fBm traffic can be served in time and consequently no packets need to wait for service in buffer and no packets are lost due to buffer overflow. Therefore, no empirical queue length and loss probability curves can be depicted. On the other hand, the arrival rate of fBm traffic in Case I is considerably large, as compared to the service capacity. Therefore, although fBm traffic is served in high priority, its arrivals cannot be served timely. As a result, some packets queue up in the dedicated buffer and lead to buffer overflow.

Another important observation is that although the total arrival rate keeps the same (i.e., 110 ) under all cases, the queue length and loss probability distributions of Poisson traffic in Figures 1 (a) and (d) are much higher than those of Poisson traffic in Figures 1 (c) and (f), respectively. The reason behind this phenomenon can be explained as follows. In Case I, fBm traffic dominates the input of the priority queueing system. As a result, the scale-invariant burstiness of fBm traffic seriously affects the service received by Poisson traffic. Further, a relatively large number of Poisson packets have to wait for service in buffer and even are lost due to buffer overflow. On the other hand, Poisson traffic dominates the input of the priority queueing system in Case III and fBm traffic has a considerably small arrival rate. Therefore, fBm traffic has relatively weak effects on Poisson traffic.

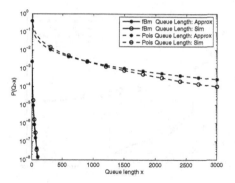

(a) Queue length distribution in Case I

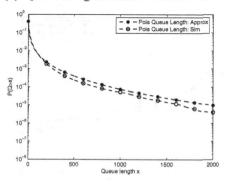

(b) Queue length distribution in Case II

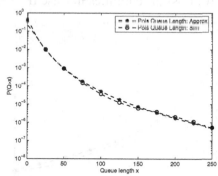

(c) Queue length distribution in Case III

**Fig. 1  Comparison between the analytical and simulation results of both queue length distribution and loss probability in Scenario I with $H_f = 0.85$.**

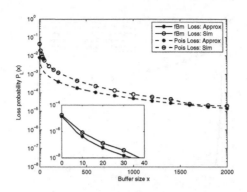

(d) Loss probabilities in Case I

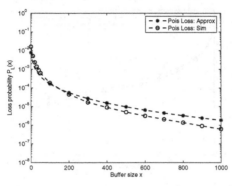

(e) Loss probabilities in Case II

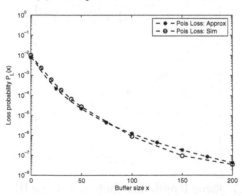

(f) Loss probabilities in Case III

**Fig. 1 (Cont.) Comparison between the analytical and simulation results of both queue length distribution and loss probability in Scenario I with $H_f = 0.85$.**

## 4.2    Scenario II: $H_f = 0.75$

It is worth noting that the observations obtained from Scenario I also hold in Scenario II (see Fig. 2), where Hurst parameter is set as $H_f = 0.75$, less than that in Scenario I. Particularly, the analytical and simulation results corresponding to the distributions of queue length as well as loss probability in Scenario II also closely match each other. This observation highlights that the analytical model performs fairly well under different scenarios.

Comparing Figs 1 and 2, we can find a very interesting phenomenon: The queue length and loss probability of traffic flows in Cases I, II, and III of Scenario II are considerably smaller than the corresponding performance measures in Scenario I, respectively. This is due to the difference of Hurst parameter of fBm traffic in Scenarios I and II. In more detail, the larger Hurst parameter $H_f$ is, the higher the probability that traffic bursts follow by each other. As a ripple effect, such scale-invariant burstiness of fBm traffic gives rise to extended periods of large queue build-ups and further leads to frequent buffer overflow.

## 5.    PERFORMANCE ANALYSIS

This section examines the performance of the priority queueing system in terms of loss probability under different settings of two important parameters, namely, variance coefficient $a_f$ of LRD fBm traffic and server utilization $U$ of the system. Here, we define the utilization as $U = (\lambda_f + \lambda_p)/C$. Besides, we investigate the effect of buffer space allocation on the QoS of both fBm and Poisson traffic.

### 5.1    Variance Coefficient $a_f$

To investigate the effects of variance coefficient $a_f$ of fBm traffic, we examine the system performance with four different values of variance coefficient, namely, $\{0.5, 1.0, 2.0, 4.0\}$, in a typical scenario where we set server capacity $C = 120$, Hurst parameter $H_f = 0.8$, and mean arrival rates $\lambda_f = 80$ and $\lambda_p = 20$. This is a representative setting in that fBm traffic has a relatively large arrival rate, while the arrival rate of Poisson traffic is relatively small. The results are shown in Fig. 3.

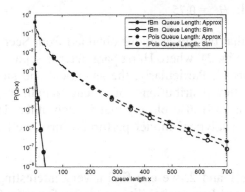

(a) Queue length distribution in Case I

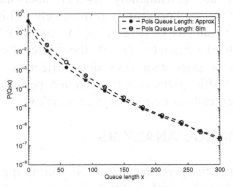

(b) Queue length distribution in Case II

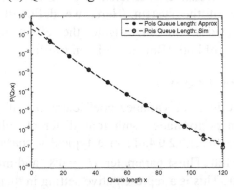

(c) Queue length distribution in Case III

**Fig. 2 Comparison between the analytical and simulation results of both queue length distribution and loss probability in Scenario II with $H_f = 0.75$.**

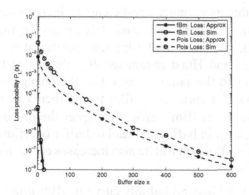

(d) Loss probabilities in Case I

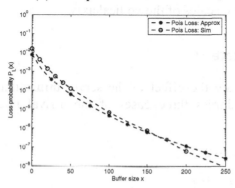

(e) Loss probabilities in Case II

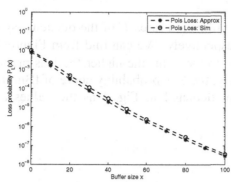

(f) Loss probabilities in Case III

**Fig. 2  (Cont.) Comparison between the analytical and simulation results of both queue length distribution and loss probability in Scenario II with $H_f = 0.75$.**

Figure 3 shows that as variance coefficient $a_f$ increases from 0.5 to 4.0, the loss probabilities of both fBm and Poisson traffic increase rapidly. From Equation (2), we know that variance coefficient $a_f$, together with mean arrival rate $\lambda_f$ and Hurst parameter $H_f$, determine the variance of fBm traffic $A_f$. Given the same $\lambda_f$ and $H_f$, the change of $a_f$ from 0.5 to 4.0 indicates that the variance of fBm traffic increases by eight times. The larger the variance of fBm traffic, the higher the probability that fBm traffic arrivals queue up in buffer and lead to buffer overflow. As an effect, the loss probability of Poisson traffic also increases as $a_f$ increases.

We can find that the loss probability curve of fBm traffic with $a_f = 0.5$ does not appear in Figure 3. This is because the loss probabilities are so small as to exceed the scales of the vertical axis.

## 5.2   Utilization Rate $U$

In order to investigate the effect of the server utilization on the system performance, we address three cases of the arrival rates of fBm and Poisson traffic:

- $\lambda_f = 95$ and $\lambda_p = 20$;
- $\lambda_f = 85$ and $\lambda_p = 15$;
- $\lambda_f = 75$ and $\lambda_p = 10$.

In these cases, the utilization rates $U$ of the queueing system are around 95%, 83%, 70%, respectively. We can find from Figure 4 that the larger the utilization rate of the system, the higher the loss probabilities of both traffic flows. Similarly, the loss probability curve of fBm traffic in the case with $U = 70\%$ is not depicted in Fig. 4 as the values are considerably small.

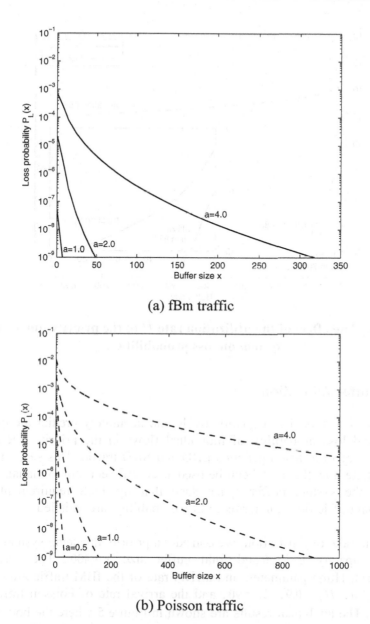

(a) fBm traffic

(b) Poisson traffic

**Fig. 3  The effect of the variance coefficient $a_f$ of fBm traffic on loss probabilities.**

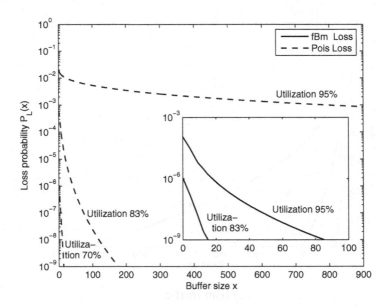

**Fig. 4 The effect of the utilization rate $U$ of the priority queueing system on loss probabilities.**

## 5.3    Buffer Allocation

The analytical model can quantitatively and accurately predict the queue length and loss probability of individual flows in the priority queueing systems subject to heterogeneous LRD and SRD traffic. This section will demonstrate how the model can be used as an efficient tool to manage and allocate the system buffer space such that the QoS requirements of individual traffic flows, in terms of loss probability, are satisfied.

For the sake of illustration, we consider a priority queueing system with service capacity $C = 120$ and total buffer size $x = 400$. The variance coefficient, Hurst parameter, and arrival rate of the fBM traffic are set to be $a_f = 1.0$, $H_f = 0.9$, $\lambda_f = 90$, and the arrival rate of Poisson traffic is $\lambda_p = 25$. The analytical results are shown in Figure 5 where the bottom x-axis and left y-axis represent the buffer size $x_f$ assigned to fBm traffic and the corresponding loss probability $P_{L,f}$ while the top x-axis and right y-axis correspond to the buffer size $x_p$ and loss probability

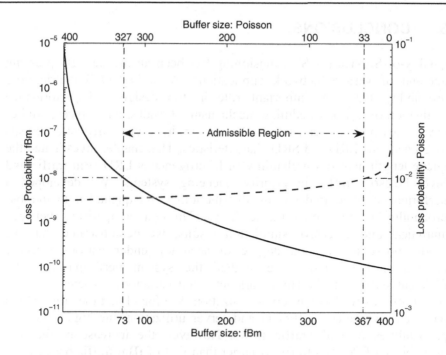

**Fig. 5 The effect of buffer allocation on the QoS received by fBm and Poisson traffic.**

$P_{L,p}$ of Poisson traffic. It is worth noting that the loss probability of fBm traffic (within the scope of $[10^{-10.0}, 10^{-5.0}]$) is much smaller than that of Poisson traffic (within the scope of $[10^{-2.2}, 10^{-1.7}]$) even if the arrival rate of fBm traffic is higher than Poisson traffic.

Assume that fBm and Poisson traffic flows have the following QoS requirement: $P_{L,f}(x_f) < 10^{-8}$ and $P_{L,p}(x_p) < 10^{-2}$. Figure 5 reveals that the minimum buffer space required by fBm and Poisson traffic is 73 and 33, respectively. Given the total buffer size is 400, the intervals $73 < x_f < 367$ and $33 < x_p < 327$ (i.e., the region between the two vertical dash-dotted lines in Figure 5) construct an admissible region. All combinations of $x_f$ and $x_p$ in this region can meet the above QoS requirements of both traffic flows.

## 6.    CONCLUSIONS

Quality-of-Service (QoS) provisioning has been an increasingly pressing demand of various network applications. As a key QoS metric, loss probability plays an important role in the design and performance evaluation of traffic scheduling mechanisms. Besides, many recent studies have shown that realistic traffic in multi-service network reveals heterogeneous LRD and SRD characteristics. This chapter investigated the queue length and loss probability of heterogeneous LRD fBm traffic and SRD Poisson traffic in priority queueing systems. We developed a performance model to derive the distributions of the queue length and loss probability of individual traffic flows. Through comparisons between analytical and extensive simulation results, we demonstrated that the model possesses a good degree of accuracy under various working conditions. Furthermore, we studied the system performance under different settings of the Hurst parameter and variance coefficient of LRD fBm traffic as well as the server utilization. We found that the larger Hurst parameter, variance coefficient and server utilization, the higher the loss probabilities of both traffic flows. However, the increase of the loss probability of Poisson traffic is larger than that of fBm traffic because the former is served with low priority. In addition, we employed the analytical model to study the buffer allocation problem and demonstrated that the model is able to determine an admissible region where the combination of different buffer sizes can meet the specific QoS requirements.

## ACKNOWLEDGEMENTS

This work is supported by the UK EPSRC research grant (EP/C525027/1).

## REFERENCES

[1]    M. Ashour and T. Le-Ngoc. Priority queuing of long-range dependent traffic. In *Proceedings of the 2004 IEEE Global Telecommunications Conference (GLOBECOM'04)*, volume 6, pages 3025–3029, 2003.

[2]    K. E. Avrachenkov, N. O. Vilchevsky, and G. L. Shevlyakov. Priority queueing with finite buffer size and randomized push-out mechanism. *Performance Evaluation*, 61(1):1–16, 2005.

[3]    A. W. Berger and W. Whitt. Effective bandwidths with priorities. *IEEE/ACM Transactions on Networking*, 6(4):447–460, 1998.

[4]    J. D. Cohn. Power spectrum and correlation function errors: Poisson vs. Gaussian shot noise. *New Astronomy*, 11(4):226–239, 2006.

[5]    M. E. Crovella and A. Bestavros. Self-similarity in World Wide Web traffic: Evidence and possible causes. *IEEE/ACM Transactions on Networking*, 5(6):835–846, 1997.

[6]    H.-W. Ferng and Y.-C. Tsai. Using priority, buffering, threshold control, and reservation techniques to improve channel-allocation schemes for the GPRS system. *IEEE Transactions on Vehicular Technology*, 54(1):286–306, 2005.

[7]    W. M. Hubbard. The approximation of a Poisson distribution by a Gaussian distribution. *Proceedings of the IEEE*, 58(9):1374–1375, 1970.

[8]    W. Hurlimann. A Gaussian exponential approximation to some compound Poisson distributions. *ASTIN Bulletin*, 33(1):41–55, 2003.

[9]    G. Iacovoni and M. Isopi. Performance analysis of a priority system fed by self-similar Gaussian traffic. http://www.coritel.it/coritel/people/iacovoni.htm, 2003.

[10]   X. Jin and G. Min. Performance analysis of priority scheduling mechanisms under heterogeneous network traffic. To Appear in Journal of Computer and System Sciences, 2007.

[11]   H. S. Kim and N. B. Shroff. Loss probability calculations and asymptotic analysis for finite buffer multiplexers. *IEEE/ACM Transactions on Networking*, 9(6):755–768, 2001.

[12]   T. H. Kim and S. Choi. Priority-based delay mitigation for event-monitoring IEEE 802.15.4 LR-WPANs. *IEEE Communication Letters*, 10(3):213–215, 2006.

[13]   W. E. Leland, M. S. Taqq, W. Willinger, and D. V. Wilson. On the self-similar nature of Ethernet traffic (extended version). *IEEE/ACM Transactions on Networking*, 2(1):1–15, 1994.

[14]   P. Mannersalo and I. Norros. Approximate formulae for Gaussian priority queues. In *Proceedings of the 17th International Teletraffic Congress (ITC-17)*, pages 991–1002, 2001.

[15]   P. Mannersalo and I. Norros. A most probable path approach to queueing systems with general Gaussian input. *Computer Networks*, 40(3):399–412, 2002.

[16]   G. Mazzini, R. Rovatti, and G. Setti. A closed form solution of Bernoullian two-classes priority queue. *Computer Communications*, 9(3):264–266, 2005.

[17]  I. Norros. A storage model with self-similar input. *Queueing Systems*, 16(3–4):387–396, 1994.

[18]  I. Norros, P. Mannersalo, and J. L. Wang. Simulation of fractional Brownian motion with conditionalized random midpoint displacement. *Advances in Performance Analysis*, 2:77–101, 1999.

[19]  V. Paxson and S. Floyd. Wide-area traffic: The failure of Poisson modeling. *IEEE/ACM Transactions on Networking*, 3(3):226–244, 1995.

[20]  Z. Quan and J.-M. Chung. Priority queueing analysis for self-similar traffic in high-speed networks. In *Proceedings of the 2003 IEEE International Conference on Communications (ICC'03)*, volume 3, pages 1606–1610, 2003.

[21]  B. Satherley, J. Oakley, C. Harrison, and C. Xydeas. Simulation of photon-limited images using video data. *Electronics Letters*, 32(6): 535–537, 1996.

[22]  S. L. Spitler and D. C. Lee. Proof of monotone loss rate of fluid priority-queue with finite buffer. *Queueing Systems*, 51(1–2):77–87, 2005.

[23]  O. Tickoo and B. Sikdar. On the impact of IEEE 802.11 MAC on traffic characteristics. *IEEE Journal on Selected Areas in Communications*, 21(2):189–203, 2003.

[24]  Y. Xiao. Performance analysis of priority schemes for IEEE 802.11 and IEEE 802.11e wireless LANs. *IEEE Transactions on Wireless Communications*, 4(4):1506–1515, 2005.

# CHAPTER 20

# Redimensioning Network Resources Based on Users' Behavior

Emiliya Saranova

IMI - Bulgarian Academy of Sciences, Sofia, Bulgaria
High College of Telecommunication and Posts, Sofia, Bulgaria

**Abstract.** *One of the main problems that has to be solved by network operators is how to determine the volume of telecommunication resources that are sufficient to serve a given input flow of demands with prescribed characteristics of QoS (Quality of Service). Usually the resource considered is the number of circuits, the value of bandwidth represented by an integral number of channels, etc.*

*The intent of this paper is to present a method of redimensioning network capacity (i.e., the number of equivalent internal switching lines) in telecommunication networks, and to propose some design parameters based on a consideration of detailed users' behavior and requested QoS. We have investigated the dependency and sensitivity of important parameters in redimensioning, and we offer a comparative analysis.*

*The approach is directly applicable for any (virtual) circuit switching telecommunication system, both for wireline and wireless systems (GSM, PSTN, ISDN and BISDN). For packet-switching networks at various layers, the proposed approach may be used as a basis for comparison in various circuit switching or circuit emulation modes (e.g. VoIP).*

*This paper presents major results and conclusions. A longer and more mathematical version of this paper is available from the author.*

## 1.    INTRODUCTION

Traffic theory enables network designers to make assumptions about their networks based on past experience. Traffic engineering addresses service issues by definition of various grade of service (GoS) parameters. A properly engineered network reflects the tradeoff between low blocking and high circuit utilization, which means there is also a tradeoff between service volume and cost.

Service traffic forecasts may not be readily available (for example, if the service has been initially developed in a different network). Similarly, users may find novel applications of services in ways not anticipated by the designer or the network operator. Thus the planning, allocation and dimensioning procedures must be flexible enough to provide, as quickly as possible, the resources required as user demand changes [14].

A process of redimensioning (sometimes called "servicing") is used on an ongoing basis to ensure maximum utilization of existing equipment, and to determine the appropriate reallocation or redimensioning when service demand changes (but before additional equipment can be installed to address the demand).

Traditional network traffic management is an activity that occurs closer to real time. Redimensioning activities are carried out at time intervals that are intermediate between full-scale dimensioning and network traffic management.

Fig. 1, based on [14], shows the various actions taken over different time scales to respond to changes in network service demand and traffic loads:

- Traffic management (short term);

- Redimensioning (medium term);

- Dimensioning (long term).

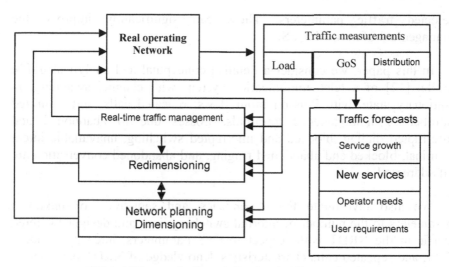

**Fig. 1 Network dimensioning/redimensioning.**

There are many different factors that need to be taken into account when analyzing traffic. QoS parameters are administratively specified in Service Level Agreements (SLA) between users and operators. These QoS parameters reflect GoS parameters [6].

Based on the sensitivity of design parameters (for example, the targeted blocking probability, handling repeated calls, etc.) and taking into account users' behavior, the goal is to create an approach for network redimensioning that will maintain the administrative contractual level of QoS (in the SLA) under static conditions.

We propose an analytical/numerical solution for finding the necessary number of internal switching lines and the values of key traffic parameters. These parameters are required to maintain the specified level of network QoS. Dependencies, based on the numerical/analytical results, are shown graphically in subsequent Sections of this paper.

The approach is as follows: (i) a system of equations based on the conceptual model and dependencies between parameters of the telecommunication system is derived; (ii) a network redimensioning task (NRDT) is formulated for the proposed conceptual model and the corresponding analytical model; (iii) the solvability of the NRDT and the necessary conditions for an analytical solution are investigated. We also propose an algorithm and computer program for calculating the corresponding number of internal switching lines, as well as the values of selected traffic parameters. These can significantly improve the management of network QoS.

In this paper, we consider a detailed conceptual and analytical traffic model [12] of a telecommunication system with channel switching, in stationary state, with Poisson input flows, repeated calls, and a limited number of homogeneous terminals. Losses due to abandoned and interrupted dialing, blocked and interrupted switching, unavailable intent terminal, blocked and abandoned ringing, and abandoned conversation are all addressed.

We also investigate the dependency and sensitivity of unknown parameters to the number of internal switching lines and designed offered traffic in the NRDT with respect to QoS parameters, intensity of input flow, and repeated calls characteristics. Knowledge of NRDT parameters' sensitivity makes evaluation of input data accuracy and correctness possible. We show some graphical results to illustrate this.

## 2.    CONCEPTUAL MODEL

The conceptual model [10] of a telecommunication system includes the paths of the calls generated from (and occupying) the A-terminals in the proposed network traffic model and its environment (shown in Fig. 2). The names of the devices are constructed according to their position in the model.

### 2.1    Comprising Virtual Devices

The following virtual devices are considered:

$a$  = comprises all the A-terminals (calling) in the system, shown with a continuous line box.

$b$  = comprises all the B-terminals (called) in the system, shown as a box with a dashed line.

$ab$ = comprises all the terminals (calling and called) in the system (not shown);

$s$  = virtual device corresponding to the switching system, shown with a dashed line box into the $a$ - devices. $Ns$ stands for the capacity or number of equivalent internal switching lines of the switching system.

## 2.2    Stages and Branches in the Conceptual Model

Service *stages*: dialing, switching, ringing and communication.

Every service stage has *branches*: enter, abandoned, blocked, interrupted, not available, carried (corresponding to the modeled possible cases of ends of the calls' service in the branch considered).

Every branch has two *exits*: repeated, and terminated (which shows what happens with calls after they leave the telecommunication system). Users may make a new bid (repeated call), or stop attempts (terminated call).

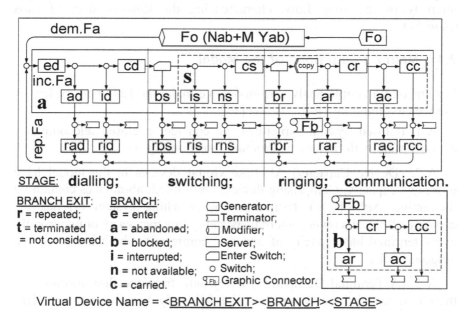

**STAGE:** dialling;         switching;         ringing;    communication.

| BRANCH EXIT: | BRANCH: | | |
| --- | --- | --- | --- |
| **r** = repeated; | **e** = enter | Generator; | |
| **t** = terminated | **a** = abandoned; | Terminator; | |
| = not considered. | **b** = blocked; | Modifier; | |
| | **i** = interrupted; | Server; | |
| | **n** = not available; | Enter Switch; | |
| | **c** = carried. | ○ Switch; | |
| | | Graphic Connector. | |

Virtual Device Name = <BRANCH EXIT><BRANCH><STAGE>

**Fig. 2 Normalized conceptual model of the telecommunication system and its environment and the paths of the calls, occupying A-terminals ( $a$ - device), switching system ( $s$ - device) and B-terminals ( $b$ - device); base virtual device types, with their names and graphic notation.**

## 2.3    Parameters and Their Notations in the Conceptual Model

$F$ = the calling rate (frequency) of the flow [calls/sec.], $P$ = probability of directing the calls of the external flow to the device considered, $T$ = mean service time in the device [sec.], $Y =$ intensity of the device traffic [Erl], and $N =$ number of service places (lines, servers) in the virtual device (capacity of the device).

In the normalized models [15] used in this paper, every base virtual device except the switch has no more than one entrance and/or one exit. Switches have one entrance and two exits. For characterizing the intensity of the flow, we use the following notation: $inc.F$ for incoming flows, and $dem.F$, $ofr.F$ and $rep.F$ for demand, offered and repeated flows respectively [5]. The same characterization is used for traffic intensity $(Y)$.

$Fo$ is the intent intensity of calls of one idle terminal; $inc.Fa = Fa$ is intensity of incoming flow, characterizing the flow of demand calls $(dem.Fa)$.

## 2.4   Main Assumptions of the Model

For creating a simple analytical model, we make the following system of fourteen assumptions (A-1 – A-14) [15]:

A-1. (Closed System Structure) We consider a closed telecommunication system with functional structure shown in Fig. 1;

A-2. (Device Capacity) All base virtual devices in the model have unlimited capacity. Comprising devices are limited: ab-devices contain all the active $Nab \in [2, \infty)$ terminals; the switching system (s) has the capacity of $Ns$ calls (every internal switching line may carry only one call); every terminal has capacity of one call, common for both incoming and outgoing calls;

A-3. (A-Terminal Occupation) Every call, from the flow incoming in the telecommunication system $(inc.Fa)$, falls only on a free terminal. This terminal becomes a busy A-terminal;

A-4. (Stationarity) The system is in stationary state. This means that in every virtual device in the model (including comprising devices like switching system), the frequency of input flow F(0, t), call holding time $T(0, t)$ and traffic intensity $Y(0, t)$ in the observed interval (0,t) converge to the correspondent finite numbers $F$, $T$ and $Y$, when $t \to \infty$. In this case we may apply Little's Theorem (1961) [11] and for every device: $Y = FT$;

A-5. (Calls' Capacity) Every call occupies one place in a base virtual device, independently from the other devices (e.g., a call may occupy one internal switching line, if it finds a free one, independently from the state of the intent B-terminal (busy or free));

A-6. (Environment) The calls in the communication systems' environment (outside the blocks $a$ and $b$ in Fig. 1) do not occupy any telecommunication system device and therefore do not create communication system load. (For example, unsuccessful calls, waiting for the next attempt, are in the mind of the user only. The calls and devices in the environment form the intent and repeated calls flows). Calls leave the environment (and the model) in the instance they enter a Terminator virtual device;

A-7. (Parameters' undependability) We consider probabilities for direction of calls to, and holding times in, the base virtual devices as independent of each other and from intensity $Fa = inc.Fa$ of incoming flow of calls. Values of these parameters are determined by users' behavior and the technical characteristics of the communication system. (Obviously, this is not applicable to the devices of type Enter Switch, and correspondingly to $Pbs$ and $Pbr$);

A-8. (Randomness) All variables in the analytical model may be random, and we are working with their mean values following Little's Theorem;

A-9. (B-Terminal Occupation) Probabilities of direction of calls to and duration of occupation of devices $ar$, $cr$, $ac$ and $cc$ are the same for A and B-calls;

A-10. (Channel Switching) Every call occupies simultaneously places in all the base virtual devices in the telecommunication system (comprised of devices $a$ or $b$) it passed through, including the base device it is in at the moment of observation. Every call releases all its occupied places in all base virtual devices of the communication system at the instant it leaves comprising devices $a$ or $b$.

A-11. (Terminals' Homogeneity) All terminals are homogeneous, e.g., all relevant characteristics are equal for every terminal;

A-12. (A-Calls Directions) Every A-terminal uniformly directs all its calls only to the other terminals, not to itself;

A-13. (B-flow ordinariness) The flow directed to B-terminals ($Fb$) is ordinary. (The importance of A-13 is limited only to the case when two or more calls may simultaneously reach a free B-terminal.)

A-14. (B-Blocking Probability for Repeated attempts) The mean probability (*Pbr*) of a call to find the same B-terminal busy at the first and at all the following repeated attempts is one and the same.

## 3.    ANALYTICAL MODEL

As noted, we have derived a detailed system of equations for the analytical model. These are described in a longer version of this paper, which is available from the author [10]. Our intention here is to describe the main points and conclusions.

Erlang's formula defines a functional relationship between the number of channels, offered traffic, and grade of service (blocking probability) and is thus a measure of the quality of the traffic services [8]. Based on the ITU definition of blocking probability (e.g., GoS parameter) [5] we consider the following GoS parameters: probability of finding B- terminal busy (*Pbr*) and probability of blocked switching (*Pbs*). The target value (*adm.Pbs*) of the probability of blocked switching is administratively determined in advance via SLAs (Service Level Agreements).

## 4.    NETWORK REDIMENSIONING TASK

### 4.1    Formulation of a Network Redimensioning Task (NRDT)

Based on previous experience, determining the volume of telecommunication resources that is sufficient to serve a given input flow of demands with prescribed characteristics of QoS is one of the main problems that have to be solved by network operators. It includes the following tasks:

1. Redimensioning a network means to find the number of internal switching lines necessary to satisfy a level of QoS that has been administratively pre-determined, and for which the values of known parameters are calculated and/or measured (in the case of an operational network).

2. Finding the values of the designed parameters describing the designed system state. For example, a system parameter describing the offered traffic intensity of the switching system (*dsn.ofr.Ys*), or the probability of finding a B terminal "busy" (*dsn.Pbr*), etc.

3. Determining the sensitivity and dependency of designed parameters with respect to QoS – i.e., the parameters and users' behavior characteristics.

The goal is to determine the number of equivalent internal switching lines *Ns*; and the values of the following:

unknown parameters:       *dsn.Pbr, dsn.Fa, dsn.dem.Fa, dsn.ofd.Ys*

**subject to:** *dsn.Pbs ≤ adm. Pbs*

There are many different traffic models used in traffic dimensioning. The key is to find the model that best suits the environment. The traffic models that have the widest acceptance for calculating the number of trunks required for network configuration are Erlang B, Extended Erlang B, and Erlang C. Other commonly used traffic models are Engset, Poisson, EART/EARC, and Neal-Wilkerson [7]. We use the Erlang B formulae and recursion form because this model well suits observed telecommunication networks; viz.:

$$Erl\_b(Ns, ofr.Ys) = \frac{\dfrac{(ofr.Ys)^{Ns}}{Ns!}}{\sum\limits_{j=0}^{Ns} \dfrac{(ofr.Ys)^{j}}{j!}}$$

where:

- *Erl_b* (*Ns, ofr.Ys*) is the probability of blocking due to an insufficient number of lines;

- *Ns* is the number of equivalent switching lines; and

- *ofr.Ys* is the traffic offered to the switching system.

## 4.2   Analytical Solution

Erlang's B formulae may be used for dimensioning/redimensioning when the offered traffic is evaluated and the level of QoS is determined administratively in advance (for example blocking probability *adm.Pbs*).

We have computed the number of internal switching lines *Ns* and the values of *dsn.ofr.Ys,* and have developed an algorithm and computer program for calculating the values of the NRDT parameters. Research has focused on parameters' dependency and sensitivity in the NRDT to GoS parameters (blocking probability) and some human behavior parameters (probability of generating of repeated calls after blocking). Knowing the sensitivity of a parameter means we can estimate the parameters' importance and necessary occupancy of its measurement (e.g., Figure 3).

We assume that loss probabilities *Pad, Pid, Pis, Pns, Par, Pac, Pcc* are fixed, except for the probabilities for repeated attempts after finding a B – terminal busy *Prbr* and after blocking due to insufficient resources *Prbs*.

It follows that $Q$, $K$, $R_1$, $R_2$ and $R_3$ are dependent on human behavior parameters and represent in case of repeated calls: a) Parameter $R_1$ represents the generalized probability of generating repeated calls and is independent both of *Prbr* and *Prbs*. In fact, $R_1$ is dependent on the loss probabilities only. b) Parameter $R_2$ is dependent on blocking probability *Prbr* of repeated calls after finding a B – terminal busy. $R_2$ is independent of *Prbs*. c) Parameter $R_3$ is dependent on *Prbs* and is independent of *Prbr*.

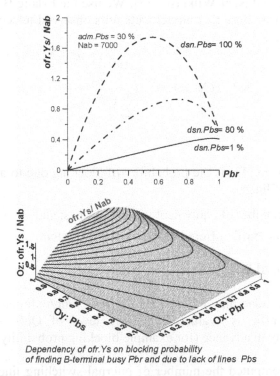

Dependency of ofr.Ys on blocking probability
of finding B-terminal busy Pbr and due to lack of lines  Pbs

**Fig. 3  and Fig. 4  Dependency of offered traffic ofr.Ys on blocking probability of finding B – terminal busy Pbr and on blocking probability due to insufficient lines Pbs.**

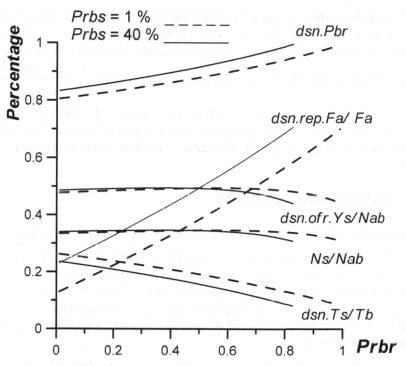

**Fig. 5 Dependency of dsn.Pbr, dsn.rep.Fa, Ns, dsn.ofr.Ys and Ts/Ta on Prbr. The values of adm.Pbs = 30 %, Nab = 7000 terminals.**

## 5.    ALGORITHM FOR CALCULATING THE UNKNOWN VALUES OF THE PARAMETERS IN THE NRDT

1.  Input data: administratively-determined values are *adm.Pbs*, *Nab* = *adm.Nab* and empirical evaluated values are *Fo*, $S_1$, $S_2$, $S_3$, $R_1$, $R_2$, $R_3$, $S_{1z}$, $S_{2z}$, *Tb*.

2.  We may always evaluate *dsn.Pbr*:

    $$\forall adm.Pbs \Rightarrow \exists dsn.Pbr$$

    *Dsn.Pbr* belongs to $(0;1)$.

3.  On the basis of *emp. Fo = dsn.Fo*, we calculate values *dsn.dem.Fa*.

4.  We find *dsn.ofr.Ys = ofr.Ys (dsn.Pbr, adm.Pbs)*.

To find the number of internal switching lines *Ns*, the recursion Erlang's B – formula is used [8]. The results for numerical inversion of the Erlang's formula (for finding the number of switching lines *Ns*) was confirmed with results of other commercial computer programs. If $Pbr \neq \dfrac{S_1 - S_3\,adm.Pbs}{1 - adm.Pbs}$

then the NRDT is solvable and there is a proposed algorithm for its solution. When $Pbr = 0$ the network loading is rather low and it is not of great practical interest, but in this case a mathematical study was also made.

## 6.    NUMERICAL RESULTS

Numerical results are obtained using the following parameters' values:

*Ted* = 3 sec, *Pad* = 0.09, *Tad* = 5 sec, *Prad* = 0.95, *Pid* = 0.01, *Tid* = 11 sec, *Prid* = 0.2, *Tcd* = 12 sec, *Tbs* = 5 sec, *Pis* = 0.01, *Tis* = 5 sec, *Pris* = 0.01, *Pns* = 0.01, *Tns* = 6 sec, *Prns* = 0.3, *Tbr* = 5 sec, *Par* = 0.65, *Tar* = 45 sec, *Prar* = 0.75, *Tcr* = 10 sec, *Pac* = 0.2, *Tac* = 13 sec, *Prac* = 0.9, *Tcc* = 180 sec, *Prcc* = 0.01, *Tb* = 139.07 sec, *Tcs* = 5 sec, *emp.Fo*=0.0125714, *Nab*=7000 terminals.

Numerical results for independent variables $Pbr \in [0;1]$ and $Pbs \in [2\times10^{-9}; 0.999917]$. The values of *Prbr* = 80 % and *Prbs* = 95 %. The number of considered values (tuples) is 62310. Results for designed traffic offered to the switching system *dsn.ofr.Ys* are:

$$0.677\times10^{-4} \le \frac{dsn.ofr.Ys}{Nab} \le 1.728311, \; dsn.ofr.Ys \in [0.473782; 12098.18].$$ Therefore,

*dsn.ofr.Ys* may exceed *Nab* by approximately 73%. This is "unproductive occupying of resources."

Absolute maximum of *dsn.ofr.Ys* = 12098.18 coincides with the relative maximum when $Pbr^* = 91.97$ % and this value is about 4.9 times greater than the calculated network capacity *Ns* = 2715. This gives reasons for using the equivalent offered traffic definition. [4]. Results for designed number of required switching lines Ns are:

$$0.000143 \le \frac{Ns}{Nab} \le 0.387857, \; \text{Designed } Ns \in [1;2715], \; Ran(Ns|Pbr) = 2714$$

Absolute maximum *Ns* = 2715 occurs when *Nab*=7000 terminals, *Ns* = 38.79% of *Nab*. This is the case if $Pbr = 0.876623 \approx 87.7\%$ and *Pbs* =

$9.28 \times 10^{-9}$, $Yab = 6136.487$ Erl $\approx 87.66$ % of $Nab$ and $ofr.Ys = 2452.021$ Erl $= crr.Ys \approx 35.0289$ % of $Nab$ and repeated flow $rep.Fa$ is about three times bigger than $dem.Fa$. Results are shown graphically in Fig. 6 and Fig 7.

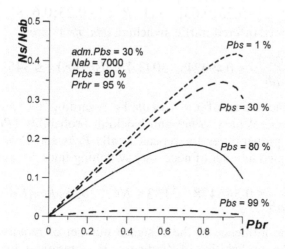

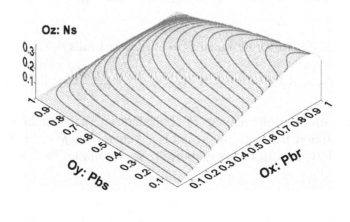

**Fig. 6 and Fig. 7 Dependency of number of equivalent switching lines Ns from probabilities for blocking switching Pbs and finding B – terminal busy Pbr . When 0 % <Pbr < 100 % and Pbs = 1% then Ns/Nab has range 4.17 % and rep.Fa/Fa - with 46 %. In case Pbs = 99 % then Ns/Nab has range 1.7 % and rep.Fa/Fa - with 0.7 %.**

Numerical results concerning network redimensioning (number of investigated value tuples is 516) regarding (independent variables) users' behavior parameters probability of generating repeated calls after finding B – terminals busy $\Pr br \in [0;1]$ and blocked switching $\Pr bs \in [0;1]$ are respectively $R_2 \in [-0.23; 0.63]$ and $R_2 \in [-0.23; 0.648]$. Numerical results for designed offered traffic switching $dsn.ofr.Ys$ are:

$$0.434765 \le \frac{dsn.ofr.Ys}{Nab} \le 0.494245, \quad 3043.4 \le dsn.ofr.Ys \le 3459.7$$

Obviously, the range of the $dsn.ofr.Ys$ regarding the probability of finding B – terminal busy ($Pbr$) and blocking probability ($Pbs$) is much larger than the probabilities for repeated calls $Prbs$ and $Prbr$. Numerical results for designed number of necessary switching lines $Ns$ are:

$$0.304714 \le \frac{Ns}{Nab} \le 0.346428, \quad 2133 \le Ns \le 2425, \; Ran(Ns|Prbr) = 292$$

Therefore, the influence of the designed number of required switching lines $Ns$ vs. the probability of finding a B – terminal busy $Pbr$ and blocking probability $Pbs$ is larger than probabilities for repeated calls $Prbs$ and $Prbr$ after the respective blocking (Fig. 8 and Fig. 9).

Numerical results for designed flow of repeated calls $rep.Fa$ are:

$$13.1235 \le rep.Fa \le 221.574, \; 0.129777 \le \frac{rep.Fa}{Fa} \le 0.715739$$

The sensitivity of the number of equivalent internal switching lines $Ns$, designed offered traffic to the switching system $dsn.ofr.Ys$, and designed incoming flow rate $dsn.Fa$ are graphically shown in Fig. 10.

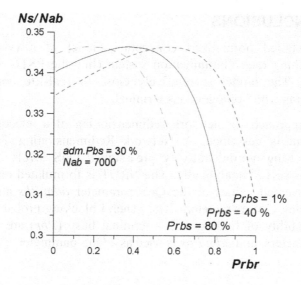

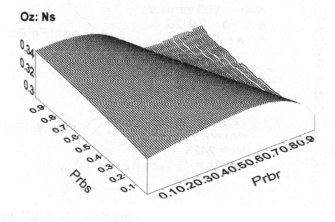

**Fig. 8 and Fig. 9 Dependency of number of equivalent switching lines Ns on probabilities for repeated attempts Prbs after blocking switching and Prbr after finding B – terminal busy. When Prbs= 80 % then Ns/Nab has range 4.2 % but rep.Fa/Fa has range 38.6 %.**

## 7.    CONCLUSIONS

1. A detailed normalized conceptual model of a (virtual) circuit switching telecommunication system (like the PSTN and GSM) is used. The model is relatively close to real-life communication systems with homogeneous terminals.

2. An approach for network redimensioning of a telecommunication system is described. A Network Redimensioning Task (NRDT) supporting administratively preassigned QoS levels is formulated and is solved analytically. The NRDT is formulated on the basis of preassigned values of the QoS parameter *adm.Pbs* and its corresponding GoS parameters. The general blocking probability *Pbs* and probability of finding a B – terminal busy (*Pbr*) are used as GoS parameters, and *adm.Pbs* is used as a QoS parameter.

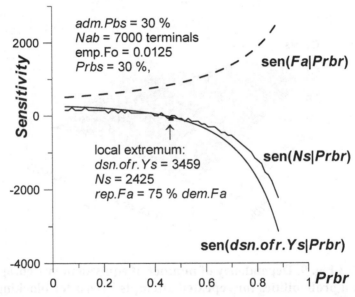

**Fig. 10  Sensitivity of the designed number of internal switching lines Ns and dsn.ofr.Ys regarding users' behavior parameter Prbr.**

3. The offered traffic *ofr.Ys* and the number of internal switching lines *Ns* are derived as a function of the probability of finding a B terminal busy *Pbr* and the probability of blocked switching *Pbs*.

4. The conditions for existence and uniqueness of a solution of the NRDT are examined, and an analytical solution of the NRDT is found.

5. An algorithm and a computer program for calculating the values of the offered (*ofr.Ys*) and carried (*crr.Ys*) traffic, and the number of equivalent switching lines *Ns* are proposed. The results of the numerical solution are derived and graphically shown.

6. The influence of repeated calls after blocking due to lack of resources (*Prbs*) or/and due to finding a B – terminal "busy" (*Prbr*) have been investigated.

7. The human behavior characteristics $R_2$ and $R_3$ addressing users' persistence in case of repeated calls under the influence of *Prbr* and *Prbs* have been investigated.

8. The influence of *Prbr* and *Prbs* over *ofr.Ys, Ns* and *rep.Fa* are ascertained.

9. The aftereffect of QoS parameters (*adm.Pbs* and *dsn.Pbr*) on *ofr.Ys* and *Ns* is evaluated in accordance with ITU definitions E.501. The solutions are investigated concerning GoS parameters' blocking probability due to insufficient of resources (*Pbs*) and finding a B terminal busy (*Pbr*). The sensitivities of the received results regarding some users' behavior parameters (*Prbr* and *Prbs*) and GoS parameters (*Pbr* and *Pbs*) are also evaluated.

10. Numerical experiments are made, and the results are graphically presented.

11. The results in NRDT make network redimensioning based on QoS requirements easy by having a clear methodology for estimating important parameters and their sensitivity.

The approach described herein is directly applicable for every (virtual) circuit switching telecommunication system (like GSM and the PSTN) and may help considerably for ISDN, BISDN and most core and access networks' dimensioning. For packet switching systems like the Internet, the proposed approach may be used for technologies that work in a circuit switching mode – e.g., MPLS tunnels, circuit emulation over packet networks, etc.

# REFERENCES

[1]    Dirschmidt, Hans Yorg, 1992 - Mathematische Grundlagen der Elektrotechnik-Braunschweig, Wiesbaden.

[2]    Dorn, William S., Daniel McCracken, 1972 – Numerical Methods with FORTRAN IV case Studies – John Wiley &Sons, Inc. New York (translated in Bulgarian 1977).

[3]    Engset, T., 1918. The Probability Calculation to Determine the Number of Switches in Automatic Telephone Exchanges. English translation by Mr. Eliot Jensen, Telektronikk, June 1991, pp. 1-5, ISSN 0085-7130. (Thore Olaus Engset (1865-1943). "Die Wahrscheinlichkeitsrechnung zur Bestimmung der Wählerzahl in automatischen Fernsprechämtern", Elektrotechnische zeitschrift, 1918, Heft 31.).

[4]    ITU-T Recommendation E.501: Estimation of traffic offered in the network. (Previously CCITT - Recommendation, revised 26. May 1997).

[5]    ITU-T Recommendation E.600: Terms and Definitions of Traffic Engineering (Melbourne, 1988; revised at Helsinki, 1993).

[6]    ITU-T Recommendation E.800: Terms and Definitions related to Quality of Service and Network Performance, including Dependability. (Helsinki, March 1-12, 1993, revised August 12, 1994).

[7]    CISCO: Traffic Analysis for Voice over IP (Version Number 1 – created 06/25/2001 and Version Number 2 incorporated editorial comments – 11/01/2001).

[8]    Iversen V. B., 2004. Teletraffic Engineering and Network Planning, Technical University of Denmark, pp. 125, 127.

[9]    Saranova E. T. Dimensioning of telecommunication network based on quality of services demand and detailed behavior of users- Proceedings of the IV International conference " Information research, applications, and education i.tech", Varna, Bulgaria, 20-25 June 2006, publ. FOI- COMMERCE- Publisher 2006, ISBN-13: 978-954-16-0036-8, pp. 245- 256.

[10]  Poryazov S. A, Saranova E. T. Some General Terminal and Network Teletraffic Equations in Virtual Circuit Switching Systems. Symposium "Modeling and Simulation Tools for Emerging Tele-communications Networks: Needs, Trends, Challenges, Solutions", (Proceedings of the European COST-285 Telecommunications Symposium) Munich, Germany, 8 - 9 September 2005, Institut für Technische Informatik, Universität der Bundeswehr München. Springer Sciences+Business Media, LLC 2006, ISBN 0-387-32921-8, pp. 471-505.

[11]  Little J. D. C., 1961. A Proof of the Queueing Formula L=λW. Operations Research, 9, 1961, 383-387.

[12]  S. A. Poryazov. What is Offered Traffic in a Real Telecommuni-cation Network? COST 285 TD/285/05/05; 19th International Teletraffic Congress, Beijing, China, August 29- September 2, 2005, Volume 6a, Liang X.J., XIN Z.H., V.B. Iversen and Kuo G.S. (Editors), Beijing University of Posts and Telecommunications Press, pp. 707-718.

[13]  E. T. Saranova. Redimensioning of Telecommunication Network based on ITU definition of Quality of Services Concept, In: Proceedings of the International Workshop "Distributed Computer and Communication Networks", Sofia, Bulgaria, 2006, Editors: V. Vishnevski and Hr. Daskalova, Technosphera publisher, Moscow, Russia, 2006, pp. 165-179.

[14]  ITU-T Recommendation E.734 (10/96), Methods for allocating and dimensioning Intelligent Network (IN) resources

[15]  Poryazov S. A. 2001. On the Two Basic Structures of the Teletraffic Models. Conference "Telecom'2001" - Varna, Bulgaria, 10-12 October 2001 – pp. 435-450.

# CHAPTER 21

# Internet Tomography in Support of Internet and Network Simulation and Emulation Modelling

A. Moloisane, I. Ganchev, M. O'Droma

Telecommunications Research Centre,
University of Limerick,
Limerick, IRELAND

**Abstract.** *Internet performance measurement data extracted through Internet Tomography techniques and metrics and how it may be used to enhance the capacity of network simulation and emulation modelling is addressed in this paper. The advantages of network simulation and emulation as a means to aid design and develop the component networks, which make up the Internet and are fundamental to its ongoing evolution, are highlighted. The Internet's rapid growth has spurred development of new protocols and algorithms to meet changing operational requirements such as security, multicast delivery, mobile networking, policy management, and quality of service (QoS) support. Both the development and evaluation of these operational tools requires the answering of many design and operational questions. Creating the technical support required by network engineers and managers in their efforts to seek answers to these questions is in itself a major challenge. Within the Internet the number and range of services supported continues to grow exponentially, from legacy and client/server applications to VoIP, multimedia streaming services and interactive multimedia services. Services have their own distinctive requirements and idiosyncrasies. They respond differently to bandwidth limitations, latency and jitter problems. They generate different types of "conversations" between end-user terminals, back-end resources and middle-tier servers. To add to the complexity, each new or enhanced* *service introduced onto the network contends for available bandwidth with every other service. In an effort to ensure networking products and resources being designed and developed handling diverse conditions encountered in real Internet environments, network simulation and emulation modelling is a valuable tool, and becoming a critical element, in networking product and application design and development. The better these laboratory tools reflect real-world environment and conditions the more helpful to designers they will be.*

*This paper describes how measurement of empirical Internet data, obtained through Internet Tomography Measurement Systems (ITMS), can serve an important role in providing these laboratory simulation and emulation modelling tools with Internet parameterization data. The data being extracted from up-to-date real-world Internet can be used to re-create such conditions within the modelling experiments. This paper sets out how such data may be captured over extended and targeted periods of time and used in the laboratory modelling and experiments to define best-, average-, and worst-case Internet scenarios likely to be encountered by the applications or network upgrades being designed. An example of real-time one-to-many global-based Internet QoS measurement data sets obtained within a collaboration in the Réseaux IP Européens (RIPE) project for this purpose is presented.*

**Keywords:** TCP/IP QoS metrics, Service Level Agreement (SLA), Internet Tomography Measurement System (ITMS), Network Simulation, Network Emulation, Empirical Network Modelling.

## 1.    INTRODUCTION

The popular and pervasive Internet continues to grow exponentially. Made up of an ever expanding range of networks, autonomous systems, meshed backbones, server farms and so forth, the effect of the Internet is characterized as a social revolution with the immense changes it has brought to every facet of daily living for all people, businesses, and economic and political communities. However while vast engineering effort is invested in developing the Internet and Internet services in all their parts, albeit in a disjointed fragmented way consonant with the nature of the Internet itself, these same "Internet engineers" face a constant technological challenge of handling, predicting, reacting to and resolving from network delays, bottlenecks and outages and so forth which compromise the Quality of Service (QoS) in various ways with varying, more or less, significant consequences, [1,2,3,4,5]. New service introductions may encounter and add to QoS problems compromising their performance as experienced or perceived by the targeted consumers resulting in significant economic consequences such as damaging or undermining business plans. Performance bottlenecks may be created where none existed before, impacting network's ability to support services that were previously running smoothly, [6]. On the other hand the Internet, particularly the core infrastructure resources are constantly changing, growing and expanding. New locations, sub-networks, autonomous systems continue to be added, backbone networks and links, and equipment, are constantly being upgraded and/or re-configured. Agreements with service providers thus also are dynamic, being modified or even switched. In some cases, new management and security tools, introduced to enhance the network operations, may have a negative QoS impact on networking environment. All this adds to the high level of dynamism and complexity for everyone today, especially "on-the-inside", associates with the Internet environment. One result is that even subtle changes can have a major, unforeseen impact on application performance and availability.

Network managers and engineers will always have particular responsibility for QoS performance to their network users. An ability to do capacity planning to make sure their networks can accommodate future growth, has to be accompanied by means to assess and validate new technologies, the value added by their implementation in terms of QoS improvements and business competitive advantages wrought. In the Internet market customers have high Internet QoS expectations when dealing with Internet vendors. Thus in turn network managers, service providers and such players will be demanding in terms of products' quality, i.e. products to be comprehensively tested and come with strong reliability guarantees. On the other hand there is constant pressure to decrease "time-to-market" to match shrinking business opportunity windows, resulting in shorter development cycles and limited testing time, cf. e.g. [7].

Service providers and network providers are in much tighter budget regimes than the telecommunication network operators of a generation ago. Managers have finite budgets. They cannot today so simply over-provision network infrastructure to make generous provision for unexpected growth, resource demands and unforeseen capacity expansion needs, e.g. increased global demand and unforeseen success of a service; or growth in new services. Basically network managers would like to be able to have readily available spare link and node bandwidth capacity to cater satisfactorily for all QoS demands of their service-provider clients and service end-users. Thus QoS performance, reliability, change and growth have to be achieved in ways, which are as cost-efficiently as directed and as measurable as possible. Network modelling and simulation and emulation tools have a growing in importance role in this. Through these, network engineering teams are better enabled to manage strategically and pro-actively the resource investments and growth of networking environments [6, 7, 8, 13].

The capabilities of these network modelling and simulation and emulation tools to provide network engineers with adequate support are related to how closely they are connected to the real-world Internet situations. As will be seen in this paper, an Internet Tomography Measurement System, ITMS, can play a vital role of being a source of empirical Internet statistical performance. ITMS measurement results and metrics are periodically updated and made available on the web for consumption by variety of Internet players such as ISPs, network operators, and of course their network engineering and service application development teams. These latter as mentioned, will require the data in formats appropriate to addressing network emulating/simulating tools requirements e.g. [10].

The rest of the paper is organised as follows. Section 2 introduces the need for non-invasive Internet Tomography measurement with associated benefits. Section 3 presents the ITMS configuration, methodology and metrics used. Section 4 covers network simulation and emulation modelling for design and analysis with relevance to Internet tomography measurement datasets. Section 5 presents an example of empirical network modelling and integrated network experimentation. Section 6 concludes this work.

## 2.     NON-INVASIVE INTERNET TOMOGRAPHY MEASUREMENT AND ASSOCIATED BENEFITS

As regional and global Internet user populations grows –in 2007 the global Internet user population is estimated at c.17% of world population; cf. Figure 1 and Table 1–, QoS expectations of users in respect of all services accessible by them monotonically grows in line with the general quality of their experience of well established services. This is evidenced by the very slow general move to IP telephony by the network providers as the risks of poorer quality with the status of today's Internet infrastructure is too great.

Users are ready to pay for better QoS (even if this is perhaps not a readiness to pay at the level network and service provider owners would like). This is not so much the problem. Rather the problem is the access provider's inability to guarantee QoS levels with reasonable confidence in an Internet environment.

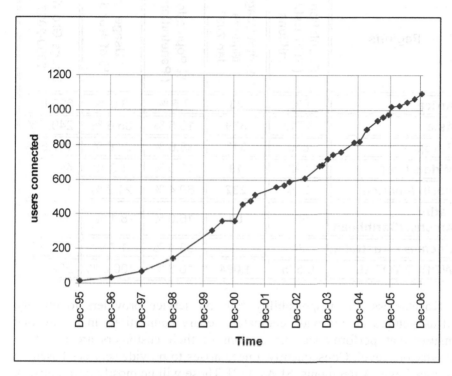

**Fig. 1  Millions of Users on the Internet**

Performance requirements among different Internet user populations vary widely. For example, the scientific research community includes high-end Internet users whose tasks often involve substantial bandwidth requirements. Users in the financial markets and online businesses sectors require secure, reliable connectivity for high-volume, high-rate, low-capacity transactions, synchronised with distributed database operations. Gaming, entertainment, peer-to-peer services and applications markets, requiring, for example, support of new real-time interactions with streaming multi-media and virtual reality, stretch the limits of existing network technologies and resources, [17,18]. Actually measuring and quantifying user/customer requirements and expectations is a significant challenge itself, cf. [11].

**Table 1: World Internet usage and population statistics as of 11 Jan 2007; Compliments of www.Internetworldstats.com . Miniwatts Marketing Group.**

| Regions | Population ( 2007 Est.) millions | Internet Usage, Millions Jan 2007 | % Population ( Penetration ) | Usage % of World | Usage Growth 2000-2007 |
|---|---|---|---|---|---|
| Africa | 933 | 33 | 3.5 % | 3.0 % | 625.8 % |
| Asia | 3,712 | 389 | 10.5 % | 35.6 % | 240.7 % |
| Europe | 810 | 313 | 38.6 % | 28.6 % | 197.6 % |
| Middle East | 193 | 19 | 10.0 % | 1.8 % | 490.1 % |
| North America | 335 | 232 | 69.4 % | 21.2 % | 114.7 % |
| Latin America/Caribbean | 557 | 89 | 16.0 % | 8.1 % | 391.3 % |
| Oceania / Australia | 34 | 18 | 53.5 % | 1.7 % | 141.9 % |
| WORLD TOTAL | 6,575 | 1,094 | 16.6 % | 100.0 % | 202.9 % |

Nonetheless, the responsibility falls on service providers to manage infrastructures and provide dedicated, secure connections in a way that ensures that performance expectations of their customers are met to a satisfactory level. Consequently a need arises to provide services based on Service Level Agreements, SLAs, [12]. These will be mostly intra-network agreements, service-provider to network-provider agreements, and users/ customers to access-networks agreements. These in turn raise a major challenge, namely to develop and implement a set of robust QoS measurement standards and end-to-end IP-based Service Level Verification (IP-SLV) solutions that can measure the user experience, completely or to a large extent, on critical paths through to end-to-end paths on an on-going basis, [6,31]. The kind of measurement process this requires is one which avoids causing possible performance degradation of normal user Internet traffic or at least has minimal impact on it, and does not in any way threaten, undermine or put in danger of compromising the network security, data integrity and privacy – concerns arising from among all stakeholders in the Internet. This has led to the development of Internet-wide non-invasive

Internet tomography measurement concepts and techniques, and has become today the preferred way for capturing of performance data, [1, 19, 23, 24, 29]. Here we refer to it as an Internet tomography measurement system, ITMS.

Both passive and active performance measurements can be invasive, as described in some of the literature sources referenced in the paragraphs above and in their bibliographies. A brief summary of this aspect is present here. Passive measurements, while by nature do not impact the user traffic, does use it for its QoS measurements. Thus user packet payloads have to be (or should be) desensitised for data privacy reasons. Intra-network QoS measurements use this approach as a norm relying on their own internal professionalism to maintain integrity on privacy and security issues. There are many tools on the market for network engineers and managers in support of such QoS measurement philosophy. However access at this level for extra-network entities no matter what the goals or who the entities are, would normally be very unusual for many reasons. For instance, the simple fact of involvement of third parties in actions like this on user traffic can be a sufficiently reasonably source of concern in a security and privacy sense to deny it.

Active measurements is where test traffic is generated, thus overcoming privacy concerns. While it may provide greater control over measurement, it does intrinsically impact on overall network and Internet traffic, even though this may be kept at an acceptably insignificant level by control of test traffic characteristics, e.g. ensuring it is composed of small bursts of precisely controlled small sized packets.

**ITMS goal:** A non-invasive ITMS has the goal of delivering short-term and long-term (even continuous), comprehensive QoS assessment/measurement of IP performance in the core, across the edge, end-to-end and even extending into customer sites without impacting negatively on normal user traffic nor especially violating security and privacy concerns in the process. Systems may be implemented in a wide variety of organised and 'unorganised' ways. Typically a system is designed to monitor what the end-user QoS experience is at different locations and has to construct a comprehensive network statistical performance picture relevant to the interested parties [15, 16]. This is the Internet QoS measurement technique used in the work being described here, i.e. an active non-invasive Internet tomography measurement. It allows control of test traffic as the Internet tomography probing stations (ITPS) generate their own traffic. QoS measuring test traffic may easily be passed through targeted links and networks with minimal cooperation from their owners just like any other Internet traffic. A major advantage of this approach is of course the absence of any need to get access to the internal QoS statistics the Internets component networks, valuable all as these may be.

The Telecommunications Research Centre at University of Limerick entered the Réseaux IP Européens, RIPE, collaboration partnership. Through this we collaborated with other groups spread throughout the globe in extracting QoS performance data. We brought to RIPE the important contribution of adding an ITMS probe test station at University of Limerick in the west of Ireland. This extended the global range of Internet Tomography measurements to the western edge of Europe.

Garnering support to create a successful widely distributed ITMS test stations greatly helps the establishment of an open dynamic and distributed database of broad statistical metrics of IP QoS over a wide spatial (geographic) and temporal range. This is well under way. From this database, it is possible to extract QoS data which serves to, e.g. cf [11, 13, 22]:

> Catalogue critical needs of the Internet networking infrastructure;
> Understand real geographic- and temporal-based performance behaviour;
> Provide real-world input data for network parameterisation in emulation and simulation modelling and experimentation;
> Set realistic geographic- and temporal-based expectations for customers;
> Identify problem areas – networks, sub-networks, autonomous systems, edge-edge links, and so forth; and
> Provide information for troubleshooting and assisting in the rationalisation of allocated resources to improve QoS and performances.

## 3.   ITMS CONFIGURATION AND METHODOLOGY

Here we describe aspects of the non-invasive probing applications and algorithms used to carry out the measurements and gather the raw data.

ITMS configuration is shown in Fig. 1. The system consists of probing stations positioned in the local area networks (LANs) of participating network sites over the Internet. Each probing station generates a pre-defined pattern of test messages. The test messages are sent through the border gateway/router of each participating network. IP QoS parameters measured are:

> latency/delay (one-way);
> delay jitter (one-way);
> packet loss rate (one-way);
> derived metrics {loss distance, loss period}). Loss distance and loss period describe loss distribution. The loss period metric captures frequency and length (burstiness) of loss once it starts whilst loss distance captures the spacing between loss periods.

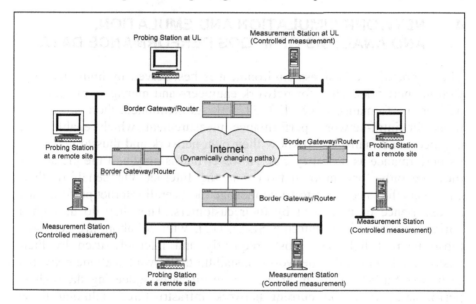

**Fig. 2  ITMS configuration**

For each routing vector, a measurement record is created and stored for post-processing of parameters under investigation.

This ITMS test station configuration and operation pose no security breach to corporate information systems, including when test stations are located within the network. In fact, as may be inferred from Fig. 2, probe test stations may be installed on the outer side (de-militarized zone, DMZ) of the firewall of the participating sites' LANs, and this is normally the case. At each, site e.g. the one at University of Limerick (UL in Figure. 1), the probing station generates probing traffic, which is sent to chosen remote measurement station(s). Receiving ITMS probing test packets is done with a filter/sniffer. Packets do receive timestamp accurately usually using a calibrated integrated GPS timing system. "Kernel level" timestamps are used as they are more accurate than "application level" timestamps. Where stations are ITMS receive-only stations, the action may be described as a non-invasive passive one.

The RIPE ITMS algorithms, measurement methodology and metrics comply with RFC 2330, RFC 2678, etc. as outlined by the IETF IPPM working group which was set up in order to maintain standardized ITMS framework [19, 20, 21]. Developments in the IP QoS performance metrics are ongoing and thus RIPE measurement strategies are updated accordingly.

## 4.    NETWORK SIMULATION AND EMULATION, AND ANALYSIS OF IP QOS PERFORMANCE DATA

The competitive e-business environment is best served by high QoS performing networks. Thus for network engineers and managers maximising network performance is key [22, 31, 32]. As mentioned, there are lots of tools for intra-network performance measurement which enables the engineers and managers to know their own network and thus to maximise its performance as best they can. However that is only half the picture, as they are only 'one more network' in the Internet. On behalf of their customers they need also to try to manage the overall Internet performance as experience or perceived by their customers. This they do through a variety of means, e.g. entering SLAs, [12], with collaborating networks those Internet links are most frequently and intensely used by their customers; buying other networks; installing their own backbone networks to bypass Internet problem areas; etc. In all cases squeezing the highest performance from the current network infrastructure, including those networks bound by SLAs, is critical. When enterprises seek the implementation of new or upgraded enterprise applications, assessing the impact of these applications on the network prior to implementation allows not only the network to be engineered for the application but the application to be modified to improve performance across the existing network. Service providers and IT organizations that seek to deliver high service levels in a cost-efficient manner, must be able to accurately model the production network environment. Accuracy in network modelling is, of course, key to effective testing, capacity planning, diagnostics and service-level assurance, [6, 7, 26, 31, 32].

Techniques used in design and validation of new and existing networking ideas include simulation, emulation and live network testing [9, 26, 27, 28, 32]. Each has its own benefits and tradeoffs. However, the different techniques need not be viewed as competing rather as complementing each other's limitations in order to better validate ideas, new concepts or verify operations. How they are used will vary from case to case; some situations they run in sequence and in others, as is more often the case, in an iterative methodology. General comparisons of these techniques are presented in table 2 under a brief description of features, benefits and limitations.

**Table 2: Network simulation, emulation and live–network analysis and design tools compared.**

| Network Modelling | Description | Benefits | Limitations |
|---|---|---|---|
| Network Simulation | • An absolutely repeatable and controlled environment for network experimentation for predicting behaviour of network and applications under different situations/scenarios. <br> • Involves creating of a model for the proposed system and sees its proper working. <br> • Two simulation methods: <br> . Discrete event simulators: create an extremely detailed, packet-by-packet model of predicted network activity; it requires extensive calculations to simulate a very brief period. <br> Analytical simulators: use mathematical equations, especially statistical models, to predict network and application performance. | • Economically feasible. <br> • Saves time, in the sense of debugging faulty or inefficient algorithms or protocols before their installation on real networks; or discovering poor application design, i.e. which makes poor or inefficient use of network resources <br> • Very efficient for medium to very large networks. | • Cannot give real-time view of how a user would experience some services using a new application or network. <br> • Testing is usually constrained, e.g. without the presence of actual protocols implementations and applications unless implementations are ported to the simulation package. <br> • Not feasible to port each version to the simulation environment for testing. |

| Network Modelling | Description | Benefits | Limitations |
|---|---|---|---|
| Network Emulation | • A technique that is usually applied to testing experimental network protocols, especially in networks that use IP as the network layer. | • Network Emulation environment is well controlled and reproducible.<br>• Economical.<br>• Saves time (relatively as for network simulation). Actual performance implementations of protocols and applications can be examined. | • Problem with accuracy of model, e.g. due to lack of parameters drawn from the real-world performance.<br>• Properties are always estimates.<br>• Time consuming - duration of an experimental session is determined by speed of the modelled network. |
| Live-network testing with Network Tomography | • Discipline that borrows techniques from signal processing and medical imaging.<br>• Uses active and passive probing methods to generate real-time performance data.<br>• Internet tomography has ability to extend beyond one's network. | • More accurate and realistic testing of new applications & protocols especially if they are already debugged.<br>• Readily provides testing platform of new protocols and applications.<br>• Provides most conclusive verification of network simulation and emulation results. | • Fully statistical by nature with Internet statistical processes, and thus lacking in a level of experimental controllability and reproducibility.<br>• More costly and time consuming.<br>• Security and privacy concerns when invasive measurements are used.<br>• Risks due to unforeseen bugs or flaws. |

## 5.   EMPIRICAL NETWORK MODELLING AND INTEGRATED NETWORK EXPERIMENTATION

Empirical network modelling and integrated network experimentation combines real elements, through real Internet data extracted using an ITMS or such like real QoS data capture means, with simulated elements in one or more instances of an existing simulation engine to model different portions of a network topology in the same experimental run [25, 26, 30]. This experimental approach leverages the advantages of using both real world and simulated elements to achieve goals such as:

➢   Validation of experimental simulation models in real traffic conditions;

➢   Exposing experimental real traffic conditions, and thus extracting likely network performance impact, to cross traffic conditions (be they congestive and/or reactive) derived from a variety of existing, validated simulation models;

➢   Scaling to larger network topologies and user activities by the multiplexing of simulated elements on physical resources other than would be the case with just real elements.

Simulation scenarios require network topologies that define links, and their characteristics and traffic models that specify sender and receiver QoS experiences and perceptions, [6]. Some parameters are selected and associated data extracted, e.g. through non-invasive Internet tomography in the case of simulation of Internet scenarios, to be used as input data suitable for simulation and emulation experimentation. This approach creates a high confidence for achieving realistic results in simulation or emulation test-beds. The combination of parameters, including number of hops with corresponding delay, jitter and packet loss rate for given routes and periods, are so chosen as to allow any simulation or emulation analysis to be performed making use of certain bounds based on the real parameter values. That is these real parameter values are based on the extracted measurement data, which is representative of realistic scenarios. The benefit of going to these lengths in modelling and simulation may eventually be seen, for instance, in successfully planned cost-efficient application or service deployment, or guaranteed secure service level assurance for services to be deployed in real networks.

A demonstrative example of a parameterisation framework for input data for evaluating an application or networking product performance in respect of robustness reliability, throughput, etc. is presented in Table 3. Possible approaches that may be followed for instance are: a point-to-many evaluation scenario, or inter-regional evaluation scenario or such like. Only the former approach is presented here. The idea is to evaluate the would-be best-, average-, worst-case IP QoS performance (one-way) between a chosen measurement point (University of Limerick – Limerick tt128) and a number of selected measurements points scattered around the globe using performance data extracted through the RIPE ITMS over a three-month 24-hour period. The structured parameter-based dataset presented in the table is comprised of delay percentiles, jitter, packet loss, number of hops, and number of routing vectors for parameterisation. The Internet link-network performances presented here would be an immense help in pre-deployment simulation or emulation studies focused on resource planning, network impact analysis, and expected performance analysis for an inter-regional IP network product or application deployment venture. The networking application scenario could be envisaged here as having a specific central point of operations, which would be typical of a company with global Internet business impact. In the example, Limerick is used as such as a specific central point of operations. The global Internet measurement points used are representative of regions around the globe, from USA west and USA east, Europe (U.K. – London), Middle East (Israel), Australia (Melbourne) and New Zealand (Waikato).

In order to test against various IP-network/Internet configurations and impairments, delay percentiles (2.5, 50, 97.5) are used to define best-, average-, worst-case performance scenarios respectively for each given route. Other corresponding parameters such as packet loss and jitter are used to further define each scenario or to check against consequent behaviour when the delay percentiles in combination with other input parameters, e.g. hop count range [minimum to maximum] and routing vectors, are applied or used. Some IP-network/Internet configurations, such as planned bandwidth, queuing and/or QoS schemes, are also used in the scenario generation. This process for instance, enables "What if ..." scenario analysis by adjusting parameters on the basis of real-time QoS time performance data.

**Table 3: Demonstrative example of parameterisation in a one-to-many global Internet scenario. Parameter values are extracted from empirically measured data gathered through the collaborative RIPE ITMS.**

| Route TO and FROM Limerick tt128 | | Delay Percentiles[1] (Delay in *msec*) | | | Packet Loss % | Jitter (ms) | Hop count Range (Min – Max) | Number of Routing Vectors |
|---|---|---|---|---|---|---|---|---|
| | | 2.5 | 50.0 | 97.5 | | | | |
| US Att 87 | To | 77.73 | 77.80 | 78.60 | 0.00 | 0.58 | 4 – 30 | 32 |
| | From | 75.92 | 76.30 | 77.64 | 0.00 | 0.73 | 9 – 30 | 18 |
| US Att 84 | To | 48.13 | 48.42 | 48.99 | 0.07 | 2.70 | 4 – 30 | 28 |
| | From | 48.97 | 49.24 | 50.10 | 0.00 | 2.40 | 13 – 30 | 13 |
| Lon don tt26 | To | 10.84 | 10.92 | 11.60 | 0.00 | 1.21 | 10 – 30 | 11 |
| | From | 12.02 | 14.29 | 15.38 | 0.10 | 2.75 | 10 – 30 | 21 |
| CE RNt t31 | To | 17.66 | 17.90 | 19.09 | 0.07 | 1.06 | 2 – 30 | 12 |
| | From | 17.66 | 17.80 | 19.09 | 0.00 | 0.82 | 9 – 30 | 8 |
| Isra eltt 88 | To | 46.84 | 50.44 | 64.35 | 0.47 | 7.70 | 5 – 30 | 38 |
| | From | 48.48 | 49.76 | 94.84 | 0.30 | 13.53 | 4 – 30 | 34 |
| Mel bou rnet t74 | To | 154.08 | 154.52 | 156.63 | 0.47 | 4.80 | 3 – 30 | 37 |
| | From | 154.08 | 154.86 | 158.35 | 0.10 | 2.92 | 6 – 30 | 42 |
| Wai kato tt47 | To | 152.58 | 153.52 | 167.14 | 0.47 | 5.73 | 2 – 30 | 49 |
| | From | 142.59 | 143.95 | 154.02 | 1.00 | 4.92 | 19 – 30 | 26 |

**Notes:** For all the queuing scheme is Weighted Fair Queuing/ Random Early Detection (WFQ/RED) and planned bandwidth upgrades for the period after these measurements were taken were 128, 256, and 512Mbs.

---

[1] The **percentile** is a way of providing estimation of proportions of the data that should fall above and below a given value. The *p*th percentile is a value such that at most (100*p*)% of the observations are less than this value and that at most 100(1 - *p*)% are greater. Thus for example, the data for "from Israel" 48.48 would mean that 2.5% had delay 48.48ms or less.

| Legend | |
|---|---|
| Limerick tt128 | University of Limerick ITPS, Ireland |
| USAtt87 | West of USA ITPS, USA |
| USAtt84 | East of USA ITPS, USA |
| Londtt26 | London ITPS, UK |
| CERN tt31 | CERN ITPS, Switzerland |
| Israel tt88 | Israel ITPS, Middle East |
| Melbournett74 | Melbourne ITPS, Australia |
| Waikatott47 | Waikato University ITPS, New Zealand |

Using the data in simulation and/or emulation will help enable realistic modelling and thus facilitate network engineers and managers in their planning, analysis, and product deployment activities. Benefits and outcomes of such testing exercises can eventually lead to building customer confidence in products, foreseeing and eliminating performance bottlenecks, avoiding cost and embarrassing mistakes in sizing and provisioning an intended/designed solution prior to deployment venture, [32].

## 6.   CONCLUSION

Internet Tomography measurement featured in Traffic-Engineering-solution space is an effort to address Internet performance shortfalls by providing QoS visibility into networks and providing raw performance data for capacity network planning, simulation and emulation modelling and experimentation. Development aspects of a pilot non-invasive Internet Tomography Measurement System (ITMS) intended to address Internet performance issues have been outlined.

Simulation, emulation, and network tomography in terms of features, benefits and limitations have been described and compared. The advantages of empirical network modelling and integrated network experimentation were highlighted, especially focusing on an experimental approach which involves usage of real-time network parameters and elements, provided by a network tomographic measurement system, being integrated into simulated elements in an existing simulation engine. This enables realistic "What if...?" scenarios to be created by making incremental adjustments to an accurate baseline network model instead of speculating about future changes in environment behavioural parameters. A demonstrative example was used to illustrate the concept of empirical network modelling and integrated network experimentation using real-time Internet performance data between measurement point at University of Limerick and various measurement points across the globe.

## REFERENCES

[1]    M.G. Rabbat, M.J. Coates, R.D. Nowak. Multiple-Source Internet Tomography; Selected Areas in Communications. IEEE Journal on. Vol. 24, Issue 12, Dec. 2006, pp. 2221–2234.

[2]    J. Gonsky, G. Jackson, D. Joncas, C. Lane and D. Olds. Middle Mile Mayhem: Solving Web Scaling Performance Problems. 2000. URL: http://developer.intel.ru/download/eBusiness/pdf/hi004603.pdf

[3]    K. Bagchi; S. Mukhopadhyay. Forecasting Global Internet Growth Using Fuzzy Regression, Genetic Algorithm and Neural Network. IEEE Int. Conf. Information Reuse and Integration, IRI. 8-10 Nov. 2004, pp. 543–548.

[4]    L.G. Roberts. Beyond Moore's law: Internet growth trends. Computer Vol. 33, Issue 1, Jan. 2000, pp 117–119.

[5]    C. Myongsu, J. Wybenga; C. K. Byung; A. Boukerche. A routing coordination protocol in a loosely-coupled massively parallel router; in proc of IEEE Workshop on Merging Optical and IP Technologies. 26-29 May 2002, pp 52–57.

[6]    K. Fall. Network Emulation in the Vint/ns Simulator. In Proc. of the 4th IEEE Symposium on Computers and Communications, 1999.

[7]    Shunra Software. My Big Fat Network: What every software developer needs to know to ensure application performance to end-users. Shunra Software White paper. 2000. URL: http://www.shunra.com/getWhitepaper.php?wpid=6

[8]    T. Bu, N. Duffield, F.L. Presti, and D. Towsley, "Network tomography on general topologies," in Proc. ACM Sigmetrics, Marina Del Rey, CA, Jun. 2002, pp. 21–30.

[9]    E. Lawrence, G. Michailidis, V.N. Nair and B. Xi. Network Tomography: A Review and Recent Developments. 2005. URL: http://www.stat.lsa.umich.edu/~gmichail/bickel_festschrift.pdf

[10]   G. Gunduz, S. Pallickara, G. Fox. An Efficient Scheme for Aggregation and Presentation of Network Performance in Distributed Brokering Systems. *Journal of Systemics, Cybernetics and Informatics*. 2003. URL: http://www.iiisci.org/Journal/SCI/pdfs/P375884.pdf

[11] K. Claffy, M. Murray. Measuring the Immeasurable: Global Internet Measurement Infrastructure. Cooperative Association for Internet Data Analysis. 2001. URL:http://www.caida.org/outreach/papers/2001/MeasInfra/measurement.pdf

[12] S. Siddiqui, "IP Service Level Agreements: Bringing Light to the End of the IP Network tunnel", Quick Eagle Networks White paper. September 2001. URL:http://www.quickeagle.com/pdf/IP_SLA_Final.pdf

[13] L. Cottrell, C. Logg, I-H. Mei. Experiences and Results from a New High Performance Network and Application Monitoring Toolkit. 2003. URL: http://moat.nlanr.net/PAM2003/PAM2003papers/3768.pdf

[14] Internet Engineering Task Force. Internet Protocol Performance Metrics Working Group Charter and Description. 2004. URL: http://www.ietf.org/html.charters/ippm-charter.html

[15] G. Vinton. Guidelines for Internet Measurement Activities. Internet Engineering Task Force RFC1262, October 1991.

[16] NetQoS, Inc. Best Practices in Network Performance Monitoring. 2004. URL:http://www.netqos.com

[17] R. Caceres, N Duffield, A. Feldmann, J.D. Friedmann, A. Greenberg, R. Greer, Johnson T.C.R. Kalmanek, B. Krishnamurthy, B. Lavelle, D. Mishra, P.P.J. Rexford, K.K. Ramakrishna, F.D. True, J.E. van der Memle. Measurement and Analysis of IP Network Usage and Behaviour. *IEEE Communications Magazine*: Vol. 38, No. 5, May 2000, pp 144–151.

[18] W. Hughes. Performance Measures for Multi-media Applications. Proc. 38th IETF Meeting, Memphis, TN. April 1997.URL: http://www.ietf.org/proceedings/97apr/ops/rtfm-2/index.htm

[19] D. Paxson, G. Almes, J Mahdavi, and M. Mathis. Framework for IP Performance Metrics. IETF RFC 2330, May 1998.

[20] G. Almes, S. Kalidindi and M. Zekauskas. A Round-trip Delay Metric for IPPM. RFC 2681, September 1999.

[21] V. Raisen, A. Morton. Network Performance Measurement with Periodic Streams. IETF RFC 3432, November 2002.

[22] R. Blum. Performance Management and Engineering. August 2002 URL: http://www.shunra.com/getWhitepaper.php?wpid=12

[23] G. Vinton. Guidelines for Internet Measurement Activities. Internet Engineering Task Force, IETF RFC1262, October 1991.

[24] A. Adams et al. The Use of End-to-end Multicast Measurements for Characterizing Internal Network Behavior. *IEEE Communications Magazine*: Vol. 38, No. 5, May 2000. pp 152–159.

[25] B. White et al. An Integrated Experimental Environment for Distributed Systems and Networks. In Proc. 5th Symposium on Operating Systems Design and Implementation, Boston, MA, December 2002. pp 255–270.

[26] L. Breslau et al. Advances in Network Simulation. *IEEE Computer*, Vol. 33, No. 5, pp 59–67, 2000.

[27] J. Heidemann et al. Effects of detail in Wireless Network Simulation. In Proc., SCS Multiconference on Distributed Simulation, USC/ISI, January 2001. pp 3–11.

[28] J. Ahn, P. Dazing, Z. Liu, and L. Yan. Evaluation of TCP Vegas: Emulation and experiment. In Proc., SIGCOMM'95, Cambridge, MA, August 1995. pp 185–195.

[29] M. Coates, A. Hero, R. Nowak and B. Yu, Internet Tomography. *IEEE Signal Processing Magazine*, May 2002. pp 47–65.

[30] B. White et al. An Integrated Experimental Environment for Distributed Systems and Networks. In Proc., 5th Symposium on Operating Systems Design and Implementation, Boston, MA, December 2002, pp 255–270.

[31] M. O'Droma, A. Moloisane, I. Ganchev and V. Dardalat. Internet Tomography Measurement in 4G System Architecture: On the Role of Network Performance Infrastructures. IEC Annual Review of Communications, Fall 2005; 58(1): 621–623.

[32] PacketStorm Communications, Inc. IP Network Emulation: Developing and Testing IP Products Under Configurable and Repeatable Network Conditions. 2006. URL: http://www.packetstorm.com/IP_Network_Emulation.pdf

# CHAPTER 22

## Emerging Requirements for Telecommunication Product Design and System Modeling

Gerta Köster[1], Stoyan Poryazov[2]

[1]Siemens AG- Corporate Technology
Otto-Hahn-Ring 6, München
[2] Institute of Mathematics and Informatics
Bulgarian Academy of Sciences

**Abstract.** *The telecommunication market and, with it, telecommunication product design has undergone drastic changes in the past years. As a consequence, modeling and simulation are confronted with new challenges.*

*In this paper we outline some requirement changes for simulation design. We believe that the focus must be on rapidity, robustness, simplicity and intuitiveness and are willing to sacrifice exactness to some extent. We base our statements on the assumption that modeling and simulation ultimately serve to facilitate decision making and that the most important decisions are made in the early design phase. We also stress that managers, who take decisions, prefer robust decisions to optimal decisions for singular cases. That is, they prefer decisions that are valid for a number of imaginable scenarios.*

*Starting from the requirement of rapidity, robustness, simplicity and intuitiveness we suggest a strategy to tackle modeling and simulation: HALDA – heterogeneous abstraction level design approach, where we develop ideas from system test and system integration test and carry them over to the early design phase.*

## 1.   INTRODUCTION

In [1] we have discussed recent trends in telecommunications and their implications on modeling and simulation for the telecommunication market. In the following section 2 we will briefly summarize these trends. Then, in section 3, we describe in which way these changes influence product design and development. In [1] we also stated some of the challenges we see in view of the development on the telecommunication market. In section 4 we try to address one of these. We look at requirements for modeling and simulation in the telecommunication industry from a new angle: Today we very often are in a much earlier stage of the decision making process when we try to throw light on a technical or business problem through modeling and simulation. In section 5 we suggest a strategy to tackle modeling and simulation in view of the challenges described before: HALDA – heterogeneous abstraction level design approach. Section 6 presents a conclusion.

## 2.   THE EVOLUTION OF THE TELECOMMUNICATION MARKET

In [1] we observed that a large part of the market has become fractal as opposed to monolithic in the past. The large state owned companies have been replaced by private enterprises. This is true for both, the Western industries, where the telecommunication business has been privatized and the former Soviet block where telecommunication has been denationalized.

This means that a large number of companies are producing and offering new - often small - products, services and devices, among which the customers, operators and consumers, may choose. Competition among providers as well as manufacturers is fierce.

Also, products of different manufactures complement each other enhancing each other's value. Hence, there remain few single solutions out of one hand.

The market for classic voice services is saturated. Providers are seeking a new "killer application" to make up for the decreasing income for voice.

At the same time operators and manufacturers try to enlarge the value chain by offering applications and services or at least middleware to enable applications and services. Thus they are entering a business known for its fast development cycles.

When products become smaller and follow, to a certain extend, the fashion of the day, development cycles shorten and design becomes more volatile.

## 3. CHANGES IN PRODUCT DESIGN AND DEVELOPMENT REQUIREMENTS

In this section we would like to investigate how shorter development cycles influence the design and development requirements and our way to process them.

For this it is helpful to look at the software development process for real-time embedded software systems (DESS) workflow, as described in [2]. It consists of the following design stages:

1. User requirements engineering.
2. System requirements engineering.
3. System design.
4. Software requirements engineering.
5. Analysis (e.g. architecture, use cases, ...) to prepare specification.
6. Specification & design.
7. Implementation.
8. Instantiation.
9. Software Integration.
10. System Integration. (Software/Hardware)
11. Deployment.

The DESS approach includes development of software and hardware product components (between points 3 and 10). Verification and validation must take place at every stage of the workflow.

It is very interesting to look at the distribution of critical problems on the design stages for complex systems: With a probability of nearly 60% critical problems are caused by the specification. Modeling and design contribute 25% to critical problems and less than 20% are caused by implementation. These critical problems can be found in hardware or in software, but often hardware and software problems are coupled. [3].

This already bad situation is likely to worsen with more pressing time demands. There remains less time for thorough requirement analysis, system design and validation before we start to specify a product. Here, modeling and simulation can help: by comparing basic design options with respect to a number of relevant use cases.

At the same time, we see competing technical options developed in parallel – often even by the same company. E.g. the WiMax standard, 802.16, satellite transmission, UMTS are developed in parallel to cover the so-called white spots on the map with respect to the availability of broadband network access. Developing competing technologies is costly – especially if only one of the technologies is expected to make the race. We also need early delivery of the products to enjoy the advantages of early market entry. Thus, we need an early proof of concept through modeling and simulation, possibly followed by rapid prototyping.

## 4. RESULTING CHANGES IN MODELING AND SIMULATION REQUIREMENTS

Before we analyze the changes in modeling and simulation requirements stimulated by these changes in the development process we would like to reflect our motives for running simulations. Why do we model and simulate telecommunication?

We believe that one of the most important – if not the most important – advantage of simulations is that they facilitate decisions.

- When we optimize a system or parts of a system, e.g. an algorithm.
- When we need to decide between design options.
- When we need to decide between technologies.
- Or even when we decide whether or not we want to venture into a business at all.

In [4] Popper, Lempert and Bankes throw some light on how humans make decision: Humans prefer robust decisions, that is, decisions that are considered "good" in a wide range of scenarios that the decision makers regard as possible or probable. They do not seek a solution that is optimal for a single scenario unless they are sure that the scenario will indeed come true.

In the old telecommunication times, researchers were very often faced with the task to optimize an existing design or to give capacity forecasts for large and extremely complex systems. At that point it was certain – or at least extremely likely – that the systems would be employed. Researchers coped with that task by refining and optimizing complicated and complex simulation tools and by building models that were sometimes even standardized. This task was as time-consuming as it was complex – and certainly intellectually rewarding. Answers were often reliable and helpful. While we believe that there will be continued demand for high precision and high reliability simulations in classic telecommunication we also believe that the real challenge is with the new technologies.

The "hot spot" has moved: In the new market segments, the products and systems we look at are usually in a very early development stage. It is by no means sure, what their final design will be, under which conditions they will be employed, or, whether they are to be employed at all. Sophisticated tools hardly exist and there is certainly no time to develop them before the answer to a question is due. In the rare case, when they do exist, they are not suitable to deal with uncertainties and the sudden apparition of unknown parameters.

When we ask how we should model and design in the future, we must therefore ask at which point in the decision making process we are. That is, when we are asked to throw light on a problem by modeling and simulation, we must look at the problem as a whole - including the question when the answer to the stated problem must be delivered and what the true need for exactness is.

Otherwise we risk finding exact and reliable answers to problems that nobody is interested in.

The authors believe that the following requirements are fundamental when modeling and simulation to support decisions in an early business phase:

- Rapidity
- Robustness

- Simplicity
- Intuitiveness

Rapidity refers to the reduced time line. Complexity of the model must adapt to the time we have to produce an answer. There certainly is a trade off between rapidity and exactness.

Robustness: We need to produce simulation results that are good in a number of imaginable future scenarios, regarding technical issues and business issues alike. E.g. does WiMax truly enable broadband transmission over radio (the answer is yes see [5]) but would it also be suitable for simple voice over IP if one chooses to employ it in developing countries where there is no classic telephone and GSM is too costly to implement? A company may choose to invest into 802.16 if the answer to both questions is yes, even if they do not find out in advance how many Mbit/s exactly they can transmit in a suburban terrain.

Simplicity: Complexity of a newly developed single component should be reduced to a minimum to save time and budget. However, the demand for simplicity conflicts with the demand for robustness and rapidity. For robustness we investigate a multitude of scenarios with a high uncertainty. This is a very complex task. To accelerate the first simulation output we may include very complex models of product components similar to the ones we need – simply because they already exist.

Intuitiveness: Models and results must be easy to understand so that the information will eventually be used by the decision makers. Decision makers in industry usually work under enormous stress. They excel in making decision based on a minimum of information and they have very limited time to assess that information. It is a very important challenge for the engineers who conduct simulations to present their results in such a way that the main message can be correctly assessed by decision makers.

The requirements stated above may well mean that we have to trade exactness of the results for rapidity and robustness, if we want to keep up or stimulate demand for simulations.

# 5.    A STRATEGY FOR MODELING AND SIMULATION: HALDA – HETEROGENEOUS ABSTRACTION LEVEL DESIGN APPROACH

## 5.1    The HALDA Approach

In section 0 we claimed that today most models are needed in an early decision phase and hence in an early design phase. We demand that models and simulations be rapid, robust, simple and intuitive. However, most telecommunication products consist of complex interworking hardware and software components.

In this section, we would like to propose an integrated design approach that we call Heterogeneous Abstraction Level Design Approach. With this ansatz we hope to at least increase our ability to fulfill our requirements and still be able to deal with complex systems.

The model of a telecommunication product consists of a model of the product itself (hardware and software) and a model of the product's working environment. Obviously, the most complete model of a product is the product itself. In this sense, the natural design process seems consecutive refinement and enrichment with details of the models - beginning from rough specifications and ending with the most complete model – the product itself. A well known paper on so called "model driven system design" is [6]. This approach is continued in "Model-Driven Engineering" [7]. A fast co-simulation of complete custom target architecture (software + hardware) for a system level design exploration is shown in [8].

But all of the mentioned design approaches use the same level of abstraction for the product component models.

In this paper, we propose to deliberately give up this common level of abstraction and to advantageously employ different abstraction levels for different components. In doing this, we follow good practise in system test and system integration test. HALDA also builds up on the High Level Architecture framework proposed for modeling and simulation for military purposes by the US department of defense. See [9] and [10].

Each component of the product, or of its environment, is presented in the model by a *presenter* – a software unit capable to interact with other component presenters. The component presenter acts as interface between a component model and other component presenters. See Figure 2.

Each component model may have different forms:

- Simulator.
- Simulating emulator. An emulator is "a model that accepts the same inputs and produces the same outputs as a given system. [11]. The simulating emulator is emulator which, in addition, simulates the response time of the modeled component.
- Natural model ("hardware in the loop" approach, see e.g. [12]).
- Real component.

The presenter may be used for storage and empirical modeling of the real components, validation of the component models etc.

As usual in modular approaches, each component model may be refined and approximated to the reality without changes in the others product components.

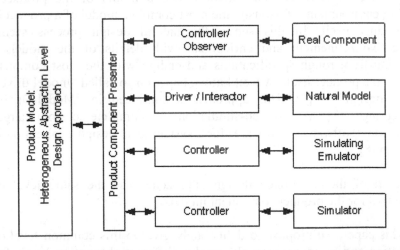

**Fig. 1   Different representations of a product component using a heterogeneous abstraction level approach. Each component may be represented by simulation, by emulating, by a so-called natural model with "hardware in the loop" or even the real component itself. The presenter is the interface of the model component to the rest of the model. The presenter remains unchanged, when the product module and its driving instance (controller, observer, driver) are replaced.**

What are the advantages of HALDA, the Heterogeneous Abstraction Level Design Approach, especially in view of the requirements we phrased earlier in the paper?

## Rapidity

The Heterogeneous Abstraction Level Design Approach means keeping newly developed component models on the absolute minimum level of refinement necessary to answer a specific question. On the other hand we can use a related model, even if it is complex, if it happens to be immediately available. Thus we can start simulations early, without waiting for each component to simultaneously reach the same level of refinement.

Model components may be in different stages of completion from simulation to prototype. In fact, we do not need modeling of all components since existing hardware components are models of themselves. Hardware in preparation may be substituted by emulators supplied e.g. by the manufacturer. Already developed software may run on an emulator. Model components may even be represented by a finished product with similar characteristics, even a competing design. This approach is already used in the system test and system integration test phases of the development cycle. Here we suggest carrying it over to the early design phases.

As usual with modular design approaches, each component model may be refined and approximated to the reality without changes in the others product components. Thus model components – or variations of model components – may be developed in parallel and by different teams, again saving time.

Many model components may be reused in other model frameworks increasing the speed at which new models can be generated from a model component library once such a library exists.

## Robustness

Model components are easily exchangeable since the interface, that is, the presenter remains in place. This facilitates the simulation of a number of scenarios, e.g. comparing competing component designs in various employment environments.

Thus, there is a higher chance that discrepancies in the design, shortage of information, mismatch of interfaces, incorrect assumptions and other problems prone to cause critical damage are detected early and that our final design decision is good for a number of imaginable deployment scenarios. Note that with the acceptance of very rough interchangeable model components we do not attempt to find a solution that is optimal for a specific scenario.

## Simplicity

By leaving newly developed model components at their lowest possible level of complexity we also keep the model relatively simple. This is especially important since we reintroduce complexity by recycling model components from other models which may be, in fact, rather refined without fitting the purpose 100%. At the same time we want to investigate a number of different scenarios with varying parameters. This is only possible if the scenarios themselves are kept simple and the number of parameters low.

## Intuitiveness

The model ensures maximal similarity to the real product and environment in those areas that are vital to fulfill the task given at that moment. Unnecessary wealth of detail does not distract the decision taker from the essence of the model and the result. Also, model components that are in fact real products do not require any form of abction.

## 5.2   HALDA in Practice – An Example

In 2004 WiMax, IEEE's 802.16 standard, was emerging. One of the questions arising at the time was: Should one produce a WiMax-WLAN converter to provide end-to-end broadband wireless access?

To answer this question a two component model – within the HALDA framework – was considered at the innovation laboratory of Siemens' Communications division. It consisted of a prototype for the combined WiMax-WLAN link as the first model component and a traffic generator as the second model component. The traffic generator was available in two versions: a traffic simulator, that is, a piece of software running on a standard computer, and real traffic such as the transfer of DVD quality video or IP telephony.

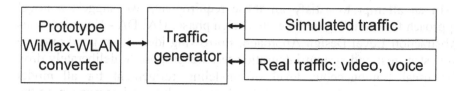

**Fig. 2 Example of HALDA use in everyday practice: A proof of concept for a combined WiMax-WLAN network to provide broadband access at the innovation lab of Siemens Communications in 2004. The traffic generator component of the model comes in two varieties: A traffic simulator to generate a challenging traffic load and real traffic such as the transfer of DVD quality video over the combined network.**

Measurements were conducted for a variety of scenarios in the laboratory and outdoors - with the conclusion that a combined WiMax-WLAN network is indeed broadband capable as long as there is at least near-line of sight on the WiMax link. In 2005 a decision in favor of the product idea was made at Siemens Communications [5].

## 6.   CONCLUSION

In this paper we claimed that growing demand for modeling and simulation must be expected in the very early phases of product design, when most product design decisions, and indeed decisions on the employment of a product as a whole, are still wide open.

Modeling and simulation must cope with that by being, at a time, rapid and robust, in the sense that valid results can be obtained for a number of varying scenarios. Hence, results are less reliable in terms of valid digits for a single scenario but more reliable regarding the validity of the result when circumstances change.

Also, simplicity and intuitiveness are a must to ensure that the results will be understood and used for decision making. Often these goals can only be achieved by making sacrifices with respect to exactness.

In an attempt to satisfy all these requirements we suggest a novel approach for modeling in the early design phase: HALDA - Heterogeneous Abstraction Level Design Approach. Borrowing ideas from good practice in system test and system integration test we propose to deliberately drop the usual homogeneous level of modeling refinement for all model components. Instead, we suggest developing each model component to the minimum level of complexity necessary to find answers. At the same time we suggest representing model components by real products with similar characteristics or prototypes – again saving time. The interface between the model components in their various stages of completion is given by component presenters that have a central role in such a modular approach.

While the idea of a heterogeneous level of abstraction for the model components may seem natural, once the necessary mind set has been established, it may not always be so easy to actually do it. As a next research step, we suggest to have a closer look at what we need to realize modeling with different levels of abstraction in terms of programming paradigms, programming language and algorithmic challenges.

## REFERENCES

[1]    Köster, G., Poryazov, S.; "Implications of Recent Trends in Telecommunications on Modeling and Simulation for the Telecommunication Industry", Fourth International Conference Information Research and Applications, Varna 2006.

[2]    Stefan Van Baelen, Joris Gorinsek & Andrew Wills (Editors). "Software Development Process for Real-Time Embedded Software Systems (DESS)", pp. 180. (http://www.dess-itea.org/deliverables/ITEA-DESS-D1-V01P.pdf) .

[3]    Horst Salzwedel, "MISSION LEVEL DESIGN OF AVIONICS." (http://wcms1.rz.tuilmenau.de/fakia/fileadmin/template/startIA/sst/V eroffentlichungen/2004/DASC2004_Salzw.pdf).

[4]    Popper, Lembert, Bankes, "Shaping the Future", Scientific American Vol. 292 2005.

[5]    Köster G., Peter H.-J, "A Prototypical Realization of a Wireless Access Network Combining WiMax and WLAN, Innovations for Europe", VDE Kongress Aachen 2006.

[6]   Loyd Baker, Paul Clemente, Bob Cohen, Larry Permenter, Byron Purves, and Pete Salmon. "FOUNDATIONAL CONCEPTS FOR MODEL DRIVEN SYSTEM DESIGN.INCOSE" Model Driven System Design Interest Group. (http://www.vitechcorp.com/whitepapers/files/200701031636590.baker_etal96.pdf).

[7]   Schmidt, "Model-Driven Engineering. Computer", February 2006, Published by the IEEE Computer Society (http://www.cs.wustl.edu/~schmidt/GEI.pdf).

[8]   Gunar Schirner, Andreas Gerstlauer and Rainer Domer. "Multifaceted Modeling of Embedded Processors for System Level Design." www.cecs.uci.edu/conference_proceedings/aspdac_2007/schirner_ASPDAC_07.pdf

[9]   [USD(A&T) Memorandum] "DoD High Level Architecture (HLA) for Simulations," September 10, 1996.

[10]  RTO Technical Report 50, NATO HLA Certification, June 2006.

[11]  DoD MODELING AND SIMULATION (M&S) GLOSSARY

[12]  [VS&S 2004] Pennsylvania Transportation Institute - Vehicle Systems and Safety Group (VS&S), 2004. (http://www.vss.psu.edu/H2VRC/h2vrc_hil_testing.htm).

# CHAPTER 23

# A Tool for Packaging and Exchanging Simulation Results

Dragan Savić[1], Francesco Potortì[2], Francesco Furfari[2],
Matevž Pustišek[1], Janez Bešter[1], Sašo Tomažič[1]

[1] Faculty of Electrical Engineering, Ljubljana (SI)
[2] ISTI-CNR, Pisa (IT)

**Abstract.** *In the field of simulations storing and exchanging simulation data are important tasks. The quantity of simulation data can be rather big and at the same time this data can appear in different formats. The conversion of big quantities of data can be extremely time-consuming. In this article we focus on simulations in telecommunications. Therefore we have studied the needs of the telecommunication community and defined a reference model of a simulation process. According to the needs we have developed a software tool CostGlue, which represents a central repository for data produced with different types of simulation tools and acts as a converter of different output formats into different input formats. CostGlue has modular software architecture. This enables further development and contributions from any other research sphere of activity. The core of the software tool represents the application CoreGlue responsible for communicating with the database. CoreGlue represents unified interface for writing to the database and reading from it. Specific functions like import and export of data and different mathematical calculations are represented as a set of self-described modules, which are loaded as*

---

[1] This work was supported by European Commission under the COST 285 Action, by the CNR/MIUR program "Legge 449/97 (project IS-Manet), and by the Ministry of Higher Education, Science and Technology of the Republic of Slovenia (program P2-0246).

*necessary. The graphic user interface is introduced as a web application
for the simplicity of use and effective remote access to the application. The
software package CostGlue is going to be released as free software with
the possibility of further development.*

## 1.    INTRODUCTION

Simulations in the field of telecommunications are known by numerous
research problem challenges, which originate from the complexity,
largeness and heterogeneity of the telecommunication networks that are
being simulated. Because of these properties simulations represent
indispensable, universal and cost efficient approach to the development of
the new networks and consequentially also the development of new
services and applications. Therefore there is a great variety of simulation
programs in use. This programs – simulators – serve the purpose of
inspecting different design approaches and studies of telecommunication
networks.

Information about the behavior and operation of the modeled system is
gathered from the simulation data, which represent the output of individual
simulation programs. In order to achieve a good flow of the gained
information among the researches and research institutions it is necessary
to take care of the exchange of the simulation data and post-processed
data. Momentarily state of simulation data exchange is to a great extent
hindered by the usage of different kinds of data formats in simulation
software packages.

This topic has been addressed [1] in the framework of the European
COST 285 Action "Modeling and Simulation Tools for Research in
Emerging Multi-service Telecommunications". A forum where researchers
from all around Europe periodically meet to address issues related to the
simulation of communications systems. The point made was that
apparently no general purpose tools exist for exchanging big quantities of
simulation data coming from different sources in different formats. Not
only was the need for a common format for exchanging data highlighted,
but also the need of feeding this data to different tools for post-processing,
each requiring a different input format.

To better understand the scope of different requirements we define a
reference model that encompasses the creation, flow and processing of
data in the analysis of telecommunications systems. The main functional

parts comprising such a model (simulators, data collectors, graphing tools, statistical tools) are covered by the many existing tools that are used by the research community; we focus on input data in form of simulation results (e.g., ns-2 [6] traces), or measurements (e.g., Tcpdump traces). Raw data can be post-processed (e.g., packet delay) and the results stored separately from the raw data or complementing them, so that further analysis is possible based on both raw and post-processed data. Finally, the results can be exported in various widespread output formats, like tabular ASCII data or XML.

Data storage is based on the HDF5 [3] data format, which was selected after the analysis of the available options. HDF5 has been successfully applied in several scientific projects; it enables efficient data storage and lookup. Among the features most relevant to our purpose, it provides support for extremely large quantities of data, meta descriptors, and embedded compression. A set of programming libraries is available in C and Python as well as in numerous others languages, which simplifies software development.

We propose a tool called CostGlue, which has modular software architecture. That makes it possible to include future development contributions from other research communities. The core is a Python application called CoreGlue, which provides HDF5 database connection for writing to and reading from the database. Specific functions, such as conversion from specific data formats and different calculations, are implemented as sets of self-descriptive loadable modules. We enriched the basic mechanism provided by the HDF5 data format to store metadata, in order to support a more useful XML Schema language in defining the significant information about simulation data. A graphical user interface is envisaged via the use of a web browser, allowing user-friendly and efficient remote access to the application.

The next sections describe the proposed architecture of CostGlue into deeper detail, particularly its core - CoreGlue.

## 2.    A MODEL OF THE SIMULATION PROCESS

In order to obtain a general and systematic overview of data creation, flow and processing, we define a reference model of the simulation process, which is depicted in Fig. 1. The model provides a layered decomposition of the main functions that are usually encountered when using simulation as a research method. There are three layers in the model.

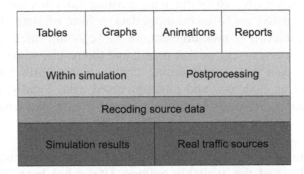

**Fig. 1  Reference model of a simulation process.**

The first layer - *source layer* - provides raw simulation output, describing a simulation run into the smallest detail. Raw data is generated with discrete event simulators (e.g., ns-2, Opnet). Usually one or more records for every event during the simulation run are created at the source layer. Structure and format of the data at this point are entirely dependent on the simulator. Most frequently they are in the form of large tabular traces, in ASCII or binary format. An optional *source recoding sublayer* handles the raw source data: its main purpose is to convert between different formats (e.g., from ASCII to binary or vice versa), data compression (e.g., Gzip, Bzip2) or removing private information, e.g., header lines, from simulation traces. The source layer supports both raw simulation data and real measurements data. In fact, during our discussions, we found out that nearly the same model can be applied to the analysis of real network traffic traces. In this case the raw data are not a result of simulation, but rather, for example, data traces captured in a network link. Apart from the different tool (traffic capture tool, like Tcpdump or Ethereal instead of a simulator) that generates raw data, all the functions of the upper layers remain the same in both cases.

The *processing layer* is responsible for simulation data analysis. At this level cumulative results can be derived from raw data (e.g., mean packet delay is calculated) or statistical confidence of the results can be deter-mined (and consequently additional simulation runs can be conducted). An important characteristic of the data processing layer is that the amount of data received from the source layer is usually much larger than the amount of results of post-processing.

The *presentation layer* is the final stage where the results are organized in a form useful for communicating the most important findings with other interested practitioners. In the case of simple tabular printouts of the results, this layer is void or only does trivial modifications of the data (e.g., changes in number formats, column spacing). However, data is frequently shown in 2- or 3-dimensional graphs (e.g., being part of scientific reports or research papers, web pages) or even presented in animated form (e.g., ns-2 NAM - Network AniMator). At this layer the predominant requirement is flexibility of presentation and a possibility to create new or modified presentation objects from new or changed simulation results without reformatting.

We can map the functionality of particular tools used in simulation to the layers of our model. Usually, a single tool provides more than one functional layer or even all of them. In the most favorable situation it would encompass all the functions needed and implement them adequately to meet all the researcher's needs. In practice this occurs very rarely and there is usually a set of complementary tools that covers the required scope of functions within the model. The selection of tools is made on arbitrary conditions, including their capabilities and performance, the researcher's past experience with a particular tool or the availability of tools.

## 3.   FORMATS FOR EXCHANGING DATA

CostGlue acts as an archive for data generated by various different simulation programs and as a converter from several output formats to several input formats. Therefore, it is important to know which programs and formats are generally used by telecommunications systems practitioners. To this end we used the information obtained from the COST 285 participants, representatives of more than ten European nations, about the kind of tools they use for their simulation work. We learned that no single simulation tool has a dominant position, but that there is a great variety of tools in use.

A specific questionnaire directed to the above mentioned people yielded some interesting results:

- apart from tabular data, other types of data organization, such as hierarchical or other elaborate structural formats are rarely used,
- most of the time, data are used for statistics or graphing, other uses such as data mining are rare,

- the most common method for evaluating the statistical accuracy of simulation data is to use independent replications with the combination of different simulation times to assure long enough stationary intervals; equivalent correlation length (single simulation run) is rarely used; these methods are generally applied on a case-by-case basis, with the help of custom Bash, Perl or Python scripts,
- a single simulation run produces anywhere from 1 MB to 2 GB of data, and a simulation campaign requires from 1 to 100 runs, in the responses we got; measurements campaigns (as opposed to simulation) required from 1 to 5 runs, each generating from 100 MB to 50 GB of data,
- storage required varies from up to 1 GB for short-term storage to anywhere from 10 MB to 10 GB and more for long-term storage,
- used metadata include type, date, parameter values and their description, version tracking, configurations, simulation scripts, location,
- metadata are stored in different locations: coded into directory and file names, in separate files, in different storage location (e.g., under root directory, shared directories) inside files, in databases.

Among those who use a predefined output format, the most common appears to be the network simulator ns-2. Among the generic tools for mathematical computation and running simulations, Matlab appears to be used by many. A large part of the simulators is composed by standard scripting or programming languages and, in general, by ad hoc simulators. Concerning the tools used for post-processing or graphing, there is an even greater variety. These observations, while limited in scope, show that some sort of tabular ASCII format is of common use, and thus that being able to read and write ASCII tabular data is certainly a requisite for our proposed archiver and converter. Nevertheless, the variety of tools used also calls for a general way of reading and writing many formats: that is why we consider the modular architecture of CostGlue a necessary feature for the tool to be useful at all.

Another interesting point is that simulation data and measurement data have a lot in common, and a tool useful for one can be also useful for the other. However, measurements like simulation results are often output in particular formats, and an input converter is very frequently needed. An interesting feature that can be made part of CoreGlue is the ability to give a similar treatment to data coming either from measurement or from simulation of the same environment, and archive them in the same format.

This is the reason why the first prototype of the CostGlue will include the ability to read ns-2 data and Tcpdump data, store them into a common format and write in Nam, ns-2 and Tcpdump formats. This capability would make it easy to use the many tools available that are able to analyze and graph data obtained by both ns-2 and Tcpdump.

All the above discussion leads to a scenario where a simulation tool is run several times, each time producing tabular data, that is, data that can be conveniently stored into a two-dimensional structure having relatively few columns and a possibly large number of rows. What about data that cannot be naturally converted to a two-dimensional format? In this case, the inner structure of the archived data needs to be different. One of the challenges is to make the tool efficient in the most common case of collections of tabular data, but still be useful in the case of non-tabular data.

## 4.    THE DATABASE

A common file format solves several problems of simulation data exchange. Therefore we made a thorough analysis of different data formats and their corresponding libraries for data manipulation. Among many, we have focused on the following set of data formats: HDF4, HDF5, netCDF, ODB, FITS and OpenDX. Beside these, we also considered using plain text formats, XML and SQL databases. The results of the analysis makes it clear that the HDF5 file format is the most suitable for this task, since it meets all the requirements of data organization e.g., separation of raw data and metadata, and different requirements of contemporary computer system architectures, such as managing big quantities of data, offering a general data model, supporting complex data structures, portability among different computer platforms, parallel data access and processing, diversity of physical file storage media, and sustained development and maintenance.

### 4.1    Database Structure

Summarizing the above, most simulation data in the computer communications area are collections of tables of numeric data: each simulation run generates a table of data having few columns and a possible large number of rows. Each table is associated with certain parameters specific to a simulation run that generated it, and is uniquely identified by the values of those parameters. We are interested in defining a database structure that is able to efficiently accommodate this type of data. HDF5 meets these requirements.

HDF5 is data format with associated software library. The software library consists of two primary objects: *dataset* and *group*. A *dataset* represents a multidimensional array of data elements, which can hold different types of data. The data stored in datasets can be either homogeneous (only one data type used within a single dataset - *simple dataset*) or compound (different number of data types within one dataset - *compound dataset*). Since tabular data collected from certain simulators often contains data with different types (e.g., integer, float, char), we use compound datasets to accommodate the nature of simulation outputs. An HDF5 *group* is a structure containing zero or more HDF5 objects. By using two primary HDF5 objects, data can be organized hierarchically by means of a tree structure where an arbitrary number of HDF5 objects are derived from the main "root" group. Groups and datasets have a logical counterpart in directories and files in a hierarchical file system and, similarly to a file system, one can refer to an object in an HDF5 file by its full path name.

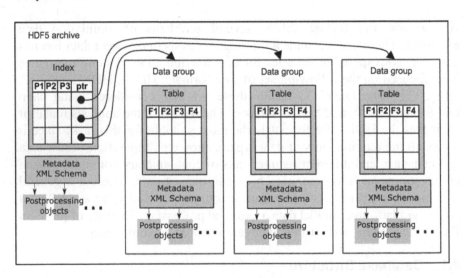

**Fig. 2  The logical structure of the database.**

To meet the requirements of efficient data storage, especially those critical to management, understanding and reuse of scientific data, each HDF5 object may have associated *metadata* stored in the HDF5 file (referred as *archive*) in a simple attributes form. Attributes usually represent a small dataset connected to a certain group or a dataset. Their purpose is to describe the nature and/or the intended usage of the object they are attached to.

In the design of the database structure our goal was a flexible representation of the stored simulation data by using one multidimensional array, where a user can easily extract a desirable portion of the simulation data. Even though HDF5 supports multidimensional arrays, it is not efficient to store large amount of data in just one array. Furthermore, due to the HDF5 primary aspect of use, which is to have data organized hierarchically, storing everything inside a single multidimensional array would be a loss on the side of flexibility. We also introduced an indexing table which maps the logical view of a multidimensional matrix into an HDF5 hierarchical structure, as shown in Fig. 2.

Fig. 3 presents a detailed overview of the proposed database structure, where the indexing table represents the logical part and all other groups and datasets represent actual data, where the raw simulation data, metadata and *post-processing data* is stored. The whole database is treated as one archive containing a "root" group from which all other groups and datasets form a two-level tree.

An immediate extension to having tables of numeric data is having tables of fixed-length data, which can be flags, numbers or strings. The PyTables library allows efficient manipulation of 2-dimensional HDF5 compound datasets from Python referred to as *tables* from now on. Each table, together with metadata and post-processing data, is attached to a data group, which usually holds the data produced during a single simulation run. Data groups are indexed by vectors of parameters. An *index* is a 2-dimensional array, referred above as the indexing table, where the *parameters* relative to each data group are stored: each column corresponds to a different parameter, and each row contains the values of the parameter relative to a data group. Therefore an index is used as the data structure for accessing a data group, using an array of parameter values relative to that data group as the key. A table is attached to each data group, where each row is filled with the values of the *fields*, each field corresponding to a column of the table.

The overall structure is a collection of 2-dimensional tables indexed by arrays of P parameters. This can be logically seen as a matrix with P+2 dimensions, where the first P dimensions are sparse and the last 2 dimensions are dense. We define the first P indices as parameters identifying a data group. As for the last two indices, the first of them represents the field in the data group table, and the second index the row number of the data group table.

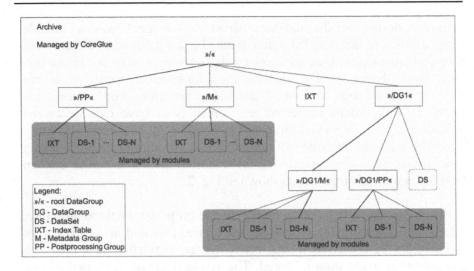

**Fig. 3  HDF5 database structure.**

Let us now describe how the results of an example real-world simulation can be stored in the described structure. We are simulating the behavior of packet switches in ns-2; each run is characterized by several parameters, such as architecture type, buffer size, number of I/O ports and traffic load. Each simulation run differs in at least one of these parameters. When storing the results of one simulation run in the archive, we populate a new row in the indexing table: values in each row uniquely identify a simulation run. Each row includes the full path to a data group, containing the table with the results of the simulation run, metadata and processing data, as shown in Fig. 3. Metadata stores information about the type of scripts used to generate that simulation run, the type of network topology, traffic patterns, etc. Post-processing data include packet loss probability, maximum, minimum and average packet delay. Metadata and processing data are also associated with the whole archive, and contain information relative to the whole set of simulation runs.

## 4.2   Metadata and Processing Data

In recent years increasing attention has been devoted to metadata for every application domain. The XML Schema language [8] provides a means for defining the structure, contents and semantics of an XML document and it is widely used to collect data about data, that is, metadata. The HDF5 data format allows metadata to be associated with every object by using a series of predefined attributes in the form of name=value pairs. This mechanism is too simple for our requirements, so we decided to use it just to replicate some relevant piece of information, in order to increase the robustness of the archiver system. Consequently, in order to insert metadata, we defined an XML Schema whose document instances can be saved together with the simulation data, as reported in Figure 2. Metadata can be associated to every Data Group; metadata referring to the archive as a whole are saved together with the indexing table, while metadata for a single simulation run are saved in the related Data Group. Metadata can make reference to any kind of additional data, which are labeled in Fig.2 as post-processing objects; examples are statistics on the raw data, charts, images, and any type of data that are produced from or relevant to the raw data.

The CostGlue metadata XML Schema is derived from the Information Model defined in the OAIS reference model [9] and from the Scientific Data Model (CSMD) [10]. The Open Archival Information System (OAIS) is a technical recommendation to provide permanent or indefinite long-term, preservation of digital information. Of particular interest is the OAIS Information Model. The preserved information is called *content information* and is accompanied by a complete set of metadata as depicted in Fig. 4, where the *content data object* is the actual preserved data (a simulation run or measurement trace in our case) and the *representation information* consists of the information that is required to render and interpret the object. This might include the specification of the data format as well as the software needed to access the data. The *reference information*, used to provide assigned identifiers to the content information, allows to univocally referring the object outside of the system. Typical identifiers could be UUIDs or terms of taxonomy. The *context information* documents the relationships between the content information and its environment, including why the object was created and how it is related to other objects. The *provenance information* specifies the origin of the content information, any changes that may have taken place and so on. Finally the *fixity information* provides *data integrity* checks to verify that the object has not been altered in an undocumented way.

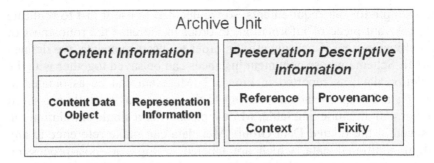

**Fig. 4 Archive package as defined in the OAIS information model.**

Our XML Schema is based on the OAIS information model with a structure specialized for describing a collection of simulation runs. Indeed, the adoption of an XML schema could facilitate further aggregation of telecommunication archives in catalogues to be published in repositories for the scientific communities [5, 11]. For this reason we have adopted in our schema the taxonomy used in the CSMD model depicted in Fig. 5, where the boxes labeled *experiment, simulation* and *measurement* contain the raw data we aim at archiving. The objective of the CSMD model is to aid interoperability of scientific information systems among research organizations. The information related to the project or investigation to which the simulation data refer are optional but, if provided, they are used in both the *reference information* and in the *context information* metadata.

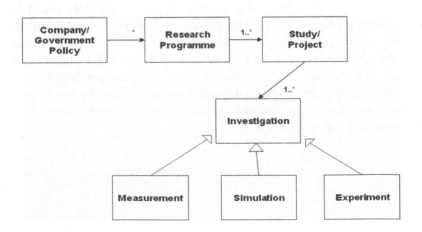

**Fig. 5 Main classes of the CSMD model version 2.**

## 5.    CostGlue ARCHITECTURE

As described, the CoreGlue manages the index and the database structure, including the tables. Modules are responsible for metadata and post-process contents, both for the single data groups and for the whole archive. The CoreGlue and the modules together constitute the whole application, which is named CostGlue.

The CostGlue is written in Python. This language was chosen because of anecdotal evidence of its efficiency both in memory usage and processing power and for its programmability ease, due to automatic garbage collection and many native functions and types. Portability among operating systems is excellent and library availability for many tasks, especially mathematical ones, is rich. With respect to its main competitor, Java, Python has a generally smaller memory footprint and since it is completely free, does not suffer from being controlled by a single entity.

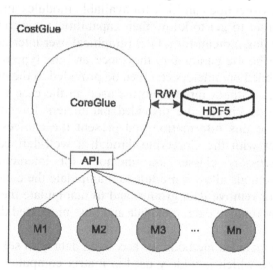

**Fig. 6  CostGlue architecture.**

The architecture of the CostGlue application, depicted in Fig. 6, consists of a core, called CoreGlue, and several specialized modules. The core takes care of reading and writing to the HDF5 archive and of the dynamic loading of modules, while the modules are devoted to specialised tasks. Modules interact with the core through an API. Examples of tasks a module can perform are:

- data import/export to/from the archive,
- statistical computations over data stored in the archive,
- data extraction from the archive with complex filters,
- transformations over the data contained in the archive,
- graphical output creating from the data in archive,
- provision of a generic graphical user interface (GUI) for exploring the data in the archive, doing simple import/export or computations and running other available modules, and
- provision of a module-specific GUI.

## 6.  OVERVIEW OF THE MODULE API

Python, like many modern languages, supports dynamic module loading. We exploit this possibility by providing a module library with a limited number of modules and leaving it open for other parties to write new modules. Modules are Python self-describing programs, which reside in a fixed place. The CoreGlue can look for available modules and query them one by one in order to get to know their capabilities; this can be used for instance for building a menu for a GUI (graphical user interface). Modules are able to describe the parameters they need and the type of output they produce. The needed parameters can then be provided to the module by the CoreGlue with or without input from the user; in the case where input is required, CoreGlue checks the provided parameters for consistency. A GUI can also use this information and present the choices to the user. Modules interact with the CoreGlue through a well-defined API which contains all necessary classes and methods for interacting with the database. The methods allow a module to manipulate the data group index in order to add or remove data groups, and to manipulate the data groups, in order to add or remove data, metadata and post-processed data.

The API also includes methods for accessing data with selectors written in index notation, which is widely used in matrix computations programs such as Matlab or Octave [4]. In this notation each of the P+2 indices can be "1", indicating the smallest index; "end", indicating the highest one; "n:m", indicating all the indices between n and m included; ":", indicating the whole range from smallest to highest, "n:s:m", indicating the range from n to m in steps of s; an array like "[1 5 6 8]" indicating the selected indices. Using the Matlab index notation one can take complex orthogonal slices of the multidimensional matrix composed of all the data in the database; in fact, the database structure can be seen as a sparse matrix with

P+2 dimensions, and being able to take a slice of this matrix could prove a powerful feature of CostGlue.

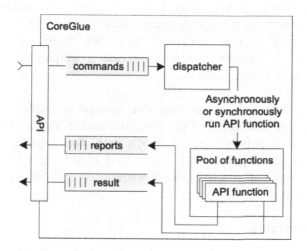

**Fig. 7 API and CoreGlue interaction.**

As shown in Figure 7, the CoreGlue contains three different queues: *command*, *result* and *report* queue, which are used for exchanging different types of messages with modules. When using the CostGlue the first step is to call the CoreGlue together with a module name and its optional arguments. A given module can work either alone, e.g., by performing a batch job, or it can depend on other modules, e.g., a command line interface can call a specialized module to do some work. Modules can also differ in the way they are built. Simple ones, after sending the command to the CoreGlue, wait for the results and are therefore not able to perform any additional tasks. Alternatively, complex modules run asynchronously with respect to the core, so they can check periodically the result queue for results and in the meantime inform the user about the current work progress by reading report messages from the report queue. Modules working as described are run as separate threads inside the core.

## 6.1 The Command Line and the HTML GUI Modules

When CoreGlue is invoked by a command line, its first argument is the module name, followed by the parameters needed by the module. When invoked with the argument `html`, the CoreGlue acts as an HTTP server, providing a graphical user interface. Through this interface, the user can look at the list of available modules and, for each of them, look at a description, at the input they require and at the output they provide. The CoreGlue provides an interface for the input of module parameters, complete with checking, thanks to the information that it reads from the modules themselves. In the simplest case, this is analogous to calling the module on the CoreGlue command line, but more convenient for interactive use. A module can also provide a graphical interface or graphical output by itself.

Currently an interactive command line module is implemented. This module is used for debugging of the CoreGlue and modules. Additionally, it can be used to import and export tabular data. This requires the user to specify options and arguments; a specialized module can automatically recognize the type of a trace and automatically provide naming, and possibly, filtering.

## 6.2   API Examples

All API commands are asynchronous, and return immediately if the NOWAIT option is given. However, modules can use the API in a more straightforward fashion, by not using the NOWAIT option; in this case, they will not be able to show any progress report, and will not be able to suspend, resume and stop a running API command. When an API command is called, the core creates a command message and enqueues it to the command queue from where it is read and executed by the *dispatcher*, which is a loop running as a separate thread. Fig. 8 sketches the implementation of the API command stub inside the core.

```
Group open (paramvals, exists, NOWAIT)
  message.name = 'OpenGroup';
  message.args = (paramvals, exists);
  retval = enqueue(message, CommandQ);
  if (NOWAIT)
    return retval;
  else
    assert(retval != error)
    dequeue(message, ResultQ);
    assert(message.name == 'OpenGroup')
    return message.result;
  endif
endfun
```

**Fig. 8  API command stub inside the CoreGLue.**

Here are some examples of commands provided by the API:

- `Archive open (filename, flags)` - opens an archive on disk: arguments are the same as in the C stdio library, returns an archive object,
- `Group open (paramvals, exists)` - `paramvals` is a list of parameter values; if `exists` is true, return the existing data group with the given parameters, else return a newly created group with the given parameters,
- `FieldList add (fieldlist)` - adds fields (that is, columns) to a table by taking a list of field names, types (e.g. Int8, Float32) and sizes of the fields.

```
open an archive for writing
create a new data group
insert parameter values in index table
create a new table with given fields
open input file for reading
read the data into the table
exit
```

**Fig. 9  Example for data import.**

```
open an archive for reading
go through index table
find the specified parameter values
get the data group name
get the table object
use selector to filter table data
create a new output file for writing
write the filtered data to the file
exit
```

**Fig. 10  Example for data export.**

Figs. 9 and 10 are snippets of example code inside a module that makes several API command calls.

## 6.3    Modules for Antenna Measurements and Simulations

We have designed two different import modules together with researchers from SSR (Signals, Systems and Radio) group at the University of Madrid. The first module deals with antenna measurements. Measurements are taken in the special antenna chamber. There are three types of different kinds of measurements depending on the way in which the probe or the testing antenna are shifted:   spherical (roll over azimuth – Θ and Φ), cylindrical or plannar. Each measurement is performed on a single frequency and the results are saved in two separate files. The first file contains the information about the organization of the raw data, which also represents the second file. The second file is in a binary form. To be stored into HDF5 database (in form of tables) it needs to be converted into ASCII format. After the import action of all the performed measurements is finished we can start using the SSR's proprietary visualization module (written in Matlab) for visualizing the antenna's directivity diagrams. Each measurement is selected by a set of parameters from the visualization module. In this case the names of parameters are: client name, project name, antenna type and working frequency. The whole import, export and visualization process is depicted in the Fig. 11.

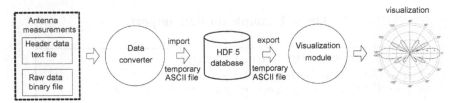

**Fig. 11   Import, export and visualization process of the antenna measurements results.**

Second specialized module is for dealing with antenna simulation results. The results are a direct output of the GRASP8 antenna simulator. The whole process (import, export and visualization) is quite similar to the one described above. The only difference is that here the simulation results are already in ASCII format and there is no additional conversion. However because of the file structure we need to first extract the information from the header lines before the actual results are imported in HDF5 database. A very useful and practical feature is the ability of comparing the measurement results with simulated ones. Therefore the visualization module supports this activity by plotting diagrams from both types of antenna data.

## 7.    CONCLUSIONS

The purpose of the conversion and storage tool described in this paper is to facilitate the exchange and management of simulation data among researchers, and to ease the task of using different simulation, measurement, data processing and visualization tools, all having different input and output data formats. This design is under active implementation, and a prototype with a debugging interface is already working. As soon as the prototype passes its testing stage, it will hopefully be enhanced by other simulation practitioners thanks to its modular structure. Possible extensions to the presented architecture include being able to accommodate non-tabular data and defining useful structures for metadata and processing data.

We believe that software developed as part of research activity should be released with a free software license, because research results should be made available for use by anyone, for any purpose and be freely modifiable, in order to further knowledge and usefulness [7]. The choice of license will be among the MIT X license, the GNU LGPL and the GNU GPL licenses, which we think best serve the purpose of free research software.

## REFERENCES

[1]    Bragg, A. Observations and thoughts on the possible approaches for addressing the tasks specified in the COST 285 work-plan. COST 285 temporary document TD/285/03/15, CNUCE-CNR (IT), 2004.

[2]    Eaton, J. W., and Rawlings, J. B. Octave – recent developments and plans for the future. In *proceedings of the 3rd International Workshop on Distributed Statistical Computing* (Mar. 2003), K. Hornik and F. Leisch, Eds.

[3]    Folk, M., McGrath, R., and Yeager, N. HDF: an update and future directions. In *International Geoscience and Remote Sensing Symposium (IGARSS'99)* (1999), IEEE, Ed., vol. 1, pp. 273–275.

[4]    Golub, and Loan, V. *Matrix Computations*, 3 ed. The Johns Hopkins University Press, 1996.

[5]    Kotz, D., and Henderson, T. Crawdad: A Community Resource for Archiving Wireless Data at Dartmouth. *IEEE Pervasive Computing 4*, 4 (Oct. 2005), 12–14.

[6]   McCanne, S., and Floyd, S. *The network simulator - ns-2*. University of Berkley, Oct. 2005.

[7]   Potortì, F. Free software and research. In *proceedings of the International Conference on Open Source Systems (OSS)* (July 2005), M. Scotto and G. Succi, Eds., ECIG Edizioni Culturali Internazionali Genova, pp. 270–271. Short paper.

[8]   http://www.w3.org/XML/Schema

[9]   ISO 14721:2003, Blue Book. Issue 1. CCSDC 650.0-r-2: Reference Model for an Open Archival Information System.

[10]  Shoaib Sufi, Brian Mathews, CCLRC scientific metadata model: Version 2, CCLRC technical report DL-TR-2004-001, September 2004.

[11]  DRIVER (http://www.driver-repository.eu/)

# SUBJECT INDEX